The Press Council

The Press Council

HISTORY, PROCEDURE AND CASES

H. Phillip Levy, M.A., LL.M., B.C.L. (OXON.)

OF GRAY'S INN, BARRISTER-AT-LAW,
HEAD OF THE LEGAL DEPARTMENT
OF THE DAILY MIRROR NEWSPAPERS LTD

WITH A PREFACE BY

Rt Hon. the Lord Devlin, P.C.

CHAIRMAN, THE PRESS COUNCIL

Macmillan

LONDON MELBOURNE TORONTO

St Martin's Press

NEW YORK

1 9 6 7

Introduction © Lord Devlin 1967
Text © H. Phillip Levy 1967

Published by
MACMILLAN & CO LTD
Little Essex Street London W C 2
and also at Bombay Calcutta and Madras
Macmillan South Africa (Publishers) Pty Ltd Johannesburg
The Macmillan Company of Australia Pty Ltd Melbourne
The Macmillan Company of Canada Ltd Toronto
St Martin's Press Inc New York

Library of Congress catalog card no. 67–24328

Printed in Great Britain by
ROBERT MACLEHOSE AND CO. LTD
The University Press, Glasgow

To Arnold and Meli

Contents

Part Three

THE COUNCIL SPEAKS FOR THE PRESS

Preface by Lord Devlin

The Press Council has now been in existence for fourteen years. During that time it has heard and adjudicated upon numerous complaints against the Press about the contents of newspapers and the behaviour of journalists. It has given many rulings, some of general application and others doing hardly more than decide a particular case. But each of these rulings, whether general or particular, expresses the considered opinion of experienced men used to editing or managing newspapers or to the daily work of the journalist on what newspapers should or should not contain, on how news and opinion should be presented, and on how in particular circumstances journalists should behave.

Inevitably a collection of rulings of this sort indicates, if it does not settle, professional standards. Even where a principle is not expressed, it can often be induced from a group of similar decisions. The Press Council has not, unlike many other professional bodies, drafted a code. It has, whether it realised it or not, adopted the methods of generations of judges who produced the common law of England. They let it grow out of the decisions they gave.

In this process there comes a stage when there is a demand for collected reports, if not for a synthesis or commentary. This stage has now been reached in the development of Press ethics by the Council. The thirteen Reports of the Council, entitled *The Press and the People*, have contained each year a summary of the principal cases decided. What was needed was a classification and commentary so that one decision could be compared with another, and the effect of several decisions on the same sort of point appraised. The demand has come not only from editors and journalists, who often have difficult professional decisions to make, but also from those in this country and abroad who want to study the working of the British Press and the Council in relation to it.

First and foremost this is a case-book. The arrangement of cases seems to me to have been admirably done and the text which introduces each group to be excellent. The text is not and does not claim to be a statement of 'Press law' on each subject, but it gives a very good guide to the way in which the Press Council is likely to approach the decision of cases on the subject. It is not based only on the cases cited; it refers also most usefully to what has been said on the subject when it has been discussed in Parliament or in the Reports of Royal Commissions.

The work of the Press Council in challenging encroachments on the freedom of the Press is just as important as its work in maintaining standards. The results are less bulky but Chapter 28 is not one that should be overlooked. Also the first four chapters, which give in brief the history of the Press Council and summarise its procedure, are as valuable as any in the book. This is at once of interest to the student and a useful reminder to the practitioner of the fundamentals which the decisions of the Press Council must respect.

In short, the platitude of prefaces is here appropriate: the book fulfils a long-felt need.

Acknowledgments

I wish to express my gratitude to Lord Devlin, the Chairman of the Press Council, for the Preface and for the invaluable advice he gave me throughout the preparation of this book.

I am also greatly indebted to the Press Council for allowing me to quote freely from the Annual Reports, *The Press and the People*; to Colonel Clissitt, the Secretary to the Council, for placing his great knowledge and experience at my disposal and for being good enough to read Chapter 4 in typescript; to his staff for being obliging at all times.

To the first three Chairmen, Lord Astor of Hever, Sir Linton Andrews and Mr George Murray, who did so much for the Council in its early difficult years, my thanks are due for giving me the benefit of their experience and permitting me to quote them.

I also wish to thank Mr Cecil M. King for information about the reactions of sections of the Press to the Press on different stages of its history. To Mr Bernard Alton, secretary of the Newspaper Proprietors' Association, and Mr James Bradley, general secretary of the National Union of Journalists, I am indebted for similar information.

Sir Richard Colville, the Press Secretary to Her Majesty the Queen, kindly read the chapter on the Royal Family in typescript and readily agreed that I could quote from his letters.

Professor J. Edward Gerald of the University of Minnesota, the distinguished American authority on journalism and the Press, provided me with much material on the right to privacy under the law in a number of the American States. I was also able to discuss the subject with him while he was on a visit to this country. Lord Mancroft also very kindly helped me with a reference to an interesting American case on the right to privacy.

Nearer home I particularly wish to thank Mr Edward Pickering for his encouragement and for reading the complete typescript; Mr Lintott and the *Daily Mirror* Library staff for producing cuttings and books of reference with characteristic efficiency and goodwill; Mr Clive Bradley for his assistance, and my secretary Miss Molly Gwyther, who sacrificed much of her own time to help.

Any personal views expressed are entirely those of the author, and none of the persons mentioned is to be held responsible for or identified with them.

H. P. L.

PART ONE

History, Constitution and Procedure

1 The First Royal Commission and the Emergence of the Press Council

I

On 29 October 1946 the House of Commons on a free vote approved a motion moved and seconded by two Members, both journalists, which called for the appointment of a Royal Commission to inquire into the finance, control, management and ownership of the Press with the object of 'furthering the free expression of opinion through the Press and the greatest practicable accuracy in the presentation of news'. The reason for the motion was 'the increasing public concern at the growth of monopolistic tendencies in the control of the Press'.

The first step towards the establishment of a Press Council had been taken. Another seven years elapsed before the Council came into existence, but its formal creation on 1 July 1953 was the culmination of a chain-reaction of events set in motion by the debate in Parliament on that October day of 1946. The Royal Commission Parliament had asked for was appointed in April 1947 with Sir David Ross of Oxford University as its Chairman.

The war had been over for less than two years; the Prime Minister of the day was Mr Attlee. Paper rationing and statutory restrictions on the allocation and use of newsprint necessitated by the war continued to weigh heavily on the Press. The public concern voiced in Parliament was not confined to the declining number of newspapers but related also to the deterioration of journalistic standards.

Speaking to the motion he presented in the House for the appointment of a Royal Commission, Mr Haydn Davies said that for years journalists had watched the freedom of the Press being whittled away. Great newspapers had been destroyed; combines had bought up and killed independent journals, and the honourable profession of journalism had been degraded by high finance and big business; as a result subservience had replaced judgment.

Seconding the motion Mr Michael Foot said that the Royal Commission should inquire into the operation of chain newspapers and devise a way of preventing the chains spreading. He believed that the serious decline in the quality of British journalism in the last thirty years was traceable to the decline in power of the editor and the encroachment of the authority of the newspaper proprietor. Many editors had become little more than 'stooges, cyphers and sycophants'.

Other members speaking in support of the motion argued that the freedom of the Press involved the freedom of the citizen to have a fair and reasonably free choice of papers of different hues and capacities. Proprietors having bought up provincial papers dictated from London a uniformity of policy and of content. Concentration of ownership was incompatible with real freedom of the Press and produced a concentration of power in the hands of a few men which was capable of dangerous abuse and was in fact being abused to suppress opinion and to distort the news. Unless progressive concentration was checked not the only the freedom of the Press but the interests of the country would also be endangered.

Opponents argued that the motion had its origin in the excessive sensitivity of Ministers to attacks in the daily newspapers and that those supporting the motion were actuated by political prejudice and by a desire to limit the freedom of the Press or of that part which opposed the Government. There was nothing approaching a monopoly in the ownership of newspapers, they said. The British Press was a shining example of freedom and independence.

The Royal Commission spent two years in a searching inquiry of the Press. Their Report was presented to Parliament in June 1949.

The Commission found that there was nothing approaching monopoly in the Press, but there had been some concentration of ownership. Between 1921 and 1948 the number of daily and Sunday newspapers published in England, Wales and Scotland fell from 169 to 128. The causes of the decrease were the intense competition of the popular national dailies with each other, and indirectly with all other dailies, and the high cost of production. Competition for circulation, which reached its peak in the twenties and thirties, took the form of grandiose insurance schemes and the lavish distribution of free gifts. The higher the popular papers forced their sales the more they tended to attract advertising away from other papers. The national papers had opened offices in Manchester and Glasgow, and provincial papers were faced with competitors whose resources, both financial and journalistic, enabled them to give readers a more extensive service. The salaries of journalists were rising, and newsprint was scarce and extremely dear.

Concentration of ownership, the Report said, took three forms: (1) the development of mammoth circulations; (2) the development of chains, that is the concentration of a number of newspapers in one ownership; (3) the development of a local monopoly, the concentration in one ownership of all the newspapers in a particular town or district (Cmd. 7700, par. 246).

In the period from 1921 to 1948, national morning newspapers decreased from twelve to nine. The Commission did not consider the number left so small as to prejudice either the free expression of opinion or the accurate presentation of news. The nine reflected the broad divisions of political opinion. There was no virtue in mere multiplicity, and the Commission did not think that the public interest required that smaller schools of thought should find expression through national newspapers. But while nine national morning papers was not alarmingly inadequate, it was not so many that any further decrease could be contemplated without anxiety.

The question whether the degree of concentration of ownership in the provincial Press was prejudicial to the free expression of opinion and the accurate presentation of news turned on the merits or demerits of newspaper chains. The Royal Commission found little to substantiate the criticism of chain groups expressed in the House of Commons debate of 29 October 1946. Their Report summarised the points made on both sides of the controversy.

On the negative side chains were said to be inimical to local independence and local diversity because they did not identify themselves as closely as independent papers with local interests. They gave too much space to national and too little to local news. Provincial members of the chain were cast in the same mould, expressed the same opinions, reproduced the same prejudice and reflected the policies of the proprietor rather than policies based on the interests and opinions of the localities they served.

Those who took the opposite view argued that chain papers could not afford to sacrifice local news to national news, or to disregard local opinion; on the contrary provincial members of the chain preserved their local character as jealously as independent undertakings, and for the same reason, namely that their survival depended on it. Chains had preserved papers which could not have survived on their own resources and the provincial dailies in a chain were better able to withstand the competition of the national dailies. By organising central purchasing, advertising, news-gathering, and other services, a chain effected economies which enabled it to produce better newspapers. It could spend more on foreign news, features, salaries and equipment, and its widespread organisation gave its readers a better service of home news than papers standing on their own could provide. (Cmd. 7700, pars. 343–4.)

The case against chains, the Commission thought, had been overstated; the tendency towards uniformity among the members of a chain was not as great as had been suggested. Chain ownership was not necessarily undesirable; in certain circumstances it might become so. It was inevitable that the chief proprietor could ensure that all the papers belonging to the chain adopted broadly the same policy on national issues and considered local issues from broadly the same point of view. If he exercised that power it would limit the expression of spontaneous local opinion and reduce the number of diverse points of view finding expression. The Commission attached importance to the preservation of newspapers which were not the mouthpiece of policies formulated in London. The provincial newspapers distinguished one area from another. They stimulated an interest in local affairs and in the work of local authorities; they provided a forum for local discussion and formulated local opinion. By fostering and reflecting diversity they contributed to the richness of the nation's life and the stability of its institutions. Hardly less valuable to their readers were the news, the gossip, the advertisements and announcements to be found in the provincial dailies which the national newspapers could not provide.

The Commission found that in the provincial Press as a whole there was nothing approaching a monopoly. The degree of concentration was considerable but not so great as to be contrary to the best interests of the public. Their Report stated that they would not be alarmed by an increase in the number of relatively small chains, but they would deplore any tendency on the part of the larger chains to expand. (Cmd. 7700, par. 350.)

Turning from the organisation of the Press to the performance of the Press, the Commission pointed out that a newspaper is produced by a profession grafted on to a highly competitive industry. The ideals of the profession can only be realised within the conditions set by the industry. The business of a newspaper undertaking is to sell newspapers; since the paper must pay or perish neither journalistic excellence nor political policies can normally be pursued in complete disregard of commercial success. But the desire to make money, the desire to form opinion and the desire to make a good newspaper can and do blend.

Though it was generally agreed that the British Press was inferior to none in the world the Commission found much to criticise. 'In assessing the standard of accuracy of the Press we have found some evidence of willingness to be satisfied with what at best corresponds only roughly to the truth and a readiness to make statements on inadequate evidence.' Political bias found expression in the mis-statement of facts and in its extreme form produced actual suppression and gross misrepresentation. Inference was presented as fact and categorical statements were made on totally inadequate evidence.

Competition for mass circulation produced a tendency to abandon national conceptions of values and to encourage reliance on sensationalism and triviality; the matrimonial adventures of a film star were presented as though they had the same intrinsic importance as events affecting the peace of a continent.

The problem was to bridge the gap between the standard of information required for healthy citizenship and the fare provided; to reconcile the claims of society and the claims of commerce. The Commission did not think the Press was doing everything it could reasonably be expected to do; some of its spokesmen were unduly complacent and deficient in self-criticism. The means of maintaining the proper relationship between the Press and society, the Commission believed, lay not in Government action but in the Press itself. It was remarkable, the Commission said, that although there were organisations to represent sectional interests within the Press there was none which represented the Press as a whole. Those engaged in newspaper production were acutely aware of the Press as an entity and jealous for its independence and its reputation. It was the more surprising, therefore, that there was no one body concerned to maintain either the freedom of the Press or the integrity on which its reputation depended.

In its modern form the Press was a young and developing institution, and, if it was to develop in the right direction, it needed to consider where it was going and consciously to foster those tendencies which made for integrity and for a sense of responsibility to the public.

For these reasons the Commission recommended that the Press itself should create a central organisation which should be called the General Council of the Press.

Although the physical production of newspapers was an industrial process, their editorial production could properly be regarded as a profession. The Commission expressed the hope that the Press would take the earliest opportunity of establishing the General Council, the principal object of which should be to maintain those standards of professional responsibility and integrity acknowledged by proprietors and journalists alike. The body they had in mind would not require powers to control entry into the profession, and would depend for its effectiveness on its moral authority rather than on any statutory sanctions. It should include persons from outside the profession and should derive its authority from the Press itself and not from statute. (Cmnd. 7700, pars. 619, 636, 638.)

Methods of newsgathering which, for example, caused distress to private persons had been condemned by both the proprietors' and the journalists' organisations. The Commission considered that it was for the profession itself to make the condemnation effective. The Press Council would perform a valuable service by enunciating afresh the principles on which professional opinion is agreed, and by drawing attention to cases in which they had been disregarded.

The Commission did not see a solution to the problems they had indicated in major changes in the ownership and control of the industry. Free enterprise was a prerequisite to a free Press, and free enterprise in the case of newspapers would generally mean commercially profitable enterprise.

II

The Report of the Royal Commission was debated by the House of Commons on 28 July 1949. The Opposition seized on the statement that 'The British Press is inferior to none in the world' and hailed the Report as a triumphant vindication of the Press; Government supporters, on the other hand, saw a condemnation of the Press on every page.

However, on the motion of Mr Herbert Morrison, the Lord President of the Council, the House resolved without a division that it would welcome all possible action on the part of the Press to give effect to the Commission's recommendations.

Following the debate in Parliament the Newspaper Proprietors' Association and the Newspaper Society met to consider how the Press Council envisaged by the Royal Commission was to be established. Two years elapsed before the proprietors were able to produce a draft constitution. Joint discussions with the journalists' organisations followed, and another two years passed in debating such questions as what the function of the Press Council was to be, what representation on the Council was to be accorded to the various constituent bodies and whether representatives of the public should be admitted to membership. Eventually to expedite progress a working committee representative of the interested organisations was formed in April 1952 under the chairmanship of the President of the Newspaper Society, Mr E. M. Clayson.

The truth is that there was no real enthusiasm in Press circles for a Press Council. While the maintenance of professional standards and integrity was an aim which all could support, there was a general feeling that an attempt to achieve this end through a disciplinary body would inevitably result in repressive measures restrictive of the freedom of the Press. In the circumstances the Press was in no hurry to forge fetters for itself.

The long-drawn-out discussions caused increasing impatience at the inordinate delay in implementing the recommendations contained in the Royal Commission's Report. In a letter to *The Times* on 19 July 1952 Lady Violet Bonham Carter, who had been a member of the Royal Commission, complained that three years had elapsed since the Report was published, and the Press Council was still not in being. Her letter was followed by others, among them one from Sir David Ross, the Chairman of the Commission, who wrote that he and others had begun to fear that the negotiations for setting up the Council would lead to nothing. By November 1952 these doubts had spread to Parliament, and a private member's Bill was introduced, to establish a Press Council by legislation. Mr C. J. Simmons, moving the second reading, reminded the House that in July 1949 it had approved a motion asking the Press to proceed with the formation of a Press Council in accordance with the recommendation of the Royal Commission. 'Nearly three and a half years after its publication,' he said, 'we are still awaiting its formation by the Press of their own volition.'

The *Manchester Guardian*, commenting on the Bill, said that its introduction would serve a useful purpose; the public had been baffled to understand why the newspaper organisations had taken such an unconscionable time in putting forward their form of Press Council. The *Newspaper World* of 20 November 1952 reported that there was no news of any fresh development in the deliberations of the Press in connection with the setting up of a voluntary Press Council; no meeting of the joint committee had been held since July, when the proprietors put forward amended proposals. The journalists' organisations had considered these proposals and submitted their views, but no meeting had since been held to see if further progress was possible. There was a plain lack of urgency in the negotiations. The *World's Press News* of 21 November 1952 observed that the Bill again raised the question of Government interference. 'The far better way is for the Press to set up its own Press Council. It is now quite likely that the interest of the House will accelerate the process.'

Mr Simmons's Bill made no further progress after the Second Reading, but the steps taken to set up a statutory body seem to have had the effect of speeding up the work of the joint committee. In February 1953 agreement was reached on a draft constitution.

After four years of serious doubt and many meetings of the constituent organisations, the Press, more under duress than of its own free will, set up a Press Council of its own making. Had it delayed doing so much longer it was virtually certain that Parliament would have imposed one by legislation. The Press might be divided in its views on a number of matters but was quite united in its opposition and resistance to statutory control, the very negation of freedom of the Press. A free Press required freedom of the Press to govern itself. The creation of the Press Council gave it the opportunity to do so.

The Press Council came formally into existence on 1 July 1953, and met for the first time on the twenty-first of that month in the Conference Room of the Press Association and Reuter headquarters in Fleet Street.

2 The Second Royal Commission — The Press Council is Reconstituted

I

The Report on the first Royal Commission had given reassurance on monopolistic tendencies. 'The present degree of concentration of ownership in the newspaper press as a whole or in any important class of it', the Report stated, 'is not so great as to prejudice the free expression of opinion or the accurate presentation of news or to be contrary to the best interests of the public.' But there was also a warning. After pointing out that one aspect of concentration was a decrease in the number of newspapers, the Commission said: 'any further decrease in the number of national newspapers would be a matter for anxiety, and a decrease in the provincial morning newspapers would be a serious loss.'

Nevertheless, the Commission saw no immediate cause for concern. A study of the figures for the period 1921 to 1948 showed that there had been a marked tendency away from concentration in the national Press, and there was no reason to expect a reversal of this tendency. In the provincial Press the trend between 1921 and 1929 had been strongly towards concentration, but it was much less pronounced after that period, and in terms of the largest single newspaper chain the trend had been reversed. 'There is no reason to expect', the Report stated, 'that the aggressive expansion of chain undertakings which characterised the earlier period will be resumed.'

Reassurance also came from another circumstance. An essential requirement, the Commission believed, which the Press should collectively fulfil was that the number and variety of newspapers should be such that the opportunity existed for all important points of view to be effectively presented in terms of the varying standards of taste, political opinion and education among the principal groups of the population. This requirement the Commission found to be fulfilled.

Excellent as was the Commission's diagnosis of the state of the Press, its forecast on future trends proved to be disappointingly wrong. By 1962 another seventeen daily and Sunday newspapers had ceased production in London and the provinces, and the ownership of those which remained had become concentrated in fewer hands. Many deaths, but fewer births, had occurred, and among periodicals large numbers had come into the ownership of one group.

The alarm was sounded in October 1960 with the death of the *News Chronicle* and the *Star*, two highly-respected newspapers, both with substantial circulations. In the House of Commons the Home Secretary, Mr Butler, said he shared the general regret. The expression of all shades of opinion in a free Press was a feature of our way of life which everybody wanted to maintain, but he refused the demand for the appointment of another Royal Commission. Pressure for an inquiry continued, and in December the House passed without a division a motion regretting the closure of the two newspapers, expressing anxiety at the increasing concentration of newspapers in fewer hands and calling for the institution of an inquiry with particular reference to the monopolistic trend and its social implications.

Further impetus was given to the demand when in January 1961 the Daily Mirror Newspapers Limited took over the *Daily Herald* and the *People*, and a large number of periodicals as a result of acquiring control of Odhams Press Limited. In February the Prime Minister, Mr Macmillan, responded to the public concern and announced that a Royal Commission would be appointed to examine the factors at work within the industry, of which the bids for the control of Odhams were felt to be 'symptomatic of some general unease in the industry as a whole'.

The Commission consisted of five members under the chairmanship of Lord Shawcross; the number had been kept small in order that the Commission could proceed quickly. The terms of reference required it to examine the economic and financial factors affecting the production and sale of newspapers, including manufacturing, printing and distribution costs, the efficiency of production, revenue from advertising, and the effect of television. The Commission was also to consider whether these factors tended to diminish the diversity of ownership and control of newspapers, or their number or variety, having regard to the importance in the public interest to the accurate presentation of news and the free expression of opinion.

The Shawcross Commission was not concerned, as was the 1947–1949 Commission, with the performance of the Press in regard to general ethical questions.

The Shawcross Report was presented in 1962. It reviewed the economic and financial factors of the industry; the high earnings and high cost of newsprint; overmanning, restrictive practices, demarcation problems, administrative and editorial efficiency and labour relations.

A more constructive spirit was needed on both sides, the Report stated. Good industrial machinery was no substitute for good relations. Individual proprietors, like the trade unions, had a duty to promote efficiency not only in the interest of the industry but also in that of the public, which relied upon the maintenance of a strong and independent Press. Although the public interest was not being seriously injured by the economic situation of the Press as the Commission found it, the future effect of the various economic pressures did cause grave anxiety. While legislative interference might check strong newspapers and bolster up weak ones, there was no way to success, the Report said, except through the quality of management and editorial direction. Legislation could not produce these qualities. (Cmnd. 1811, pars. 74–108, 278.)

The Commission considered various schemes to improve the competitive position of the smaller circulation newspapers by reducing the advantages which sprang simply from having a large circulation. Here again they concluded that there was no acceptable legislative or fiscal way of regulating the competitive and economic forces to ensure a sufficient diversity of newspapers. The only hope of the weaker newspapers was to secure managers and editors of such enterprise and originality as would enable these publications to overcome the economic forces affecting them. (Cmnd. 1811, par. 313.)

The Report stated that the concentration of ownership had a number of aspects which could not be measured by any single numerical formula. Whether the degree of concentration was assessed by reference to circulations or to the number of newspapers controlled by single undertakings, it was important to dissociate the facts of concentration from any sinister implication the word conveyed. There was more than one view on the question whether the public interest was injured by the degree of concentration of ownership and control existing at a particular time, and no reliable view was possible unless all the facts were known. The growth of circulations or of the number of newspapers controlled by one undertaking was not necessarily to be attributed to aggressive empire-building. It could result from expansionist policies, but it could indicate the growing popularity of an undertaking's journals or its enterprise in starting new publications; it could also result from the reduction in the number of other journals. The obvious danger of concentration of ownership lay in the possibility that variety of opinion might be stifled if one proprietor came to control a number of newspapers which formerly presented varied and independent views. Nevertheless, the Commission were satisfied that in the quality Press the accurate presentation of news and the free expression of opinion seemed unlikely to be threatened by amalgamation, and that even in the popular Press common ownership did not necessarily entail a suppression of independent editorial policies. (Cmnd. 1811, pars. 15, 33, 36.)

There was no doubt, the Commission stated, that several of the previously independent publications which had been absorbed into group ownership would not have been able to remain economically viable on their own. But whatever might be the economic implications, there was a special public interest in Press amalgamations because they involved the power to influence public manners and political opinions. The potential political and social influences of the multiple ownership of newspapers, although not to be exaggerated, remained of serious concern. A considerable range of choice in the national and Sunday Press remained, but it was less than it had been in 1949, and it would be better if there were more.

The Commission were not in favour of the wholesale prohibition of all future amalgamations or expansions. There was no public interest in preventing mergers when the newspaper merged would have gone out of existence in any event. Some amalgamations, however, might be contrary to the public interest, for instance, where the group taken over could have survived economically on its own. In the case of the *News Chronicle*, for instance, the Commission said they could not escape the conclusion that the failure of the newspaper was not entirely the result of an inevitable law of newspaper economics; a different and more consistent managerial and editorial policy might have saved it.

There were, however, other circumstances in which amalgamations might take place, some of which could be contrary to the public interest and which required scrutiny. The Commission cited the acquisition of Odhams Press Limited by the Daily Mirror group. Odhams, they said, could have survived economically on its own. A body of opinion, including some of its own directors, thought that if it were to be taken over at all it would have been more in the public interest for it to be amalgamated with a group other than the Daily Mirror group; others took the opposite view. What in fact happened was decided wholly by the financial interests of shareholders who were not, as such, concerned with the national interest.

The Commission recommended the establishment of a Press Amalgamations Court to scrutinise transactions involving the purchase of newspapers or the controlling interests in companies which owned newspapers. The scheme was to be limited to daily and Sunday newspapers and a transaction would be scrutinised if the purchaser controlled aggregate weekly sales of daily or Sunday newspapers of more than three million copies either before or as a result of the purchase. The Amalgamations Court would consent to a transaction only if it were shown to be in the public interest. The Court would be established by statute, which would also specify the criteria for determining whether transactions were in the public interest. (Cmnd. 1811, par. 337.)

The Commission realised that objection might be raised to legislation of this kind on the ground that it involved an interference with the freedom of the Press. The Commission, however, did not think that this was so and in their Report referred to an American case (Associated Press *v.* The United States, 325 U.S. 1), which raised the question whether anti-trust legislation and the First Amendment which guaranteed the freedom of the Press could be reconciled; the Commission cited the following passage from the judgment of Mr Justice Douglas:

> Finally, the argument is made that to apply the Sherman Act to this association of publishers constitutes an abridgment of the freedom of the press guaranteed by the First Amendment. . . . It would be strange indeed however if the grave concern for freedom of the press which prompted adoption of the First Amendment should be read as a command that the government was without power to protect that freedom. The First Amendment, far from providing an argument against application of the Sherman Act, here provides powerful reasons to the contrary. That Amendment rests on the assumption that the widest possible dissemination of information from diverse and antagonistic sources is essential to the welfare of the public, that a free press is a condition of a free society. Surely a command that the government itself shall not impede the free flow of ideas does not afford non-governmental combinations a refuge if they impose restraints upon that constitutionally guaranteed freedom. Freedom to publish means freedom for all and not

for some. Freedom to publish is guaranteed by the Constitution but freedom to combine and keep others from publishing is not. Freedom of the press from governmental interference under the First Amendment does not sanction repression of that freedom by private interests. The First Amendment affords not the slightest support for the contention that a combination to restrain trade in news and views has any constitutional immunity.

The proposed Court was also likely to be objected to because it would interfere with the proprietory rights of shareholders and involved treating the newspaper industry differently from industry in general. The answer, the Commission said, was that the public interest in relation to the newspaper industry was different. Discrimination was based on the proposition that freedom and variety in the expression of opinion and presentation of news was an element which did not enter into the conduct of other competitive industries and that it was a paramount public interest. (Cmnd. 1811, pars. 339, 340.)

The action taken by the Government on this part of the Shawcross Report is dealt with in Chapter 27.

II

The Press Council had been in existence nearly ten years when the Shawcross Commission considered the Council's performance in relation to certain of its objectives.

The 1949 Commission had recommended that the Council should study the long-term development of the Press and the economic and social factors which affect it, particularly any tendency to produce greater concentration or monopoly as well as matters of research. The Shawcross Report stated that had these recommendations been carried out much of their inquiry might have been unnecessary. The constitution of the Council differed significantly from that recommended by the 1949 Commission, and though one of the objects of the Council was 'to study developments in the Press which may tend towards greater concentration or monopoly', the Council's study of economic problems had been mainly confined to the preparation of a factual account of some of the changes in the number and ownership of newspapers which had occurred in each year.

In its evidence to the Commission, the Press Council explained the difficulties in the way of discharging its economic functions. It lacked the power to call for information and could take no action to control trends of which it might disapprove. Furthermore its financial resources limited the activities they could undertake. The Commission's Report, however, pointed out that these limitations were entirely the result of policies pursued by the Council's constituent bodies; there was no evidence that the Council had ever pressed for a substantial increase of funds.

The Shawcross Report went on to state that the more valid the excuses for the Council's inactivity in the economic field were, the greater was the criticism against the constituent bodies which had denied it the necessary power and finance. The Council as then constituted had not been able to make any significant contribution to the solution of the broad problems the Commission had had to consider.

While the Shawcross Commission did not disagree with the 1949 Commission that there were important advantages in the Council having a voluntary basis, the Commission said that if the Press was not willing to invest the Press Council with the necessary authority and contribute the necessary finance, the case for a statutory body with definite powers and the right to levy the industry was a clear one.

The Commission thought the revision of the Council's constitution should be undertaken as a matter of urgency, to comply with the recommendations of the 1949 Commission on the appointment of an independent chairman and the inclusion of lay members and functions, and to ensure that the Council had the necessary powers, including the power to call for information about ownership and control, and the necessary funds to enable it to carry out all its objectives to the fullest degree. The Press should be given another opportunity to establish voluntarily an authoritative Council with a lay element, but a time limit should be set for this to be done and, failing compliance, a statutory body should be established. (Cmnd. 1811, par. 325.)

The Commission hoped that the reformed Council would devote itself more effectively to its stated objectives and in addition would undertake to (a) scrutinise and give publicity to changes in ownership and control of newspapers, (b) publish up-to-date statistics, (c) ensure that newspapers carried the name of the company or individual in ultimate control of its affairs, (d) hear complaints from journalists of undue influence by advertisers.

This last objective, the Commission hoped, could be extended to include complaints by editors or other journalists that they had been improperly obliged by their employer to suppress opinion, distort the truth or otherwise engage in unprofessional conduct. Anyone making such a complaint might be unable or unwilling to stay with the newspaper, but the existence of a forum for such complaints would act as a deterrent to undue pressures.

The Press had not accepted the recommendation of the 1949 Commission that the Chairman of the Press Council should be a person unconnected with the Press, nor had it accepted the recommendation that the Council should contain lay members. The spectacular 'monopolistic tendencies' revealed in 1960 and 1961 and the categorical pronouncement by the Shawcross Commission made reconstitution inevitable.

A new constitution was adopted 1 July 1963. The General Council of the Press met for the last time in June 1963 and made final arrangements to hand over its duties to the new Council. A period of transition followed during which the duties of the Chairman were discharged by the Vice-Chairman, Mr Henry Bate.

The new Council with its independent Chairman, Lord Devlin, and the lay members who had been appointed, held its first meeting on 14 January 1964.

3 The Constitution of the Press Council

The Press Council began its history in 1953 under a constitution which did not provide for representation on the Council of members of the public outside the profession of journalism and a Chairman also unconnected with the Press, as the first Royal Commission had recommended. Until 1963 the Press Council was a professional body consisting entirely of representatives of the newspaper industry and having as Chairman a member of the Press. When, however, the Shawcross Report categorically supported the recommendations of the first Royal Commission and said that unless the Press Council should have an independent Chairman and lay members, the Press no longer resisted the recommendations, and the constitution of the Council was amended to give effect to them.

The 1963 constitution also revoked the former title, 'The General Council of the Press', and substituted the new title, 'The Press Council'. Responsibility was accepted by the Press Council for all acts done by the General Council of the Press as though they had been done by the Press Council.

The objects of the Press Council set out in the 1953 constitution were the objects recommended by the first Royal Commission. They were re-adopted, slightly amended, when the constitution was re-written in 1963.

OBJECTS OF THE PRESS COUNCIL

As they stand today the objects are:

(i) To preserve the established freedom of the British Press.

(ii) To maintain the character of the British Press in accordance with the highest professional and commercial standards.

(iii) To consider complaints about the conduct of the Press or the conduct

B

of persons and organisations towards the Press; to deal with these complaints in whatever manner might seem practical and appropriate and record resultant action.

(iv) To keep under review developments likely to restrict the supply of information of public interest and importance.

(v) To report publicly on developments that may tend towards greater concentration or monopoly in the Press (including changes in ownership, control and growth of Press undertakings) and to publish statistical information relating to them.

(vi) To make representations on appropriate occasions to the Government, organs of the United Nations and to Press organisations abroad.

(vii) To publish periodical reports recording the Council's work and to review from time to time developments in the Press and the factors affecting them.

The first is the prime object in every sense. It is cardinal to the existence and independence of the Press; it is vital to the democratic society the Press serves. 'The liberty of the Press', Blackstone declared two hundred years ago, 'is indeed essential to the nature of a Free State'. Freedom of the Press means that the free flow of ideas shall not be impeded; in the words of an American judge it means 'the widest possible dissemination of information from diverse and antagonistic sources'. The freedom of the Press, which the constitution describes as 'established', became so only after a long constitutional struggle which endured for several centuries. It is the Press Council which must 'preserve' this freedom against insidious and even open attempts constantly made to restrict it.

While the objects of the constitution are important, none is of the same importance as the first; those that follow contribute to and help safeguard a vital freedom without which the remaining objects would be of little consequence. The support of public opinion, by which the freedom of the Press is maintained, depends on the observance by the Press of ethical standards. The function of the Press Council to declare and uphold these standards is reflected in object (ii).

There is a widespread but mistaken belief that the Press Council's judicial function is limited to the consideration of complaints against the Press. Object (iii) shows that the Council's jurisdiction is not so circumscribed. Clearly the Press cannot fulfil its function of gathering and publishing the news if it is prevented by the conduct of others from doing so.

Attempts by local authorities, hospital boards, business concerns or anyone else to suppress information or to obstruct or mislead the Press in gathering information of public importance, which should be made known to the public, constitute a dereliction of duty by those responsible and an interference with the proper activities of the Press. The Council will undoubtedly investigate such cases and expose them. Object (iv) emphasises the Council's right to do so.

Under the 1953 constitution the Council in dealing with complaints about the conduct of the Press was required to consider complaints only from persons actually affected. This was a substantial limitation on the recommendation of the Royal Commission that the Council should consider any complaint received. Those who drafted the constitution feared that the Council would be deluged with complaints and the limitation was intended as a breakwater. In fact, however, the limitation was never operated. At the outset of its work the Council put on record its view that it did not consider itself precluded from considering complaints from whatever source they came. When the constitution was rewritten in 1963 the words of limitation were deleted.

The Prime Minister, Mr Wilson, has said that a free and democratic country is entitled to a free Press representing every point of view. Concentration of ownership reduces the opportunities for this and tends to stifle variety of opinion. The Shawcross Commission considered that the Press Council had not sufficiently realised the importance of or given anything like sufficient attention to what is now object (v) of the constitution.

In its evidence to the Commission the Press Council explained that it considered its most useful work lay in maintaining professional standards. A Council composed of employers and working journalists was not a body that was likely to reach unanimous decisions on industrial or economic matters. Moreover it was questionable whether the Council which acted as a court of honour dealing with professional standards was a suitable body to watch and report on developments tending towards concentration or monopoly in the Press. In any case, the Council did not have the financial resources, or the staff, or the power to call for information on economic matters. Its revenue which came from the subscriptions of the constituent bodies had been fixed at £2,500 in the first year, and, although it had increased since then, it was at the time of the sitting of the Shawcross Commission in 1961–2 still under £6,000.

The Commission was not persuaded or influenced by these considerations and reported that if the Press was not willing to invest the Council with the necessary authority and to contribute the necessary finance the case for a statutory body with definite powers and the right to levy the industry was a clear one.

A levy, of course, proved unnecessary. In 1965 the Council's revenue had risen to over £20,000.

The amount of respect the Council's representations will command under object (vi) will depend on the recognition it achieves by its own exertions to be the genuine and authoritative voice of the Press. The Council's performance to date is dealt with in Chapter 28.

Object (vii) is chiefly fulfilled by the Council's Annual Report entitled *The Press and the People*. It contains all the important adjudications made by the Council during the year and other aspects of the Council's work and articles on subjects of interest to the Press.

MEMBERSHIP

Under the 1953 constitution the Council contained no representatives of the public, but consisted of twenty members, all representative of, and appointed by, the constituent organisations on an agreed allocation. When the Council was reconstituted in 1963 to include lay members no increase in the size of the Council was made; the professional representatives were reduced by five, and five lay members were appointed in their place. In this way the first Royal Commission's recommendation that the Council should consist of twenty-five members, representing proprietors, newspaper and other journalists, and lay members amounting to twenty per cent including the Chairman, was met. The Press, however, kept in its own hands the appointment of the independent Chairman and the lay members, although the Royal Commission had recommended that they should be nominated jointly by the Lord Chief Justice of England and the Lord President of the Court of Session of Scotland. The first independent Chairman chosen was Lord Devlin, a judge whose exceptional legal talents had taken him to the House of Lords, and who had the further advantage of great experience of public service in other fields.

The lay members are co-opted to the Council by the Chairman and other members in consultation. They have the same rights and privileges as the professional representatives, except that they are not eligible for the office of vice-chairman.

The constituent organisations which elect the professional members are eight in number. They are:

1. The Newspaper Proprietors' Association Limited, consisting of undertakings which publish the national morning and Sunday newspapers with their Manchester editions and the two London evening newspapers (the *Evening News* and *Evening Standard*). The Association negotiates rates and conditions of service with the trade unions and concerns itself with matters of common interest to the national newspapers. It has no function in regard to the editorial content of its members' newspapers.

2. The Newspaper Society consists of the provincial morning, evening and Sunday newspapers and the London suburban newspapers.

3. The Periodical Proprietors' Association Limited represents the interests of the general periodical press and the trade and technical journals.

4. The Scottish Daily Newspaper Society consists of the proprietors of the daily and Sunday newspapers published in Scotland.

5. Scottish Newspaper Proprietors' Association represents the proprietors of the weekly newspapers in Scotland.

6. The National Union of Journalists is a registered trade union and consists of working journalists employed by newspapers and news agencies and those employed regularly by periodicals; some members are freelance, and a considerable number are employed in sound and television broadcasting and in public relations.

7. The Institute of Journalists is a professional organisation of journalists incorporated by Royal Charter; membership also includes proprietors who have at some time worked as journalists. It is a registered trade union considerably smaller in membership than the N.U.J.

8. The Guild of British Newspaper Editors consists of London and provincial newspaper editors whose newspapers are in membership of the Newspaper Society, the Scottish Daily Newspaper Society or the Scottish News-

paper Proprietors' Association. Editors of certain other newspapers are eligible for associate membership.

(*Note*: From 1 January 1967 all members of the Institute become members of the National Union of Journalists and *vice versa*. The Institute will serve the professional interests and the N.U.J. the trade union interests of the whole joint membership.)

Members nominated by the constituent bodies must be full-time directors or employees of the newspaper industry. Any person ceasing to be so qualified ceases to be eligible as a member and must vacate his place on the Council.

All members are elected for three years but are eligible for re-election. A vacancy which occurs on the Council will be filled by a replacement made by the electors of the person causing the vacancy.

Each constituent body, in addition to its ordinary representation, is entitled to nominate one of its officials to attend meetings of the Council in a consultative capacity; these officials may speak but may not vote.

AMENDMENT OF THE CONSTITUTION

Twenty-eight days' notice is necessary for a resolution to amend the constitution. A two-thirds majority of those present and voting at a meeting is required, and the majority must not be less than a simple majority of the membership of the Council.

REVENUE

The revenue to meet the estimated expenditure of the Council is raised by subscriptions from the constituent bodies on an agreed scale of contributions.

MEETINGS

Meetings of the Council are held at least five times a year but the Chairman may call a special meeting where in his opinion the circumstances warrant this. A special meeting will also be convened by the Secretary on the requisition of not fewer than eight members.

Other details relating to the conduct of the business of the Council are set out in the constitution, a copy of which is reproduced in Appendix I.

4 The Council in Action

THE COMMITTEES

Like other organisations with a wide range of responsibilities the Press Council works through standing committees. The Council has two, the General Purposes Committee and the Complaints Committee. On both the lay membership is generously represented. The General Purposes Committee deals with what has been described as the positive side of the Council's work; this includes keeping under review the law on such matters as censorship, contempt of court and libel, developments tending towards greater concentration or monopoly in the Press and the statistical information demonstrating these developments which the Council publishes for the benefit of the public. The Complaints Committee handles the negative side of the Council's work, complaints about the conduct of the Press. Any complaint about the conduct of persons towards the Press is a matter for the General Purposes Committee.

WHO MAY MAKE A COMPLAINT?

Any member of the public is entitled to lodge a complaint against a newspaper, provided the complaint is one of unethical conduct. The person making the complaint need not be directly or personally affected by the publication; for instance, where the victim of a sexual offence is named, complaint is not limited to the victim, any member of the public can complain to the Press Council.

The Press Council deals with complaints against newspapers, not against individual journalists; the editor accepts responsibility not only for what appears in his newspaper, but also for the behaviour of his staff.

Following the reconstitution of the Council and the admission of representatives of the public to membership the number of complaints greatly increased, rising from 283 for the year 1963–4 to 436 for 1965–6, which was a forty-three per cent increase over the year 1964–5. An interesting feature of the latest figures is that they cover far more publications than ever before. The complaints are given a preliminary screening and as a result about twenty per cent are rejected as frivolous or because they disclose no case to answer. These include complaints that are outside the terms of the Council's constitution or seek denunciation by the Council of a newspaper for doing something it has an established right to do — such as publishing a will, reporting a court hearing or refusing an advertisement.

The Complaints Committee can halt a case after it has survived all preliminary screening if the Committee finds that the case is not substantial, but here again, if there is the slightest doubt, the benefit is given to the complainant and the matter referred to the Council for decision.

Of the effective cases about half are upheld and half rejected. The participation of lay members in the work of the Complaints Committee ensures that the public point of view is heard and disposes of the criticism that the Press is a judge in its own cause.

It is a firm rule of the Press Council that before it will accept a complaint the aggrieved person must first seek redress from the editor of the newspaper said to be at fault. There are two reasons for this rule. In the first place the editor, on having his attention drawn to the complaint, may agree to publish a correction or apology or adopt some other course which will redress and dispose of the complaint. If a grievance is settled in this way the Press Council does not need to be troubled at all. The second reason for the rule is that, as the Council is the ultimate arbiter between the complainant and the newspaper, it is preferable that it should not appear on the scene until after the parties have failed to settle their differences and there is an issue between them to be adjudicated. By delaying its intervention the Council preserves a judicial detachment and avoids acting as both accuser and judge.

Should an aggrieved person fail to obtain satisfaction from the Editor he can then make his complaint to the Press Council. He should state the grounds of his complaint in a letter addressed to the Secretary of the Council and enclose copies of the correspondence he has had with the Editor, a copy of the paper or of the page of the paper showing the date and the report or article complained of; he should also give the names and addresses of any witnesses he relies upon and any additional information he may wish to tender in support of the complaint. The complaint will then have been properly prepared and effectively notified.

At this stage the Press Council will accept the complaint for investigation. After notifying the Editor of the newspaper concerned of the complaint and inviting his observations and any supporting statement he wishes to submit, the Secretary will make such additional inquiries as he thinks necessary and then prepare the case for hearing by the Complaints Committee.

The Press Council will not deal with any complaint if legal proceedings have been instituted or are threatened until after the proceedings have been concluded or abandoned. If such proceedings are threatened, or if the Council considers they are likely, it will require the complainant either to abandon the proceedings or to wait until they have been disposed of by the court. Where the complainant decides to abandon legal proceedings and proceed with his complaint before the Council, a formula exists designed to protect the newspaper from subsequent legal action. The object of this is twofold. First it is obviously undesirable that two sets of proceedings should be running at the same time; in any case Press Council proceedings must give way to court proceedings.

In the second place the Press Council will not allow process before it to be used as a means of 'discovery' to enable a complainant to obtain material for a legal action.

HOW A COMPLAINT IS DEALT WITH

The Complaints Committee frames its decision in the form of a recommendation to the Council; a similar procedure is followed by the General Purposes Committee. The Committee usually arrives at its recommendation upon the written statements and representations furnished by the two sides. Where these provide a clear conflict on material facts the persons concerned will be invited to appear before the Committee and give oral evidence. The Committee in this way has the advantage of observing the demeanour of witnesses and being able to put further questions to them. If the editor or any other journalist wishes to appear before the Council in person in order to supplement his statement or to put his point of view, the Committee will readily hear him.

Although a complaint is regarded by the Press Council as directed primarily against the newspaper rather than individual journalists, on the basis that the Editor is responsible both for what is in his newspaper and for the behaviour of his staff, the Council reserves the right to apportion blame to an individual journalist if his conduct seems to warrant it.

After the Complaints Committee reaches its decision, the Secretary prepares a note of the proceedings of the Committee which is at once the minutes of the Committee and the summary of its work. The Secretary's note includes a statement of the facts and the adjudication recommended; if oral evidence has been given the note will also contain the substance of this. The complete dossier is sent to each member of the Council in advance of the meeting to give members the opportunity of considering the recommendation of the Complaints Committee so that when the Council comes to deal with the case all the members will be fully informed of the facts on which the recommendation is based.

Many recommended adjudications are accepted by the Council without comment, but some do lead to a prolonged discussion, and on occasion the recommendation of the Complaints Committee will be reversed; sometimes the recommendation is accepted with some amendment of the wording. If there is a division of opinion in the Council, a vote is taken, and the decision of the majority prevails.

After a decision in Council is reached a summary of the facts and of the recommendation is released for publication.

To remove misunderstanding about the method of adjudication of complaints, and to clarify the procedure the Press Council in May 1964 issued the following statement of its practice:

Complaints about the conduct of the Press are considered by the Council on the report of the Complaints Committee which investigates every matter where it thinks that there is a case to answer and submits to the Council both a recommendation and the documents in the case.

The Committee usually arrives at its recommendation upon written statements and representations. But whenever it considers it necessary, e.g. where there is a conflict of evidence about a material fact, it invites the persons concerned to appear before it and give evidence. If any journalist wishes to appear before the Council in person in order to supplement his statement or to put his point of view, the Committee will hear him; in fact it has never refused to hear a journalist who has asked to appear before it.

PROCEEDINGS ARE IN PRIVATE

The adjudication of complaints is held in private. Neither the Press nor the public is present.

In considering its procedure after it was created the Council decided that it would not sit in public or permit reporters to attend its meetings. The decision to proceed with caution and to avoid unnecessary risks was understandable. The Council, still far from sure of itself, did not wish to lessen its chance of survival. Commenting on the decision to exclude the Press the *Observer* in a leading article of 28 March 1954 said: 'Newspapers which claim the right of free reporting in the public interest should be ready to apply the same principle to their own affairs.'

The Council explained that its position was an ambiguous one. It was a voluntary body in a different category from the statutory societies which could hold their meetings in public. Whether the Council was covered by legal privilege in respect of its proceeding was open to argument. If it was not it might be involved in heavy damages for defamation since its work consisted of the investigation of charges that might affect the livelihood of journalists or the credit of business undertakings. In the circumstances the Council felt that while it had nothing to hide it could not take the risk of conducting its affairs in open session. The meetings of the Council are still held in private.

Nevertheless the Council could not disregard the public interest in its adjudications, and it was decided to issue a statement of the result of adjudications at the close of each meeting and whenever possible to supplement the statement with additional particulars. The procedure was first adopted at the meeting of 4 May 1954 and gave rise to allegations that the Council was allowing itself to be hampered by excessive fear of the law of libel. The Council denied this, and said that on no occasion had it shirked the duty of investigation or toned down its judgments for publication because of fear of a suit for libel.

Some hundreds of cases have now been dealt with; judgment in many of them has contained severe criticism; the facts and the adjudications have been published in the Council's Annual Reports, which are on sale to the public, and in the Press. Often the judgments express criticism and censure of newspapers, editors and journalists in the most forthright terms. Yet there is no record of any proceedings for libel ever being started against the Council or its members or against the printers of the Council's reports or the newspapers that carry the reports. This was a great surprise and disappointment to the early opponents of the Council who had hoped and expected that it would be silenced and its activities ended by the crippling damages awarded against it in actions for libel.

The procedure for dealing with complaints in private was not changed when the Council was reconstituted in 1963.

LEGAL REPRESENTATION

Proceedings before the Council are informal. So far the Council has refused to permit legal representation to prevent its proceedings becoming too formal and legalistic. The Minister without Portfolio, Mr William Deedes on 6 May 1964 in answer to a question in Parliament whether he would introduce legislation to formalise the procedure of the Press Council said he would not. The Council had its own procedure and it did not provide for legal representation. Nevertheless, there are those who think that a journalist facing a charge of serious professional misconduct where an adverse finding could be very damaging to him should be permitted legal representation before the Council.

There are those also who think that if the Press Council conducted its proceedings in open session it would dispose of the reproach that the Press is less ready than it expects others to be whose affairs are of public interest to conduct them in public. If it is the fact that legal privilege does not attach to the proceedings of the Press Council, and this has yet to be tested in a court of law, a strong case would exist for adding such proceedings to the list of statutory privileged occasions.

SANCTIONS

The Press Council is concerned with the maintenance of the character of the British Press in accordance with the highest professional standards. This is plainly stated in the constitution. How then does the Council enforce compliance with these standards? A study of the constitution from which the Council derives its authority shows that it contains no provision for sanctions. The simple fact is that there are no sanctions, and the absence of provision for them was not an oversight.

The Royal Commission gave much thought to the matter. They were told that the best way to foster a sense of responsibility in the Press was to put behind the standards of the working journalist a sanction sufficiently strong to make him resist any temptation to depart from them. A Registration Council with power to keep a roll of qualified journalists and to strike off for professional misconduct, or a single professional association embracing all staff journalists with power to expel were some of the suggestions made. Such arrangements could only work if employers were debarred from employing journalists struck off or expelled or any others not on the roll. These conditions could only be created by turning journalism into a closed profession. This the Commission said would be disastrous. Their Report stated:

> The body we have in mind would not require the powers to control entry into the profession which characterise the statutory professional bodies and would depend for its effectiveness on its moral authority rather than on any statutory sanctions. It would derive its authority from the Press itself and not from statute. (Cmd. 7700, par. 656.)

Those who had urged that the Council should be a statutory body answerable to Parliament, with authority to discipline the Press and power to punish objectionable journalistic practices by fine, suspension or expulsion were disappointed that the Press Council when established did not have its origin in an Act of Parliament, that it was not answerable to Parliament and that it had no power of punishment. They were convinced that a Council without sanctions would be a Council without authority.

In the absence of sanctions the Council exerts its influence entirely by the exercise of its moral authority in the form of admonition and, in more serious cases, by censure. The Council is a court of honour concerned with conduct affecting the good name and good repute of the Press. Since no newspaper welcomes being held up to public condemnation for unprofessional conduct the Council's reprimands are not taken lightly. Moreover the offending newspaper is not only expected but is also morally bound to publish a statement of the case against it and the Council's ruling. An indication of the extent to which the newspapers observe this obligation was given by the Press Council following a question in Parliament. On 20 January 1964 the Minister without Portfolio was asked if he would introduce legislation to permit the Press Council to take space in the advertising columns of newspapers to publish its reports where newspapers had failed to publish them and to provide the Council with up to £100,000 for the purpose.

The Minister's reply was 'No'.

A few days later the Press Council issued a statement saying that the member's question might have given a wholly misleading impression of the attitude of editors and proprietors. The Council stated that in the previous three years there were only two recorded cases of offending newspapers not publishing an adjudication critical of their conduct.

PART TWO

The Press Council
Case-Book

This case-book is based on the Annual Reports of the Press Council and includes the cases in the first thirteen Reports. Each case dealt with bears a reference, for example 1966/43, to indicate the date of the Annual Report and the page in it where the case is reported.

In addition the book also includes the cases adjudicated by the Press Council in the first six months of 1967. These will appear in due course in the Fourteenth Annual Report. Meanwhile they are identified by the date 1967.

Cross-references to cases in other chapters are generally made by citing the newspaper concerned rather than the title.

5 Confidential Documents and Occasions

Documents marked 'confidential' or 'private and confidential' frequently come into the possession of a newspaper sometimes by chance, sometimes as the result of being sent by persons who have obtained them and think the newspaper should know of the contents. The documents are clearly not intended by their authors for newspapers or for publication although they may be of public interest. An editor wishing to publish a document of this nature may feel scruples about doing so because of its confidential marking. Is he morally bound by journalistic standards to refrain from doing so?

In its First Annual Report the Press Council gave some forthright advice.

Some critics, the Council stated, cherished the belief that they could suppress a document of which the public should know by labelling it 'private and confidential', and that the Press should consider themselves bound in honour to respect the injunction. Many a fussy little 'jack-in-office' would like to set up his own Official Secrets Act in this way. But every experienced editor would refuse to be fenced off. If hushing up a matter was against the public interest, the duty of the Press was clear, it must tell the public what was happening.

The Council gave some examples. It was wrong, for instance, for members of a town council to treat the public affairs entrusted to them as if they were a matter of their own private concern and to make arrangements for spending public money without giving the ratepayers the opportunity of expressing their views. Again, the planning of a strike or lock-out which would cause acute inconvenience to the public could not be treated as a private and confidential matter which the Press must not mention.

The Council later qualified its earlier declaration that documents did not become sacrosanct merely because they were labelled 'private and confidential'. The restriction should not be disregarded in all circumstances. A letter marked 'private and confidential' sent to a newspaper unquestionably imposed an obligation of honour on the editor not to publish it. This, however, did not mean that the information given in the letter was to be regarded for journalistic purposes as 'permanently vetoed'. The information could come to the editor from other sources, or the confidential letter accompanying it might be an attempt to suppress information that ought to be known. The editor, when deciding whether or not to publish it, must consider whether the confidentiality attributed to a document was well founded. He should not suppress information merely because an official or a public authority would find it more convenient if the Press kept quiet about it. (1955/6–8)

On the other hand the Press must not adopt unethical methods to obtain information, even about matters of public interest. See p. 307 (*Ilford Recorder*) for an example of this.

CONFIDENTIAL OCCASIONS

PARLIAMENTARY PARTY MEETINGS

The question whether the Press should publish information obtained unofficially about the proceedings at private meetings of Parliamentary parties was considered by the Press Council on a complaint by Mr Herbert Morrison (later Lord Morrison). He maintained that confidential matters discussed at private meetings should not be revealed in the newspapers. The newspapers argued in reply that the business of the Press was not to help politicians to keep their secrets, but to let the public know what was happening on issues of vital importance to the nation.

The Press Council approved this view, and stated it would be wrong for the Press to co-operate in a caucus policy of jealous concealment of the truth for partisan gain. (1954/7–8)

PUBLIC OR PRIVATE MEETINGS

Two years later the Managing Editor of the *Salisbury Journal*, Mr Robert Bennett, sought the advice of the Press Council in a dispute which had arisen between the Town Clerk acting on behalf of the City Council and himself.

The Town Clerk had protested that the newspaper had published a report of the meeting between tenants of the housing estate and representatives of the City Council to which the Press had not been invited.

The Town Clerk asked for an apology, but the proprietors of the newspaper said that they would not give one unless the Press Council advised that they should. There was no good reason shown, they said, and there could be no good reason why this particular meeting, which was clearly of interest to every ratepayer in the city, should have been held in private. If there was nothing to hide, why hold it in secret? If there was anything to hide, it was the duty of the newspaper to reveal it. They quoted Mr Aneurin Bevan as saying 'a representative of the people has no right to secrecy'.

The Press Council said that no apology was necessary and that the newspaper had behaved with complete propriety.

The City Council was also informed that while differences of opinion might arise between a city council and the editor of a local newspaper as to whether meetings ought to be held in public or in private, the Press Council considered that in this case the City Council was wrong in deciding to hold a private meeting about a matter in which not only the four hundred tenants of the estate but also the general body of the ratepayers of Salisbury were vitally interested. The Editor had acted quite rightly in deciding that the public should be able to read a report of the meeting. (1956/31, 47–9)

ROYAL SOCIETY OF MEDICINE

The President of the Royal Society of Medicine on behalf of his Council complained that the *Evening Standard* committed a 'serious breach of confidence' in blatantly publishing to a lay readership a contribution to a private meeting arranged for a professional audience.

The news story, which dealt with a hormone discovery, contained a brief statement said to have been made by a Fellow of the Royal Society of Medicine in a commentary on papers read at a London meeting of endocrinologists that day. It was alleged that written notices were displayed announcing the privacy of the meeting, and, if confidence in the privacy of such meetings was destroyed, it would be difficult to prevail upon speakers to take part in them, which would be damaging to the Society and to medicine as a whole.

The Editor, Mr Charles Wintour, replied that the use of drugs as rejuvenators was a matter of acute public interest. The newspaper's Science Correspondent saw a paper in the American Geriatrics Society's journal bearing on the subject. The Royal Society of Medicine did not give the newspaper any information about the meeting, and no representative was present who might have seen the warning poster. He denied the breach of confidence.

The Press Council held that although reference was made to the London meeting the newspaper report was clearly based on material previously published. The Council did not agree that the report was a breach of confidence and saw no valid objection to it. (1964/73–4)

REPORTER'S CONDUCT ATTACKED

A reporter of the *Northamptonshire Evening Telegraph* was alleged to have gained access to a private meeting of the local group of the Association of Supervisory Staffs Executives and Technicians by a subterfuge. The complainants said that the newspaper itself had been guilty of 'gross impropriety' in publishing the report.

The Editor and the reporter both strongly denied the allegations.

The Press Council held that there had been no impropriety whatever in the published statement about the meeting or in the method by which it was obtained by the newspaper.

The company which had made the complaint informed the Press Council that unless its decision was rescinded and a proper opportunity given for a representative of the company and the trade unions to appear before the Council, the matter would be raised immediately in the House of Commons.

The Council declined to reopen the matter on the ground that the mass of documentary evidence furnished by both sides provided all the required information. (1956/32)

See also p. 300, 'Anonymous Buyers at Public Auctions'.

CONFIDENTIAL DOCUMENTS

EDITOR'S RIGHT TO PUBLISH

The Darlington Borough Council complained of the publication by the *Northern Echo* and the *Northern Dispatch* of a document marked 'confidential'. The document was a report to members of the Borough Council of the discussion that had taken place between a Borough Council deputation and Dr Beeching about the future of the town's railway interests. The parties had agreed that public announcements about the talk should be confined to a joint communication. A confidential report of the talks was circulated to the members of the Council with an indication that publication would be a breach of faith with the Transport Commission.

The Borough Council alleged that the publication by the two newspapers was reprehensible and showed a lack of responsibility; it bred suspicion and ill-feeling when the relationship between the local authorities and local newspapers should be one of trust. The complaint was not that the newspapers broke a confidence reposed in them by the Borough Council, but that publication of a document intended for the private information of members did not accord with the highest professional standards.

The document had been handed to the Press by a councillor who objected to the report being confidential. The whole purpose of sending a deputation to see Dr Beeching, he said, was to give an anxious public more information on a matter of local importance, and as far as he was concerned the report was not confidential.

The Managing Director of the *Northern Dispatch*, Mr Frank Staniforth, said that he decided that publication was an inescapable duty. The Editor of the *Northern Echo*, Mr Harold Evans, was of the same opinion, and added that in his opinion the delegation ought not to have been pledged to secrecy.

The Press Council ruled:

1. The fact that the Borough Council treated the reports as confidential did not preclude the editors from making their own decisions on whether it should be published in the public interest.

2. The decision was entirely a matter for the editors, and the Press Council did not agree with the Borough Council's view that the editor's decision to publish was not in accordance with the highest professional standards.

3. The Press Council noted that it was a member of the Borough Council who gave the report to the Press. (1963/35–7)

CONFIDENTIALITY NOT BINDING ON THIRD PARTY

A similar issue arose on a complaint by the Brierley Hill Urban District Council that the Wolverhampton *Express and Star* had published a confidential memorandum about the rates proposed by the Treasurer for the consideration of the Finance Committee before the Committee had discussed it.

The publication was described by the complainants as a serious and disturbing departure from the standard of conduct expected from a newspaper. Permission to publish had neither been sought nor given.

When asked by the Finance Committee to reveal the source of his information, the Editor, Mr J. Clement Jones, refused to do so, but said the information was volunteered to a reporter without any indication that it was confidential, and that it was published because of the keen public interest in the rates.

He added that the Brierley Hill Council did not seem to understand the difference between information supplied on the basis of mutual recognition that it was confidential and information supplied without restriction as to its use. He did not agree that the seal of confidence automatically applied to a third party.

The Press Council upheld the Editor. It noted that the newspaper had given considerable space to the Brierley Hill Council's views of the publication. (1963/51–2)

LEGITIMATE POSSESSION VITAL TO PUBLICATION

The principle governing the publication of confidential documents was again considered when a complaint was made by the Magistrates' Association about the publication of a document which dealt with suggested penalties for motoring offences. The document, which was addressed to members, was marked 'To members of the Association only'; in addition each page was marked 'Confidential. Not for publication.' The *Daily Mail* published the report. The Secretary of the Association thereupon sent a letter for publication 'as of right' in which he pointed out that the suggestions circulated were only 'starting points'. He also complained of breach of confidence.

The Managing Editor of the *Daily Mail*, Mr E. V. Matthewman, was willing to publish that part of the letter deemed to be of general interest, but maintained that marking the document 'Confidential. Not for publication' could not be interpreted as an instruction to a newspaper to which it had not been addressed.

The Press Council upheld this view, and laid down the principle that a newspaper which comes legitimately into possession of a document issued confidentially to members of an organisation is not bound by the confidence enjoined on the persons to whom it is addressed. (1965/62–3)

LONDON STOCK EXCHANGE CASE

The *Sunday Telegraph* published a report headed 'Two Beatles Offered at 7/9*d* a Share' which stated that within a fortnight two Beatles would be quoted on the London Stock Exchange. The pair were John Lennon and Paul McCartney who were behind Northern Songs, a company seeking quotation and offering for sale 1,250,000 2*s* shares. The article gave the expected revenue and profit figures and the names of the directors.

The solicitors for the company and the brokers complained that the *Sunday Telegraph* details must have been obtained from an underwriting proof marked 'private and confidential' and 'not for publication'. The information could only have been obtained in an unethical way and should not have been published, because the Financial Editor must have known the unvarying practice of keeping arrangements for forthcoming public offers private and confidential.

The solicitor conceded that if the *Sunday Telegraph* had been given the information by a third party whom they believed authorised to give it, and the newspaper had not been given it on a confidential basis, the newspaper could not be criticised for publishing the information.

The City Editor of the newspaper, Mr Kenneth Fleet, maintained that the information published was given to him in the knowledge that it would be used in the newspaper. He was not bound by the words 'private and confidential' or 'not for publication' stamped on the documents, which were not the subject of an agreement to which he was a party. The publication of details of news issued in advance of the formal publication of financial documents was an accepted part of a City Editor's job.

The Press Council held there was no evidence that the information published was obtained improperly, and rejected the complaint. (1966/77–8)

THE MIDLAND LIBERALS

A complaint against the *Birmingham Planet* raised the question whether an editor in publishing extracts from a confidential report of an inquiry of public interest had a duty to obtain permission of the writers to reproduce official correspondence relating to the findings.

The newspaper published what it described as 'the document that has shocked the Liberals'; it was the report of an inquiry conducted by Mr John

Baker, Q.C., into the affairs of the Birmingham and West Midlands Liberal Federation.

Letters critical of the report were stated to have been sent to Liberal Party Headquarters and were extensively quoted.

The Editor of the *Planet*, Mr M. H. Guy, said the contents of the publication were given to the newspaper by a senior officer who asked that his name should not be mentioned. The newspaper was not bound to advise officers of the Liberal Organisations of its intention to publish extracts from the report.

The Press Council held that there was no unethical conduct by the *Birmingham Planet* in publishing, without reference to the parties concerned, information in its possession about the affairs of Liberal organisations in the region which the Editor considered to be of public interest. The complaint was rejected. (1966/78–9)

COMPREHENSIVE SCHOOLS CONTROVERSY

An article in the Stoke-on-Trent *Evening Sentinel* which dealt with plans for comprehensive education in Newcastle-under-Lyme was described by an alderman as 'a mockery of journalistic integrity'. The article referred to anxieties expressed by teachers, parents, and others, and claimed that the Education Committee of the Council had shown 'a perverse reluctance to reveal details of their intentions'. Teachers, it was said, were denied a sight of the documents setting out proposals, but the secrecy efforts were farcical because the details leaked out and were published in the article.

The alderman complained of untruths, half-truths, and innuendoes in the article. He had always attempted to keep people informed of the Education Committee's intentions; the first indications he had that the teachers were refused copies of the proposals was the report in the *Evening Sentinel*. He believed that consultative teachers had been given copies.

The Editor, Mr J. H. S. Tupholme, said the article was written in good faith and based on reasonable conclusions. The burden of the complaint seemed to be resentment over the suggestion that teachers were not being properly consulted. The alderman had not disclosed the fact that he had opposed the holding of a further consultation with the teachers; copies of the proposals might have been given to consultative teachers but they were unknown to the general body. He would willingly have given the alderman space if he had offered a rebuttal of the criticism.

A reporter claimed that he had been given a copy of the document containing the proposals.

The Press Council held that the newspaper was fully entitled to publish its views on the comprehensive schools controversy. The objection to the newspaper's criticisms largely turned on whether a document handed to the Press at a sub-committee meeting was available for immediate publication or not. On this point the evidence was conflicting. The Council noted, however, that the newspaper had published lengthy statements from the official side replying to criticisms and points of detail. The allegation that the article was 'a mockery of journalistic integrity' was not substantiated, and the complaint was rejected. (1966/73-4)

In 1955 a series of inquiries was put to the Press Council by official bodies on the interpretation and effect of the endorsement of documents with the words 'private and confidential'.

The circumstances and the replies of the Press Council are contained in the four cases that follow.

THE EDUCATIONAL INSTITUTE OF SCOTLAND

The Educational Institute of Scotland complained that the Glasgow *Sunday Post* had published in full a plebiscite form issued to members on the establishment of a strike fund to advance professional interests. The form was marked 'Private and confidential. Not to be communicated to the Press'.

The Press Council took the view that the mere marking of a document as 'private and confidential' did not prevent a newspaper from publishing it, if it considered that the subject was one of general importance and not merely of interest to those to whom the document was primarily addressed. (1955/16)

POOLE COUNCIL

The *Poole and Dorset Herald* published a report prepared by the Borough Surveyor and circulated to a limited number of members of the local authority. The document was not marked 'confidential', as all papers issued to members of committees were in fact confidential. The Town Clerk of Poole asked the Press Council whether the newspaper was justified in publishing the report. He also raised the question whether the newspaper was justified in refusing to disclose the identity of the person from whom the document had been obtained.

The Press Council replied that even if the document had been marked 'private and confidential' this would not prevent the newspaper from publishing it if it considered that the matter was one of general importance.

In reply to the other question the Council said that the normal procedure was for the Editor not to disclose a source of information unless he was ordered to do so by Parliament or by a court of law. (1955/16)

COUNTY COUNCILS ASSOCIATION

The County Councils Association stated that among papers that they had sent to the Press from time to time were a number dealing with 'private and confidential matters'. The Association inquired of the Press Council whether in the event of a newspaper receiving information in this way which was clearly private and confidential the newspaper would be entitled to publish it.

The Press Council replied as follows:

> The obligation not to disclose genuinely confidential information rests upon newspaper editors as upon other members of the community. Experience has shown, however, that documents are sometimes marked 'Private and confidential' in order to prevent publication of matters which in the public interest ought to be published. Where a document marked private is handed to a newspaper by someone who thinks it contains information which ought to be made public the editor must use his own judgment in deciding whether the document has been marked private for good or bad reasons, and he should naturally take this decision with a keen sense of responsibility.
>
> Public bodies will of course decide for themselves the extent to which they wish to take a newspaper into their confidence, bearing in mind that an editor's decision whether to publish or not will be taken in the light of all the facts he has been able to ascertain. (1955/17)

LLANELLY COUNCIL

Complaint was made that the *Llanelly Star* had published a confidential report prepared by the Borough Treasurer on the rents of council houses. The report was submitted to the Council at two private meetings, but no statement was given to the Press. Subsequently extracts from the document were published in the *Llanelly Star*. The Town Clerk had been unable to ascertain how the Editor obtained a copy of it. When questioned the Editor quoted a ruling by the Press Council that the mere marking of a document as 'private and confidential' would not preclude a newspaper from publishing it if it was considered that the subject was one of general importance.

The Town Clerk asked the Press Council whether an editor in interpreting this ruling should have regard to local or other circumstances containing the consideration of a private and confidential report.

The Press Council replied that it did not consider that the Editor had been guilty of a breach of privilege in publishing the contents of the report. (1955/17–18)

'NOT FOR PUBLICATION'

A minute of the Earby Urban District Council dealing with the proposed conversion of a local cinema into a public hall and swimming-bath was marked 'not for publication'. The *Barnoldswick and Earby Times* published an article relating to the matter, but not until after the matter had been considered in open Council at a later date. The Urban District Council complained to the Press Council and decided to exclude representatives of the local newspaper from future meetings and to cease to supply agenda, reports and minutes to the Editor.

The Press Council declared that the Editor had a full right to publish the news, once it had come before the full meeting of the Council, and regretted the action taken against the newspaper. (1960/29–30)

PERMISSIBLE BREACH OF MEDICAL CONFIDENCE

A decision by the Press Council in 1962 led to a lively discussion in *The Times* and other newspapers. The question at issue was whether a newspaper, in seeking a reprieve for a man condemned to death, had the right to publish extracts from confidential medical documents concerning his mental health.

The case came before the Council as the result of its attention being drawn by a Harley Street surgeon to the publication in the *Observer* of medical evidence which showed that Hanratty, who was about to be executed for murder, as a boy had been diagnosed as a mental defective. The surgeon said that a serious breach of confidence had occurred unless the disclosures had been sanctioned by the patient, by the doctor who wrote the letter which was quoted and by the hospital authorities whose case record had been photographed.

The Deputy Editor of the *Observer*, Mr J. M. D. Pringle, said that the documents — copies not originals — were given to Mr Sydney Silverman, M.P., by the condemned man's solicitor with the object of obtaining publicity and were published by the newspaper in furtherance of that objective. It had not been possible to reveal the facts at the trial because the defence was based on wrong identification. Before publishing the documents the *Observer* had tried to contact all the doctors mentioned in them, including one in Australia, and succeeded in doing so in several instances. None of them objected to publication, and the newspaper felt that it was clearly a matter of public interest, even of duty, to make the facts known.

The Press Council held that the documents had been handed by the condemned man's solicitor to a Member of Parliament for the purpose of obtaining publicity in his interest, but, in any case, it was a matter of profound public importance, and to insist that traditional confidences should be preserved would seem, in the circumstances of the case, not to be justified. The Council was of the opinion that the *Observer* was fully justified in publishing what it did and upheld its right to do so. (1962/40–1)

For another case of breach of medical confidence see p. 345, *Daily Telegraph*.

TENANTS' 'SECRET' MEETING

When a West Indian family moved into a flat on an estate in Earlsfield demonstrations of colour prejudice occurred. The Committee of the Estate Tenants' Association arranged with representatives of the three main political parties and Wandsworth Borough Council to discuss the problem.

A leaflet was distributed to estate tenants announcing the meeting, and a copy was sent to local newspapers. The newspapers were requested not to publish the information in it.

The Tenants' Association complained that the *Balham and Tooting News and Mercury* announced that the tenants were to hold a secret meeting and gave particulars from the leaflet as a statement by the Association's Secretary. It was contended that the way in which the matter was published was not in the public interest in view of the violent demonstrations that had occurred previously.

The Assistant Editor, Mr B. Murray, denied any betrayal of confidence and said it had never been his desire to exacerbate the problem on the estate.

The adjudication stated that the Press Council noted that the official handout about the tenants' meeting was supplied to the local newspapers on the basis that, in the public interest, the announcement was not for publication. The newspaper in its next issue published details taken from this communication.

The Press Council rejected the newspaper's explanation for this and censured it for its irresponsible action. It was wrong to describe as 'secret' a meeting to which the Press had been invited. (1964/66–7).

DELETED PASSAGE OF SCRIPT PUBLISHED

When Princess Margaret addressed two R.A.F. squadrons in Germany, an official script of her speech supplied to the Press after delivery contained a clearly marked deletion of seven words which referred to the number of enemy aircraft destroyed in the Battle of Britain by one of the squadrons. The Princess did not say the words. In most national newspapers the following day reference was made to this omission. The *Daily Express* carried the heading 'Margaret censored' and quoted the words deleted. The *Daily Sketch* said the deletion was to avoid hurting German feelings. *The Times, Daily Herald, Daily Telegraph* and *Daily Mail* also called attention to the omission, and quoted an R.A.F. spokesman who said that the cut was made as a mark of respect to the host country.

Princess Margaret's Press Secretary asked the Press Council to say whether the reporting of part of a written speech omitted in delivery, or comment on officially supplied script of a speech, was in accord with journalistic ethics.

Editorial views expressed to the Council differed. The following opinions were expressed by editors.

1. If the deletion was to be regarded as confidential the script should have said so.

2. The reporting of part of a written speech deliberately omitted in delivery, or comment on the omission is undesirable except where an 'on-the-record' statement is given explaining the reasons for the omission.

3. It should be the accepted practice of all newspapers not to refer to passages deleted from scripts and not delivered unless the originators of the script give their permission.

The judgment of the Press Council was: Scripts are supplied for the assistance of the Press, and where alterations have been made by the speaker the original draft should not be reported without the speaker's permission. (1965/47–8)

EAVESDROPPING

LISTENING IN ON TELEPHONE

In his column in *Reynolds News*, Mr Tom Driberg, M.P., quoted from a telephone call he had accidentally overheard through a technical fault. The speakers were checking information for a lecture to be given by the Duke of Edinburgh. In making the point that the telephone service was at fault, Mr Driberg revealed something of what the Duke was to say.

In reply to a complaint to the Press Council that it was intolerable for a journalist to publish a private conversation overheard on the telephone, Mr Driberg described the complaint as frivolous and trivial. He denied that the article could have caused any serious embarrassment to the Duke of Edinburgh.

The Press Council protested in vigorous terms about the light-minded way the matter was dealt with by Mr Driberg and the Editor of *Reynolds News*, Mr W. R. Richardson. It thought that criticism of the telephone service could have been made quite as effectively without divulging the contents of a private conversation. It deplored eavesdropping of this kind, and considered it detrimental to the standards of journalism which was the Council's duty to protect. (1955/19, 38–40)

OVERHEARD CONVERSATION

The director of a jeweller's shop in Colchester was shot in the thigh as he tackled two raiders.

A report of the incident in the *News of the World* attributed a statement to the director which he denied having made.

A local correspondent who had supplied the report said that he was present at the police station when the director went there, after having had the bullet extracted at the County Hospital, and he had overheard what the director said to the police. He gave the substance of what was said, but when asked by the newspaper for quotes he provided them, making it clear at the time that the remarks were not addressed to him.

The Editor of the newspaper said that he saw no reason to doubt that the statement quoted in the report had been made. In any case, the report did not say the statement had been made to the correspondent.

The Press Council held that the article was misleading in presenting a personal statement by the director in a way which suggested that he had made it to a press representative.

The action of the journalist in reporting a private conversation accidentally overheard was unethical. (1966/70–1)

LORD DENNING — AN ABUSE OF CONFIDENCE

The *Sunday Times* published a picture of Lord Denning, who at the time was investigating security questions arising out of the Profumo affair. The pictured showed Lord Denning with an open file of letters before him. The newspaper's columnist disclosed the contents of one of the letters, which had been magnified by the camera lens. The paragraph was headed: 'Security leak' and underneath it said: 'It is ironic to say the least that the gentleman dedicated to investigating security leaks should have been so unlucky with his own. So who, oh who, will guard the guards?'

The complainant stated that the disclosure was against the decencies of life. People who examined the photograph were morally in the position of people who happened to see private papers on somebody else's desk. To read them was ill-mannered and dishonourable; to repeat what one read was far worse; and to publish it for all the world to read was unforgivable.

Lord Denning told the Press Council that he allowed pictures of himself at work because he felt public interest warranted it. The photographs were taken at some distance, and he did not dream that modern science enabled photographs to be 'blown-up' and the contents of letters read, or that his confidence in the photographer would be abused.

The Editor of the *Sunday Times*, Mr C. D. Hamilton, stated that by permitting a private letter to appear in a photograph, Lord Denning had removed that letter from the category of 'private'. He did not agree that this instance could be compared with reading private papers on somebody else's desk.

But the Press Council held that the letter published in the *Sunday Times* was clearly a private document and condemned its publication as a breach of faith. (1964/52)

6 Embargoes

The Press Council has given the following description of the purpose and object of the embargo system: 'It is customary to issue important [public documents] with a statement giving the time at which they may be published. The object of the system is to give newspaper staffs plenty of time to prepare adequate summaries and considered comment.' The Council went on to say that the embargo system had worked well, and if it were abandoned the Press would be gravely handicapped by having to handle long and important documents under conditions of unnecessary rush, and both the newspapers and the public would not be as well served with information and enlightenment as they should be.

The growing complexity of public affairs made the additional time provided by the embargo essential if newspapers were to be able to prepare intelligible explanations of many of the technical and voluminous documents of interest and importance to the public.

The effectiveness of the embargo clearly depends on its strict observance. An infringement destroys its validity and, besides threatening the benefit it confers on the Press as a whole, an infringement brings the honour and good name of the Press into disrepute.

The following cases have been dealt with by the Press Council.

NOTIFICATION OF EMBARGOES

An important decision on the notification of embargoes arose out of a protest made by a number of provincial newspapers.

EMBARGO DATE — ALL NEWSPAPERS SHOULD BE NOTIFIED

The London Editors of the *Bristol Evening Post*, Wolverhampton *Express and Star*, *Nottingham Evening Post*, *Yorkshire Evening Post* and *Manchester Evening News*, drew the attention of the Press Council to stories published in the *Sunday Express* and *Observer* divulging the British Railways Reorganisation Plan in detail. The completeness and accuracy of the accounts, they said, left little room for doubt that they had been derived from a preview of the British Transport Commission's document setting out the scheme, copies of which were issued in advance to certain sections of the Press under strict embargo.

The Sunday papers had not received these advance copies, and it was appreciated that the *Sunday Express* and the *Observer* may have acted in innocence of the embargo. Nevertheless, the provincial editors wrote, there was a strong case needing investigation of a serious lapse which threatened to jeopardise good relations between all Fleet Street offices, Government departments and organisations like the British Transport Commission.

The Editor of the *Observer*, Mr David Astor, gave an absolute assurance that neither the economic correspondent nor anyone else on the staff had seen or sought to obtain any information about the contents of the document setting out the British Transport Commission's scheme. The report in the *Observer*, he said, was entirely based on the British Transport Commission's

Sixth Annual Report. All the facts cited in the article were contained in that Report.

The Editor of the *Sunday Express*, Mr John Junor, also denied that his newspaper had had an advance copy of the Report. They were quite unaware of any embargo, and their story had reached them through normal news channels and was printed in good faith. He added that so long as he was an editor he had no intention of breaking embargoes, which he realised were for the convenience of newspapers. He could not, however, be expected to honour embargoes the existence of which he was unaware.

The Press Council found that the embargo had not been deliberately broken by either newspaper. A good deal of confusion, however, had arisen because the Transport Commission's document had not been sent to the Press generally.

The Council recommended that the notification of an embargo should in future be forwarded to all morning, evening and Sunday newspapers with a copy of the Press statement.

The recommendation was forwarded to the Transport Commission and also to the Government's Central Office of Information with the request that it be communicated to the public relations officers of all Government departments. (1955/22–3, 29–30)

COMPLAINTS UPHELD

A CALCULATED BREACH

A case which attracted a great amount of interest was a quite deliberate breach of an embargo in order to register a protest. It occurred in 1956 and related to the New Year's Honours List. That year 1 January fell on a Sunday, and the authorities decided that the List should not be published until the Monday. Advance copies of the List were sent to newspapers and news agencies with an embargo that it was not to be published until Monday 2 January. The Editor of the Sunday newspaper, the *People*, Mr Stuart Campbell, angered at the denial to the Sunday newspapers of the right to print the List ahead of the dailies on one of the few occasions when 1 January fell on a Sunday, decided to ignore the embargo. He told the Press Council that he did so by way of protest. The embargo, he contended, was a breach of the principles of fair comment and common sense. As the *London Gazette* was not published on a Sunday it was nonsense not to allow the newspapers to publish the List on the grounds that they would be scooping the official publication. He hoped, he said, that his action would lead to fairer treatment for the Sunday newspapers.

Among the organisations which protested against the breach were the Parliamentary Lobby correspondents whose duty it is to collect the Honours List for their newspapers.

Pending the adjudication of the complaint and the consideration of Mr Campbell's protest on behalf of the Sunday newspapers, he undertook to honour all existing embargo arrangements.

The Press Council rejected the arguments advanced by the Editor and strongly condemned and censured him for the calculated breach of an embargo that was in clear terms. No newspaper, the Council declared, had a right to disregard an embargo for its own ends. The action of the *People* placed the system of issuing information in advance on a confidential basis in jeopardy. The Council took the opportunity to commend the restraint of the other Sunday newspapers which loyally observed the embargo, although they were aware that the *People* intended to disregard it. (1956/27–8)

AN INTERNATIONAL EMBARGO

Two national newspapers, *The Times* and the *Manchester Guardian*, complained that the *Daily Telegraph* had infringed an embargo on the publication of the United Nations report on the Hungarian revolt. The report should not have appeared in the Press before 11.00 G.M.T. on 20 June 1957, which meant that it was available for the evening but not the morning papers that day. The *Daily Telegraph*, however, published the report in its late morning editions.

The complaining newspapers stated that it was in the interest of all newspapers that the trust reposed in them should be safeguarded. If embargoes were broken by some, they would soon be broken by all. It would become impossible for national and international bodies to issue documents in advance on a confidential basis, and this would be harmful both to newspapers and the public.

The *Daily Telegraph* said it had received information that the embargo might be broken in the United States, and it had therefore prepared extracts from the report in case they should be needed suddenly. Two British national newspapers had printed a summary of the report in their early editions, and the *Telegraph* decided that the embargo was effectively broken. It released the prepared extracts at 1 a.m. The newspaper did not inform other newspapers or the news agencies of its intention to disregard the embargo.

The Press Council condemned the *Daily Telegraph* for its breach of confidence in publishing an embargoed document before the hour fixed for its publication throughout the world. (1957/24–5, 37–9)

FOOTBALL LEAGUE FIXTURES

The Secretary of the Football League Limited submitted a complaint about the *Enfield Gazette and Observer*. A year previously the newspaper had published information about the Football League's provisional fixtures for the 1965–6 season and had been told that the information was the copyright of the Football League. The Editor had apologised and said that the sub-editor who had dealt with the copy was unaware of the copyright in the list.

The newspaper had printed a provisional list of Tottenham Hotspur fixtures which had been sent to the club marked 'private and confidential' with a request circulated through the Press Association that sports editors should not print anything until the approved fixture list was issued.

The Editor of the newspaper, Mr C. R. Maunder, said that he assumed that the matter raised the previous year referred to the League's copyright. He gave instructions that the next list of fixtures should carry the wording 'Copyright of the Football League Ltd' and this was done. The newspaper did not, he added, receive the Press Association memorandum. Had he done so, he would have honoured it.

The Secretary of the League said that the provisional list for 1966–7 from which the newspaper obtained its information was not sent to any newspaper or news agency by the League.

The Editor claimed that it was not until the League wrote at length that the newspaper was aware of an embargo on the fixtures. When he became aware of it he withheld publication of Arsenal F.C. fixtures. In the absence of knowledge of the embargo he thought that they were entitled to publish the list.

The Press Council adjudication was that the basis of publication of Football League fixtures free of copyright fee by newspapers is generally agreed. The request that there should not be any publication until the final form was printed by the Football League was reasonable and should have been complied with. The *Enfield Gazette and Observer* should have been aware of this arrangement. (1967)

COMPLAINTS REJECTED

INFORMATION INDEPENDENTLY OBTAINED

An embargo on information contained in a document does not, however, rule out the publication of information already in the possession of a newspaper.

The matter was considered when the *Guardian* on 18 February 1961 published the news that Lord James of Rusholme had been appointed first Vice-Chancellor of York University. The official announcement was embargoed until 20 February. When a complaint was made of what appeared to be an obvious breach of the embargo, the Editor of the *Guardian*, Mr Alastair Hetherington, said that he had obtained the news legitimately in time for publication before receipt of the official announcement, but had withheld publication for twenty-four hours. As the news was then known in a fairly wide circle, he felt that it was impossible to hold up publication until 20 February. The complainant argued that for an editor to observe or ignore an embargo as it suited his convenience was unfair to other editors.

The Press Council decided that having regard to all the circumstances, the *Guardian* had not acted improperly. (1961/28–9)

WHAT AN EMBARGO DOES NOT MEAN

A similar question was considered in the hearing of a complaint made by Mr Alan Hardaker, Secretary of the Football League against the *Daily Express* and the *Daily Mirror* for alleged infringement of an embargo on information about amendments to the Football League Rules. Mr Hardaker complained that both newspapers printed articles which infringed the ban the day before the embargo expired. He maintained the embargo prevented discussion of the subject matter of the embargo until the ban ended.

The Editor of the *Daily Express*, Mr Robert Edwards, stated that he was meticulous in ensuring that nothing learned exclusively from the embargoed statement appeared in the newspaper. What was published in his newspaper was information given by Mr Hardaker at a Press Conference in Dublin some time previously, and the new proposals relating to the employment of players had been common knowledge for some time.

The Editor of the *Daily Mirror*, Mr L. A. Lee Howard, said that the content of the article of which Mr Hardaker complained was either common knowledge or the result of inquiries and deductions made independently of the embargoed material. He did not accept Mr Hardaker's interpretation of the meaning of a Press embargo. The *Mirror* report was a preliminary report to draw attention to whatever findings were to be made public later. The proposals in the embargoed document were not discussed, and no information from it was disclosed.

The Press Council stated that it was an established practice for newspapers to publish preliminary articles based partly on known facts and partly on anticipation when they dealt with impending Government and other announcements of particular public interest. There could not be any reasonable objection to this, and the Council could not accept the view of the Football League that the issue of an embargoed document implied that there should be no reference to the subject before the document was available for publication. The Council considered that there was no misuse of information by either the *Daily Mirror* or the *Daily Express*. (1964/68–9)

An embargo can operate against a single newspaper. It need not even be in writing but can rise out of an undertaking given by a reporter. For a case of this kind see p. 342 (*South London Press*).

7 Fair Comment

COMMENT MUST BE FAIR AND BASED ON FACT

COMMENT MUST BE ON A MATTER OF PUBLIC INTEREST

COMMENT MUST NOT BE REPORTED AS FACT

COMMENT BASED ON FACTS KNOWN AT THE TIME

Lord Birkett in the course of a judgment in the Court of Appeal (Kemsley *v*. Foot (1951) 1 All E.R. 331) stated that fair comment was now recognised to be one of the most valuable parts of the law of libel and slander.

> It is an essential part of the greater right of free speech. It is the right of every man to comment freely, fairly, and honestly on any matter of public interest, and this is not a privilege which belongs to particular persons in particular circumstances. It matters not whether the comments are made to the few or to the many. Whether they are made by a powerful newspaper or by an individual, whether they are written or spoken, the defence that the words are fair comment on a matter of

public interest is open to all. When defendants who wish to rely on this defence are deprived of it, the importance of the matter is manifest to all.

It is the exercise of this right 'to comment freely, fairly and honestly on any matter of public interest' which the Press Council safeguards when dealing with complaints of unfair reporting.

The right of the Press to comment freely has a significance and importance far beyond the interests of the Press itself. In its First Annual Report, the Press Council pointed out that a free and trusted Press is the only ultimate safeguard of our democracy, and since the rights of the individual to express himself are precisely the same as those of his newspaper, it follows that if the rights of the newspaper are whittled away those of the individual will as surely diminish.

Freedom of speech, however, whether it be the spoken, the written or the printed word is freedom under the law. The law balances the right of the individual to his reputation against the equally important right of the public to express their views honestly and fearlessly on matters of public interest. A newspaper has exactly the same rights, neither more nor less than the individual citizen, but it commands a vastly greater audience. The power this gives the newspaper involves a responsibility not to abuse the power or use it tyrannically.

The defence of fair comment in an action for libel or slander will only succeed if the comment is on a matter of public interest, if the facts on which the comment is based are correctly stated, and if the comment is the fair and honest opinion of the person making it. When considering whether an article of which complaint is made is fair, the Press Council will probably have regard to the same tests as does a court of law in dealing with a plea of fair comment. The Council will not, however, in accordance with its practice, investigate the ethical aspects of a report if it is the subject of a libel action until the legal proceedings are over.

The legendary C. P. Scott of the *Manchester Guardian* expressed in a simple phrase what can be described as a golden rule of journalism: 'Comment is free, but facts are sacred'. The fairness of a comment does not depend on whether other people agree with it. In an action for libel against an eminent newspaper columnist, Mr Justice Salmon told the jury 'The enthusiast, the crank, the man with deep feelings, with strong and even prejudiced and obstinate views is just as much entitled to express his honest opinion as the meek and mild, the sweetly reasonable man'. People, said the judge, were free to state fearlessly to anyone their real opinion honestly held upon a matter of public interest. They could state such opinions in any way they liked, 'diffidently, decorously, politely and discreetly, or pungently, provocatively, rudely and even brutally' ('Liberace *v. Daily Mirror* and W. Connor (Cassandra)').

But when a journalist invents or distorts facts or presents as a fact what is only a deduction or an assumption from particular circumstances any comment that follows is as dangerous as the bogus fact on which it is based. It was a situation of this kind that the Tribunal of Inquiry, appointed after the conviction of Vassall for espionage, had to deal with.

In the course of the debate in the House of Commons on 6 May 1963 on the Report of the Radcliffe Tribunal, the Prime Minister, Mr Macmillan, recalled the atmosphere of hysteria which prevailed after Vassall's exposure and arrest. As a result serious allegations were made against Ministers, security officers and civil servants. He went on to state that newspapers in their task of finding out the truth and publishing it, may have a feeling that in some cases Government or other officials tended to push out the frontiers of what are called 'secrets' too far. In times of war there was a very careful and strong censorship on the Press; in peace this had normally not been necessary.

'But,' said the Prime Minister, 'I am afraid we must face the fact that in this unhappy twilight world in which we live in a state of truce — neither war nor peace — it is not always easy for the Government and their officers, or the Press, to know exactly where the line should be drawn, and that the system can only work on the basis of mutual confidence.'

Apart from security matters, the Press had a right and a duty to find out the truth, to publish it and comment on it as it thought fit. The advantages of a free Press, Mr Macmillan said, far outweighed any of its disadvantages, but as with every right there was a corresponding obligation. Men in public life must expect, whether by the reporter's words or the cartoonist's pencil, to suffer some wounding blows, but they had the right to expect that while they might be wounded they should not be hounded.

On its side, the Prime Minister continued, Parliament should recognise the difficult circumstances under which journalists and the Press laboured, with editions having to be brought out by night and day. But he thought they had the right to complain if 'statements are made as fact when they are only inference and have no foundation, and then, from them, deductions are drawn which I feel certain are realised, within a day or two of their being printed, by those responsible for them to have been fantastic'.

The Press Council, when it considered the report of the Radcliffe Tribunal, expressed very much the same views. About some of the newspaper articles which the Tribunal had been obliged to review in the course of its inquiries, the Press Council said:

> The Press has the right and indeed the duty to investigate and comment on matters concerning national security, but the Council condemns the publication, in some London newspapers, of false information and damaging innuendos based on nothing more than conjecture, assumption and speculation. It regards these reports as a serious lowering of the standards of a responsible Press.

The cases that follow have been classified as far as possible in accordance with the principles the Press Council has stated should determine whether the standards of fair comment have been observed or transgressed.

THE RIGHT TO COMMENT

EDITORIAL COMMENT UNOBJECTIONABLE

The Middlesbrough Trades Council, one of six bodies which had organised a demonstration against unemployment, complained that the *Yorkshire Post* had deliberately distorted the facts in their report of the meeting to denigrate the motives of the organisers. The Chairman was reported to have asked his 'unemployed audience' to give generously to a collection to defray expenses, but, it was claimed, he had said categorically that his call was not to the unemployed. In an editorial the paper criticised the organisers for what it thought to be a political stunt to exploit unemployment.

Mr W. T. Oliver, Deputy Editor of the newspaper, stated that there had been no deliberate distortion and said that the editorial was written in genuine indignation because the demonstration looked like a stunt to exploit unemployment. The reporter had not heard the Chairman's remarks about the exemption of the unemployed from the collection.

The Press Council found that no objection could be taken to the strong editorial views, but that the news report was not objective. This had been met by printing a lengthy letter of protest. (1963/38)

UNAUTHORISED USE OF PICTURE

In thanking the crofter weavers of the Outer Hebrides for a gift of tweed Mrs Kennedy, wife of the American President, sent signed copies of a photograph of herself. Reproductions of the photograph were sent with a story to the Press by a public relations company. The *Sunday Telegraph* reproduced the picture and alleged that its use in this way was dishonourable commercial conduct.

The public relations company said the photograph was attached to the news story as authentication and was not intended for publication.

The Press Council ruled that the newspaper was entitled to draw attention to the fact that a picture of Mrs Kennedy had been used in commercial publicity without her permission. (1963/48–9)

C.N.D. PROTESTS

In an editorial comment on a suggestion made at a meeting of the Chislehurst and Sidcup Urban District Council that the Campaign for Nuclear Disarmament movement had been, or was, subversive, the *Sidcup and Kentish Times* stated that the C.N.D. had been infiltrated by persons concerned with furthering destructive and disruptive aims and asked whether or not the movement was now some sort of national security risk. It was plain, the article stated, that the C.N.D. people were planning a campaign of infiltration into the Civil Defence Corps.

The organiser of the local branch of the C.N.D. complained that the newspaper had imputed corrupt practices to the C.N.D. and dishonesty and subversive intent to him. Another complainant said that scathing criticism was permissible, but smearing was not.

The Editor-in-Chief of the *Kentish Times* series, Mr J. S. Massey, said that the title of the leading article was 'Subversive or Not?' The article made due acknowledgment that there were 'genuinely pacifist and idealist' members. The article was fair comment.

The Press Council in its adjudication held that the newspaper editorial was fair comment on a matter of public interest raised at a meeting of the Urban District Council.

In its 'Letters' columns the newspaper gave its readers adequate opportunity to reply to the criticisms in the editorial. (1964/63–4)

ATTACK ON LOCAL COUNCIL

The Chairman of the Stockport Borough Council's Housing Committee complained that a report in the *Stockport Advertiser* of a Borough Council debate was not objective news reporting but was garbled, distorted, and an exercise in party propaganda. In the issue after the report, it published a letter from the alderman setting out his points of grievance, and also an editorial entitled 'Dismal Record' which criticised the housing achievement of the Socialist Council.

The complaint to the Press Council said that the editorial was 'the meanest method of again publishing the abusive rubbish'. The Press Council accepted the reply of Mr Ian Pearson Walsh, the Editor, that the report was a balanced and unbiased account of the Borough Council's debate; it deplored the alderman's attitude to the newspaper's editorial comment and upheld the right to free expression of opinion. (1963/41–2)

'THIS STRIKE WAS SHAMEFUL'

Under the heading 'This Strike was Shameful' the *Daily Mirror* published an article on the circumstances surrounding a dispute at the London Docks in 1954. A branch official of the Transport and General Workers' Union, complained that the article was a complete travesty of the truth.

The Press Council decided that the complaint was unjustified and that the *Daily Mirror* was fully entitled to say what it did on a matter of vital public interest. (1955/25)

REST HOMES FOR HORSES AND DONKEYS

An article in the *People* on the financial administration of rest homes for horses and donkeys advised readers to restrict their support until the finances were put on a good basis. The writer said that the rest homes' bills were mounting and that the secretary had told subscribers that it was now a regis-tered charity, which was not true. He added that the secretary of the homes had admitted she was in need of ready cash. She should join forces, he said, with some bigger organisation where her kindness could find an outlet. 'If she won't, then it is up to the Charity Commissioners to stop her calling her fund a charity and raising money from the public.' The secretary complained that the story was 'malicious, unfair and harmful', and said that had it not been for the article she would have been registered as a charity, and funds to help the cause would have been received.

Mr Stuart Campbell, Editor of the *People*, said the secretary should give up trying to undertake the work without adequate support. He told the Press Council that on two or three occasions the *People* had tried to help by printing her appeals for help, but readers had begun to complain, and a reporter had spent two weeks investigating the rest homes' affairs. He came to the conclusion that the secretary was not dishonest, but was unbusinesslike in handling the monetary side of her homes. Nowhere was it stated or implied in the article that the main object in running the homes was to make a personal profit.

The adjudication of the Press Council was that in the circumstances it was the duty of the Editor to inquire into the position and inform his readers. The inquiry was made honestly and carefully, and the criticisms resulting from it were made in good faith. The complaint was rejected. (1966/43–4)

DISAGREEMENT ABOUT THE FACTS

An article in the *People* criticised a local council for what were regarded as unduly heavy duties for a warden in aged people's flatlets. The official advertisement for the appointment stated that the person appointed would be provided with a flatlet. It went on to set out the thirty-five duties involved in six sections: supervisory; cleaning; laundry and heating installations; inspection and maintenance; social welfare and miscellaneous. The post was offered as a part-time job at £5 a week.

The article stated: 'My deepest sympathy with the successful applicant — and my utmost contempt for an authority with such meanness and audacity'. The Urban District Council complained and said the majority of the warden's duties were of an occasional nature only. The *People* had published its comments without approaching the Council, which indicated its desire for sensationalism instead of the truth.

The Editor of the *People*, Mr Stuart Campbell, said that if the complaint was based on the view that the thirty-five duties listed in the document were within the compass of a £5-a-week part-time warden it was derisory.

The Press Council held that the article was not misleading. Although the criticism was strong, it expressed a point of view that could reasonably be held. The complaint was rejected. (1965/58)

WHO MAKES THE LOCAL COUNCIL DECISIONS?

An article in the *Journal*, a Birmingham Trades Council publication, implied that officers of Birmingham City Council were deciding matters of principle which should be the function of elected members. The article was written by Professor David Eversley and was headed: 'The Lid Off Birmingham's Traffic Chaos. No proper planning, car-parking muddle. Who makes the decisions?' The writer suggested that the City Engineer had not shown the appropriate Council committee a Government department letter about land usage.

It was suggested that fewer and fewer decisions were submitted to the elected Council members and that even matters of fundamental principle were left entirely to the officers.

The Town Clerk of Birmingham complained that the article was based on inaccurate information, of which the author ought to have satisfied himself beforehand, and that it was untrue and unfair to members and officers of the City Council. An inquiry had been held which made it clear that the letter from the Government department had reached the Public Works Committee within a week of arrival.

These complaints were contested by the author of the article, and the Press Council found that it was not proved that the article was untrue and unfair, and rejected the complaint. (1965/72)

PARTISAN PHRASEOLOGY

The *Sunday Express*, in a leading article on the Rhodesian crisis, wrote, 'The people of Britain have been watching Mr Ian Smith. And they like what they see. They have learned to respect his integrity and straightforwardness. Does Mr Wilson not realise that, by contrast, they are angered by his own Government's hypocrisy?' A reader complained to the Press Council that this leader was an example of flagrant malpractice and abuse of the responsibility which must go with the freedom of the Press. The complainant said that he was a British subject, and the statement in the article purported to have been written in his name. He added that although the Editor had the right to express whatever opinions he chose in his newspaper, he had no right whatever to impute those opinions to the complainant.

The Editor of the *Sunday Express*, Mr John Junor, argued that even if the opinion about the British people's attitude to Mr Smith was mistaken it was a view the newspaper was entitled to express.

The Press Council said that the partisan phraseology used was within the discretion of the Editor, and in the opinion of the Press Council it would not mislead readers. The Council rejected the complaint. (1966/45–6)

THE RHODESIAN CRISIS

A leading article in the *Daily Express* on the Rhodesian situation led to a complaint that it was based on a false premise. The article said that it was now inevitable that Mr Ian Smith would soon issue his declaration of independence, and there was 'no doubt whatever that this step would have the full support of the Rhodesian people. . . . For they, like us, are British. . . .'

The complaint said that it was totally wrong that in a column designed to mould the opinion of readers, the *Daily Express* should base its arguments on the false premise that all Rhodesians were white and British. Such distortions of fact, it was alleged, could have been carried out only with mischievous intent.

The Editor of the *Daily Express*, Mr Derek Marks, contended that there was no ambiguity about the meaning of the article. In the context of the article 'Rhodesian people' clearly referred only to Europeans. He claimed it to be permissible for a newspaper to assume that its readers had knowledge of certain facts, such as the presence in Rhodesia of a substantial coloured population. He thought it was ridiculous to assert that the article could mislead anybody, as the situation had been reported at such length day after day that it was unnecessary to restate the background to it in a comment column.

The Press Council rejected the complaint on the grounds that the leader would not have misled readers. (1966/47)

CRITICISM OF FLATS WAS NOT UNFOUNDED

The Housing Committee of Leeds City Council complained about an article in the *Sunday Pictorial* which contained statements that at the Council's

Quarry Hill Flats there were 'worse cases of overcrowding than Leeds can ever have known' and 'flats dirtier and filthier than any slum'. The Committee described the adverse comment as undesirable and unfounded, and said the report had caused distress to the many good tenants living in the flats.

The Press Council obtained statements from two of the three people quoted in the article and then wrote to the Leeds Town Clerk, saying that it did not share his Committee's opinion that the comment was undesirable or unfounded. (1954/24)

ANACHRONISM IN THE NUCLEAR AGE

A disparaging reference to Woolwich Arsenal occurred in a *Daily Herald* article. It called the institution 'an anachronism in the nuclear age', and 'one of our quieter national scandals'. This led to a complaint on behalf of fifty-eight Arsenal signatories.

The Editor, Mr Sydney Jacobson, claimed that the writer was entitled to hold and express the view that the Arsenal had outlived its function.

The Press Council rejected the complaint. (1965/55–6)

A BARRISTERS' PRIVILEGE ATTACKED

An article in the *Sunday Express* which criticised the practice whereby barristers have the privilege of not paying tax on fees paid after they have retired led to a complaint that this was an unfair attack on an individual who was given as an example. The article said that some eminent barristers, such as Sir Patrick Hastings, Q.C., had claimed the privilege three times. 'Lawyers know how to look after themselves', the writer stated. The complaint came from Sir Patrick Hastings' daughter, who said that the article carried the innuendo that her father was a cheat, and that it gave great pain to her mother. It had been asserted, quite falsely, that for the purpose of tax avoidance her father had made a practice of retiring and returning to the Bar.

The Editor, Mr John Junor, replied that though the financial privilege had been a matter of controversy for many years, there could not be any suggestion that a barrister who availed himself of it was guilty of cheating. If any error of fact had arisen he would correct it.

The Press Council held that the article was fair comment on a legal situation which had been much criticised, and it did not bear the innuendo complained of. (1965/84-5)

'THUMBNAIL' REVIEWS

In a Christmas holiday 'round-up' of current theatre productions the *Sunday Telegraph* critic presented 'thumbnail' reviews of twenty-seven shows. Mr Harold Fielding complained that it was wrong to write a review from which the public might be falsely led to believe that the criticism was based on a recent visit.

The Editor, Mr Donald McLachlan, said no reasonable reader would assume that a critic summing up twenty-seven shows in one article would have specially revisited the productions for that purpose.

The Press Council agreed that it would be unreasonable to expect the critic to revisit all the shows mentioned. (1963/43)

DISCLOSURE OF INTEREST

Should a newspaper possessing a financial stake in a matter declare this fact when it reports and comments on it?

When the Pilkington Report on the future of broadcasting was published, a complainant said that some newspapers would be adversely affected if the Government accepted the Report, and that non-disclosure of their financial interest when they criticised the document was a travesty of objective reporting. He added that providing the interest was declared, he agreed that newspapers could be as one-sided as they liked in their observations.

The Editor of one of the newspapers concerned, the *Daily Sketch*, Mr Howard French, said that newspapers were still independent, and Editors could be relied upon to give their views without fear or favour whatever the interests of their proprietors might be.

The Editor of the *Guardian*, Mr Alastair Hetherington, regretted the omission of a declaration of his newspaper's interest in Anglia Television. It was not deliberate, and the fact had been mentioned in the newspaper on a number of occasions. His newspaper's leading article was warmly favourable to most of the Pilkington Committee's recommendations, but did not deal with the point of ownership interests.

The Press Council held that it was not necessary for newspapers to disclose financial interests when presenting objective news reports, but in regard to editorial comment it might be desirable to declare such interest. The decision must lie within the discretion of the editor. (1963/59–60)

RIVAL AUTHOR REVIEWS BOOK

The book, *Captain Scott: The Full Story* by Mr Harry Ludlam, was reviewed in the *Sunday Telegraph* by Reginald Pound. The review stated that the book made no original contribution to the knowledge of the expeditions made by Scott in 1901–4 and 1910–13. Nor, said Mr Pound, did the book take account of the archives of the Royal Geographic Society and the Royal Society; without the backing of these institutions the expeditions would not have been possible. 'There are other equally significant omissions', the review stated.

The author complained that Mr Pound had publicly announced that he was engaged in writing a biography of Captain Scott; it should have been made clear that the review was that of a competitor, not of a disinterested reviewer. His book was the first to give a full account of the two expeditions, and the first Captain Scott's son, Mr Peter Scott, had seen fit to lend his name to it. The newspaper was asked to publish a letter complaining of biased comment.

The *Sunday Telegraph* replied that Mr Pound was entitled to draw attention to important sources not consulted. The Editor, Mr Donald McLachlan, said that the criticisms in the review were serious ones which had not been seriously answered. If the author had challenged the criticisms in a letter to the Editor it would have been published. In the newspaper's opinion the book was not the full story of Captain Scott based on original research into all the available documents.

The Press Council held that the Editor of the *Sunday Telegraph* was entitled to select as reviewer an expert of his own choice and was not required to disclose that the reviewer was the author of a forthcoming book on the same subject. The complaint was rejected, but the Council felt that it would have been helpful if the Editor had offered to publish a brief letter on the subject from the author. (1966/101–2)

A FAIR INFERENCE

An article in the *People* advised motor-car purchasers to collect their new cars at the factory because some delivery drivers caused damage by driving the vehicles too fast. The Delivery Agents' Association complained that the article was unfair and said that the generalisation implicated every reputable collection agency.

The Editor, Mr Stuart Campbell, said the facts were obtained from official documents of a major collecting firm and had been matched by similar firms in various parts of the country.

The Press Council expressed the opinion that the newspaper's facts appeared to be well authenticated so far as its inquiries went. It noted that the newspaper had published letters giving information to the contrary. (1962/48–9)

ROUGH RUGBY TACTICS

An article in the *Western Mail* arising out of a game between schoolboys was headed: 'Schools must stamp out rough tactics' criticised methods adopted by a schoolboy forward and went on to say that, 'Llanelli officials should demand clean and fair scrummaging and eliminate neck locks'. The Hon. Secretary of the Llanelli and District Schoolboys' Rugby Union complained that his Committee considered the report cast an unfair and unjust reflection on the Llanelli players. It imputed that their play lacked sportsmanship, and that they employed tactics contrary to the laws of the game. It was also a slur on a body of professional people, and in particular on the coaches.

After hearing evidence from the referee, the reporter and the Editor, Mr John Davies, the Press Council held that the *Western Mail* was fully entitled to express an honest opinion, however critical, on various aspects of Rugby football play. Where readers disagreed with criticism, it was open to them to submit their points of view in letters for publication. In the opinion of the Press Council, such action would have been appropriate in this case. (1966/47–8)

PHOTOGRAPHY SCHOOLS CRITICISED

In an article in the *British Journal of Photography*, the author declared that tuition in photography schools needed the strongest discipline and called for energetic and dedicated teachers. Students from three schools had spoken to him about conditions that seemed deplorable. The names of the schools were not disclosed, but the author condemned them as hindrances to professional morality.

The Principal of Ealing Technical College in London complained that the strictures went beyond legitimate criticism and that a letter he sent to the *Journal* expressing this view was not published. The failure to name the schools caused eight or ten schools to work under the shadow of the implications.

The Press Council found that the Editor of the *Journal*, Mr A. J. Dalladay, was entitled to draw attention to what he believed to be deficiencies in some schools of photography. The Council was satisfied that his motive was to advance the interests of the profession; the *Journal* had published letters criticising the article. (1963/50)

OPINION WAS REASONABLE

Mr Malcolm Muggeridge complained that two newspapers, the *Sunday Express* and the *People*, criticised him for an article in the *Saturday Evening Post* of New York entitled 'Does England really need a Queen?' He alleged that the criticisms were inaccurate and distorted and gave a completely misleading impression of what he wrote. The attacks upon him, he said, had had disagreeable consequences to him both personally and professionally.

The Press Council rejected the complaint on the grounds that the critical opinions were honestly held, and that the newspapers had the right to say that Mr Muggeridge's article contained a number of unfair, untimely and wounding disparagements of the Royal Family.

The Press Council regretted that neither of the critical articles saw fit to quote anything that Mr Muggeridge had written to the credit of the Royal Family and the Monarchy, but recognised that his long analytical article would cause different impressions in the minds of different people. (1958/27–8)

GROSS MISREPRESENTATION ALLEGED — AND REJECTED

Dr John Highet of Glasgow University delivered an address on 'Likely Trends in Life and Leisure' which was reported in the Scottish but not the English editions of the *Daily Herald*. A later article on the speech written by

Mr John Akass appeared in all editions of the newspaper, and Dr Highet complained that it was a 'gross misrepresentation'. He asked the Editor of the *Daily Herald* for a public apology, the publication of an article he had written and the payment of a fee of about £35. The *Daily Herald* refused.

The Press Council held that the article was fair comment on a speech to the report of which no objection had been taken. (1959/23)

MAYOR CRITICISED

The Mayor of Woolwich was described by the *Daily Sketch* as the 'Scrooge Mayor' because he refused to allow Woolwich schoolchildren to receive free tickets to a circus dress rehearsal which was to be held in school hours.

The Metropolitan Mayors' Association complained that the reference was derogatory to the office of mayor, but the Press Council held that the criticism was directed against the Mayor of Woolwich personally, and rejected the complaint. (1955/24)

See also p. 342 (*Northern Echo*).

COMMENT MUST BE FAIR AND BASED ON FACT

To be fair, the facts on which a comment is based must be accurate, though minor inaccuracies may not by themselves make the comment unfair so long as the opinion can reasonably be held on the facts shown to be true. The fairness of the comment will often depend on fairness of the reporting of the facts and the care taken to verify them. Selective reporting as a basis for comment will vitiate the fairness of the comment: to be fair the comment must be justified not only by the known facts but also by the facts readily available if sought.

SELECTIVE REPORTING FOR THE PURPOSE OF ADVERSE COMMENT

The Chief Constable of Southend complained about an item in the John Gordon column in the *Sunday Express* which said his force had 'hauled' a boy into the Juvenile Court on a charge of stealing a torch, but the owner said: 'That's not mine'. The item continued: 'Immediate collapse of the case. Wouldn't you think the police would have established a simple fact like that before bringing the boy into court?' The Chief Constable said that the column gave a misleading impression of the local police. The boy was accused of other offences relating to taking and driving away a motor-cycle without the owner's consent. In court he pleaded guilty to these charges.

The Press Council held that the article gave a partial and misleading view of the proceedings, and condemned the distortion caused by the use of only those parts of the case suitable for making an unfounded and unfair criticism of the police. (1964/56)

INSUFFICIENT CARE ABOUT THE FACTS

An article criticising councillors for double standards and favouritism when granting planning permission was the subject of a complaint against the *Oldham Chronicle*. The complainant said unworthy motives had been imputed to members of the council in approving a local councillor's application to build a bungalow in the Green Belt. An article said the approval suggested different standards for the nobodies and the somebodies, as a similar application by a farmer had been refused. Later the paper admitted the two cases were not comparable. In an editorial it disclaimed any imputation of unworthy motives to the councillors, and expressed regret if the facts had been misinterpreted by any readers. It added that if the relative merits of the different applications had been pointed out to the public when the Press gave the opportunity of explanation, justice would have been seen to be done.

Mr Kenneth Hirst, the Editor, told the Press Council that the local council had been criticised not for showing favouritism but for allowing a situation to arise in which other people were led to believe that there had been favouritism. He admitted that his newspaper had been at fault in blaming all the members of the council, when only half of them were on the committee that had dealt with the applications. The accusation of favouritism had been made by a reader, and before it had been printed council members and officials were given the opportunity to refute the allegation.

The Press Council held that while newspapers must always be vigilant in the public interest in cases of this kind, in this case insufficient care had been taken to check the facts, and as a result the account was inaccurate and the criticism unfair. It added that it was unfortunate that the newspaper's apology for its attitude was accompanied by further criticism. (1962/49–50)

PART OF ARTICLE UNFAIR

'Is this how a city cares for a child?' was the headline to an article in the *News of the World* which criticised the Manchester City Council's Childrens' Department for the way in which it had looked after a child put in its care for playing truant. The child continued to play truant, and while in the Council's care he and a friend stole a cabin-cruiser. The day before he was to appear before the magistrates, the article said, the mother received a curt note from the Department telling her of this.

The City Council complained that the story was factually inaccurate, unfair in its criticism and comment and ill-balanced because it gave a misleading impression of the letter to the mother.

On behalf of the newspaper it was admitted that the letter to the mother was not quoted in full, nor was the Council asked to comment. But the crux of the problem was the boy's truancy, and it was pitiable that a public authority should state that there was nothing they could do when a boy in its care played truant except talk to him or send him to an approved school. It was the undisputed right of a newspaper to criticise what it believed a misuse of power.

The findings of the Press Council were that the criticism of the City Council following the fact that a boy for whom they were caring was able to play truant and commit offences was fair comment, and the Press Council rejected the major complaint.

But in an important aspect the article was unfair: it contained an untrue statement about the way in which the Council had acquired responsibility for the boy; it also unfairly attributed indifference to the official concerned, by misquoting his letter to the mother. The Press Council thought that the Council should have been given the opportunity to submit its version of the affair before the article was published. (1956/68–70)

EXAGGERATED STATEMENTS

An article in the *Daily Sketch* criticising the child care arrangements of the Kent County Council questioned the fitness of the Council to have the care of children. Court orders were made as the result of secret reports handed to magistrates but not shown to the parents.

The complaint was that the article was 'laced with inaccurate statistics and other inaccurate information'. Three illustrative cases were cited.

The Press Council held that while the child care arrangements by local authorities are a proper subject for reports and comments in the Press, the article in the *Daily Sketch* contained a number of exaggerated and misleading statements. An offensive reference to the chairman of the Children's Committee and to the Children's Officer was deprecated. (1965/66–7)

IMPORTANT FACTS DISREGARDED

Anglian Pig Breeders claimed that an article in the *People* dealing with the firm's activities was so slanted by a mixture of untruths, half-truths and suppression of relevant material that it distorted the image of the company beyond recognition, leaving the reader with the impression that the firm was shady and shaky.

It was contended that the article contained not a single favourable word, although the newspaper's representatives who visited the firm's headquarters were given all the information they required. The article described the author's visits to four farms where sows purchased by subscribing members of the public were tended by sub-contractors. The four sub-contractors criticised the newspaper's presentation and denied some of the statements attributed to them.

The Editor of the *People*, Mr Stuart Campbell, claimed the article was fair comment and accurate. The financial stability of the company had not been criticised; only the conditions in which many of the pigs were kept. The words attributed to the sub-contractors had been made in the presence of witnesses. The farms the author had visited were chosen at random, and he felt he was justified in assuming they were a representative cross section of the company's farms.

The Press Council held that, although the newspaper claimed to have made a thorough and comprehensive investigation, it failed to take due account of other facts which were made available by the company in a very full and open manner. This being so, the Council considered that the report was biased and to that extent fell below expected standards. (1963/49–50)

EVIDENCE TOO SLIGHT

An article in the *Sunday Telegraph* described Woolwich Arsenal as 'probably the country's most assiduous centre for do-it-yourself (in the firm's time)' illicit production of goods. The newspaper declared that restoration work on cannon featured in national monuments had led to the practice of putting down overtime to the 'big gun'.

In reply to a complaint, the Editor, Mr Donald McLachlan, said that the article was based on the experience of a number of workers in the arsenal, and the correspondent who had written the story said that the people who worked in the arsenal spoke freely to him and had taken him on a tour of homes where he had been shown items which had been made on 'homework'.

The Press Council did not doubt that the article had been written in good faith and had a basis of information given to the correspondent, but considered that the basis was too slight to justify the impression of widespread malpractice. (1965/55–6)

COMMENT MUST BE ON A MATTER OF PUBLIC INTEREST

LORD'S DAY OBSERVANCE SOCIETY LINKED WITH CONVICTED MAN

The *People* reported the conviction of a member of the staff of the Lord's Day Observance Society for indecent assault, under the heading 'Lord's Day Saint was a man of sin'. The General Secretary of the Society complained about the revelation in the article that the defendant was a member of its staff, saying that this had not come up in the court proceedings. He called the incident a 'disgrace to our national Press', and in a letter to the newspaper said that the Society could not be held responsible for what its workers might do in private life.

The Editor, Mr Stuart Campbell, said that the article was fair comment on a matter of public interest, and he was upheld by the Press Council, which added the rider that in its opinion the newspaper had performed a public service. (1959/19)

IMPRESSIONISTIC REPORT ON TOWN

Goole and District Chamber of Trade took exception to a descriptive article in the *Daily Herald* on the port and borough of Goole, and complained that it was misleading, unwarranted and harmful. The Press Council, however, decided that though the impressionistic tone and point of view might be disliked by citizens with a warm affection for Goole, the article was fair comment on a matter of public interest. (1959/23)

TOO MANY ACCOUNTANTS

An article in the *Sunday Express* suggesting that the number of financial experts on the boards of companies was getting out of balance was said to be a slur on chartered accountants. The complainant said that when he had asked the newspaper to identify a company which the article alleged had 'burned their fingers badly' because of the preponderance of chartered accountants and lawyers on its board, his request had been refused on the grounds of journalistic etiquette. He thought that if the umbrella of etiquette excused a misinformed statement there was cause for apprehension about the freedom given to journalists.

The Editor, Mr John Junor, replied that the article sought only to consider whether it was a good thing that so many company directors should be chartered accountants, and the Press Council's adjudication agreed that it was an expression of opinion on a matter of public interest. (1962/54)

'IS LIFE TOO LUSH FOR THE LAWYERS?'

The Law Society complained about an article which appeared in the *Sunday Express* under the headings: 'Men at the Top', 'Is Life too lush for the Lawyers?' and expressed the hope that the Press Council 'did not regard it as in accordance with the proper standards of reporting that a national newspaper should publish defamatory remarks about the Law Society as a professional organisation of solicitors of the Supreme Court and make other sweeping allegations designed to damage an entire profession in the eyes of the public'.

The Press Council issued the following statement:

> The Press may infrequently use its freedom to attack other professions, but it has an undoubted right to do so and the Press Council intends to maintain that right. The *Sunday Express* criticism of the legal profession and the Law Society in particular did not constitute a breach of journalistic ethics provided that it was fair and accurate.
>
> The Council notes that the *Sunday Express* published a short letter from a member of the legal profession replying to a number of alleged inaccuracies in the article. But, in view of the scale of the newspaper's

attack on the whole profession, the Council feels that the Law Society would be justified in making a request to the Editor to give space for an article or a statement by the secretary or other spokesman of the Law Society giving the public its side of the picture. The Council considers that if such a request is made the Editor ought to grant it.

The newspaper published the statement, but the Editor, Mr John Junor, protested that at no time had he refused to print a letter from the Law Society, and no letter for publication was ever sent by the Society (1956/32)

N.F.U. PRESIDENT CRITICISED

A complaint was made about a leading article in the *Daily Express* which criticised the President of the National Farmers' Union. The Editor replied that as the President was a public figure, the newspaper must reserve the right to criticise him.

The Press Council upheld the newspaper in that the article was fair comment on a matter of public interest. (1954/24)

A GERMAN OFFICIAL AT BRITISH WAR MEMORIAL

When a member of the staff of the German War Graves Commission attended in uniform on the occasion of the Queen's visit to the British War Memorial at Tobruk, the *Daily Sketch* protested about the German being present on such an occasion. The German complained to the Press Council, saying that the uniform was the 'tropical service kit' of the Commission.

The Editor, Mr Herbert Gunn, said the article was not a criticism of an individual but a protest against a German in uniform being present on such an occasion at all.

The Press Council upheld the Editor's view that the question whether it was desirable that a former enemy should attend such a ceremony was a matter of public interest on which the newspaper was fully entitled to comment. (1955/25)

DRUGS OVER THE COUNTER

'Drugs over the counter. Getting "high" costs pennies,' was the heading of an article which appeared in the *Swindon Echo*. The article stated that habit-forming drugs were readily available over the counter at most Swindon chemists' shops despite the tightening of the restrictions on sales. One of the drugs contained morphine, and for a matter of shillings any youngster knowing what to ask for could get 'high' without arousing the suspicions of the chemist. Reporters had made test purchases, and details were given of the ease with which they obtained drugs without prescription.

The Pharmaceutical Society of Great Britain complained that part of its work was educating the public about the dangers of indiscriminate drug taking, and this was undone by irresponsible reports which appeared in certain sections of the national press. In this case the newspaper had named drugs which might assist young people to embark on drug-taking.

The Editor of the *Swindon Echo*, Mr Peter Young, said that a small minority of young people were bent on drug-taking and were far better informed on sources of supply than the newspaper would be. The article would neither encourage nor discourage that minority. If substances had not been named there would have been no point in the story. The article brought home to the public the fact that these stimulants, however mild, were readily available and was a warning to parents of the inherent dangers of these substances.

The Press Council considered that the article was of value to parents and others concerned about the availability of certain drugs, and did not regard it as contrary to the public interest. (1967)

Other cases of fair comment in the public interest will be found on pp. 328 (*Scottish Daily Express*), and 344 (*Sunday Pictorial*).

COMMENT MUST NOT BE REPORTED AS FACT

SPECULATION REBUKED

A complaint was made that a headline in the *Belfast Telegraph* made a comment which was speculation by a political correspondent appear to be a matter of fact. A statement by the Prime Minister of Northern Ireland condemning some riots was said in the opening passages of the report to be a tacit rebuke of Mr Paisley, the clergyman concerned. The headline ran: 'Provocation by men associated with the I.R.A., says Capt. O'Neill. Premier rebukes Mr Paisley.'

The Rev. Ian R. K. Paisley complained that as the Prime Minister had mentioned no names in his speech, he could not see how such a headline was justified. Mr John E. Sayers, Editor-in-Chief of the newspaper, told the Press Council that the headline was based on the report by the political correspondent, but that he did not favour an interpretative story which used the word 'tacit' being given so positive a headline, and a change had been ordered for the next edition.

The Press Council held that although the newspaper may have been justified in inferring that the Prime Minister's rebuke was directed against a named person, it was misleading to present this speculation as a fact in the headline. This the Editor himself recognised by changing the headline in later editions. (1965/40)

COMMENT BASED ON FACTS KNOWN AT THE TIME

BEHEADED SOLDIERS

A complaint was made about a *Daily Express* editorial based on a news story in the same edition, and which also appeared in other British newspapers, that two British soldiers had been shot in an ambush in the Yemen, and that their heads had been cut off and exhibited in Taiz. The editorial said that it was President Nasser who must bear the ultimate responsibility and the guilt of murder. The complaint said that the newspaper had handled a story, which was later partly discredited, irresponsibly, headlining it as though it were undisputed fact and repeating it in a misleading and inflammatory form in an editorial. The editorial, it was alleged, tried to implant a picture of British soldiers being brutally murdered by having their heads hacked off, when in fact they were killed in action and then decapitated.

The Editor of the *Daily Express*, Mr Robert Edwards, replied that the story was based on an official statement from the G.O.C.-in-C., Middle East Land Forces. The claim that the newspaper had suggested that the soldiers were killed by beheading was ridiculous when the first paragraph of the story said that they were shot down, and the comment did not represent the beheadings as murder but claimed that 'he who screamed at the mob to sweep the British out of Aden, stirred them to frenzy, organised them, armed them and gave them their opportunity, bore the guilt of murder'.

The Press Council held that the *Daily Express* was entitled to express its opinion on the day's news, and that on the facts known at the time the comment was not irresponsible. (1964/79)

8 Misreporting and Misrepresentation

D

A newspaper is one of the most remarkable products of modern society, the First Royal Commission stated in its Report in 1949. It gathers news from five continents, prints it and distributes it so fast that what happens before dawn in India can be read before breakfast in England; it performs the feat every twenty-four hours and sells the product for a few pence. Without some conception of how it is done and the conditions of time and space within which it is done it is impossible to realise the problems which beset the production of a newspaper.

Since 1949 new techniques have increased the speed of production and widened the scope of coverage. Technical genius, however, is not a substitute for reliability, and, while speed may explain errors, it does not excuse them. If the public cannot rely on the accuracy of what it reads it will soon cease to trust any information it is given.

Misreporting is generally the result of inadvertence or negligence; misrepresentation, on the other hand, while it may be innocent in the sense of being unintentional, can also be calculated and intended to mislead. A deliberate misstatement of the facts is one form misrepresentation can take, suppression of the facts or their distortion is another. The Press Council assesses the degree of culpability in the light of the circumstances of each case.

A Fleet Stret editor of great experience told the Royal Commission of a message on accuracy he once addressed to his sub-editors and reporters. In the course of it he said that the plain fact was that whenever they saw a story in a newspaper concerning something they knew about it was more often wrong than right. The Commission thought that applied to the Press as a whole the statement was too extreme; nevertheless from their own experience they believed it contained a substantial element of truth. The reason was that in the collection of news from a number of sources of varying trustworthiness, its transmission by cable, telephone or teleprinter, its sub-editing and its translation into type, the opportunities for error were enormous. The risks were increased by the speed at which the work had to be done and the number of people who had a share in doing it.

Much of the information published in a daily newspaper is obtained by one fallible human being from another. If the informant is reliable he may be misunderstood; if he is not certain of his facts he may mislead the journalist. Even an eye-witness account, as practitioners in the courts know very well, may be untrustworthy, particularly if the witness is a person not trained to observe accurately and tells his story in an atmosphere of tension.

The Commission accepted the assurances they were given that newspapers took the greatest care to check their facts. No newspaper welcomed being detected in an inaccuracy. But the limitations imposed by shortage of time made it impossible to check facts in the sense of making certain that statements which could not be verified from a reference book were indeed true. The inaccuracy which the informed reader noticed, said the Commission, was not so much the misreporting of the kind of facts that could be checked as in the general impression conveyed by a report. The basic facts might in themselves be correct, but they were fitted together to make the wrong picture.

There is an almost endless variety of ways of publishing information that will render it inaccurate and misleading. Striving for the attractive headline which will catch the reader's attention, is one. An instance brought to the notice of the Royal Commission was the headline over a news report of

5 July 1947 of a speech by Mr Ernest Bevin at the Annual Independence Day dinner at the American Society in London.

BEVIN TO U.S.
'Your humble servant'

The report recorded that Mr Bevin had said:

> 'As long as I am Foreign Secretary, I will work with you. My country will do all it can to harmonise with you.'
>
> 'Speaking for the British people', he said, 'I say to Mr Marshall, "We take you and the American nation at your word. We do not question it." '

The words quoted in the headline did not appear in the report. They were what the Commission described as 'an inference masquerading as quotation'.

The pressure of competition can sometimes induce a newspaper to rely on a dishonest form of imaginative reporting in which a reasonable assumption is presented as a fact. An example presented to the Commission was a report in a national newspaper of Hitler's entry into Prague in March 1939. A sub-editor who dealt with the report said that as an authentic account of the event could not be received in time for the early editions, he was instructed to 'jump' the news by writing an imaginative account and to attribute it to 'our Prague Reporter'. The proprietor of the newspaper said he thought that such a thing could happen in any newspaper office.

A final example concerned the Royal Commission itself. While their Report was being written a Sunday newspaper published an article by its political correspondent in which he stated the Commission would propose a Press Council appointed by the Government and he went on to report the opinions of members of the Commission. The Commission referred to the article as a flagrant breach of standards in presenting speculations as categorical statements of facts. The Commission neither recommended nor even proposed to recommend a government-appointed Press Council; the opinions attributed to members were not only untrue but devoid of any resemblance to the truth.

Among the points illustrated by the cases that follow is one that shows that the public has a contribution to make to the accuracy of what is published in the newspapers. For instance, it is the duty of a reporter when he obtains information critical of some person or organisation to obtain if possible the other point of view so that what is published is not a one-sided account. If the other side refuses to comment, the newspaper will not be entirely to blame if its report is not accurate. Cases illustrating the point are headed 'Melksham Urban District Council — Complaint of Biased Reporting', 'Firm Refused Information' and ' "Hush-Hush" Robbery' (pp. 98, 100 and 101).

Another point of interest illustrated under the heading 'Altering Copy Without Writer's Consent' (p. 122) is that not members of the public but journalists also have the right to complain to the Press Council.

Other cases of misrepresentation and alleged misrepresentation are considered in Chapter Nine: Sensationalism and Distortion, pp. 145–57.

MISLEADING REPORTS

A FESTIVAL POEM

A story in the *Daily Sketch* relating to the Autumn Cheltenham Literary Festival which involved Mr Stirling Moss was the subject of a complaint. The story stated that with other distinguished people Mr Moss had been invited to contribute 'My Favourite Poem When I Was Young' to the Festival. Mr Moss had told the Festival organisers that he could not remember any particular poem which caught his fancy when he was young, but he sent a few lines of a poem written by a friend of his. The poem was not recited at the Festival, but the *Daily Sketch* reported that it was, and that the Honorary Director of the Festival had described it as 'the worst piece of poetry I have ever heard'. The Director complained that the report was wholly untrue, and that he did not make the statement attributed to him. The *Daily Sketch* did not correct the story or publish his denial.

The Editor of the paper, Mr Howard French, stated that the report was from a correspondent and was published in good faith. The correspondent maintained that, in fact, the poem had been read by the Director's secretary in an ante-room to about half-a-dozen people, and that the Director had made the statement alleged.

The Press Council said that the report was grossly misleading and contained a number of falsehoods. It condemned the correspondent and stated that the *Daily Sketch* should have exercised greater care in checking the information obtained. (1964/40)

AN ARTICLE ON JOURNALISM

The Press Council was invited to examine an article which appeared not in a newspaper but a publication issued by the National Union of Students. The article purported to describe the day in the life of a Fleet Street reporter.

The President of the Union said the article had been intended to be a humorous contribution, he regretted that it had been found to be offensive, hoped that it would not prove damaging, withdrew unreservedly the statements complained of and added that instructions would be given for the immediate withdrawal of all remaining copies.

The Council expressed its satisfaction.

(The Union later published an excellent article written by the President of the Guild of British Newspaper Editors.) (1958/28)

CHEAP HOLIDAYS FOR OLD-AGE PENSIONERS

A front-page story in the *People* was headed: 'Cheap Holiday Ramp. Hotels Protest. "Phoney Pensioners are getting cut rates".' The article said that Britain's hoteliers were threatening to ban cheap holidays for old-age pensioners, as many of the people who went on them were not old-age pensioners at all, and the cut-price holidays were a racket run by the coach companies.

The Director and General Manager of a coach company wrote to the *People* complaining that the headlines were untrue and unjust so far as his company was concerned and constituted a slur on its good character. He was told by the Editor of the *People*, Mr Stuart Campbell, that the article did not suggest that all coach companies were operating this practice. But the solicitors of the coach company complained to the Press Council that the article did not say that it was referring to a minority of operators as suggested by the Editor.

The Editor told the Press Council that he believed the newspaper could rely upon the common sense of readers to know that such improper practices were not carried on by everyone in a trade or industry. But the Press Council upheld the complaint, saying that it should have been made clear that the article referred only to a minority of coach operators. (1966/35–6)

TRANSPORT HOUSE PAY

The Chairman of the Staff Council at Labour Party headquarters complained that a report in the *Daily Express* about the rejection of a pay rise for the staff at Transport House was wholly incorrect. A correction published when attention was called to the matter was also erroneous. The complainant suggested that the inaccuracy was printed on the front page because it was anti-Labour propaganda.

The Editor, Mr Roger Wood, denied this suggestion and said that the report, from a hitherto reliable source, had been printed in good faith. The error had been corrected eight days later in a story dealing with pay rise negotiations concerning seven organisations.

The Press Council found that the *Daily Express* was at fault in publishing two inaccurate versions, but noted that the error was later corrected in a third reference to the subject. (1962/41)

UNBALANCED PRESENTATION

A case involving the Duke of Edinburgh's award for youth was an example of selective and exaggerated criticism. An article in the *People* suggested that the scheme was in danger of being made a laughing-stock. A panel inset in the article stated: 'He got a gold award for making a rug. She swotted up the top pops for a bronze. He won a "gold" with his home-made wines.' Later in the article, it was disclosed that the 'pursuits and projects' section was only one of four in which candidates had to reach a required standard to win an award.

A complaint to the Press Council alleged that the article distorted the facts, and presented them in such a way that the boys and girls working towards the awards were ridiculed. The Editor, Mr Stuart Campbell, replied that the newspaper's policy was to print facts accurately, coupling them with vivid and crisp comment.

The Press Council upheld the right of newspapers to comment on matters of public interest, but said that the article was unbalanced in presentation and was likely to mislead readers as to the full requirements needed for gaining one of the awards. (1964/65)

VIGILANTES AND THE GIPSIES

A report in the *Evening News* stated that vigilantes armed with truncheons were to carry out nightly patrols in the unlit streets of the Kentish village of Cobham, to prevent any of the fifty families of gipsies camping in the area from misbehaving and annoying residents. The vigilantes were said to have a secret call-sign to summon assistance.

The Parish of Cobham Association, which was said to have drawn up a plan of campaign to get rid of the gipsies, denied that there were any patrols, truncheons, secret call-signs or secret meetings, as the story alleged, or that there was any hostility to the caravanners.

The news agency which supplied the story stated that it was based on the avowed intentions of the local residents, the fears of the gipsies who anticipated violence from the villagers, and on the 'ugly' solid anti-gipsy feeling in the village. Oral evidence given by two reporters employed by the news agency was that the information about the vigilantes was obtained from casual conversations with people in the village. Neither knew the names or addresses of any of their informants.

The Press Council's adjudication was that, while some people in the village might have wanted militant action against the gipsies, there was no evidence apart from village talk that the type of action suggested in the report was contemplated. The Council strongly condemned the coupling of the Parish Association with the alleged patrols which gave a misleading impression. (1964/44–5)

DOPING RACEHORSES

Under the heading 'Doped or Poisoned? Quick probe needed if owner is correct' the *Daily Express* printed a news story which described how an owner had said that his horse had either been doped or poisoned, and suggested that if the dope test showed a positive reaction it must be the death-knell for bookmakers in this country. There could be no other solution if the sport were to survive. 'I wonder, for instance, if our racecourse security agents have been tracking the activities and movements of a certain bookmaker,' commented the author of the article.

The Public Relations Officer of the National Association of Bookmakers complained to the Editor of the *Daily Express* about the outrageous insinuation 'that bookmakers as a body must be held responsible for doping racehorses.' Only an extract from this letter was published with other criticisms of the article.

The newspaper then published another article saying that if a certain filly was found to have been doped 'The whole sordid business of the doping menace would be reopened, even if the few greedy participants are book-makers virtually only in name.'

After further correspondence the National Association of Bookmakers referred their complaint to the Press Council.

The Editor of the *Daily Express*, Mr Robert Edwards, told the Press Council that the author of the article had information which led him to believe that a man with bookmaking interests might be involved in a recurrence of the doping scandal, but until he had more concrete evidence the laws of defamation prevented him from being more specific. In oral evidence the author said that there had been many cases of doping which were ruining the industry, and that bookmakers were conniving. They were not responsible, he said, but with the laws of libel as they were, they could not put that in the paper.

The Press Council held that, while the article arose out of the writer's concern for the future of racing, he did not have sufficient material to justify a general attack on bookmakers. The complaint was upheld. (1966/39–41)

AN ESSAY IN IRONY

A leading article in the *Guardian* headed 'Forward with the Conservatives' was the subject of a complaint on the grounds that, although it was intended to be ironical, it was capable of being read by some people as a serious state-ment of fact. The article welcomed 'the annual report of the Conservative Party . . . as much for the insight it provides into one of the nation's best known institutions as for its handsome binding.' The article went on to refer to a foreword by Lord Blakenham.

The complainant, a Conservative Chief Agent, wrote to the *Guardian* asking by whom the Report was published and was told that the article was an essay in irony. He alleged that the article was 'a complete and unadulter-ated attempt to mislead readers'. He had received three telephone calls from readers who had thought that the document did exist.

The Press Council accepted the *Guardian*'s statement that the editorial was intended to be satirical, but said that the fact remained that it was misleading, and as such it was open to criticism. (1964/61–2)

DENIAL OF TAKE-OVER OMITTED

Three days before the *Sun* published a paragraph about a market rumour of a bid for a paint company the newspaper's reporter was told by a director that he had not heard of such a deal. He denied that a bid had been on the company's desk for two months. The *Sun* did not refer to the interview or the denial of the rumour.

The company complained that the omission constituted irresponsible journalism.

Mr. R. L. Dinsdale, Editor of the *Sun*, said that in denying the rumour the director stated he did not wish his name to be mentioned as the source of the information. The newspaper regarded anonymous denials as of little value. Had the director agreed to his name being given the statement would have been published. The company had not issued any public denial although there had been subsequent references to the take-over rumour in other newspapers.

The Secretary of the company said that a copy of the complaint made to the Press Council had been sent to the Stock Exchange which might be regarded as an official denial of the rumour. As the Stock Exchange Council took the view that the copy-letter did not conform to the terms of the undertaking to give sufficient information to enable shareholders to appraise the position of the company and to avoid establishment of a false market, no action was taken.

The Press Council held that the *Sun* report of the rumoured take-over bid should have included the company spokesman's denial. The complaint was upheld. (1966/67–8)

A COLLIERY DISASTER

The *Daily Mail* published a report headed 'Ten bolts left undone, so 31 miners die', 'Two guilty men'.

The report stated that the negligence of two electricians had caused the tragedy. They had ignored safety regulations and left the cover off a switch they were testing, as a result of which a spark ignited fire-damp gas in the pit.

The National Union of Mineworkers complained to the Press Council that the headlines and what was stated in the article could mean only that two men were responsible for the disaster, a statement or inference which could not be found anywhere in the report of the Chief Inspector. It was improper to lay the blame on two men when there were others not less guilty.

The Editor, Mr Michael Randall, said that in retrospect he felt that a perfectly balanced story would have included more of the ventilation aspect of the tragedy, but he could not accept that the official findings warranted a statement in a letter to the *Daily Mail* that lack of ventilation was the prime cause of the explosion. He agreed that the leaving off the cover of the switch was an unnecessarily loose description of what had occurred.

The Press Council stated that the headlines and the opening paragraph of the report overstressed the responsibility of the unnamed electricians and contained an error of fact. The complaint was upheld. (1966/58–9)

FOOTBALL ASSOCIATION AND SPORTS WRITERS AT ODDS

The Football Association complained about the standards of Press reporting and coverage of the 1959 England International Football tour of Brazil, Peru, Mexico and the United States. The reports in the London newspapers were said to have contained 'errors of fact, mistruths and mis-statements'. The attitude of the Press towards the officials was said to have changed from reasonable friendliness to 'increasing antagonism' and the writing from 'straightforward comment and reporting' to that of 'complete irresponsibility'.

A deputation of the Football Association met the Council and subsequently some of the football journalists appeared at another meeting.

A story in the *Daily Mail* (27 May 1959) stated that Billy Wright, the captain of the England team, referring to the last matches had said: 'It's much better that I take the blame than some youngster setting out on his international career.' This appeared under the heading ' "I'll take the can," says Billy Wright'. Mr Wright denied the statement or that it was made in Disneyland as reported.

The Press Council regretted the mis-statement which necessarily weakened the authenticity of the story as a whole.

A story in the *Daily Mirror* (26 May 1959) headed 'Now The Cry is "Go Home England" ' said that the 'ultimate insult' of 'this miserable tour' was that the American Football Association would rather the England team did not play the Americans at Los Angeles as arranged because 'American fans just ain't interested in failures'. The quotation was attributed to an American official, one of fifteen, who had flown down from California to see England's 'humiliating defeat' by Mexico. The Football Association produced a letter from the U.S. Soccer Association Inc. denying that any official was present at the match.

The Press Council held that the reporter fell into an error in implying that the tourists were officials of the American Soccer Association.

The *Daily Telegraph* commented that either 'these teams are incompetently managed' or that 'the comfort and efficiency of the players are being sacrificed for the profit of the Football Association'. The Council considered that the comments were not without justification.

The Football Association said that up to a few years ago relations with the Press had been perfectly happy. A Press witness agreed, and said relations had deteriorated because the old style of football reporter had reflected the official view, whereas the new-style reporter criticised the Association, and the officials resented it.

He thought the change was a healthy one.

The Press Council reached the following conclusions:

1. It was clear that bad feeling had developed but the charge of complete irresponsibility was not substantiated.

2. The Council condemned the mis-statements in the reports but found that these did not justify the Football Association's sweeping indictment of the Press.

3. The Council was much concerned at the differences and misunderstandings which had developed between the Football Association and some football writers. These were contrary to the best interests of the game and of journalism.

4. The Council made the suggestion in the circumstances that representatives of the Football Association and the Sports Writers' Association should meet and try to restore harmony.

In a subsequent issue of *F.A. News*, the official journal of the Football Association, the Association declared that the Council's statement was inconclusive and unsatisfactory. While the Association would be happy to meet the Sports Writers Association, as the Press Council had suggested, this was, like the Press Council, a body without ultimate power and a meeting with editors and proprietors of newspapers might be more effective. (1960/30, 35–8)

MR FRANK COUSINS' RESIGNATION

Events which culminated in the decision of Mr Frank Cousins not to continue as a Member of Parliament resulted in a complaint against the *Nuneaton Observer*.

The newspaper in a front-page story stated 'Nuneaton Labour Party, which has asked for a special meeting with Mr Frank Cousins to persuade him to continue as their constituency M.P., yesterday got what amounted to a brush-off from Mr Cousins.'

The article went on to say that the Transport and General Workers' Union was said to have advised Mr Cousins to tell the Party to put their request in writing to the Executive. When the Secretary of the Nuneaton Constituency Labour Party was asked whether he considered this was a brush-off from Mr Cousins, he was reported as saying, 'One thing I know there will be no brush-off as far as Mr Cousins is concerned. He is very concerned about Nuneaton.'

When the Secretary heard that the Executive of the T.G.W.U. was to consider the matter he telephoned the newspaper and said that the brush-off report was not true. No correction, however, was published. The local Constituency party had not requested a personal meeting with Mr Cousins but a meeting with the T.G.W.U., and a deputation had been cordially received by the Executive Committee.

The Editor of the *Nuneaton Observer*, Mr Neil Coates, said that the news story was supplied by the newspaper's London staff, who had confirmed that the basic facts were true. The story was read before publication to the Secretary of the constituency party and his comments obtained, and when a reporter some days later spoke to the Secretary no mention of a correction was made.

The Press Council held that the statement in the newspaper that the Nuneaton Constituency Labour Party asked for an interview with Mr Cousins and received a 'brush-off' was inaccurate. (1967)

CITY COLUMN ERROR

A man complained that, after reading in the financial column of the *Evening Standard* about a fast expanding investment bingo hall concern and a statement by the directors that they expected it would go public in about a year, he invested £1,000 in the concern. The report also stated that the business had already attracted take-over offers, one from Mecca.

The complainant said that hardly a word of the *Evening Standard*'s report was true, including the reference to Mecca.

The Editor, Mr Charles Wintour, said that the writer had been severely rebuked for his failure to check the reference to Mecca. It was impossible to check every statement made by company directors. He expressed regret that the complainant had been misled.

The reporter told of statements said to have been made by one of the directors that Mecca was interested. He thought that this was true because a director of Mecca had told him many times that his company was always looking for opportunities.

The complainant said that he considered that the *Evening Standard* should reimburse him for the loss of his investment.

The Press Council's adjudication was that the complaint against the newspaper was that it had published an inaccurate and unchecked statement. The *Evening Standard* had acknowledged the fault and apologised. The Council saw no need for any finding on the claim for compensation. (1967)

MELKSHAM URBAN DISTRICT — COMPLAINT OF
BIASED REPORTING

The Melksham Urban District Council complained that the *Western Daily Press* by the manner of its reporting had wrongly placed the Urban Council in an unfavourable light in the eyes of the public. Three instances were cited.

In the first the headline to a report read 'Wife, 64, might have to leave her husband. Too many in their home, says Council.' The report stated that the wife after forty years of marriage might have to leave her husband to please the Council; because the council house they occupied with a daughter and five children was overcrowded.

The Clerk to the Urban Council told the Press Council that the newspaper had not checked the facts. The woman lived in a council house but also owned a bungalow where the Council wanted her to go with her husband. The daughter and five children slept in a tiny bedroom, and until recently another daughter and two children had also lived in the house. The woman had five cats.

In the second instance the report was headed 'Widow fights for nine banned homes'. The report stated that she owned nine of thirteen condemned houses, but she heard a Public Health Inspector admit that he did not know why they were under a demolition order. The Health Inspector was reported as saying that the houses were subject to rot and rising damp, but that he did not know the reasons for demolition.

The Clerk to the Urban Council said that the Council wanted to knock the houses down so that tenants could be re-housed and the road widened. He further said it was rubbish for the newspaper to report that she heard the Health Inspector admit that he did not know why the houses were under a demolition order. The Health Inspector was the man who reported to the Council that they ought to come down because of their condition.

In the third instance the report was headlined 'Still Mr B—— fights for more money' and went on to state that Mr B—— was looking for a short-hand typist to take a note of his meeting with the Urban Council which he hoped would end the months-old dispute on compensation for land the Council had bought from him under a compulsory purchase order.

The Clerk to the Urban Council said there was no compulsory purchase. Mr B—— had sold the land to the Council for an agreed figure. Mr B—— then started a campaign for more money, which the Council had resisted.

All three cases, he said, were examples of biased reporting against the Council. They bore no relation to the true facts and gave the public a wrong impression.

The *Western Daily Press* in a leading article said of the complaint to the Press Council 'It is unfortunate that many Melksham Councillors are anti-newspaper. Not just the *Western Daily Press*, but all newspapers. Unfortunate because newspapers could be a Council's best friend.'

The Editor, Mr Eric Price, denied to the Press Council that his newspaper had sought to tarnish the Urban Council's reputation. It was nonsense to say of the first case that the reporter had not checked the facts. The Chairman of the Housing Committee had refused to make a proper statement. The report was entirely factual.

In the second case as soon as the misinterpretation of a statement by the Health Officer was discovered an explanatory paragraph was published. The real reason for the complaint was that the newspaper ventilated a matter which the Urban Council would rather not have had discussed.

The Press Council's adjudication was:

The newspaper was clearly critical of the activities of the Urban Council.

It was part of the newspaper's function to criticise local authorities if it had cause to do so, but it should be careful to get its facts right.

In regard to the first report the newspaper would not have published the article if it had known the full facts. The newspaper, however, was not to blame because it had offered the Chairman of the Housing Committee an opportunity of stating the facts which he did not take.

In the case relating to the Public Health Inspector in which it was alleged that he had said that he did not know the purpose of the demolition, a correction was published, but the serious misinterpretation had made the Health Inspector look ridiculous.

In the third case the newspaper was in error in describing the struggle as one for compensation for land which the Council had bought under a compulsory purchase order which implied that £700 compensation was inadequate. There was no compulsory purchase, and the land was sold by Mr B——at an agreed figure.

Taking the complaint as a whole the Council was of the opinion that it was justified. (1966/61–4)

FIRM REFUSED INFORMATION

A firm complained that a report in the *Stratford Express* was 'recklessly inaccurate'. An empty naphthalene tank was said to have exploded causing three workmen to run for their lives and that twenty firemen had fought the blaze for half-an-hour. In fact there was no explosion, and the blaze at the works was extinguished by the works fire crew in ten minutes as the professional firemen arrived.

The Editor-in-Chief, Mr Ivan W. Smith, said that all endeavours by his reporters to obtain an official statement from a responsible official of the firm were rebuffed. They were refused permission to enter the works, or to speak to a member of the management. The story printed was obtained from policemen, firemen and employees of the firm.

The firm informed the Press Council that they had no wish to see reporters. The fire was not of public interest; it had taken place some distance from public property, and adequate precautions for safety of workpeople had been taken.

The Press Council found that if the firm had given information to the newspaper the complaint of inaccuracy might not have arisen. An industrial fire with attendant risks to life and limb was in no sense a private matter, and the firm was at fault in so regarding it. The Council condemned the firm's attitude as 'inimical to the public interest'. (1963/34)

'HUSH-HUSH' ROBBERY

Under the heading 'Robbery is hush-hush' the *Streatham News* stated that a local firm had thrown a curtain of secrecy over the entire incident and that when reporters called at the firm's offices on two occasions they were told that no comment would be made.

Nine days after the publication of the report the firm stated that its reason for wishing to avoid publicity was to protect its staff from attacks in the street. It complained that statements in the report that a safe had been blown open and that the discovery of the robbery had been made by a member of the staff were untrue.

The newspaper had relied on information given by Scotland Yard.

The Press Council pointed out that the firm had been twice approached by the newspaper for information. It should have realised the public importance of the robbery and made a statement. (1962/28-9)

A GRIMY FIRE STATION

A story in the *Evening Standard* that East Ham firemen had not lifted a finger in three years to clean their fire station caused the local branch of the Fire Brigades' Union to complain to the Press Council that the story was distorted. The Branch Chairman denied the allegation that the washing of paintwork had been declared 'black' and that the grime continued to grow. In fact after discussions with the Amalgamated Society of Painters and Decorators, a committee had recommended that the established practice of the firemen washing the paintwork for cleanliness and painters doing it before repainting, should continue.

The branch union complained to Mr Charles Wintour, the Editor, and the *Evening Standard* sent a representative to see the Branch Chairman. According to the Chairman, they reached agreement that the complaint was justified and that the errors should be rectified. But two days later the Editor wrote saying that he understood that the Chairman objected only to the presentation of the story.

The Editor of the paper told the Press Council that the story had been supplied by a news agency. The Council traced the reporter concerned, who had since left the agency, and he told the Council that he had obtained his information by telephone, though he had been told to visit the fire station personally. He felt that the inferences he drew from what he had been told were fair, but the Press Council agreed that the story was distorted and deplored its publication. (1964/80–1)

DEATH OF BABY DAUGHTERS

A father complained that a reporter from the Glasgow *Daily Record* had entered his home without permission; that he had written a story about the death of his baby daughters which contained statements attributed to him which he had not made; and that he had had described an incident involving the complainant's son which could not have happened because the son had been moved to the home of relatives a few days earlier. The father also complained that the reporter had obtained a photograph from a local photographer of which he (the father) owned the copyright, by representing that he had permission to obtain it.

The reporter claimed that he did not say he had the father's permission to ask for the photograph, but the photographer denied this and said that he had twice asked whether permission had been given and was assured that it had. The reporter agreed that the incident about the little boy had not, in fact, happened. He claimed that he had about fifteen minutes' conversation with the father, but the father denied this. Mr Alex Little, Editor of the *Daily Record*, told the Press Council that he had reproved the reporter for his report, but that he accepted his version of the alleged intrusion.

The Press Council censured the newspaper for publishing a story which the reporter admitted was untrue in important particulars. The newspaper was also seriously at fault in publishing a photograph without the consent of a member of the family which held the copyright. (1962/26–7)

INTERVIEW FABRICATED

Wolverhampton Wanderers Football Club claimed that an interview with one of the club's directors published by the *Daily Sketch* was a complete fabrication. Their complaint said that the interview had not taken place at all.

The situation arose when the club dismissed its manager. The Press naturally wanted to know the details, but the directors of the club agreed among themselves that no one would speak individually to the Press.

The journalist concerned had attempted to contact the directors of the club to obtain information. At the office of one of them the journalist said he was promised information later, but the director said he ordered the journalist off the premises. The following day, an article in the *News of the World* said that the director was one of two directors who had fought strenuously against the manager's dismissal. A few days later, the *Daily Sketch* published a report by the journalist recording an alleged conversation he had had with the director who described his support for the manager. The journalist told the Press Council that he had not seen the report in the *News of the World*, but had himself been told the information contained in it. He said that the interview with the director had been made by telephone on the Monday morning. He was surprised that the director had decided to talk, but had asked his wife to listen in on an extension. She took a few notes but did not bother to keep them, as her husband told her that nothing controversial had emerged. The director denied that there had been any conversation at all, or that he had been in his office when the telephone conversation was alleged to have taken place.

In its adjudication, the Press Council stated that after exhaustive investigation it found that the interview was fabricated by the journalist who was condemned accordingly. (1966/75-7)

ATTACK ON NEW TOWN

An article in the *Daily Sketch* about Harlow New Town headed 'The Town that lost its way' was described by the Urban District Council as a scathing attack on Harlow based on spurious interviews and published without adequate investigation. No one was approached on behalf of the Harlow Council for an interview. The article stated, 'Everyone I spoke to in Harlow wants to get out of it. What's wrong? After living there for a week I found the answer.'

The Clerk said the Council did not question the right of the Press or anyone else to comment fairly and honestly on a matter of public opinion, and they appreciated that the opinions of others would not necessarily coincide with their own. But the article was deliberately biased, and the reputation of Harlow and its residents had been sacrificed for the sake of sensationalism.

The Editor, Mr Herbert Gunn, disputed most of the allegations, and, on the point that the reporter had not in fact done all the interviews himself, he said that it was customary where two or more reporters were working on a story together to print it under one name. The reporter had in fact made several visits to the town.

After considering the arguments the Press Council found that the article was misleading and irresponsible, and based on cursory and inadequate enquiries. The evidence showed that the writer had only made several visits to Harlow, and had not, as claimed, 'lived there for a week'. The Council noted, however, that the paper had already published the gist of a letter from the chairman of the Harlow Council contradicting some of the statements made in the article. (1959/21, 32–5)

See also p. 207 (*Daily Mail*).

ABRIDGMENT CAUSING INACCURACY

ERRORS IN STRIKE REPORT

The Transport and General Workers' Union complained that a report in the *Daily Express* about a stoppage of work in the London Docks was a flagrant and inexcusable misreport of the incident, and said that it would cause bad feeling between the staffs concerned. The men were not tally clerks as reported, and it was not true that they planned to call for support from other docks. The members in arrears over whom the dispute arose, had not at any time been banned from membership.

The Editor of the *Daily Express*, Mr Robert Edwards, told the Transport and General Workers' Union that the reporter's original copy had been condensed, which had led to the inaccuracy about the tally clerks. The reporter told the Press Council that he had been assured by two union men that they were calling for support from other docks if a satisfactory conclusion to the dispute was not reached. He had no reason to doubt the information he had received that the two men in heavy arrears had been automatically suspended.

The Press Council held that the report contained serious errors, and upheld the complaint. (1966/36–7)

EXPERTS MUST BE QUOTED ACCURATELY

Two members of the Department of Psychology at Edinburgh University complained that a report in the *Sun*, though reasonably accurate, gave a wrong attribution to a quotation.

The Editor, Mr R. L. Dinsdale, said that the reporter who recorded the interview had for the sake of brevity and smoother reading combined two separate sentences from her notes and moulded two quotations into one. If the report was capable of being misunderstood he would have corrected it at the time had he been informed by the complainants.

The Press Council held that the report was substantially accurate, but when dealing with experts greater care should be taken to quote the exact words spoken. (1967)

See also p. 351 (*Western Daily Press*).

Cases of abridgment of matter within quotation marks will be found on pp. 116 and 118.

NEGLIGENCE — FACTS INACCURATE

STORY UNTRUE

The *Sunday Pictorial* reported that two local councils had sold a list of the names of tenants who were bad at paying their rent on time to a private credit traders' association. The story was not in fact true, and the newspaper published a correction. But the Press Council said that more care should have been taken to obtain accurate information from the local authorities before publication. (1960/33–4)

'A SPY IN THE COUNCIL OFFICE'

The *Essex Weekly News* published a story headed: 'Is there a spy in the Council Office?' which told how a woman had inquired at the Brentwood Urban District Council offices about building permission for a plot of land she had been offered 'for a song'. Within an hour, the story said, she returned to the owner of the plot only to find that a local building contractor had bought the land for a higher figure than she had been asked. She stated that nobody else could possibly have known about the proposed deal, and was reported to have said: 'It all points to there being someone at the Council tipping off the big building contractors . . . I feel sure there is something shady going on and it ought to be investigated.' The story described the woman as wishing to remain anonymous, and the newspaper observed: 'We cannot vouch for her story. We give it because we feel it should be investigated.'

The complainant told the Press Council that he thought the publication was despicable because it sought to cast doubts on the integrity of Council employees without a whiff of evidence. The Clerk of the Council described the innuendo as damaging, distressing and unjustified.

Mr E. L. Waring, the Editor, in his evidence said that he felt the matter should be aired because the woman was so emphatic about the story. He still felt he did right in throwing the matter open for inquiry and reply. But the Press Council found that the newspaper should not have published the story which was based on the unsubstantiated assumption of an aggrieved person. There was no evidence to support it, nor was the newspaper able to obtain any. (1963/40–1)

A FORGED LETTER FROM WORMWOOD SCRUBS

Mr X, a prisoner at Wormwood Scrubs and then Editor of the prison magazine *New Horizon*, complained about a news story in the *Daily Sketch* which opened with the words, 'A disturbing letter, written on notepaper headed Wormwood Scrubs Prison reached the *Daily Sketch* yesterday. It came from five prison officers who are angry and embittered by what is happening in this gaol.' Naming Mr X, the article continued: 'He, according to these prison officers, is often to be seen taking tea in George Blake's cell. And another regular at these cosy *tête-à-têtes* is apparently Y' another prisoner serving a sentence for fraud, perjury and forgery.

The newspaper article went on to accuse these 'intelligent and unprincipled men' of spreading among their less intellectual fellow-prisoners, the idea that George Blake, who was serving a sentence of forty- two years for espionage, somehow had been done an injustice. It reported that George Blake himself contributed an article to the magazine attacking religion. The newspaper criticised the prison administration for allowing the prisoners too much freedom.

In his complaint Mr X said that everything in the newspaper article was false. He had never planned any campaign to whitewash Blake's crimes; he had never drunk tea in Blake's cell, and had never been in the cell at the same time as the other person mentioned. The leading article in the magazine criticised by the *Daily Sketch* had been written by him alone and approved by the Governor. The article attributed to George Blake by the newspaper was written by a group of persons calling themselves The Humanist Group, and it had been given a by-line accordingly.

The Managing Editor of the *Daily Sketch*, Mr Robert Johnston, produced to the Press Council the letter upon which the news item was based. The letter was unsigned and undated, typed on notepaper bearing the printed address of Wormwood Scrubs Prison. The telephone number had been obliterated. The writer described himself as a prison officer and referred to the 'limitless editorial freedom' allowed to the prison magazine which was being used for dubious purposes, and the letter was signed 'Five dissatisfied prison officers'.

Mr Johnston also produced to the Council copies of the prison magazine received with the letter. One contained an editorial entitled 'The Morality of Spying'. Another contained a letter attributed to one of the train robbers criticising the editorial and an article by another prisoner praising it; there was also an article entitled 'Knaves and Fools' attacking religion 'By George Blake'.

When its investigations disclosed that the article 'Knaves and Fools' was attributed in one copy of the magazine to George Blake and in official copies of the same issue to The Humanist Group the Press Council reported the matter to the Home Office. The Home Office subsequently informed the Council that it appeared that the copy of the magazine sent to the *Daily Sketch* was a forgery and the only one in existence attributing the article to George Blake. It had not been possible to establish who was responsible for the forgery or for conveying it out of the prison.

Mr X contended that the opening paragraphs of the news story in the newspaper would lead readers to believe that the Editor had in his possession the signatures of the five prison officers, and that he had satisfied himself beyond all doubt that the signatures were genuine. The complainant contended that he had been the victim of a false, malicious and totally groundless attack by a national newspaper acting upon evidence which had been proved to be completely fraudulent.

Mr Johnston had earlier informed the Council that the newspaper was satisfied that the letter was genuine and had checked with the prison officers themselves. In oral evidence at a later date he said that he was not now so sure of his information as he was at the time the inquiry began.

A journalist on the staff of the newspaper said that after publication of the article he had investigated the authenticity of the letter. He did not know the names of the writers, but he was satisfied that the letter was genuine. He was not prepared to disclose the 'contacts' among whom he made his numerous inquiries into the origin of the letter.

The newspaper was asked to produce evidence of inquiries made before the publication of the article, but Mr Johnston submitted that whether it had been the victim of a hoax or not, the circumstances indicated that there was room for improvement in the supervision of the prison.

The fact that the letter was written on official prison notepaper and accompanied by evidence in the form of a magazine gave no reason to believe that it was other than a genuine grievance. He did not think that a reader of the article would necessarily come to the conclusion that the newspaper knew the names of the five prison officers. It was now known, he said, that inquiries had not been made into the source of the news story before publication. When told that the Council's investigations had shown that the telephone number obscured on the printed prison notepaper was that of a nurse's flat and that it had not been used by Wormwood Scrubs Prison for more than seven years, Mr Johnston said that the newspaper might have attached importance to the alteration and the fact that no new telephone number had been inserted if its attention had been drawn to the point or if it had any reason to suspect the significance of the obscured number.

The Press Council held that a reader of the article in the newspaper would have assumed that there were in fact five prison officers known to the newspaper who were dissatisfied with conditions at Wormwood Scrubs. In fact the letter was anonymous, and the newspaper did not before publication check either the authenticity of the letter or the substance of the allegations in it. The Council deplored such irresponsible conduct. (1967)

See also p. 332 (*Sunday Telegraph*) and p. 344 (*People*).

MISLEADING HEADLINES

DANGER OF FOOD-POISONING

During an outbreak of food-poisoning the *Daily Express* reported that various foodstuffs were listed as suspect by a Rural District Medical Officer of Health. The heading of the story was: 'Beware cream buns, "Poison", Doctor warns.' The introduction to the story read: 'Cut down on cream buns, a medical officer warned housewives. . . .'

The local branch of the National Association of Master Bakers complained about the singling out of one item when six were listed equally. On the day after publication sales of cream buns fell substantially. In answer to the complaint, Mr Roger Wood, Editor of the *Daily Express*, stated that his reporter was assured by the health authorities that all foods were suspect and that cream buns and pastries were of particular danger, but the Press Council found that the headline placed unfavourable emphasis on one of the suspected foodstuffs, and in so doing distorted the balance of the report. (1963/51)

BABY KILLED BY WEED-KILLER

The report of the death of a baby in the *Scottish Daily Express* was headlined: 'Baby Boy Killed by "Bottle of Orange".' In fact the story clearly stated that the child died after he had been seen to play with an orange-juice bottle which had been used to hold liquid weed-killer, and the Scottish Federation of Aerated Water Manufacturers and Bottlers Associations complained to the Press Council that the headline was misleading.

Mr Ian McColl, the Editor, submitted that as the words 'Bottle of Orange' were in inverted commas, it should have been clear to the reader that the expression was not what it appeared to be. But the Council agreed that the headline was undoubtedly misleading. In fact the child had been poisoned by weed-killer and 'orange' had nothing to do with the tragedy. (1962/31)

NON-UNION MEN AND LABOUR CLUB

The omission of some of the facts led the Press Council to censure a news agency for a misleading story. The report, published in several newspapers, was about the opening of a Labour club which was said to have been built by men who were not members of a union. In fact one or two men were not members of a union, but had been persuaded to join while on the job. No mention of this was made in the report. The news agency was censured for circulating a misleading report, and the Press Council said that the *Daily Herald* and the *Daily Express*, the two papers complained of, should have tried to put the matter into proper perspective by ascertaining the facts.

The *Daily Herald* headline, 'Non-union men built the union club', was considered to be seriously at fault, but no objection was taken to the *Daily Express* headline, 'The club that Ted Hill [Chairman of the T.U.C.] opened: Non-union labour helped to build it', which was more nearly accurate. (1962/53–4)

SPEECH ON THE COMMON MARKET

Viscount Amory, Britain's High Commissioner in Canada, was reported by the *Daily Express* to have said in a speech: 'Whether Britain joins the Common Market or not, big economic and commercial readjustments to the pattern of our trade will be forced upon us. We in Britain know we are going to face some extremely painful changes — some of our industries going ahead but others contracting sharply.' The report carried the headline: 'Amory lets it out — Common Market will bring painful changes.' The complaint stated that since Lord Amory did not say that the Common Market would bring the changes, the choice of headline would seem to exemplify deliberate misreporting.

Mr Roger Wood, the Editor of the *Daily Express*, said that he could not agree that the headline misrepresented the speech or that the text was unfair. Most of the points in the speech favourable to the Common Market had been made many times before, but it was rare that a person of Lord Amory's political standing had been so forthright in public about the disadvantages. This was the real news in the speech. After studying a full copy of the speech, the Press Council found that it favoured Britain's entry into the Common Market and that the headline was misleading. (1962/42–3)

CHILD TO CLIMB MATTERHORN

The *Stockport County Express* published a story headlined 'N.S.P.C.C. fear danger to girl of three in Matterhorn venture. "Stop Climb" plea to parents. Tiny mountaineer has much experience, would be roped between us, says mother.'

An N.S.P.C.C. inspector denied having called on the parents and appealing to them to call off the venture. The newspaper said its only mistake was in saying that the inspector had called on the parents, and it corrected this and apologised.

The father complained that it was absurd to suggest that his three-year-old daughter was going to climb the Matterhorn, and the mother denied any reference to the N.S.P.C.C. when she was interviewed by the newspaper.

Mr Norman A. Kellie, the Managing Editor of the newspaper, stated that the mother's remark that the child was to be roped to the parents was made in the presence of four witnesses.

The Press Council condemned the newspaper story as seriously inaccurate. (1963/45)

BOOK ON CIVIL LIBERTIES

'Amazing advice to public shocks the law. "Run away from the police" '. This headline to a report in the *People* of the publication of the National Council of Civil Liberties' book *A Handbook of Citizens' Rights* led to a complaint that it distorted the facts.

The National Council complained that the headline 'Run away from the police' was quite misleading. The sentence, 'If innocent, you would be quite within your rights in running away', was an accurate legal account of the law and, within the context of the whole chapter, could not be advice to run away from the police.

The Editor, Mr Stuart Campbell, said that the headline was based upon the general tone of advice of the handbook. Far from counselling the public to give assistance to the police, the publication seemed to be directed to telling readers the best way to obstruct them.

The complaint was upheld. The Press Council agreed that a newspaper was entitled to publish a critical review, but the headlines gave a distorted impression of the contents of the book. (1965/50–1)

A HURTFUL IMPRESSION

The report of an inquest in the *Surbiton Borough News* bore the heading 'Girl accepted lift from a party at 3 a.m. and died'. It went on to say that a young man 'who was giving her a lift in his van' told the inquest jury that he hit a lamp post after being at a party with her.

The girl's parents complained that the report implied that their daughter had accepted a lift from a stranger at 3 a.m., when in fact the man was her fiancé. Complaint was also made that the phrases 'accepted a lift' and 'the girl sitting in the front seat beside me' conveyed a wrong impression of the girl. The father called at the newspaper office and asked for an apology.

The Editor, Mr R. G. Hills said the parents had not troubled to write to him: all he had received was a typed letter on copy paper without a hand-written signature. He had not heard that the father had called at the office. He denied that the report suggested that the girl accepted a lift from a stranger, but agreed that the words 'accepted a lift' could have been better expressed.

The Press Council held that the headline and report gave a hurtful and misleading impression. Although a letter was received by the Editor and a personal call made at the office no acknowledgment was made by the newspaper. The complaint was upheld. (1965/43-4)

INQUEST ON FOOTBALLER

Following an inquest on A.B., a professional footballer, who died of injuries received in a road collision between the motor-car he was driving and an omnibus, the *Eastern Evening News* reported the opening of the inquest under the headline 'A.B. had been drinking inquest told'.

The report, however, stated that the medical evidence was given that the alcohol content of his blood was not unduly high, and that the injuries received would have caused instant death. At an adjourned hearing a month later the Coroner recorded a verdict of accidental death.

After the first hearing the newspaper published a letter signed by six readers expressing anger that such a headline should have been printed, when the medical evidence showed that A.B. was not under the influence of drink.

The Editor, Mr M. Beales, said there was no thought that anyone would interpret the headline in the way suggested, and when it was found that people were reading more into it than was justified an explanatory statement was published in a prominent position on the front page. This was unprecedented because the inquest had not then been completed.

The Press Council held the headline of the report was grossly careless. A prompt correction had been published, but there should also have been an apology. (1967)

HOW FINAL IS 'FINAL'?

Complaint was made that the title 'West End Final' on two copies of the *Evening Standard*, which were different in appearance and content and evidently with an interval of about two hours between them, was a 'flagrant and deliberate attempt . . . to deceive the public'.

The Editor, Mr Charles Wintour, explained that the system was highly complicated and arose from a large circulation. It was possible to change one or two pages during production runs, but to alter the name of the edition would cause confusion in distribution.

The Press Council found that in the evening newspaper distribution the edition marking on many thousands of copies could not possibly coincide with the actual time of delivery or purchase. The Council felt, however, that these markings should be such as would not confuse or mislead the public. (1963/44)

See also p. 202 (*Stafford Newsletter*)

FAKED PHOTOGRAPHS

ROBBERY NEAR NAIROBI

The Kenya Government complained that photographs in the magazine *Weekend* showing a murder and robbery on a highway near Nairobi were forgeries. The complaint said that the alleged murder did not take place, and that exhaustive inquiries had been made which revealed that no inquest had been held, and that there was no record of the person who was alleged to have taken the photographs having visited Kenya.

The Government statement described the report as 'what must be one of the most loathsome forgeries ever known to 'journalism'.

The Editor of *Weekend*, Mr David Hill, said that the pictures were submitted by the London representative of a reputable German magazine, and he had been prepared to accept their guarantee of authenticity.

The Editor-in-Chief of the German magazine said that the photographer had sent them an original negative which could not have been forged.

When the Press Council asked for an affidavit from the photographer it was not produced.

The Press Council said that no evidence had been produced to satisfy the Council of the authenticity of the photographs and the truth of the report. The Council noted that the material was supplied to the Editor of *Weekend* by a reputable organisation but felt that in the unusual circumstances the Editor, although acting in good faith, would have been well advised to have made special inquiries before publishing the photographs. (1966/80–1)

ENGLISH NURSE AND KENYAN BABY

The *Sunday Telegraph* published a photograph of a white nurse holding a coloured baby with a headline 'A British nurse spells prestige in Kenya'. The caption stated that a white nanny, particularly if she was a trained nurse, was a new mark of social prestige among better-off Africans in Kenya, and that many were being recruited through advertisements in British newspapers.

A complainant writing from Nairobi said that he had enquired at all levels of society but could not find a single case of an African employing a British trained nurse. The Kenya Government had told him that a permit would not be granted for such work, and the British High Commissioner had no trace of a single British girl having gone to Kenya for employment of this kind. The publication was a slur on newly affluent Africans.

The Editor, Mr Brian Roberts, said the publication rights in the picture had been bought from a French newspaper. He had since discovered that it was a faked picture, but had no reason to believe this at the time it was published. He did not publish a letter from the complainant because it was unsuitable, but he had offered to print a suitable one.

The Press Council held that the Editor had acted within his discretion in refusing to print the complainant's letter of correction if he thought it was offensive. When, however, he discovered that the picture was not genuine and the headline and caption were seriously misleading, he should have published a correction. (1966/86–7)

DR NKRUMAH AND A CHALLENGED PICTURE

The *Daily Express* in the course of a campaign against alleged oppression and tyranny in Ghana published across the full width of a page a picture purporting to show some Ghanaian politicians sitting in chains in a prison in Ghana. The caption read, 'Shackled together like slaves of a bygone era . . . Ghana politicians and Opposition Party officials in a Ghanaian prison.'

The accompanying article stated that the shackled men were members of Ghana's Loyal 'Opposition'. Among them were politicians, officials of the Opposition United Party and leading citizens who had been critical of Dr Nkrumah. The picture was said to have been obtained from Mr Asigri, a Ghanaian Member of Parliament, who had spent two years in a Government prison camp before escaping.

A letter addressed to the Prime Minister, Mr Wilson appealing for British intervention, was said to have been smuggled out of the prison. Reference was also made to the reported death in prison of Dr Joseph Danquah, Dr Nkrumah's chief political opponent.

After publication of the picture Dr Nkrumah in a speech in the National Assembly described it as a forgery. The *Daily Express* published a challenge and said that three of the men in the picture were personally known to Mr Asigri and two others to the Press Officer of the Opposition United Party in London. Subsequently, at a press conference in Accra, the Ghana Minister of Information stated that the picture had been posed by former Togolese prisoners after the overthrow of the President of Togoland in 1963.

The High Commissioner for Ghana in London complained to the Press Council, and six Ghanaian journalists to the Editor of the *Daily Express*, that the photograph was false. The Editor asserted that the picture had been vouched for by exiled officials, and some of the men had been identified.

Three months after publication, following investigations in West Africa, the *Daily Express* published a retraction; it explained the circumstances in which the picture had been received and expressed its regret for the error. The High Commissioner withdrew his complaint to the Council, but the six journalists pursued theirs.

Mr Derek Marks, who had succeeded Mr Edwards as Editor, told the Press Council that the newspaper had no reason to doubt the reliability of the photograph sent to it by a man of the standing of Mr Asigri. When the authenticity was challenged they had approached Dr Busia, a distinguished Ghanaian who lived in Britain, who said that he did not doubt the authenticity of the photograph. The members of the United Party of Ghana were also firmly of the belief that the photograph was genuine. Mr Marks refuted allegations made by Lord Brockway and Lord Francis-Williams that the photograph had been in circulation in Togoland.

The Press Council considered sworn statements and other evidence, but following the overthrow of Dr Nkrumah the complainants found themselves unable to pursue the matter.

The Council, however, after considering the representations made by Lord Brockway and Lord Francis-Williams, decided to complete its enquiries into whether the publication was the result of deliberate malice on the part of the *Daily Express* and whether adequate steps were taken by the newspaper to investigate the authenticity of the photograph.

E   L.T.P.C.

On this part of the enquiry the Press Council found that there was no evidence to support the serious allegations that the photograph was published by the *Daily Express* with malice.

On the contrary, in the particular circumstances, it was not unreasonable for the newspaper to have published the picture. (1966/108–11)

QUOTATION MARKS MISUSED

QUOTED IN FIRST PERSON

A lady complained that she had been quoted in the first person in the *Sunday Express*, when in fact, she had never spoken or written to anyone connected with the newspaper. The words ascribed to her — the effects of weedkiller on hedgerows, insects and birds — had been taken from other correspondence, out of context, and slightly altered. The journalist who had contributed the story to the *Sunday Express* stated that he had written to the lady asking for her views, telling her clearly that he required them for publication. He considered he had her full co-operation and permission to use the comments contained in the letters she had written to another newspaper, and to quote her in the first person. But Mr John Junor, the Editor of the *Sunday Express*, told the Press Council that it was utterly wrong of the correspondent to suggest that he had had a conversation with the lady when, in fact, the remarks he attributed to her were made in a letter; but it was not true that the facts of the story itself were incorrect and he could not agree that the whole story should be withdrawn.

The Press Council held that the report was misleading, and it deprecated the failure to publish a correction. (1965/38–9)

SCIENCE FOR THE LAYMAN

The *Daily Mail* reported the content of a scientific article in an academic journal, but, as the result of a cut, the quotation marks at the end of an extract were removed and two paragraphs of comment by the Science Correspondent were attributed to the professor who had written the original article. The professor also complained that the article misrepresented what he had written.

The Press Council stated that greater care should have been taken in simplifying the article for the lay reader, and the quotation marks which had surrounded the quotation taken from the original article should not have been deleted in cutting. But the Press Council noted that the journal had sought publicity for the article by sending a copy of it to the *Daily Mail*, and accepted that this mitigated the offence to some extent. (1960/34)

PROFESSOR INCORRECTLY QUOTED

A professor complained of a report in *Reynolds News* about his discovery that a number of premature babies developed blindness because they received too much oxygen in the tents in which they were reared. The report contained a first-person quotation which he denied making. He said the statements held him up to ridicule and contempt as a doctor who gave self-adulatory interviews to the Press. After his secretary had informed the newspaper that he would not be interviewed, the reporter submitted four questions through the Institute of Ophthalmology which he answered in writing. When the Institute telephoned the reporter to give him the answers the Institute was told the article had already been written. The answers did not appear in the news story, but the professor agreed that apart from the first-person quotation the facts were accurate.

The reporter said that the Institute had given him authority to quote the professor and had approved a draft of the article. This was denied by the Institute, which said that permission was given to quote only the answers to the questions.

The Press Council accepted that the professor had made it clear that he was not prepared to give Press interviews and in fact had not done so on this occasion. The newspaper was at fault in wrongly attributing statements to him as direct quotations and had erroneously described him as a surgeon in a headline. It should have published a correction as requested. (1962/35–6)

AN ALDERMAN MISREPORTED

Complaint was made of a report in the *Daventry and District Weekly Express* of a meeting of the Finance and General Purposes Committee of a local council at which a development scheme was discussed. The report attributed to an alderman a statement he had not made, and said of another councillor that he had not taken part in the discussion when in fact he had.

In a later issue the *Weekly Express* published a front-page story which said that it had been threatened with a complaint to the Press Council. Then followed the full text of a letter of complaint from the Town Clerk. In a feature article in the same issue, the newspaper said its report was based on information received from two members of the Council who were perhaps not as accurate as experienced journalists.

The Press Council ruling was that the *Daventry and District Weekly Express* was wrong to report words said to have been used by a Council member at a meeting which no newspaper representative had attended in the form of a direct quotation; the publication of the letter of correction from the Town Clerk was, however, sufficient to balance the report, and the complaint was rejected. (1966/49–50)

AN ABBREVIATED RESOLUTION

The Newbury Constituency Labour Party complained that a resolution which had been passed at a meeting for submission to the national conference was reported in the *Newbury Weekly News* in condensed form, but was published in quotation marks as though it were a full copy of the original resolution. This, it was stated, gave rise to an inaccurate heading. Eight weeks later the newspaper published the correct text of the resolution but did not refer to its original publication.

In evidence to the Press Council the Editor, Mr G. E. Willis, claimed that the abbreviated version gave the substance of the resolution.

The Press Council held that editors must have the right to condense material, but that the condensed version should not be given in quotation marks. However, the Council thought that the Newbury Labour Party should have been satisfied when the full text of its involved and lengthy resolution was published. (1962/29)

REPORT OF COMPANY MEETING

When *Sporting Life* printed an abbreviated version of the statement by the company chairman of Hackney and Hendon Greyhounds Ltd in quotation marks, the company complained that this implied that it was a verbatim report, though in fact the reasons advanced by the chairman for reported reduction in revenue were omitted. The company also contended that the report of the statement, combined with some comments on it, showed bias, caused inaccuracy and affected the company's interests.

The Press Council agreed that the newspaper was at fault for omitting a section of an official statement which was presented as quoted throughout and, therefore, purported to be a verbatim report. (1963/47)

A related complaint will be found on p. 139 (*Daily Mail*).

HONEST MISTAKES

BROTHER MISTAKEN FOR HUSBAND

The *Daily Mirror* reported a tragedy at Beachy Head in which a mother and her three-year-old son plunged in a car over the cliffs. The husband was said to have telephoned the police and accompanied the police down the cliffs in a search. In fact, the husband denied having done either of these things, and complained to the Press Council. Investigation revealed that the Chief Constable of Eastbourne had given the information to the Press, saying that the person concerned was not the husband but one of his brothers. The Chief Constable suggested that the reporter concerned had made the honest mistake of assuming it was the husband from the wording of the police statement, and the Press Council agreed that this was so. In fact the complainant had been informed of the mistake before he complained to the Press Council. (1961/37–8)

REPORT OF A PUBLIC INQUIRY

A local councillor complained of a report in the *Guardian* of the evidence he gave at a public inquiry when opposing a compulsory purchase order for land. He was reported to have said: 'Most of the vice and crime of Manchester flourishes in the slums and much of this would be expected to come with overspill to Wilmslow.' The councillor said that his words were: 'Some of the vice and crime . . .' and that the story gave a wrong slant to his evidence by reporting little else of what he had said, and left the reader with the impression that his sole objection was based on the habits and character of the people. The Editor of the *Guardian*, Mr Alastair Hetherington, said that the sense of the passage was that the movement of families from the slum areas in Manchester would bring crime and vice; there was no deliberate intention to alter the meaning; the reporter's note said 'much' and the report gave the general sense of the councillor's remarks. The Press Council accepted the explanation and rejected the complaint. (1964/41–2)

INACCURACY NOT NEWSPAPER'S FAULT

A complaint was made that the *Daily Mail* (and several other newspapers) reported that Dag Hammarskjöld, the U.N. Secretary-General, had arrived at Ndola airport when in fact he had been killed in an air crash. The Editor of the *Daily Mail*, Mr William Hardcastle, explained that he had based the story on a reputable news agency's message, and that the news agency itself had got confirmation of Mr Hammarskjöld's arrival (though wrongly) from the airport control tower. The Press Council found that the *Daily Mail* was not to blame, and that it corrected the error as soon as it was known. The information came from Ndola airport control tower, and the error arose from the state of confusion that existed in the area at the time. (1962/29–30)

A JUSTIFIED INFERENCE

The *Kentish Independent* published an article which was said to convey to the reader that a quoted statement was taken from an official bulletin by a co-operative society but was in fact the personal composition of an individual.

The bulletin was issued by the secretary of the Political Purposes Committee in conjunction with the chairman under a majority decision to use every possible support for the rules revision proposals.

The Press Council decided that Mr L. W. Neves, Managing Editor of the *Kentish Independent*, was entitled to regard it as an official statement. (1963/44–5)

SUSPECTED MURDER

On a night when Brockworth was shrouded in thick mist the body of a woman was found lying in a garden in a pool of blood. The police thought at first that it might be a case of murder, and the early edition of the Gloucester *Citizen* discussed this possibility. Later in the day the police were satisfied that the woman had fallen from an upstairs window.

Complaint was made that the newspaper had been guilty of 'alarming sensationalism' in its handling of an accident.

The Editor told the Press Council that the newspaper reflected the changing course of the investigations in editions published throughout the day.

The Press Council accepted his explanation and said the attack on the newspaper was not justified. (1959/21–2)

CONJECTURE REPORTED AS FACT

SPECULATION ON MORTGAGE INTEREST

A news story about house loan mortage rates in the *Scottish Daily Express* stated that couples buying their homes with loans from Building Societies would have to pay 7 per cent mortgage interest. The heading read: ' "Blame Callaghan" say the Building Society Chiefs'. The later textual matter revealed that the statements of fact were only predictions.

Some time later the newspaper reported a meeting of the Building Societies Association Council, when it was disclosed that the bid to put up the mortgage rate had been defeated.

The Editor, Mr Ian McColl, said that the report should be read as a whole. This would dispel any possible confusion.

The Press Council held that the article stated as fact what was conjecture; this the Council strongly deplored. The complaint was upheld. (1966/65)

ABOLITION OF CAPITAL PUNISHMENT

On the morning after the second reading of a Bill for the abolition of the death penalty, the *Daily Sketch* reported that the previous night three men in condemned cells learned that they would not be hanged by listening to a B.B.C. bulletin on ear-phone radio sets. Complaint was made that the statement was inaccurate.

The evidence showed that in two of the cases the condemned men had not been listening in, and in the third it was thought most unlikely, although there was a radio set in the cell.

The Editor of the *Daily Sketch*, Mr Herbert Gunn, admitted that the newspaper had no knowledge that the three prisoners did listen in to the wireless and that its statement was an assumption.

The Press Council held that the statement was admittedly without justification and misleading. A correction should have been published. (1956/30)

TRANSFER OF FOOTBALLER FORECAST

A *Daily Express* article reported that Tottenham Hotspur Football Club was planning to buy a player from West Bromwich Albion. The article discussed the ability of the player and stated that the manager of the Tottenham Club had watched him play in a match. The story was headlined '£60,000 Kaye is Spurs' Target.'

The West Bromwich Albion club complained to the Press Council that the statement completely misrepresented the facts. The Tottenham manager had certainly visited the West Bromwich club's ground, but it was purely speculation on the part of the reporter that he went there purposely to cover Kaye. The article could have led the player to believe that he had an opportunity to go to another club. It also gave supporters the impression that the club was likely to lose an important player and could affect confidence in club management, and attendance at matches.

The Editor, Mr Robert Edwards, said that the writer of the article had made a great number of inquiries before he wrote his story, and he was convinced that Tottenham were considering the possibility of making an offer for Kaye. He had offered to publish a categorical denial that there was any truth in the news story, but the letter which the manager had written to the Sports Editor did not contain any such denial.

The Press Council held that the *Daily Express* article was speculative, and the headline was misleading because it did not make this fact clear. (1965/42–3)

ALTERING COPY WITHOUT WRITER'S CONSENT

AUTHOR ASKED FOR PROOF

The writer of an article published in the former periodical *Today* complained that, although he had agreed to the amendment of his contribution, substantial changes were made without his approval and misrepresented him. The article dealt with his personal experiences in the treatment of cancer, and before he submitted the article he had it read by medical consultants who were anxious that false hopes should not be raised amongst cancer sufferers. The changes made in his article implied that he had been cured of cancer, that he had not lived the life of an ordinary man, and that he had smoked and drunk excessively. He had requested a proof of the amended article, but it had not been supplied.

The journalist who handled the story for *Today* said that the author had made some changes as a result of a personal meeting, that some additional information had been obtained by telephone, that he had agreed in detail to the changes made and had not asked to see a proof.

The Editor, Mr Charles Stansby, said that provision of proofs would have been unusual, since the greater part of the article consisted of the original submission, and the changes were made in consultation with the author who was a professional journalist. No proof had been promised. The published story did not misrepresent the author.

In its findings, the Press Council said that there were substantial alterations in the article, and that the author's request for a proof should have been complied with. (1965/87)

FILM REVIEW TAMPERED WITH

Mr Tom Hopkinson, a former editor of *Picture Post*, had accepted an invitation from the Editor of the *Daily Sketch*, Mr Herbert Gunn, to act as guest film critic for one month, his name to appear with his articles.

The main subject of his article in the first week was a film of newspaper life entitled 'Front Page Story'. In its original form Mr Hopkinson's article expressed the opinion 'This is not a great film'. After handing in his copy he was telephoned by a member of the features staff and told there was only one word that they suggested should be changed; this was the word 'not', so that the opinion should read 'This is a great film'.

Mr Hopkinson replied that he did not think the film was a great one, and he could not say that it was. He was agreeable, however that the phrase should be altered to read: 'This is not a great film, but it is a good one'.

When the article appeared additions and further alterations had been made. Mr Hopkinson complained that a review had appeared over his name which misrepresented his opinion of the film and paid an undeserved compliment to the film's technical adviser, the wife of the Editor who commissioned the article.

Evidence before the Press Council showed that a proof of the article was sent to the Editor who made alterations about which Mr Hopkinson was not consulted, although his name appeared as the author of the article. The Editor said he had given instructions for Mr Hopkinson's name to be removed, but through a misunderstanding this was not done. He had tendered a private apology to Mr Hopkinson, but it had not been published in the *Daily Sketch*.

E 2

The Press Council decided that the Editor's action had fallen below the best journalistic standards and deserved professional censure. The Council's decision was based on three principles of journalistic ethics:

1. The retention on an article of the name of the author after his article has been materially altered, without consultation with him.

2. The right of the author treated in this way to ask for a public rather than a private apology.

3. The propriety of an editor allowing his own association with a work to affect his newspaper's judgment upon it. (1954/22–4, 38–40)

WRITER'S VIEW DISTORTED

A local councillor complained that his letter to the *Huddersfield Daily Examiner* about an alleged General Election pact was so altered as to misrepresent his view. Without consulting the writer, substantial passages of the letter were deleted and the remainder rewritten.

The Editor, Mr J. W. Dicks, said the letter had been received on the eve of a General Election, when there was heavy pressure on space. He had tried to pick out the main points of the letter, and did not feel he had misrepresented the writer. There was no time to submit his amended letter for approval.

The Press Council held that although the condensation of readers' letters is often necessary, the newspaper was in error in publishing a rewritten version, which had not been agreed with the writer and which was in fact an inaccurate statement of his views. (1965/75)

CUTS MADE LETTER RIDICULOUS

The *West London Observer* cut a letter in a way that altered the view the correspondent had expressed. He asked for a correction and, when he received no acknowledgment, he repeated his request. The Managing Editor, Mr Eric E. Carter, then wrote saying that a small deletion had been made for reasons of space.

The writer protested that this was no justification for altering the sense of his letter. He received no answer, and a fortnight later he wrote again. A week later the Editor wrote stating that as far as he was concerned the correspondence was closed.

The Press Council censured the newspaper for cutting a reader's letter in a way that made the author's view appear ridiculous, for failing to observe ordinary courtesy in replying to a request for a correction and for failing to publish a correction. (1965/77)

REPORTS — ACCURATE OR SUBSTANTIALLY SO

A REPORT OF A WEDDING

' "Cad" weds heiress — again' was the heading of a story in the *Sunday Mirror* which reported the wedding of Mr and Mrs L. T. Gardner-Bell. The report began: 'Laurence Bell, 27, self-confessed "cad" from London's East End, who hoaxed the Brigade of Guards by posing as a "former officer", was married yesterday. To an heiress . . .' and said that none of the bride's family were present and that barely a dozen friends attended the ceremony. It described Mr Bell's family background 'in a humble terrace-house in Wanstead', and said that he would make his future home in Ascot in a house for which the couple were believed to have paid more than £50,000.

A firm of solicitors acting for Mr Bell complained that the report carried the connotation that the couple had been socially ostracised, and that the passage about the family background was objectionable and unjustified colouring for a news story.

The Editor of the *Sunday Mirror*, Mr Michael Christiansen, said that the report about the number of people at the wedding was factually correct, and that Mr Bell had himself described his background in a series of Sunday newspaper articles himself. He had also published a statement that he had 'hoaxed the cream of British aristocracy', that he had been a 'High Priest in a strange religious movement', that his bride had given him £30,000 and that he had left behind him 'a trail of broken hearts'. The Council held that the report was substantially correct and rejected the complaint. (1965/32–3)

'SPIDER MAN'S' OPINIONS OMITTED

A 'spider man' who had given an interview to the *Daily Mail* about an industrial dispute complained that, although the facts he had provided were correctly stated, he had also given his opinions, which had been omitted. The

Press Council agreed with the Editor, Mr William Hardcastle, that the report was not unfair. The facts had been published, but opinion had been ignored; as presumably the point of the interview was to obtain facts about the dispute, the story was not inaccurate in any way. (1962/51)

'ADDICTION' TO DRUGS

A complaint was made that an article in the *People* which stated that marijuana smoking led to addiction was false, lacked authority, and disseminated 'lies and baseless prejudice'. In reply, the Editor, Mr Stuart Campbell, contended that many social workers thought that marijuana smoking could lead to drug addiction.

The Press Council saw no objection to the article and considered that the word 'addiction' was used in its proper general meaning. (1962/51)

MAN KILLED BY PIRATES

The wife of a man who had been killed by pirates off Borneo complained of the inaccuracy of a *Daily Sketch* report that she had said that the Admiralty had been heartless in breaking the news to her by telegram, instead of sending someone to see her personally, and that she was furious that her husband had been buried in Borneo when she wanted him brought home. She denied that she had expressed such statements when interviewed. The Admiralty, she said, had been very helpful throughout. The reporter for the news agency, which supplied the story, said that the wife had made the remarks not in answer to questions from him, but as observations on something said by a member of the family in general conversation.

The Press Council held that the wife had made the statements attributed to her when in a state of distress and that the report was substantially accurate. (1964/47–8)

CHARACTERS OF JURORS

The *Daily Sketch* reported that a Government committee of inquiry had been told that eleven out of thirty-three people called for jury service at an Old Bailey session had criminal records. The report said that the inquiry had also heard complaints by Scotland Yard detectives that guilty men were being freed because jurors with criminal records could swing a verdict.

A complaint was made that the article gave the impression that the method of selecting jurors was wrong, or that one in three of the citizens of London were criminals. The article was calculated to bring discredit on British justice.

In evidence to the Press Council, the Clerk to the Central Criminal Court confirmed that 'out of a group of 38 jurors four had convictions and nine others appeared to have records'. When the Report of the Government inquiry was published, the statement was substantiated. The Press Council held that the *Daily Sketch* report was accurate and that the article was not irresponsible. The complaint was rejected. (1965/33–4)

PETS DESTROYED BEFORE HOLIDAYS

When the *Daily Express* and the *Daily Mirror* reported that veterinary surgeons in Luton were inundated with calls to destroy unwanted pets before the summer holidays, a veterinary surgeon in Luton complained that the report was inaccurate. In letters to the Editors of the newspapers he said that in two out of three veterinary practices treating pets in Luton, there had not been a single instance of an animal being destroyed because the owner was going on holiday. He asked for the publication of a correction.

The Assistant Editor of the *Daily Mirror*, Mr Bryan Parker, told the complainant that the information in the article came from a veterinary surgeon with a large practice and from an R.S.P.C.A. Inspector.

Mr Robert Edwards, Editor of the *Daily Express*, sent a similar reply.

After hearing evidence from the Editors of the newspapers the Press Council found that there was substance in both reports and rejected the complaint. (1965/39–40)

DAILY HERALD STAFF

The Central London Branch of the National Union of Journalists complained of a report in the *Daily Telegraph* about a meeting of the T.U.C. General Council, at which one of the members was stated to have said that the troubles of the *Daily Herald* were not due to its links with the T.U.C., but to the incompetence of its staff. An apology was demanded by the Father of the *Daily Herald* Chapel but was refused.

The Press Council did not consider an apology was called for. The passage complained of was not the expressed opinion of the newspaper but what it believed was an accurate report of a remark made. (1961/25)

ROWDYISM AT A SEASIDE RESORT

An article in the Newcastle *Evening Chronicle* entitled 'Whitley Bay concern over Teddy Boys' reported rowdyism at weekends and stated the local hoodlums were preparing for full-scale warfare with gangs from outside areas. The Whitley Bay Borough Council felt that the article could cause unnecessary public alarm and could have a serious effect on the activities and revenue of the town as a seaside resort by attracting youths to come in to commit acts of hooliganism. The complaint described what the town had done to advertise itself as an attractive seaside resort and went on to say that the Council made every attempt to provide full facilities for the Press, including admission to all standing committees other than Establishments. 'This article affronts the simplest canons of fair play,' it said. The complaint was backed by members of the public, the Hotel and Boarding House Association and major entertainment enterprises. The local Council appealed to the Press Council to make representations to the Editor of the newspaper to avoid similar complaints.

The case for the newspaper was that gang warfare was increasing in the town, and the newspaper had a duty to give publicity to it. What was published was factually correct.

The Press Council rejected the complaint, saying it did not believe that the article was untrue or blameworthy in any respect. It was right that the facts should be made known to the public. (1958/26, 42–5)

TIME-AND-MOTION STUDY AT THE DOCKS

A group of dockers complained about an article in the *People*, reporting the findings of a time-and-motion expert who had stood on London Bridge and watched dockers at work through a telescope. He had described them as 'bone idle'. With the report the *People* published a statement from the General Secretary of the Institute of Work Study saying that he would have thought that a study of a vast field such as the docks required more observations than the expert had made; the article also included an interview with the docks chief of the Transport and General Workers' Union, who described the observations as 'too hit-and-miss'.

The dockers protested against the allegations of slackness and demanded an apology, which was refused.

The Editor of the paper, Mr Stuart Campbell, said that the article was not an attack on the dockers but a report of an expert's view with the replies of a senior union official.

The Press Council rejected the complaint. (1965/63)

OCCUPATIONS OF UNMARRIED MOTHERS

The Guild of Hairdressers, Wigmakers and Perfumers protested to the Council about a *Daily Mirror* report that the Medical Officer of Health for Bournemouth had said that he believed that hairdressers provided the greatest number of unmarried mothers in the town. The Medical Officer of Health denied making the remark attributed to him, and the Guild complained of 'inaccurate, repulsive and injurious reporting.'

The Editor of the *Daily Mirror*, Mr L. A. Lee Howard, said the report was obtained from a reputable news agency, and any suggestion that the newspaper deliberately set out to besmirch hairdressers was nonsense. The news agency produced its notes of the telephone conversation with the medical officer. The Press Council accepted this evidence and the complaint of inaccurate reporting was rejected. (1965/48–9)

THREATENED COMPULSORY PURCHASE ORDER

The *South London Observer* printed a story under the heading: ' "Blackmail" bid by Council alleged in take-over grab'. It said that an old couple had been threatened by the Camberwell Borough Council with a compulsory purchase order if they did not retain tenants they did not want. The daughter of the couple had written to the Minister of Housing and Local Government stating that she was told by the local Housing Department that if she and her children moved in with her parents, and allowed the quitting tenants to have her house, the claim for possession would be dropped. The daughter had refused, and declared that the proposition savoured of blackmail. Subsequently, a public inquiry was held, and the Minister decided against the Council. The newspaper's report of the inquiry was headed 'Blackmail allegations denied by Council'.

The report contained the Council references to the 'completely unethical and apparently successful attempt by a local newspaper to prejudice the interest of justice by this unwarrantable attack on the Council'. The newspaper criticised the Council for alleged 'hole and corner secrecy'.

The Borough Council complained to the Press Council alleging unfair reporting over a period of nearly three months. The reference to blackmail, it said, had appeared only in a letter from a private person to the Minister, and the newspaper had not published the fact that the Leader of the Council had told it that the Council's action in the matter accorded with general policy.

In his evidence, the Editor of the *South London Observer*, Mr Ian McKenzie, said that the Leader of the Council was not available for comment until 9 p.m., and all that he then said was reported. Mr McKenzie denied the charge that the newspaper's reports had prejudiced the interests of justice during the inquiry, and maintained that an inquiry did not make discussion of the relevant matters *sub judice*. The newspaper had 'leaned over backwards' to be fair to the Council, but they had been dealing with an attempt by the Council to circumvent the principle of the Housing Act.

The Press Council held that the *South London Observer* was not guilty of unfair reporting. (1965/44–5)

CYCLING ACCIDENTS

Reports in the *Daily Telegraph* and the *Sun* of a lecture on the incidence of cycling accidents led to complaints of misreporting and unfairness to the cycling community.

As the *Sun* had apologised and offered to print an explanation to put the matter right, the Press Council decided not to take any further action against that newspaper. It held that a substantial case had not been made out against the *Daily Telegraph*. (1965/61–2)

A POLITICALLY DAMAGING RUMOUR

A complaint was made about an article in the *Observer* headed: 'The Time Bomb under Sir Alec'. The complainant stated that the story represented a political rumour as having a basis in established fact, as instanced by the use of the phrase, 'the latest sex scandal'. The complaint alleged that although the allegations were found to be without foundation, the *Observer* made no attempt to retract the story except when at a later date it criticised the Daily Mirror Group for having published the rumour originally. Mr Charles Davy, the Assistant Editor of the *Observer*, said that the article was concerned with the rumour's political consequences, and that the later article described in detail the way in which the *Sunday Mirror* had handled the story, and had then retracted it. The readers were left in no doubt that the story was baseless and unjustified.

Mr Michael Davie, the Deputy Editor of the *Observer*, said that, far from encouraging the spread of the rumour, the *Observer* article went to some lengths to show it was groundless, and there was no delay in bringing the facts to the attention of readers.

The Press Council rejected the complaint. (1965/83–4)

RUMOURS DENIED

The Portsmouth *Evening News* printed a report denying local rumours that there would be a large-scale redundancy in a local firm. The firm complained that the publication of the story, although it was a denial, had caused alarm in the area and had shaken the faith of customers and workers. It did much to undo the company's attempts to avoid creating any major disturbance in the area, and resulted in loss to the firm of status and prestige.

The Editor, Mr E. T. Symons, claimed that he had every right to publish the story which, in his opinion, was a matter of vital interest to the public his newspaper served. The published statement was factual and was obtained from the company's publicity manager at its headquarters — and this was stated in the report. The Press Council upheld the Editor. (1961/29–30)

AN 'ARCHBISHOP'S' YOUTH CLUB

Two articles in the *People* criticised a youth club run by a sect called the Old Roman Catholic Church (English Rite), revealing that four of the six 'priests' had been in gaol, and two of them had been convicted for indecency. The 'Archbishop' of the sect had described them as lambs that had strayed who were now being given the chance to redeem themselves.

The Archbishop complained that the articles were persecution, and that the interview recorded in a second article was a fabrication, as he had not spoken the words which had been attributed to him in the first person.

After hearing the reporters responsible for the story, the Press Council found that the articles were substantially correct, and that the disputed interview did in fact take place. In the circumstances, the exposure of the criminal record of the people concerned was a material factor, and the disclosure was justified. (1965/70–1)

TELEVISION VIGILANTES

A television play entitled 'Up the Junction' resulted in considerable public controversy. The *Daily Mirror* arranged a debate between Mrs Mary Whitehouse, Founder of the Clean TV Campaign, and Mrs Avril Fox, leader of the Freedom for TV movement.

Mrs Fox complained that the newspaper, in reporting the discussion, attributed to her a number of statements she did not make and which were harmful to the movement she represented. She denied saying 'the more "Up the Junctions", four-letter words, bedsheet wrestling, murders and irreverencies the merrier'. There were other passages in the report attributed to her by the newspaper which she also denied.

Mr L. A. Lee Howard, Editor of the *Daily Mirror*, said that the reporter's notes showed that she had been accurately reported; the reporter also affirmed that his article fairly reproduced the statements made by Mrs Fox.

Mrs Whitehouse told the Council that she did not think the report was unfair.

The Press Council's adjudication was that the report in the *Daily Mirror* was substantially accurate and rejected the complaint. (1966/54–5)

ACCURATE SUMMARY OF CASE

The President of the Hull University Union complained that the Hull *Daily Mail* had unfairly reported a case that came before the Magistrates involving a student convicted of taking a motor-cycle without the owner's consent and driving without insurance. The police had made an application to take the student's finger-prints on the grounds that it might help to clear up a spate of petty thefts, some of which were thought to involve students.

Their application was refused. In the newspaper the story was headlined:

' "Irresponsible" ones in petty thefts. Hull student should be finger-printed — Police application'.

The complaint suggested that this was an unfair summary and in 'the worst possible taste'. In defence of the paper, the Managing Editor, Mr G. H. Giles, said that the application had been made in open court, was in pursuance of police policy, and was obviously of great significance in a university city. The Press Council found that the report was accurate, and rejected the complaint. (1965/53)

RISK OF DEFAMATION

When the *Express and Star* of Wolverhampton reported that Rowley Regis Council committee had recommended non-payment of an extra charge requested by the contractor for better quality turf he proposed for tennis courts and bowling greens it cut part of the Committee's report on the grounds, the Editor, Mr J. Clement Jones, said, that the document carried only qualified privilege and to include it might result in a libel action. The Rowley Regis Council claimed that the story gave a wrong impression.

In evidence, the Press Council was told that a reporter had requested further information from the Town Clerk without success.

The Council rejected the contention that the newspaper had failed to make the necessary inquiries to check the accuracy of the facts. The first report published by the newspaper was inadequate because it omitted essential information about the local Council's position, but this deficiency was made good in the lengthy report of the proceedings of the local Council meeting in the following day's issue. There was, therefore, no need for the complaint to the Press Council. (1965/59–60)

A SATIRICAL QUESTION

The Yeovil Borough Council allowed a retired employee to sub-let his council house, furnished, at a rent to be approved by the Housing Committee, while he was away in Australia for two years. The *People* criticised the Borough Council and said there was no mention of 'This unusual concession' in the Commiteee minutes; the article concluded with the question, 'Will the Council get a commission on this private deal?'

The Town Clerk complained that there was nothing unusual about the arrangement, that the usual procedure had been followed, and the implication of the last sentence amounted to an accusation of corruption. The Editor, Mr Stuart Campbell, expressed astonishment that the Borough Council had failed to recognise the satire. The writer of the article would be ready to say that it was satirical.

The Press Council said that the question was patently satirical. The Editor had offered to make this clear to his readers. (1964/81)

WOOLWICH ARSENAL TO BE CLOSED

An announcement in the *Daily Express* that Woolwich Arsenal was to be closed, published a month before the official announcement in Parliament, led to a complaint to the Press Council that the report caused alarm and despondency which could be very well unfounded. The report said that Mr Fred Mulley, the Army Minister, had found no reasons to reverse the previous Government's decision that the factory should be closed. The complaint from a member of the Arsenal staff said that he had been told by the Ministry of Defence that the re-examination was not yet complete.

The Editor of the *Daily Express*, Mr Robert Edwards, said he was sure that when the report was published the *Daily Express* would be found to be right. However, the Director of Public Relations at the War Office said the re-examination was not complete, and that the department was not aware of any basis on which the writer of the article would have been justified in assuming that the decision would be as the *Daily Express* stated.

In fact, a month later an announcement was made in Parliament that the Arsenal was to be shut, and the Editor told the Press Council that it would be absurd to criticise a reporter for fulfilling his first duty, which was to report news accurately.

The Press Council rejected the complaint on the grounds that although the report was published before the official announcement it was correct in substance. (1965/65)

REPORT NOT BIASED

The President of the Glastonbury Chamber of Commerce complained that his integrity had been impugned and that he had been unfairly treated in a news story in the *Central Somerset Gazette* about Glastonbury's one-way traffic scheme.

The report stated that at a private meeting of the Chamber a vote of no confidence in the President had been proposed but not supported. The mover when interviewed alleged that the President had been in communication with the County Council without the knowledge of the Chamber. The article included a denial by the President.

Five weeks later the President reviewed the traffic negotiations at a meeting of the Chamber, but the *Gazette* reported only that he had opened the meeting with a lengthy résumé.

The President complained that the original interview with him had been obtained by telephone and that he had not been given sufficient time to make a considered reply. In his address to the Chamber he had presented all the facts.

The Editor of the *Gazette*, Mr Kenneth Meadows, said that the complainant had not asked on the telephone for more time. The report did not impugn his integrity.

The Press Council was satisfied that reasonable facilities had been given to the complainant to reply to the allegations against him, and the newspaper did not show bias in not re-opening the controversy more than five weeks later. (1964/74–5)

ANTI-POLARIS DEMONSTRATORS OBJECT

A husband and his wife who had been arrested and fined for their part in an anti-Polaris demonstration complained about reports in the *Scottish Daily Express* and the *Lennox Herald*.

It appeared that the husband's fine had been paid but the wife had elected to take the alternative punishment of thirty days in gaol. After she had been in prison one day the *Scottish Daily Express* gave her husband the money to pay the fine and she was released. She did not then know the source of the payment.

The *Scottish Daily Express* published a report, with a picture, of the release. This described her as 'rushing to the arms of her husband', sobbing 'It was horrible', and saying she had been scrubbing floors all day. She denied this conduct, and said that if she had known who had paid the fine she would have been very angry. The husband said that when his wife discovered who had paid the fine it caused a terrible row between them.

The Editor of the *Scottish Daily Express*, Mr Ian McColl, said that the money had been given to the husband for humanitarian reasons, as he was unable to cope with the house and two young children. His wife was patently delighted when she was released. He could not help feeling that subsequent reflection on the shortened duration of her prison sentence had detracted from her vision of martyrdom and hurt her pride. The newspaper reporter and photographer confirmed the accuracy of her reported speech and actions.

The complaint against the *Lennox Herald* said that the newspaper had also misrepresented the facts and that a letter written by the wife to the newspaper had not been published. The Editor, Mr David G. Cattan, disclaimed responsibility.

The Press Council said that the complaints had not been substantiated. (1963/58-9)

RESCUE BY A CRIPPLE

A report appeared in the *Daily Express* that a crippled boy was to be awarded a Royal Humane Society testimonial for saving a legless friend from drowning. The father of the rescued boy complained that his son had not been in danger, that he was standing only waist deep in water at the time and that he was a certified swimmer.

The Press Council consulted the Secretary of the Royal Humane Society who said the award was confirmed after independent inquiry.

The rescued boy's swimming certificate applied only when he was not wearing artificial legs. On the occasion of the rescue he was wearing them. They filled with water, and this added considerably to the weight of the irons. Although it appeared afterwards that he was not in much danger, there was considerable danger to his rescuer who was crippled with polio.

The Council declared that the complaint of misreporting was unfounded. (1962/44)

REMARKS ABOUT MORMONS

The *Crawley Advertiser* recorded in a leading news story that a local woman Councillor had said at a Community Association meeting that she and other members of the Community Centre Committee 'charged the Mormons a high rent for their Sunday services in an attempt to "frighten them away" '. She had said later: 'I should not have said it. It was just my joking sort of way.'

The following week, the newspaper published a full page about the Mormon faith and local adherents, and also a letter from a local resident saying that the newspaper had viciously attacked the Councillor and made a mountain out of a molehill.

The Councillor complained to the Press Council denying that she used the words 'frighten them away' or 'higher rent'. She had not complained when the *Advertiser* first published the report because people in the public eye had to take a good deal from the Press.

The reporter told the Press Council that no one else at the meeting had made any accusations of inaccuracy about his report.

The Press Council said that this was not a case of dishonest or careless reporting, and rejected the complaint. (1964/45–6)

REDEVELOPMENT PLAN ABANDONED

When Surrey County Council abandoned its East Molesey redevelopment plan the *Daily Express* credited Molesey Residents' Association with victory. The claim was contested by members of Esher Urban District Council who said that the abandonment of the plan was due to the concerted action by the East Molesey Councillors. The newspaper was accused of errors of fact and in not having sought views other than those of one association. The author of the article was said to have muddled facts with an imaginative fiction.

The Editor of the *Daily Express*, Mr Derek Marks, said that the complaint was essentially an airing of a dispute between local politicians and the Residents' Association. It was an attempt to belittle the efforts of the residents' organisation which had succeeded in stirring up opposition to the proposed plan.

The Press Council held that the newspaper article was substantially accurate as seen by the writer of the article. The question of whether the report should have included some reference to the local authorities' side was a matter within the discretion of the Editor. The complaint was rejected. (1966/72–3)

AN INQUEST JURY'S VERDICT

A member of a Coroner's jury complained that the report of an inquest in the *Welwyn Times* inaccurately recorded a rider to the effect that the state of the vehicle's tyres had contributed to the fatal motor crash.

The Editor, Miss M. Thomas, denied that the report was inaccurate.

The Coroner told the Council that juries often added riders to their verdicts, but were not encouraged to do so. In this case the jury did mention points about the state of the tyres and the road, but no rider was recorded.

The Press Council found that, although the view expressed was not formally recorded as a rider, the jury did call attention to the question of bald tyres, and the Council was satisfied that the newspaper report was substantially accurate. (1966/70)

POOLS WIN DENIED

The Reading *Evening Post* reported that Mr S., a newspaper seller had won more than £5,000 on a football pool and that he had stated that he was going to carry on with the job. The man had fourteen grandchildren.

The man in question alleged that he had denied to the reporter that he had won the money and telephoned the newspaper and repeated his denial when he saw the report, which he said was wrong in every particular except that he had fourteen grandchildren.

The reporter, a man of thirty-five years' experience, confirmed the man himself had said that he had won £5,000.

The Editor, Mr Howard Green, said the information had first been given by a Mr S. on the telephone, but when contacted personally Mr S. had denied making the call.

The newspaper seller said the story was a concoction and said that he did not give the reporter any reason to think that he had won £5,000.

The Press Council was not satisfied that the interview with the newspaper seller was incorrectly reported and rejected the complaint. (1966/60–1)

RADIO PIRATE STATION DISMISSAL

A man who was employed by Radio City, the broadcasting station on Shivering Sands in the Thames Estuary, complained that as the result of inaccuracies in a report in the *Romford Times* he was dismissed.

The report stated that a man in fear of his life had said that explosives were to be taken to the pirate broadcasting station to protect the crew. Any unidentified ship visiting the station would be sunk first and questions asked afterwards. Death threats were also said to have been made against the complainant and other members of the crew.

The complainant said that these statements were untrue. He said that he did not use the actual phrases, though basically the article was true.

Mr Ivan W. Smith, Editor-in-Chief of the *Stratford Express and Romford Times*, said that the reporter who wrote the story had checked his notes, which accorded with the statements published.

The complainant's former employers assured the Council that he was not dismissed because of the newspaper article.

The Press Council rejected the complaint. (1967)

'EXCUSE ME, SIR OR MADAM'

The *Scottish Daily Express* report on an assault charge against three young men stated: 'Trouble flared when four long-haired teenagers were greeted "Excuse me, sir or madam." A few seconds later there was a scuffle at the entrance of a Dumfries lavatory and a university student was stabbed.'

The father of the man who had made the remark complained that the report was inaccurate and misleading because it implied that his son's remark had led to the scuffle. The scuffle occurred outside the lavatory while his son was inside.

The Managing Editor of the newspaper, Mr J. E. Campbell said that the reporter insisted that his report of the court proceedings was accurate. Reporters from other newspapers also said that it was the man's remark which sparked off the fighting.

The Press Council said that the remark in question had been over-emphasised in the report but the Council was not prepared to criticise the newspaper report as a whole as being misleading. The complaint was rejected. (1967)

SUMMARISED REPORT 'FAIR AND REASONABLE'

In a case relating to Hackney and Hendon Greyhounds Ltd the chairman complained that a *Daily Mail* summary of his statement in the Annual Report was unbalanced because of omissions, and was, therefore, damaging to the company's interests. The company claimed that the newspaper report created a sense of despondency which did not exist, and failed to record that difficulties were attributed by the chairman to the new Betting and Gaming Act. Mr Michael Randall, the Editor of the *Daily Mail*, denied that the story justified this criticism.

The Press Council decided that the newspaper's report was a fair and reasonable condensation of a lengthy statement. (1963/40)

UNOFFICIAL STRIKE — COMMENT UNREPORTED

The Clerk to the St Albans Rural District Council complained that although he had been asked by the *Herts Advertiser* for his comments on remarks made by Council employees on unofficial strike, his replies had not been included in the report. As a result, the report did not give a balanced view of the situation.

The Editor, Mr A. A. Booth, said that the men had complained that earlier reports of the strike had not included their point of view, and they had invited the newspaper to send a reporter to one of their meetings. The Clerk's comments did not seem to alter the basic points at issue.

The Press Council found that the reports were not unfair. (1965/47)

C.N.D. IN DOWNING STREET

When about four hundred people broke away from a rally in Trafalgar Square at the end of a C.N.D. march and thronged Downing Street, the *Daily Mirror* published a story headed: 'Ten held on C.N.D. siege of No. 10.'

This heading misrepresented the facts, a complainant told the Press Council, as the C.N.D. did not plan or approve the action and had expressly repudiated any such gesture in advance. But the Press Council held that, as the report made it clear that the incident was not an official C.N.D. action, readers would not be misled by the headline. (1965/51)

GIRL KILLED ON WAY TO TELEPHONE

The *Daily Mail* reported that a girl who left her home to walk to a telephone-box to speak to her boy-friend had been found gagged and stabbed. The headline was: 'Phone-call girl, 16, knifed to death.' The complainant stated that the expression 'Phone-call girl' was accepted to mean a prostitute, and this would mean extra suffering for her parents.

The Press Council rejected the complaint, and stated that neither the headline nor the text of the story sustained the implication. (1963/55–6)

TWO STORIES OF RAILWAY ACCIDENT

At the inquest on a man who had fallen in front of a train, one witness had said that the fall looked like a deliberate act, another that the man seemed to slip and fall. The verdict was 'accidental death'. The *Acton Gazette* headed its report: 'Two stories of death on rail lines.' A complaint was made to the Press Council that the headline gave a misleading inference to the story in that evidence suggesting suicide was printed in larger type than the remainder of the story, and that some of the rebutting evidence was omitted. The complainant also said that the evidence of the witness who thought that the fall was a deliberate act had been rebutted at the inquest and that this was not mentioned in the report. However, the Coroner told the Council that this was not so, but that the jury had preferred the weight of the testimony that pointed to accident.

Mr R. Summerhayes, the Editor of the *Acton Gazette*, told the Press Council that the report fairly summarised the proceedings, that the use of larger type in the introductory paragraph was normal newspaper practice, and that the omitted evidence did not add anything to the other evidence in rebuttal that had been published.

The Press Council held that the headline was not unfair or misleading, but that a balanced report would have included the pathologist's evidence that the victim had symptoms of heart disease. (1962/45–6)

A HEADLINE QUOTATION

The *Ilford Recorder* reported a meeting of the Dagenham Council under the heading, 'Council has Death on its Hands'. The Town Clerk complained to the Press Council; no objection was made to the report itself, but the headline, it was said, gave a false impression.

The Press Council held that, as the headline statement had been used in the discussion, no objection could be taken to it, more particularly as it had been published in quotation marks. (1955/24)

THE ECONOMIC SQUEEZE

A front-page news story in the *Evening Standard* carried a three-line, three-column heading, 'Pay Freeze, Smokes Up, Forces Cut'. Below in smaller type was the heading 'Now Wilson must choose'. The article made it clear that a statutory freeze of all wage and price increases for a year or so was a key proposal in a mixed bag of measures before the Cabinet to fight the economic crisis. Various proposals affecting home and overseas expenditure were listed, including the use of the regulation to increase duty on drink and tobacco.

A reader complained to the *Evening Standard* that he had bought the newspaper expecting to be given direct information that the price of cigarettes had been raised. Contrary to his expectation the newspaper had no information on final decisions but only on possibilities. In the circumstances different headlines should have been used. In his complaint to the Press Council the reader said that all too often one saw a deceptive tendency on the part of headline writers to make their headlines appear as facts when the text was based only on supposition.

The Editor of the newspaper, Mr Charles Wintour, said that it was extremely difficult to convey in a short space the full implications of the story. 'Perfection in headline writing', he said, 'is simply never entirely possible owing to the very small number of letters that can be used in bold type on a lead story. But in this case I felt that the words "Now Wilson must choose" were bold enough to be seen by anybody looking at the front page casually.' The intention was to tell readers that a really mighty deflationary blow was in preparation, a prediction that was rapidly justified by the facts.

The Press Council held that the headlines were not misleading, and the complaint was rejected. (1967)

FUN MADE OF OLD-FASHIONED ATTITUDE

A retired army officer complained of an article in the *Camberley News* which made fun of him for what it regarded as an old-fashioned attitude. He was reported to have looked at an Ian Fleming book in the public library, and to have been so shocked by what he read that he asked the librarian to put it under the counter. He had, however, dropped his request when the librarian explained that 'things which were regarded as unforgivable 15 years ago are now a matter of course'.

The officer complained to the Press Council that the article was 'a travesty of the truth'. In reply, the Editor, Mr R. A. Jones, said that he was willing to publish a list of specific inaccuracies, but that he had in fact already corrected some admitted inaccuracies.

The Press Council held that it was legitimate for a newspaper to make fun of an attitude which, rightly or wrongly, it regarded as being stuffy and old-fashioned. The article was not malicious, it did not distort the incident, and it did not exceed the bounds of what is permissible. (1965/64)

HO CHI MINH'S 'RESPONSE'

A leading article in the *Daily Express*, which stated that the truce in the bombing of North Vietnam by the Americans had produced no response from the North Vietnamese, led to a complaint that the article was inaccurate, one-sided, distorted, misleading and only partially correct.

The complainant alleged that Ho Chi Minh, the North Vietnamese Premier, had sent a letter to the Queen and replied to the Pope's peace appeal. He told the Council that he regarded a flat rejection of a truce as a response.

The Editor of the *Daily Express*, Mr Derek Marks, said that all the North Vietnamese had done in response to the truce was to harden the conditions on which they would confer. To say that was a response was an abuse of language.

The Press Council held that the leading article was not inaccurate, and the complaint was dismissed. (1966/58)

'ICE CREAM CHAOS'

The Ice Cream Alliance complained of a *Daily Express* headline, 'Ice Cream Chaos. Four Britons Ill', and of the repeated lack of responsibility by the newspaper in casting reflections on the ice cream trade.

The report related to the Tour of Britain cycling event when four of the British team suffered stomach trouble after eating ice cream. The team manager stated that the upsets must have been caused by the ice cream. The tour organiser had stated that he had not been able to establish the positive cause of the outbreak, but he had established that not every member of the team had ice cream although they were all ill.

The Editor, Mr Derek Marks, stated that the four members of the team who ate ice cream were ill. The precise nature of the trouble was not known.

Later, when it was known to be due to stomach chills, the fact was reported.

The Press Council held there was no allegation that the team manager was misrepresented. In the circumstances neither the article nor the headline in the newspaper was irresponsible. (1967)

COMPLAINT MUST BE MADE WITHIN A REASONABLE TIME

DISTASTEFUL FILMS

An article in the *People* on 22 August 1965 stated that two men were engaged in making films to be sold in America for showing on home-movie projectors. The films were not pornographic, but one of the two men who made them was said to have told the writer of the article that they were not the sort of films he would show to his wife.

The heading of the article read: 'He lures girls into making nasty films to sell to America'. The films showed lightly-clad girls wrestling, girls in punch-ups or realistic sword fights. The accent was strongly pitched on violence and was said to be quite distasteful.

An investigator from the newspaper posing as a potential customer with a market in America was shown a number of films and was quoted £50–£60 for each. The author of the article recommended the makers of the films 'for the good name of Britain' to switch their talents to more wholesome films.

The makers of the films complained on 4 April 1966 that the article contained factual inaccuracies, of the improper methods in obtaining information and of the unethical motives that prompted publication. The films were privately made and were not salacious or illegal.

The Editor of the *People*, Mr Robert Edwards, said the films were of an unsavoury nature, and the two makers were exposed by the traditional method adopted by reporters of not identifying themselves until a later stage.

The Press Council held that in all the circumstances of the case, and having regard to the long delay in the presentation of the complaint against the *People*, the Council did not consider that it should be upheld. (1967)

9 Sensationalism and Distortion

Sensationalism was described in the Report of the First Royal Commission as partly an extreme manifestation of the peculiar values reflected in the popular newspapers, partly a desire to provide the excitement which the reader is believed, and has been taught, to expect. It consists in publishing prominent and detailed stories which, in the words of one witness, minister to the personal gratification of the reader such as news of crime, the relation between the sexes, scandalous behaviour and the private lives of individuals who are victims of some misfortune.

Another form is presenting news not itself sensational so that it appears to be either more exciting or more important than it is. The effect is achieved by banner and bold headlines in large type. This is largely a matter of layout designed to attract the reader by its appearance. Under this technique an item of news of no particular importance can be given a quite misleading significance.

The Royal Commission thought that this practice might merely increase slightly the gulf separating the world presented by the popular newspapers from the world of sober reality; but in times of tension, and particularly international tension, it might dangerously stimulate public excitement.

Nevertheless the Commission considered that it was legitimate and indeed desirable for a newspaper to present complicated subjects in such a way that its readers would be attracted to them. The Editor of a mass-circulation paper frankly stated that his newspaper believed in the sensational presentation of important news and views as a necessary and valuable public service. This method of giving the news consisted of presentation that was vivid, writing that was vigorous and in everyday language everyone could understand, and arresting headlines. The intention was to make an impact on the readers' minds.

It is a matter of opinion at what point legitimate liveliness of presentation becomes mere sensationalism. Headlines aimed at producing a dramatic effect frequently produce a grossly misleading one. The headline should be justified by the text; it ought not convey a stronger and more significant meaning than the report beneath it.

The first Annual Report of the Press Council pointed out that the readership of newspapers in Britain was huge; readers ranged from the most highly educated to the least literate. To maintain the circulations on which their existence depended, newspapers had to flavour themselves according to their public's requirements and to compete hourly with others catering for a similar public. 'The local newspaper must serve its locality. The quality newspaper must serve its quality. The popular newspaper must serve its populace.'

A newspaper, however, which reports only matters that interest and entertain can easily lose sight of the distinction between what is interesting and entertaining to the readers and what is intrinsically important, and it will finally come to judge importance in terms only of reader appeal.

The First Royal Commission came to the conclusion that the failure of the Press to keep pace with the requirements of society was largely attributable to the plain fact that an industry that lives by the sale of its products must give the public what the public will buy. A newspaper cannot raise its standards far above those of its public and may even seek to attract profit by lowering them in order to gain advantage over a competitor. This tendency was not always resisted as firmly as the public interest required, nor did the Press do all it might to encourage its public to accept or demand a higher quality of reporting than was given. The years since the Commission reported in 1949 have shown a considerable improvement and a greater realisation and acceptance of the moral responsibility involved in the production of a newspaper.

The Press Council has dealt with the following complaints alleging sensationalism and distortion.

SENSATIONAL AND EXAGGERATED REPORTS

HOOLIGANISM IN HONITON

'Honiton is today a place of grim-faced men and frightened women', the *Evening Chronicle* of Newcastle upon Tyne stated in a report about the return of the First Battalion of the Durham Light Infantry to their camp at Honiton. Headlined 'North Soldiers no longer welcome, say Devonshire people — Town in fear as D.L.I. return — Week-end of violence', the article spoke of 'scenes of violence and damage as groups of soldiers . . . swept through the main street . . .'.

The Mayor and Corporation of Honiton complained that the story exaggerated and misrepresented incidents in a way that discredited both a famous regiment and the good name of the townspeople. The freelance journalist who supplied the story told the Press Council that his report was founded on statements made to him by townspeople, that it fairly represented the facts and was in accord with court records of offences committed by members of the Durham Light Infantry since they had been stationed in Devon. The Commanding Officer denied there had been scenes of violence

F

during the week-end, and said that the conduct of his troops had not been abnormal.

In its adjudication the Press Council expressed the view that there was some hooliganism in Honiton when the battalion returned. There was also a background of previous incidents. The Council held, however, that the headlines and certain introductory phrases in the report, exaggerated both what took place and its effect upon the inhabitants of the town. (1961/23–4)

AN ATTEMPTED ASSASSINATION

A complaint from Malta alleged that the *Sunday Times* had given a distorted account of events in Malta during a visit of a three-man delegation appointed by the Socialist Congress in Rome. The story referred to an 'attempted assassination of the three-man delegation' and stated that the assailant had escaped in a van; it added that the island's 1,100-strong police force would all be on week-end duty to prevent serious clashes and bloodshed in a full-strength trial between supporters of Mr Mintoff and Archbishop Gonzi.

The complainant stated that the shooting was directed at only one of the delegates and that the police had made a statement to that effect; the van story had been officially discredited, and no bloodshed was anticipated by the police, who were not issued with riot equipment, and the account omitted a statement by the Archbishop deploring the shooting incident.

The newspaper's correspondent said that the police statement did not reach him until the day after he had filed his story. After the shooting, crowds of Labour supporters roamed Valletta and were ready for retaliation. The Editor, Mr C. D. Hamilton, said that the Archbishop's statement was omitted through a head office error.

In its adjudication, the Press Council found that there was some exaggeration in the report, which spoke of an assassination attempt on a three-man delegation, but omitted to say that the three were travelling in different cars, that only one car was hit by shots from a shotgun and that the delegate in the car was unhurt. Nevertheless since there had been an assassination attempt there would be a good deal of tension in the island, leading naturally to extra police precaution. The Council regretted the omission of the Archbishop's statement. (1962/33–4)

THE STORM WAS NOT A 'NEAR DISASTER'

Canvey Island Urban District Council described a report in the *Daily Express* as inaccurate, irresponsible and calculated to cause undue anxiety in the minds of the residents.

The report stated that the island had escaped disaster 'by the skin of its teeth as huge waves battered the new defences. The stonework cracked; parts of it crumpled and but for the massive steel piling the sea would have swept through'. The storm was termed a 'near disaster'.

The Clerk of the Urban District Council said that at no time during the storm was there any danger of the sea wall being pierced. There was severe damage to the outer stonework, but the stone facing was there for the purpose of protecting the earth sea wall behind it. The Engineer to the Essex River Board gave corroborative evidence and stated that there had been no danger of the wall being breached or of flooding.

Mr Robert Edwards, the Editor of the newspaper, said everyone agreed the damage to the wall was extensive. The wind had dropped at a crucial time.

The Press Council considered that the *Daily Express* was not justified in using the phrase 'near disaster' in reporting the high tides and gale. (1965/31–2)

PRINCE PHILIP RUMOUR

The *Daily Mirror* devoted the whole of its front page to a news story headed 'Prince Philip and the Profumo Scandal. Rumour is utterly unfounded'. The story was to the effect that 'the foulest rumour which is being circulated about the Profumo Scandal' had involved Prince Philip. The report did not state the terms of the rumour other than by inference.

A complaint was made that the story was an example of the practice of blackening somebody's name by concocting an unpleasant rumour and then refuting it. The complainant could not offer any fact in support of this contention, but said that even if the newspaper did wish to rebut an unpleasant rumour, the publicity given in the article was bound to spread the gossip far and wide.

The Editor, Mr L. A. Lee Howard, said that the complainant was not justified in his allegation that, because he was not aware of the rumour, the

Daily Mirror had invented it. The rumour was so widespread that a forthright repudiation had become necessary.

The Press Council found that it had no clear evidence as to the extent to which the rumour had spread among the public, and it could not, therefore, judge whether the stage had been reached when the newspaper was justified in repudiating it and thereby giving it greater publicity, but the sensational treatment of the story was distasteful and did not accord with the newspaper's attitude of being activated by the highest motives. (1964/57–8)

'POLICE CHARGE CROWD'

Complaint was made of a news report in the *Daily Telegraph* under the headline: 'Mounted Police Charge Crowd', which described the advance of mounted police on a crowd of 4,000 unemployed outside the House of Commons. The report stated that scores of people were knocked down and that many policemen lost their helmets in the scuffles.

The Commissioner of Metropolitan Police told the Council that the desired movement of the crowd was effected by a steady co-ordinated movement of mounted men at a slow walk. To have advanced faster would have been completely contrary to the conception of police duty.

The Editor of the newspaper, Sir Colin Coote, said that the word 'charge' was used by an experienced reporter because at one stage the police advanced not at a walk but at a trot. The people were knocked down not only as the result of pressure from the crowd but also as a direct result of the use of horses.

The Press Council held that the report was exaggerated. (1963/46)

A 'MAN-EATING SHARK' IN BOURNEMOUTH BAY

The *Sunday Citizen* published a story that a man who had disappeared, and whose clothes had been found on a beach, might have been killed by a man-eating shark. In fact, he was found in Birmingham suffering from loss of memory. The man's father complained that the story was a piece of sensationalism, and though there could be no objection to publicity about his son's possible drowning, to sensationalise the provable facts made the publication horrific to the extent of showing utter disregard for the humanities.

The Editor of the newspaper, Mr W. R. Richardson, contended that sharks had been harpooned in Bournemouth bay in recent years, and that an encounter with such a creature could bring about the death of a swimmer. A dead shark had been washed ashore on the day the story was published.

The Press Council held that 'This was a highly speculative report and the Press Council regrets its publication.' (1963/42–3)

'ROAD BLOCKS' FOR MENTAL PATIENT

A three-line paragraph in the *Daily Express* said that police had set up road blocks in a search for a mental patient who had escaped from hospital. As a result, a reader asked the secretary of the hospital for an assurance of protection for children and other defenceless citizens should there be further escapes. He was assured that there was no danger to the community from the type of inmate treated at the hospital.

The reader then complained to the Press Council that the story unnecessarily alarmed the public.

The Chief Constable of Essex said that no road blocks were set up, and that the two local journalists who had been given information at a police station were informed that the missing patient was neither dangerous nor likely to be violent.

The Managing Editor of the *Daily Express*, Mr Derek Marks, said, that when police circulated a description of a mental patient believed to be missing, it was not unreasonable to refer to the incident as an escape. The inaccuracy about the road blocks was due to a misunderstanding and was regretted.

The Press Council found that the report was undoubtedly exaggerated, and considered that the newspaper should have made more thorough inquiries. (1963/63–4)

'VIOLENT' MENTAL ESCAPEE

A warning of the need for newspapers to check facts in incidents reported to them from outside sources was given by the Press Council in respect of a report in the *South London Press*. The report was headlined ' "Violent" mental escapee' and stated that a mental patient believed to be violent had escaped in Forest Hill. He was named and described as an inmate of a local home for the mentally ill. The complainant said that the home named was a hostel for people with mental problems who were at work. As they were free to leave when they wished such words as 'escapee' and 'inmate' were positively harmful.

The Editor of the newspaper, Mr Eric Kinton, told the Press Council that the information for the report had been given by a police station sergeant. When it was found that the name had not been given correctly a correction was published, and it was then made clear that the home was a voluntary hospital and that the patients were free to come and go as they like.

The Press Council's adjudication was that the *South London Press* was wrong in describing a patient at the home as an escaped inmate. The case served to emphasise the necessity to make careful inquiries into incidents of this kind. The Council noted that the newspaper had published a correction. (1966/44–5)

A TELEPHONE INTERVIEW

Replies to questions in a five-minute telephone interview with the Chairman of East Ham Ratepayers' Association, conducted by a junior reporter, were described in a news lead story in the *Stratford Express* as 'a bitter attack' on the planners of the borough's newly-built £1,000,000 technical college 'launched by the borough's Ratepayers' Association', and an 'all-out onslaught on East Ham's Education Committee' by the Councillor.

The Town Clerk of East Ham complained to the Press Council that the article was biased and completely misleading, and was based on statements the Councillor denied having made. The Councillor, in evidence to the Press Council, described statements attributed to him as 'pure fiction'. He said some of his statements had been split up and different interpretations given to them.

At the hearing by the Council of oral evidence, the reporter's notes were examined. Some of the expressions used in the report, though not all of them, were recorded, but the reporter said that he had typed the story with the points freshly in mind. He did not describe the Councillor's remarks as 'a bitter attack' nor did he use the expression 'all-out onslaught'.

The Editor of the *Stratford Express*, Mr Ivan W. Smith, said that the Councillor did not complain that he had been misquoted until the matter was taken up by the East Ham Council.

The Press Council adjudication was: The interview recorded in this case was made by telephone and lasted about five minutes. The reporter's notes, produced for examination, contained the phrases 'disgraceful situation' and 'gross misuse of money' which the Councillor denied having used, although he did not dispute the accuracy of the general tenor of the views attributed to him.

While it was not possible finally to resolve this issue, the Council felt that the *Stratford Express* in its headlines, presentation and sub-editing exaggerated the report. (1964/43–4)

COLOUR BAR DENIED

A complaint alleged that reports in the *Evening Star*, Ipswich, about the deposition of an Arab chairman of Ipswich Civic College Students' Union was a 'deliberate distortion of truth aimed at turning a trivial incident into something sensational, disregarding the inevitable harmful social effects of such distortion'.

One of the reports was headed: 'Students' Arab Chairman sacked. Colour bar row is denied. Whispering campaign'. The story began: 'Allegations that the Arab chairman of the Students' Union at Ipswich Civic College was sacked from that office on the grounds of colour are being strongly denied, it was revealed today'.

The report said the chairman refused to resign when the Union Council objected to his conduct of a Council Meeting and passed a vote of no confidence; but he had to quit when a similar motion was passed by a general assembly of the members.

Two days later the paper ran a follow-up story headed: 'Colour Bar Allegations "Whispered" Around College. "Completely Refuted"'. It reported that the Editor of the students' magazine had stated that allegations being made in the college that the Arab chairman was sacked on racial grounds were untrue.

The complaint alleged that the reports were slanted, and, far from airing and eradicating rumours of colour prejudice, the article magnified an absence of colour prejudice into a whole front-page sensation.

The Editor, Mr J. O. Carter, said that the reports were true, factual and fair. The newspaper had never attempted to slant the situation. Its policy was based on decent, honest, vigorous journalism that was a service to the people. This meant they did not avoid controversy because it might relate to a nasty subject. He believed that in presenting unbiased, factual reports the paper rendered both town and college a service.

The Press Council upheld the complaint, saying that the newspaper turned a trivial incident of a domestic nature into something sensational and disregarded the harmful social effects. (1965/60–1)

'RIOTS IN HAYES AND SOUTHALL'

The Hayes and Harlington Urban District Council complained about an article in the *Hayes Post* carrying the heading, 'Race Riots in Hayes and Southall'. The local council felt that the report contained exaggerated and inaccurate statements and tended to alarm and inflame residents in the area.

The Press Council agreed that the article was sensational and exaggerated, but noted that the Editor had offered to publish a statement from the Urban District Council, which the Press Council thought should have been accepted. (1959/23–4)

DEATH BUT NOT MURDER

The *Daily Sketch* published a report that a publican in Southall, Middlesex, had died in an alleyway fight after ejecting two coloured men from his hotel. It also stated that the barman heard his calls for help and had found him with knife wounds. The police were said to want to see two West Indians. At the inquest it was disclosed that death was due to natural causes, and that there was nothing to suggest that there had been an affray.

The Southall International Friendship Committee complained that the report could have caused a difficult situation because there was a large number of coloured immigrants in the area.

The Managing Editor of the newspaper, Mr Robert Johnston, said that every effort had been made to check the facts, but it was not until the following day that there appeared to be real doubt about whether the licensee had been murdered. He agreed that a message had been received from a news agency timed at 1.25 a.m. on the day of publication, reporting that the police had stated that the licensee might have died from a heart attack after the fight, but that they were not ruling out murder, and that it was in time for the last edition. He did not know why it was not used. The erroneous story was not corrected, nor did the newspaper publish an account of the inquest proceedings. The correction was overlooked because of the week-end interruption.

The agency reporter stated that his information came from three sources, a telephone call to the Southall police, a police officer at the scene and an ambulance driver. The agency copy included the passage, 'Knives flashed and Mr Cooper, 64, was left dying in a pool of blood; ambulance men found cuts on his face and one arm and police were looking for the weapon'.

Scotland Yard said that the reference to knife wounds was completely untrue. The Press representatives and their photographers obtained their information from ill-informed bystanders and jumped to the wrong conclusion without waiting for verification.

The Council censured the agency for supplying a report which was grossly exaggerated and based on inadequate inquiry. The newspaper was also censured for publishing a report despite doubts thrown upon it by a late message. It was also censured for failure to report the true facts as revealed at the inquest. (1965/34–6)

For another case of inadequate investigation see p. 103 (*Daily Sketch*), and for one of a picture giving a wrong impression see p. 202 (*Scottish Daily Express*).

TREATMENT WITHIN EDITOR'S DISCRETION

CHILD DIED IN DENTIST'S CHAIR

The Council of the British Dental Association complained about a news item which appeared in the Manchester editions of the *Daily Express*. No objection was taken to the factual report of the inquest on a child who had died in a dentist's chair, but the Dental Association objected to the headlines which were three-quarters of an inch high.

The Press Council stated that the method of treatment of a story of an exceptional and dramatic character properly came within the discretion of the Editor. (1959/24–5)

WHY A GIRL LOST HER LIFE

The Editor of the *South London Press*, Mr Eric Kinton, who was reproved by a Coroner for overstepping the boundary between factual reporting and a

L.T.P.C.

form of speculation which might influence a jury and interfere with the course of justice, asked the Press Council for guidance on whether he was wrong in publishing a pre-inquest report about a girl who was killed crossing the road as she left school. The report, which was headed: 'She was killed as school broke up for holiday. Ten minutes that may have cost a life', said that the Coroner would have to decide how the girl managed to be outside the school grounds ten minutes before the rest of the pupils were released.

At the end of the inquest a legal representative of the parents complained that this remark, with its implication of truancy, had distressed the mother and father of the girl. The Coroner remarked that the implication was not justified by the evidence, and he wrote to the Editor of the paper saying that the report tried to sensationalise the girl's death.

The Press Council held that the Editor was entitled to draw attention, before the inquest, to the circumstances in which the girl was killed, including the time factor. The Council did not think the report was unduly sensational. (1961/25–6, 53–4)

'A BITTER TWO-HOUR MEETING'

A second complaint was made against the *Balham and Tooting News and Mercury*, following the case, described on p. 47, in which that newspaper was censured for publishing a confidential communication about a tenants' meeting over West Indian tenants in a local flat.

The second complaint alleged that the report of the tenants' meeting was biased and inaccurate.

The report described the event as 'a bitter two-hour meeting', said that women screamed abuse and men roared their disapproval at the Council policy being outlined, that the meeting threatened violent outbreaks, and that the complainant 'faced violent opposition and threats of more trouble'.

The complainant, a member of the Borough Council, told the Press Council that although the meeting was lively, it was courteous. The report was likely to 'make matters worse and cause racial friction'.

The newspaper contended that according to their reporter the meeting lasted over two hours and, apart from a few minutes here and there, was in uproar. This version, he said, was confirmed by other speakers and by another local reporter.

The Press Council found that the temper of the meeting must necessarily be a matter of personal impression, and it was not satisfied, on the evidence, that the newspaper report was inaccurate. (1964/67–8)

FLUORIDATION OF WATER SUPPLIES

The Birmingham City Council complained to the Press Council that an article in the *Birmingham Planet* campaigning against fluoridation of public water supplies was untrue, biased and designed to spread public alarm and fear amongst the city's population. The article was headed: 'It kills rats — Will it kill Brummies?' and claimed that Birmingham City Council had perpetrated a major public scandal. It went on: 'At a cost of thousands of pounds of ratepayers' money it has begun to put poison in your water.' The fluoride, 'which every Brummie will be forced to drink', might well cause serious injury and early death, it was claimed.

Mr M. H. Guy, the Editor, said that the facts were true and the article was a justified expression of opinion. The free Press would disappear if such criticism was discouraged.

In its adjudication the Press Council rejected the complaint. It considered that fluoridation was a matter which excited violent controversy and that the newspaper was entitled to campaign against it if it considered such action to be in the public interest. The Council thought the paper's treatment of the subject was sensational, but did not agree it was reckless or irresponsible. (1965/55)

10 Letters to the Editor

PUBLICATION UNNECESSARY

OFFENSIVE AND ABUSIVE LETTERS

THE COURTESY OF A REPLY

WHERE A LETTER COULD HAVE RESTORED BALANCE

Correspondence columns have been described as the part of the newspaper which readers write themselves. Their letters constitute one of its most read and diversified features; every point of view ranging from the eccentric to the authoritative, on every possible subject, is reflected in them.

A letter to the editor is the accepted way of endorsing, challenging or contradicting editorial opinion. The correspondence column offers readers a forum for the expression and exchange of views and acts as a safety valve for those who demand to be heard. For the editor the letters are an invaluable guide to the minds of his readers.

Most people who write to the editor do so because they believe that they have something original and worth while to say. They write in the expectation that their letters will be published, and if they are not, however reasonable and resigned they try to be, it is almost inevitable that they feel rebuffed and resentful.

A correspondent has no legal right to space for his letter, though circumstances may give him a strong moral right and create a corresponding moral obligation on the editor to publish it. The Press Council has frequently pointed out that the publication of a letter can restore the balance between the newspaper and the person who, directly or indirectly, has been put at a disadvantage by editorial comment; the publication of a letter in reply gives him the opportunity of answering criticism. Failure by an editor to publish a letter might on occasion, if legal proceedings ensue, be evidence of malice on the part of the newspaper.

By publishing a letter of correction, an editor will often be able to mitigate the Press Council's censure; see, for instance, p. 154 (*Hayes Post*).

An editor cannot, of course, be expected to publish all the letters addressed to him, but it is not unreasonable to expect that in making a selection for publication he will try to make a fair and representative choice. His task will be considerably lightened if those who write have regard to the limited space available and keep their letters short. By doing so they will also leave room for others.

Many factors will no doubt influence the editor's selection, the authority of the writer, the nature of the subject matter, the suitability of the letter to the readership of the newspaper, the correspondent's right of reply, the light relief a humorous letter will provide, and so on. He may reject a letter because its adds nothing to what has already been said or because it is defamatory, abusive or in bad taste. He may not want to open a correspondence on a particular subject or may think that a correspondence has gone on long enough and should be terminated. Whatever the editor decides will not please everybody, and a great many complaints made to the Press Council are from disappointed correspondents whose letters have not been published.

A letter should not be abridged without the author's consent in such a way as to misrepresent its meaning. See, for instance, p. 124 (*Huddersfield Daily Examiner*) and (*West London Observer*).

The judgments of the Press Council in respect of complaints arising out of letters addressed to the editor will be a help to editors as indicating the considerations they ought to have in mind when deciding which letters should and which need not be published. The cases reviewed by the Press Council have been decided in the light of their particular circumstances, and an editor must use them with this fact in mind.

In the cases that follow an endeavour has been made to classify them to illustrate governing principles which emerge from the decisions.

THE EDITOR'S DISCRETION

The Press Council has been quite emphatic in its recognition of the basic discretion of the editor to select letters for publication. So long as the discretion is properly exercised, the editor's decision is final. It is his right to decide which letters shall be published and which shall not. If, in accordance with the practice of his newspaper, he refuses to publish a letter because it has already appeared in another journal, or for any other good reason, he is entitled to do so.

OPENING AND CLOSING A CORRESPONDENCE

It is the editor who decides whether and when to open a correspondence on a particular matter.

OCTALS AND DECIMALS — WHO WROTE FIRST?

The Times published a letter from Professor Fred Hoyle, the distinguished mathematician and astronomer, on the use of octals instead of decimals. Another reader contended that as a matter of fair play she was entitled to an acknowledgment that a week before the professor's letter was published she had advocated precisely the same idea in a letter sent for publication. The Editor, Sir William Haley, said that the question of credit did not arise because the idea advocated in the letters was widespread.

The Press Council said that the choice of date for opening a correspondence on a particular subject, and of a suitable opening letter, were matters within the discretion of the Editor. (1962/38–9)

MURDER OF KING ALEXANDER

In its introduction to Lord Avon's memoirs *The Times* described the murderer of King Alexander of Yugoslavia and Louis Barthou, the French Foreign Minister, as 'a Croat terrorist'.

A complainant wrote to the Editor denying this and claimed that the assassin was 'a Bulgarian nationalist'.

The Editor, Sir William Haley, refused to publish the letter on the ground that there were differing views about the origin of the assassin, and he was not prepared to allow a correspondence on the disputed point.

The Press Council upheld his right to refuse publication of the letter. (1963/40)

CHRISTIAN PACIFISM

The General Secretary of the Peace Pledge Union complained that *The Times* had closed a correspondence on Christian Pacifism without publishing a reply from the Peace Pledge Union, which it had attacked.

The Press Council stated that an editor had the undoubted right to close a correspondence at any moment he considered suitable. (1955/22)

THE COST OF LIVING

A correspondent complained that his letter to *The Times* on the cost of living had not been published although it had reached the newspaper before the correspondence was closed.

The Press Council informed the complainant that the right of publishing or refusing to publish a letter in any correspondence rested solely with the editor. (1955/22)

NO ABSOLUTE RIGHT OF REPLY

Mr John Gordon writing in the *Sunday Express* quoted a statement by Professor Colin Clark, Director of the Oxford Agricultural Economic Research Unit, that the much-mentioned figure that two-thirds of the world's people went hungry was an arithmetical error made by Lord Boyd-Orr, and that the number of people receiving insufficient calories was probably about fifteen per cent of the world's population.

The Professor was also quoted as saying that although the real position had been known to experts for some years, most of the general public still believed Lord Boyd-Orr's figure to be correct, and a lot of officials had a vested interest in letting it continue to circulate.

The General Secretary of the United Kingdom Committee of the Freedom from Hunger Campaign said that the Professor's statements and the newspaper's comments on them might damage his society's work. He had written to the *Sunday Express* criticising the Professor's views, but his letter had not been published. He did not deny the accuracy of the newspapers' quotation.

The Press Council ruled that the *Sunday Express*'s comments were based on a correct quotation, and that an absolute right of reply did not exist. The decision was one for the discretion of the Editor. (1963/53–4)

LORD GLADWYN

In a leading article entitled 'The Foolish Experts' the *Sunday Express* said Lord Gladwyn had stated that if Britain did not join the Six in the Common Market disaster would follow. He had now changed his tune and was saying that no responsible person would suggest it would be disastrous if Britain continued to keep out of the Six.

Lord Gladwyn asked for the right of reply in the next issue of the newspaper. The Editor, Mr John Junor, told him that the letter he had submitted was too long, but said that he would print a shorter one. Lord Gladwyn thereupon telephoned a shorter letter, but this, too, was not printed, because, so the Editor decided, it added little to what was already known about Lord Gladwyn's views on the Common Market. Lord Gladwyn complained that to be denied the right to reply, even briefly, to the representation of his attitude on a matter of national importance, was unfair.

In its adjudication the Press Council said that Lord Gladwyn's letter was controversial rather than factual, and that publication was properly one for the Editor's discretion. (1964/50)

LIFE UNDER THE TORIES AND SOCIALISTS

Lord Williams of Barnburgh, a former Cabinet Minister, objected to a political feature article in the *Sunday Express* about conditions under a previous Labour Government, on the ground that it contained misrepresentation and distortion.

The Editor, Mr John Junor, refused to publish a rebutting letter because the feature writer was not concerned with what England was like under the Tories before 1945 but was giving a factual account of what life was like under Socialism in 1951. No inaccuracies in the article had been pointed out.

Lord Williams described the article as a scandalous piece of partisan journalism which violated every decency of what was expected from a privileged free Press.

The Press Council ruled that feature articles dealing with political questions normally contained a good deal of partisan opinion, and that publication of letters replying to such articles was a matter within the discretion of the editor. (1965/85–6)

'ALL OR NONE'

The Secretary of the Southwark Diocesan Catholic Parents' and Electors' Association complained that the *South London Press* had invited the Association to submit a letter for publication and then failed to publish it, but had unfairly printed comment on the letter without disclosing its contents.

The newspaper had published a feature protesting against State subsidies for Catholic schools. In his letter to the Editor, the Secretary of the Association challenged the accuracy of the facts, but added a proviso that his letter was to be published in full or not at all. The newspaper thereupon published another article, headed 'All or none', which stated: 'So it is not at all, since everything that appears in this newspaper has to be sub-edited for length and clarity owing to the high price of newsprint'.

The Secretary of the Association said he had not been invited to reduce the length of the letter, and told the Editor he should have been given the opportunity to do so. Mr Eric Kinton, the Editor, replied that a letter would be printed if the all-or-nothing embargo was withdrawn.

The Editor told the Press Council that his newspaper had not commented on a letter that had not been published.

The Press Council ruled that an editor has a discretion whether or not to publish a letter and is entitled to take into consideration its news value and length. But in this case the Editor had not handled the situation in a way calculated to improve relations between the Press and public, and the complaint was upheld. (1966/87)

TEACHERS' PANEL

The Chairman and Secretary of the Teachers' Panel on the Burnham (Main) Committee complained that, after the Education Correspondent of *The Times* had written an article which they alleged contained misleading criticism of teachers' leaders over delay in arbitration proceedings, the Editor of *The Times* declined to publish a letter in reply from them. They were informed that the substance of their letter had been published in a teachers' journal, and, although it was not possible to use it in *The Times*, the points raised would be taken up by the Education Correspondent in the paper. This was done, although the substance of the letter was not reproduced.

The complainants contended that it was unreasonable for the Editor of *The Times* to withhold from his readers the nature of their reply to his Education Correspondent on the ground that they had taken action through other channels to inform those to whom they were responsible.

The Editor of *The Times* told the Press Council that the letter made such a direct attack on the competence of the Education Correspondent that the charge had to be investigated before it was published. By then extracts from the letter had appeared in the teachers' journal, and it was the practice of *The Times* not to publish a letter which had appeared elsewhere.

The Press Council decided that the Editor acted correctly within his discretion in not publishing the letter, and the complaint was rejected. (1966/90–1)

CAR SAFETY BELTS

The *Guardian* published a letter with statistics on the value of car safety belts. Another reader submitted a letter which expressed amazement and challenged the value of safety belts. A few days after his letter was received another letter making much the same points, but not including the factual evidence, was published.

The complainant made the point that having begun correspondence on a controversial subject the newspaper was morally bound to publish his point of view.

The Editor of the *Guardian* explained that the complainant's letter was longer and less interesting than the one published in reply to the letter on the value of safety belts.

The Press Council held that the Editor had properly acted within his discretion in not publishing the complainant's letter. (1966/91)

MOTOR-CARS, NOT POLITICS

The Editor of *Motor Sport*, Mr W. Boddy, published a long letter of political comment on a motoring theme, but declined to publish a second letter from the same correspondent on the grounds that he had had his say and that the journal was concerned with motoring, not political wrangling.

The Press Council rejected the correspondent's complaint and upheld the Editor's discretion to end correspondence on a particular subject. (1963/39–40)

LETTER CRITICISED IN EDITORIAL

In response to an invitation in the *South Notts Echo* to send in views on proposals made by the Boundary Commissioners for the inclusion of certain urban districts within the City of Nottingham, a reader wrote a letter in support of the proposals. His letter was published, and criticised in the editorial.

The reader felt that he had been held up to ridicule, and sent a reasoned reply for publication. This and two further letters were ignored.

The Press Council held that as the newspaper had already published a lengthy statement of his views, the reader's complaint that his second reply should have been published was unreasonable. But the Council considered that the Editor should have acknowledged the reader's inquiry. (1963/42)

QUEEN FREDERIKA

The *Guardian* published a letter by Mr Francis Noel-Baker, M.P., on the proposed visit to Britain of King Paul and Queen Frederika of Greece, in which he referred to Earl Russell. Earl Russell replied; and his letter was published.

The *Guardian* later published another letter from Mr Noel-Baker referring to Earl Russell, but Earl Russell's reply was not published. The Editor of the *Guardian*, Mr Alastair Hetherington, said that both Earl Russell and Mr Noel-Baker had already contributed two letters each on the subject (the first from Earl Russell at an earlier date), and nothing was to be gained by a third round.

The Press Council ruled that the question whether a further round of letters should be allowed was properly a matter for the Editor. (1964/48–9)

BERTRAND RUSSELL PEACE FOUNDATION

The *Guardian* published a letter from a member of the Bertrand Russell Peace Foundation, criticising a leading article. Later, three letters criticising the correspondent were published.

The correspondent wrote in reply to the three letters, and complained when his letter was not published.

The Editor, Mr Alastair Hetherington, said that too long a gap had elapsed for the correspondent's letter to appear. The correspondent had re-submitted his letter later with a new tailpiece in reply to a separate matter, and this letter had been published.

Three more letters referring to the correspondent's letter were published, and he submitted a further reply. The Editor said that each side had had its say twice and the newspaper could not carry the correspondence further.

The Press Council rejected the correspondent's complaint. (1966/89–90)

GRADUATES IN INDUSTRY

An article in the *Sunday Times* dealing with the dwindling intake of arts graduates into industry was alleged to present an inaccurate picture, and the complainant said that a letter he sent for publication was 'mutilated' without his consent. This letter contraverting some of the conclusions in the article was published, but a further letter replying to one from another reader was declined.

Mr C. D. Hamilton, Editor of the *Sunday Times*, said the letter was refused because it re-stated views already published.

The Press Council rejected the complaint. (1966/46)

RHODESIA — FAIR COVERAGE

A correspondent complained that the news and letters in the *Guardian* were heavily loaded against the Smith régime in Rhodesia. He said that a second letter replying to one commenting on his first letter was not published. He claimed that there was an obligation on editors to give fair coverage to the views of both sides in matters of controversy.

The Editor of the *Guardian*, Mr Alastair Hetherington, conceded that perhaps he should have published the further letter. To have done so, however, would have extended the field of controversy and inevitably led to still further correspondence. In the past two years the *Guardian* had carried extensive correspondence giving all points of view including the Rhodesian Government's.

The Press Council held that the question whether or not the particular letter should have been published was a borderline case and therefore a matter for editorial discretion. (1967)

LETTERS SELECTED SHOULD REFLECT
ALL SHADES OF OPINION

ALDERMASTON MARCH

In a report of the Aldermaston march, *The Times* stated that more than seventy people were arrested when thousands of 'Ban-the-Bomb' marchers fought with police on their way through the West End to Hyde Park.

A correspondent wrote to the Editor pointing out that although there were many thousands of marchers only a small number were in trouble with the police.

Letters critical of the report were published, but none made the point contained in this letter which was not published.

The Press Council were of the opinion that although *The Times* had published two columns of readers' letters critical of the report, nevertheless inclusion of the letter challenging the number of marchers said to have been involved in scenes with the police would have been advisable. (1964/46–7)

EDUCATION (SCOTLAND) ACT

The *Scottish Educational Journal*, commenting on a judgment of the Court of Sessions, said that its effect was to render a section in the Education (Scotland) Act, 1962, inoperable.

A reader challenged this view and said the article was liable to mislead; he alleged that the Editor had a duty to print a correction. Mr R. Thomasson, the Editor, declined to do so.

The Press Council stated that in general terms it was advisable that, while an editor should give publicity to all shades of opinion, the publication of any particular letter must be a matter within his discretion, and the Council was not prepared to say his decision was wrong in this case. (1965/76)

NINETY-DAYS DETENTION CLAUSE

The day before publishing an advertisement for one of her books *The Times* published a letter from the writer in which she criticised the South African Government's use of the ninety-days detention clause.

A letter defending the South African Government was not published, and the correspondent complained to the Press Council. Readers were entitled to assume, he said, that the letters published represented a fair selection of the views received by the newspaper on any subject, and that no other motive influenced the selection. He alleged that publication of the letter critical of the South African Government was evidence on this occasion that selection of letters was rigged for commercial and propaganda purposes.

The Editor of *The Times*, Sir William Haley, said that only a fraction of the letters received on the subject could be printed. An important test of selection in controversial matters was that letters made a useful contribution to the discussion. In his view the letter from the complainant did not do so.

The Press Council rejected as unwarranted the suggestion that the selection of letters by the newspaper was based on commercial and propaganda considerations. (1964/59)

OFFICIAL REPLIES WHICH SHOULD HAVE BEEN PUBLISHED

ARSON AT A SYNAGOGUE

The *South London Advertiser* published an article stating that the Jewish households in the district were praying that the fire that had swept through the local synagogue hall was not the signal for race war. The article said that the police had little doubt that the fire was arson by fanatical anti-Semitics, and that in an earlier incident a few weeks previously the synagogue was desecrated on the Sabbath by the nailing of a pig's head on the doors.

In a letter to the Editor, the minister of the synagogue denied the story of the pig's head, and said there was no truth in the report that Jewish citizens were praying that the fire was not the signal for a race war. The Editor, Mr A. S. Hitchings, did not print the letter.

The Press Council deplored the exaggerated tone of the article, and censured the Editor for failing to correct the mis-statement by publishing the minister's letter. (1956/29–30, 42–6)

BUYING A HOUSE

An article in the *Sunday Express* on the subject of buying a house was alleged to contain misleading advice and to cast adverse reflection on valuers. The Secretary of the Valuers' Institution complained that the Editor refused to publish any letter stating their case. The Editor, Mr John Junor, claimed that none of the letters received pointed out any factual inaccuracy.

The Press Council held that the essential parts of the letter submitted by the Valuers' Institution should have been published, and it regretted that this had not been done. (1961/23)

A STRAIGHT DENIAL

The *Daily Sketch* reported that half a million copies of the pamphlet, *The Future Labour Offers You*, were lying in store in cellars in Transport House and elsewhere. When the General Secretary of the Labour Party, Mr Morgan Phillips, wrote to the Editor denying this, the Editor, Mr Herbert Gunn, asked if the writer of the article could inspect the stock. The request was refused on the grounds that Mr Phillips's letter had been a straight denial.

The Press Council found that this was a case in which the *Daily Sketch* should have agreed to publish an official reply by Mr Phillips on behalf of the Labour Party. (1960/26)

CANON COLLINS AND MOSCOW RADIO

Moscow Radio broadcast a recorded interview with Canon L. John Collins during his visit to Moscow in June 1961. In announcing this the *Daily Telegraph* stated that he was reported by Moscow Radio to have given his full approval to Mr Khrushchev's proposals on Berlin and the German peace treaty.

In a letter to the Editor, Canon Collins stated that the newspaper report was erroneous and he gave his version of what had taken place at the interview. The Editor replied that he did not consider there had been misrepresentation.

Canon Collins told the Press Council that he was not concerned with the apportionment of blame, but merely with the correction of error, and contended that it was not in keeping with the traditions of British journalism for a newspaper which claimed to be responsible and trustworthy to refuse to allow correction of a false impression even though created inadvertently.

The Council held that the newspaper should have published a letter from Canon Collins giving his version. (1962/28)

CHRISTIAN SOCIALIST MOVEMENT

The *Catholic Times* published a letter from a correspondent attacking the Christian Socialist Movement.

The Movement replied through its Chairman, Dr (now Lord) Soper, but the letter was not published. The Editor, Mr Mark Fawdry, said that Dr Soper had plenty of opportunities to explain himself elsewhere, and he did not feel under a moral obligation to afford him space to air his views.

The Press Council's adjudication was that the Editor, having printed a letter strongly critical of the Christian Socialist Movement, was under a moral obligation to publish an official reply. (1962/31)

AUTHOR'S LAST WORD

The Times Literary Supplement printed an unfavourable review of a book. The author complained that some of the reviewer's comments were based on a misrepresentation of what had been written, and alleged that such practice approached distortion.

The Editor, Mr Arthur Crook, told the Press Council it was not possible to print all the letters received from disgruntled or disappointed authors. These letters were sent to reviewers for comment and a selection made of those of substance or public interest for publication.

The Press Council expressed the opinion that where there is a substantial difference of opinion between reviewer and author, the author's reasoned answer should be published in the form of a letter to the editor. (1963/63)

For another case concerning an author's complaint about a review see p. 71 (*Sunday Telegraph*).

ADOPTION OF A PARLIAMENTARY CANDIDATE

An article by the Political Correspondent of the *Sunday Telegraph* commented that the Left's greatest weakness was that it was leaderless, and that

Mr Ian Mikardo, their ablest and potential leader, was inhibited by the fact that the Labour Party in Poplar, where he had been adopted as Parliamentary candidate, was Right-wing with a strong Roman Catholic influence. Furthermore, the article continued, he was not the first choice of the Poplar party, but was adopted after the candidature of the favourite had been invalidated on technical grounds.

Mr Mikardo wrote to the newspaper and denied that any inhibitions had been placed on him. He also stated that he had defeated the person generally considered to be favourite, a fact which could easily have been verified at the time the article was written. The letter was not published; the Editor, Mr Donald McLachlan, said he would have published it had he thought Mr Mikardo had been harmed by the inaccurate story.

The Press Council took the view that he should have published at least that part of Mr Mikardo's letter correcting the mis-statement about the circumstances of his adoption as Parliamentary candidate. (1964/49–50)

SMOKING AND CANCER

The *Sunday Telegraph* invited replies to an article on smoking and cancer and stated that the Editor would publish 'authoritative answers'.

A doctor, who was Secretary of the Royal College of Physicians Commission on Smoking and Health, sent a detailed reply saying that, although he was not writing officially, he expected his reply to be regarded as authoritative. The letter was not printed, and the newspaper published a statement that no authoritative answer had been received.

The doctor then wrote a shorter letter, which was published with excisions, and he complained to the Press Council about the newspaper's statement that no authoritative replies had been received.

The Editor, Mr Donald McLachlan, explained to the Press Council that the doctor's letter, written in his private capacity, was not the authoritative answer the newspaper invited and that it did not deal with the principal point in the article.

The Press Council held that the statement that the newspaper had received no authoritative replies was a regrettable inaccuracy which remained uncorrected. (1965/74)

AN OFFICIAL REPLY

The Newcastle *Evening Chronicle* published an article criticising a service charge made by traders for hire-purchase facilities, but closed the correspondence which followed without publishing an official reply from the National Association representing the traders.

The Editor, Mr W. Moth, told the Press Council that, though many letters had been received, only one of them from the general manager of a local firm defended the service charge, and this had been published in a box to emphasise its importance.

The Press Council stated that while it upheld the right of an editor to close the correspondence at his discretion, the Council felt that in this case the letter from the National Association was an official one, sent within a reasonable time of the publication of the article, and that it should have been published to inform the public of the views of the traders. (1955/21–2, 40–2)

LONDON UNIVERSITY

The *Observer* published two articles criticising aspects of the administration of London University. A member of the Senate replied to comments alleged to be damaging to the good name of the University, but the letter was not published.

The Press Council recognised the Editor's right to select letters for publication, but considered that in this instance there was clearly a case for publishing a reasoned reply from an authoritative representative of the University. (1963/38–9)

THREE NURSES WHO WENT TO AMERICA

The *Daily Mirror* and the *Daily Sketch* published a story, supplied by a news agency, that three nurses had left Clayton Hospital in Yorkshire for similar posts in America because they had to help mop the ward floors. The local Hospital Management Committee wrote to both newspapers asking them to print its letter denying that the nurses had to undertake domestic duties, and saying that the nurses concerned had asked the Committee to protest against the interpretation put on their statements. Neither newspaper published this letter. Both Mr L. A. Lee Howard, Editor of the *Daily Mirror*, and Mr Howard French, Editor of the *Daily Sketch*, commended the news agency's standard of service.

The Press Council in view of the conflict of evidence was unable to determine the facts fully because the nurses were not available to give evidence, but it declared that the *Daily Mirror* and the *Daily Sketch* should have agreed to publish the Committee's statement. (1963/37–8)

PUBLICATION UNNECESSARY

THE BIBLE IN SPAIN

In a letter to *The Times* a reader complained about a report from the newspaper's Madrid correspondent that all Bibles of the Bible Society in Spain had been confiscated and that it was illegal to import the Bible or print or distribute it in Spain.

The reader said that a Spanish translation from the Vulgate was printed, published and freely sold in Spain. His letter was not published.

The Press Council considered that it was clear that *The Times* was referring to English Bibles such as the Revised and Authorised Versions, and it would be well known to readers of *The Times* that Catholic countries like Spain had their own translations from the Vulgate. (1959/20)

DR BEECHING'S PLANS

An article in *The Times* on the re-shaping of British Railways stated that the Rugby route was being electrified and that the Leamington route was expected to be closed beyond the Home Counties. The Banbury Borough Council said the article had caused anxiety and embarrassment in Banbury and to industrialists proposing to move factory premises to the town. The British Railways Divisional Manager described the newspaper's statement as speculation. *The Times*, however, declined to publish a letter containing the Divisional Manager's statement on the ground that no question of fact was involved and that the 'expected' closure did not denote a decision but indicated a likelihood foreshadowed in the Beeching Report.

The Press Council's adjudication was that *The Times* was justified in declining to publish the letter submitted by the Town Clerk of Banbury. (1964/50–1)

A RHETORICAL QUESTION

In an editorial article the *Sunday Express* asked rhetorically whether anyone could recall a single memorable thing that a certain cleric had said about Christianity. A reader wrote to the Editor saying that he could remember quite a number. He did not recount what they were, but said he would be glad to list them if invited to do so; his letter proceeded to praise the cleric for his work of a political and social nature. The letter was not published, and the reader complained to the Press Council.

Mr John Junor, the Editor of the newspaper, said that the complainant did not answer the question asked in the editorial.

The Press Council rejected the complaint. (1964, 78–9)

THE PRACTICE OF PSYCHIATRY

An article in the *Spectator* by Mr Alan Brien criticised the practice of psychiatry. A reader wrote a letter of about 800 words replying to the points in the article, but was told that pressure of space did not permit criticism. The Deputy Editor, Mr J. W. M. Thompson, said that Mr Brien's article was a minority complaint against a widely held attitude, and that different viewpoints were in no danger of being overlooked.

In reply to a complaint to the Press Council, the Editor of the *Spectator*, the Rt Hon. Iain Macleod, M.P., said that the article was almost entirely opinion, and the Press Council upheld his view that there was no obligation to publish a reply, especially as the columnist discussed the range of reactions from readers in a further article. (1964/76)

THE WARREN REPORT

A Director of the Bertrand Russell Peace Foundation complained that the *Evening Standard* refused to publish a letter from him in reply to personal attacks in their editorial and Diary columns. The Diary item recorded that Lord Russell had criticised the Warren Commission Report on the assassination of President Kennedy. After recording that it had been said that Lord Russell had not read the Report, the article stated that it was a pity that Lord Russell did not apply to politics the rigorous standards of inquiry and proof that had made his great reputation as a logician.

When the Director of the Peace Foundation alleged that the Warren Report ignored sinister contradictions and suppressions of evidence the Editor, Mr Charles Wintour, replied that he could only conclude that the Director had not read the Report or that he did not understand plain English.

The Press Council accepted the views of the *Evening Standard* and rejected the complaint. (1965/73–4)

OFFENSIVE AND ABUSIVE LETTERS

A BOGUS SIGNATURE

The Chairman of the Association of Jewish Ex-Servicemen and Women objected to a letter published in the *West London Observer* over the signature 'G.A.S. Chambers' which gave great offence to the Jewish community.

In a letter to the Editor, Mr Eric Carter, he said: 'Whilst we are not unaccustomed to seeing in the correspondence columns of newspapers the venomous vapourings of the lunatic fringe who appear to thrive by poisoning relations between various religious and racial groups, nevertheless, we had thought where such letters were sent to newspapers, the genuineness of the signature was a matter to be examined with some care.' He went on to say that the signature was not merely an obvious fake, but it was also a reminder to readers of the logical conclusion of similar ideas in Nazi Germany, namely the gas chambers in which millions perished. He informed the Press Council that he had had no acknowledgment or reply from the Editor.

The Editor told the Press Council that he had not received the letter. Had he done so he would have suggested to the writer that he was at liberty to reply to the one in the correspondence columns with which he disagreed. As regards the letter complained of, it was published in good faith; the signature was assumed to be genuine.

Commenting on the Editor's offer to publish a reply in the correspondence column, the Chairman of the Association said that this would have been wholly unacceptable because he would not have been prepared to enter into controversy with an anonymous correspondent, and also because the Editor was guilty of gross negligence in publishing the letter.

The Press Council severely condemned the newspaper for publishing an anti-Semitic letter over a signature which should have put the Editor on his guard as to its purpose. (1959/22, 35–7)

PRESIDENT NKRUMAH AND DR BUSIA

The High Commissioner for Ghana complained that the *Daily Telegraph* had declined to publish his letter in reply to one from Dr K. A. Busia of Oxford, which he said was a direct personal attack on President Nkrumah.

The Editor, Mr Maurice Green, told the Press Council that the first half of the High Commissioner's reply was devoted entirely to a strong personal attack on Dr Busia, and that an effort to get the personal attack moderated was unsuccessful.

The Press Council rejected the High Commissioner's complaint, and said that the publication of the letter in the form submitted was entirely a matter for the discretion of the Editor. He had exercised it by offering to publish an amended version, but the offer had not been accepted. (1965/75–6)

UNION OFFICIALS AT LOGGERHEADS

A man who described himself as Organiser of the Union of Skilled Engineers complained to the Press Council that although he had been attacked in the local newspaper, the *Craven Herald*, by an official of the A.E.U., he had been denied the right of reply.

On investigation, the complainant agreed that he had previously criticised the A.E.U. in a Press interview, and that the official's letter was in reply to that criticism.

The Editor-Manager, Mr John Mitchell, explained that the reason the letter was not published was because it was 'full of personal abuse'.

The Press Council upheld the Editor's right to reject the letter, and noted his willingness to publish letters from the complainant if they were not too personal in character. (1962/55)

THE COURTESY OF A REPLY

MR GRESHAM COOKE'S REQUEST FOR A RULING

Mr R. Gresham Cooke, M.P., asked the Press Council to declare that Members of Parliament should be accorded the courtesy of reply in a newspaper which made a substantial attack on them. He referred to a leading article in the *Daily Mirror* that had criticised a speech in which he said that M.P.s were getting too many letters. He said that M.P.s did not object to ordinary comment and criticism.

The Editor of the *Daily Mirror*, Mr L. A. Lee Howard, told the Council that, although he agreed that a right of reply should be given where there had been substantial criticism, he did not agree that his newspaper's comment in this case was substantial criticism.

The Press Council decided against a general ruling. It was of the opinion that the right to publication of a reply to criticism depended on the facts of the particular case. (1961/37)

The following year Mr Gresham Cooke again raised the matter and asked the Press Council to rule that replies on matters of public interest from responsible sources should be published.

The Press Council issued the following statement:

> It is obviously impossible to lay down any such ruling, if only because in times of acute public controversy the newspapers would consist, to a large extent, of letters from readers. While it is desirable that newspapers should give a right of reply to persons criticised, it is one which must necessarily be exercised at the Editor's discretion.

(1961/37, 1962/37)

WHERE A LETTER COULD HAVE RESTORED BALANCE

COMMENT WENT TOO FAR

'If the ratepayers of Feltham, in Middlesex, have consciences, I hope they will revolt at the news that they have just robbed a charity of £100,000.' This was part of a story in the *People* that told of the vain endeavours of the Crusade of Rescue to get planning permission for industrial building on a site near London Airport so that it might be sold to enable homes to be built away from the noise of aeroplanes. Because of the failure to get building permission the charity sold the site to Feltham Council for £200,000. Feltham Council then obtained permission to erect warehouses, and the site was sold within a few weeks for £300,000.

Feltham Council complained that the report was inaccurate, misleading and damaging because they were forced to buy the site after the charity obtained a judgment from the Land Tribunal that the amount payable by the local authority should be that of reinstatement of the homes elsewhere. The figure was mutually agreed at £200,000, which would have had to be met by the ratepayers had the Council not succeeded in selling the land. An application by the Council for permission to build warehouses on the site was granted, and the Council had a duty to the ratepayers to obtain the best price for the property.

The Press Council held that the *People* was justified in publicising the affair, which was of considerable public interest. The newspaper was quite accurate in its report that the Feltham Council had made a substantial profit, but the statement that the Council had robbed the charity went too far. The Local Authority should have asked the *People* to publish an immediate letter putting its case. (1962/55–6)

COUNCIL SHOULD HAVE CORRECTED REPORT

The *Sunday Times* and the *News of the World* reported that angry members of the St Albans Rural Council had ordered an investigation into the harsh action of an official in giving notice to quit to a Council tenant when he refused to pay a repair bill of £1. The Councillors complained that the reports were a gross misrepresentation of their views which were concerned with Council policy and not with the action of the official.

The Press Council found that the cause of the notice to quit was correctly reported, but it was untrue to say that there was to be an investigation into the harsh action of an official. The Rural Council should have sent a prompt correction to the newspapers. (1962/54–5)

AN ALLEGED 'BABY SNATCH'

An article in the *People* criticised the Croydon Corporation and its Children's Committee for the treatment of a homeless family turned out of the one room they occupied. The newspaper described the taking of the children into care as a 'baby snatch' and spoke of the distraught parents 'robbed of their children'.

The Town Clerk complained that the tone of the article was offensive and unwarranted in light of the help given by the Council. The children had not been forcibly removed from their parents as the article suggested, and there was no prohibition on the parents seeing their children.

The Editor of the *People*, Mr Stuart Campbell, offered the Town Clerk space for a letter in reply to the article. The offer was refused.

The Press Council's adjudication was that if the Editor's offer to publish a letter had been accepted the letter would have gone far to meet the objections made. (1963/60–1)

THE REASON THE CHAIRMAN RESIGNED

The Exeter *Express and Echo* published the explanation given by the Chairman of a Ratepayers' Association for resigning his chairmanship. The new Chairman and other officers contended that the Editor should have satisfied himself before he published the statements made by the former Chairman that they were accurate, and they called upon him to correct them.

The Editor, Mr M. Hoare, claimed that in view of the ex-Chairman's standing a check was not necessary, and he was entitled to rely on what he said. He offered, however, to publish the letter of correction submitted subject to the deletion of imputations on the former Chairman.

The Press Council was of the opinion that the letter the Editor was prepared to publish was a fair and adequate statement of the views of the Association and should have been acceptable to the Chairman and officers. (1964/51–2)

EARL RUSSELL'S SECRETARIES

The Secretary to Earl Russell complained of an article in the *Guardian* which stated that a screen of private secretaries protected the 91-year-old Earl from interviewers, and that the secretariat was largely identified with the Bertrand Russell Peace Foundation directorate and heavily weighted with members of the Committee of 100.

The complainant denied the allegations in the article and said they were made for the purpose of casting doubts on Lord Russell's capacity and integrity.

The Press Council held that the complaint could have been dealt with by a letter for publication in the *Guardian*. (1964/59–60)

ALLEGED CONSISTENT DENIGRATION

The South Warwickshire Water Board complained of 'consistent denigration' by the *Leamington Spa Courier* following a series of articles criticising the Board's lavish expenditure.

The Chairman of the Board pointed out that two members reported by the newspaper to have criticised the Board's expenditure did not vote against the expenditure they had criticised, and that particulars of the expenditure given in the newspaper were inaccurate.

The Press Council was of the opinion that when the expenditure of the Water Board was criticised the Chairman of the Board should have sent the newspaper a letter for publication stating the Board's case. The complaint of constant denigration was held not to be substantiated. The newspaper was at fault, however, in not publishing the proceedings at a later meeting when the charges of extravagance which the newspaper had prominently reported and criticised were refuted. (1964/64–5)

UNBALANCED REPORT

A report in the *Cambridge News* that some members of Royston, Herts, Chamber of Commerce had asked that the town should be transferred to Cambridgeshire was described as 'neither accurate, balanced nor complete'. The complainant said that the report 'gave a completely false impression by omitting to mention the considerable opposition to the point of view reported'.

The Editor of the newspaper, Mr Keith Whetstone, said that the argument over the future of Royston had a long history, and both sides had been given fully. Publication was restricted because of pressure of space; the population of Royston was under three per cent of that of the circulation area.

The Press Council found that the report was a little unbalanced, but could have been corrected by the publication of a factual letter from the complainant. (1965/50)

A FOURTH APPEAL

An auctioneer and estate agent who was making a fourth appeal against a planning authority's refusal to permit development on a site at Cannock complained that a leading article in the *Cannock Advertiser and Courier* was calculated to influence the decision.

The article, the complainant said, implied that his fourth appeal was futile, improperly suggested that legislation limiting appeals should be introduced to limit 'a shocking waste of money' and failed to make clear that the circumstances of the fourth appeal were different from those of the previous appeals.

The newspaper reported that the complainant had stated that the Minister of Housing and Local Government, in refusing previous appeals, had not supported the reasons given by the local authority.

A leading article in the same issue declared that the right of appeal should remain an integral part of our democracy, but a fourth appeal was ludicrous and a shocking waste of money.

The Editor of the newspaper, Mr B. Dawson, told the Press Council that the leading article was intended to expose what was considered to be a loophole in the law, namely that repeated inquiries had to be held by the Minister if the appellant could produce a fresh point. He maintained that four inquiries should not be necessary. The report had made it clear that the circumstances of the fourth appeal were different from the others.

The Editor added that the complainant would have been allowed to comment in the correspondence column if he had wished to do so; alternatively an explanatory paragraph would have been considered for it was the newspaper's policy to rectify a mistake immediately.

The Press Council held that there was a case for an explanatory letter or correction which the Editor would have been willing to publish, and accordingly there was no basis for the complaint. (1966/41–2)

RATEPAYERS AND 'MAFIA'

Complaint was made that a report of a meeting in the *Oadby and Wigston Advertiser* was an unbalanced one, that the headline was unfair and the withdrawal of certain words spoken at the meeting was not recorded. The headline read 'Wigston Ratepayers' Association told of "Mafia" Council'.

The report recorded that the Wigston Ratepayers' Association was launched at the meeting and that the meeting was featured by an attack on the policy of news delay by the Council to the Press. Mr T., had asked 'Is Wigston Council some sort of "Mafia"? It is a closed club? Ratepayers under the present system of news release from council committees don't know enough, soon enough . . .'. He complained that the report unduly featured the attack on the Council; that it was discourteous to the Council and to himself to headline words which were withdrawn.

The Editor of the newspaper, Mr L. Wilkes, said that the reporter who attended the meeting was not aware that Mr T. had withdrawn any of his remarks. Although 'Mafia' was used in the form of a question at the meeting, subsequent remarks made by Mr T. turned the question more into a statement and this gave rise to the headline. The reporter concerned was a man of considerable experience; he had no note of the withdrawal of the word, nor had the newspaper been able to confirm that they were withdrawn. If Mr T. had complained at once and asked for space for a fuller explanation this would have been given to him. The reporter said that Mr T.'s remarks were taken down in shorthand and he had the notebook with the report. He could supply the names and addresses of people present who agreed that the report was a fair one.

The Press Council held that there was no journalistic misconduct on the part of the *Oadby and Wigston Advertiser*, and the whole of the matter could have been dealt with by a letter to the Editor. (1967)

LETTERS SHOULD GENERALLY APPEAR IN CORRESPONDENCE COLUMNS

LETTERS PUBLISHED IN GOSSIP COLUMN

Two letters printed in the *South London Press* as part of a gossip feature by 'Wanderer' were brought to the notice of the Press Council.

One letter was printed without interruption, but with what the complainant regarded as a disparaging reference at the beginning and a critical commentary at the end. The second letter was interspersed with 'Wanderer's' comments.

The complainant said that in the case of the first letter the comments were not separated from the letter and were printed in the same type, which detracted from the expression of his views, because the Editor had the last word. In the second letter the interspersion of comment was still more objectionable.

Mr Eric Kinton, the Editor of the newspaper, said that although editorial comment might reduce the effect of the reader's letter, the journalist had equal freedom with readers. The second letter with the Editor's comment interspersed was not a new contribution; it had been published in a previous issue and was quoted only in part, for 'Wanderer's' comment.

The Press Council held: As a general rule it is desirable that letters written for publication should be printed in the correspondence columns. In this particular case a letter arose out of a comment in 'Wanderer's' column. It had been the practice for twenty years for 'Wanderer' to deal with such matters in his column, and the letter was printed in full. The Press Council did not consider this objectionable. (1967)

11 Corrections and Apologies

In adjudication of a complaint the Press Council has stated:

> It should be accepted as a journalistic principle that where a mis-statement of fact is made, and a person or group of persons likely to suffer by it calls the editor's attention to it, there should be a frank correction and apology on a page where the correction and apology are likely to be seen by those who read the original mis-statement.

The case was decided at an early stage in the Press Council's history, but the principle stated has been frequently confirmed. It is a principle founded both in ethics and justice. The only elaboration perhaps needed is that the correction should be published without delay.

The newspaper itself generally drafts the form of correction. Sometimes it is advisable to submit the proposed correction to the complainant for approval. If the complaint is made through solicitors it is generally accompanied by a request that the correction be approved before publication. Where, however, agreement on the wording cannot be reached the newspaper will nevertheless be well advised to publish a correction, since it is better to be able to produce a published correction than a good excuse for not publishing one at all, should court proceedings or a complaint to the Press Council follow.

A question often arises whether a correction should be accompanied by an apology. The answer will depend on the circumstances. A correction deals with the facts, an apology with the injury done by their mis-statement. A bare correction sometimes is sufficient; sometimes an apology will clearly be necessary. In case of doubt it should be borne in mind that a correction will not suffer if accompanied by a courteous expression of regret.

The Press Council has held that where an inaccuracy has caused embarrassment and distress a formal correction is insufficient; there should, in addition, be an expression of regret. Occasions occur, although they are rare, where even a mis-statement needs no correction. Where, for instance, an obvious numerical error appeared in a headline, but was correctly stated in the text, the Council held that a correction was not needed; the reader would at once recognise the mistake.

More frequently the Council has held that a formal correction is unnecessary where the newspaper has published a letter from the complainant correcting the inaccuracy or where the Council thinks that he should have written such a letter. Again the Council may decide in a particular case that the mere publication of a letter without an expression of editorial regret is inadequate.

The position in the newspaper in which the correction is to be published and the size of the type to be used are often matters of contention. The original report may have been published under a block headline in large type and taken up a considerable amount of space. A person asking for a correction will expect and generally demands that it should be given the same prominence including publication on the front page if that is where the offending article appeared. Legislation has even been suggested to impose on newspapers the legal obligation to give equal prominence to the correction as was given to the inaccuracy.

It is possible if the newspaper so contrives for a correction to be published in such a position as to be virtually concealed. Or the correction can be so worded as to have the effect of aggravating the offence already given. These are questions of fact for the consideration of the Press Council when dealing with complaints of this nature.

There is no general rule on the matter. The Press Council has stated that corrections and apologies should be on a page where they are likely to be seen by those who read the original mis-statement. It has also ruled that a reply to criticism contained in the leading article does not have to be printed in the leader column. The Council has further expressed the view that there can be few better positions for a correction than at the end of a further report of the matter that has given rise to the complaint

Cases considered by the Council are the following:

CORRECTION SHOULD HAVE BEEN PUBLISHED

CORRECTION REFUSED

A reader wrote to the Editor-in-Chief of the *Sunday Express*, Mr John Gordon, stating that a report in the newspaper that twenty houses were to be built for policemen at an average cost of £5,709 was inaccurate and that in fact the cost per house was £2,718. A request was made for a correction to be published.

Mr Gordon replied that the figure he quoted had been published in the

Daily Mail, and that if the reader could persuade that newspaper to correct its statement he would print a similar correction. He also said that the County Council had not questioned his figures.

The reader made further appeals to Mr Gordon and finally informed him that he would bring the matter to the Press Council.

Mr Gordon replied: 'I do not think it is worth while pursuing this long forgotten matter. As for your threat you can report me to the Press Council, Madame Tussauds, the Society for the Protection of Sputniks, N.A.T.O., U.N.E.S.C.O., or the Dancing Dervishes Association as you wish. May you enjoy yourself.'

The Press Council expressed its regret that Mr Gordon, having allowed the mistake to appear in his newspaper, had failed to correct it although asked to do so on four occasions. (1958/25)

PILGRIMAGES TO LOURDES

An article in the Dundee *People's Journal* said that typhoid outbreaks in Britain could be traced to the number of people going to the Continent for holidays and in particular on pilgrimages to Lourdes.

A reader complained that the newspaper declined to publish his letter contesting the accuracy in relation to the pilgrimages.

The Editor, Mr J. B. Hood, said the article was based on information supplied by the Medical Officer of Health for Dundee. Publication of the reader's letter was considered inadvisable.

The Chief Medical Officer at the Ministry of Health informed the Press Council that nearly half of all the cases notified since 1960 were presumed to have been infected abroad. There was no evidence that any were infected at Lourdes. The Medical Officer for Dundee agreed that it would be very difficult to prove that Lourdes was the actual source of infection.

The Press Council held that the evidence showed conclusively that the article was incorrect in its reference to Lourdes. The newspaper should have published a correction. (1965/52–3)

ERROR NOT CORRECTED

A report in the *Paisley Daily Express* said that Independent candidates had complained to the Returning Officer that Labour supporters at the entrance to the poll had given voters wrong information about the number of votes they were entitled to in the local District and County Council Elections.

The Labour Election Agent asked the Returning Officer for details and discovered that no complaint had been made to him.

A request was then made to the Editor, Mr A. W. Lochhead, to correct the report, but this was not complied with nor was it acknowledged.

The Editor said that had the letter of complaint not been marked 'Not for publication' it would have appeared promptly in the newspaper. The first check seemed to confirm the accuracy of the report, and no action was taken.

The Press Council expressed the view that the error should have been corrected. (1965/60)

SUICIDE AFTER CRUELTY CHARGE

A solicitor acting on behalf of the widow of a man who committed suicide the day after his conviction on a cruelty charge complained of the reports of the proceedings in three newspapers, the *News of the World*, the *Sunday Express* and the *Sunday Dispatch*. The reports had included the allegation that the defendant had gagged his daughter by putting adhesive plaster over her lips before chastising her. No mention, however, was made of the fact that when the Chairman of the Bench announced that the defendant would be fined he said the penalty was imposed because of the severity of the beating of the child, and that the Court were not satisfied that the allegation of gagging had been substantiated.

The *News of the World* had published a correction, but the *Sunday Express* and the *Sunday Dispatch* had not, though asked to do so.

The Press Council expressed the view that it was unfortunate that these two newspapers had not seen their way to publish an immediate correction. (1954/25)

THE COST OF LIVING

In an article headlined 'Mr Rising Price is put in his place', the *Daily Express* said the cost of living in Britain had risen less in the previous year than in many other countries. Complaint was made that the newspaper had given only the food indexes of other countries, not the percentage increase. Moreover five countries had been omitted from the *Daily Express* list where the index figures were lower than Britain's. A correction was asked for.

The Editor of the newspaper, Mr Derek Marks, said that in regard to certain parts of the complaint their report was a fair summary of the *Ministry of Labour Gazette*, but there was substance in one part of the complaint.

The Industrial Correspondent agreed that a mistake had been made in comparing the full price index of this country with the food index of other countries, but the complaint that the newspaper had grossly misled the public was an exaggeration. Distortion was minimal.

The Press Council decided that a mistake had been made in the presentation of essential facts, and the newspaper should have corrected it promptly. (1966/51)

MR JACK DASH

The *Daily Express* in three news stories in an issue in connection with the Devlin Committee's Report on the Port Transport Industry labelled Mr Jack Dash as a 'wrecker'.

Solicitors on behalf of Mr Dash told the Press Council that the Devlin Report did not at any time label or call him a 'wrecker'. They had requested a correction of the three reports, but none had been published. Lord Devlin, in a letter to the Secretary of Mr Dash's Liaison Committee, had stated that he did not think it right to say that the Report branded any individuals as 'wreckers'.

The Editor, Mr Derek Marks, said that the Report had been widely read as applying the comment 'wreckers' to unofficial committee leaders, and in particular to Mr Dash. He offered to publish an interview with Mr Dash by one of the newspaper's senior feature writers which could include references to the question of wreckers.

Mr Dash's solicitors refused the offer and said that there was no need for the suggested interview. A completely wrong statement had been made, and it should be corrected.

The Press Council in its adjudication said that the newspaper was in error in stating that Mr Jack Dash was labelled in the Docks Inquiry Report as a 'wrecker'. The newspaper should have published a correction on being requested to do so. (1966/52–4)

QUEEN'S VISIT TO GHANA

The *Daily Mail* in its news column said that a spokesman of the Ghanaian High Commissioner's office in London had suggested the arrests of President Nkrumah's political opponents were a possible move to prevent demonstrations during the Queen's forthcoming visit (1961). In an adjacent leading article the newspaper wrongly attributed to the High Commissioner the comment that the arrests had been made to protect the Queen. The High Commissioner asked for an unconditional apology for attributing to him a statement which was a complete fabrication.

The Editor of the *Daily Mail*, Mr William Hardcastle, offered to publish a correction of an error in attribution, but with an explanation that the remark had been made by the Press Office.

The High Commissioner objected and said that the member of the staff cited was a junior employee not authorised to make statements. The employee denied making the statement, and he was corroborated by other members of the staff. The parties could not agree on the wording of a correction.

Because of the conflict of evidence the Press Council invited the representatives of the *Daily Mail* and the Ghanaian officials to attend personally to give oral evidence. The newspaper's representatives did so, but the Ghanaian officials did not. The Press Council was unable to adjudicate on what transpired at the interview in the absence of the Ghanaian witnesses. But two errors were undisputed, the reporter's account of the interview was misquoted and a statement was erroneously attributed to the High Commissioner. The *Daily Mail* should have taken prompt action to correct them, irrespective of being unable to reach agreement on the wording. (1962/31–2, 71–3)

NO AGREEMENT ON FORM OF CORRECTION

A Scottish minister of religion complained that the *Scottish Daily Express* had inaccurately reported him and another minister as objecting to the nail varnish worn by a woman church organist.

Mr Roger Wood, Editor of the newspaper, said that attempts to reach a form of correction had failed. He was satisfied that the facts of the story, as published, were correct.

The Press Council declared that this was a case in which a correction should have been published at the earliest opportunity. The Editor had not written to the complainants suggesting this. The Council found it hard to believe that to devise a form of words was beyond professional journalists. (1961/28)

CONDUCTRESSES AND COLOURED WORKERS

The Birmingham Liberal Organisation criticised *Reynolds News* for stating that 1,400 conductresses had threatened to strike if coloured people were employed on the corporation buses. Other newspapers had correctly stated that the women had threatened to resign.

The Press Council informed *Reynolds News* that a paragraph should have been published clarifying the position. (1955/26)

DISTORTED PICTURE OF OLD LADY

A complaint was made of an article in the *Daily Herald* about an old lady printed after the publication of her will. Her relatives alleged that several statements in the article were incorrect, and that it gave an unfair and distorted picture of a quiet old lady who had spent her strength in giving attention to an ailing sister.

After considering letters from the Editorial Manager of the *Daily Herald*, Mr Andrew Mellor, the Press Council expressed its regret that the newspaper did not take the earliest opportunity of correcting statements in the story when they were found to be incorrect. (1958/29)

EARL RUSSELL'S ATLANTIC PEACE FOUNDATION

An article in the *Sunday Telegraph* headed 'Lord Russell Charity Raises Only £3,000' was said to contain falsehoods and complaint was made that Earl Russell was refused the right of reply.

The article described the Atlantic Peace Foundation, founded by Earl Russell in 1963 to establish international centres for the study of war and peace, as a 'massive disappointment' for its founder. The Foundation was said to work in co-operation with the Bertrand Russell Peace Foundation, a political and propaganda organisation which had unsuccessfully sought charity status. Little progress had been made by the Atlantic Peace Foundation towards its stated aims and the only disbursement shown in the accounts was a cash grant of £410 to one recipient. Earl Russell complained that there had been no failure to establish international centres nor had such 'mythical failure' been a 'massive disappointment'. 'Almost all our income,' wrote Earl Russell, 'is contributed directly to the Bertrand Russell Peace Foundation' and the Foundation had never sought charitable status.

The Managing Editor of the *Sunday Telegraph*, Mr Brian Roberts, declined to publish a letter because what Lord Russell had to say about the Russell Peace Foundation appeared irrelevant to an article which dealt with the Atlantic Peace Foundation. The application for charity status was on the files of the Charity Commissioners.

When the Press Council informed Mr Roberts that the Charity Commissioners were unable to trace any application by the Bertrand Russell Peace Foundation he said he now recognised that there was a measure of doubt about it.

The Press Council decided that the only mis-statement of fact in the article was the assertion that the Russell Peace Foundation unsuccessfully sought charity status. The statement could have been checked before publication and certainly should have been checked when its accuracy was questioned by Lord Russell. To this extent the complaint was upheld.
(1966/57–8)

CORRECTION 'TOO LONG FOR PUBLICATION'

Mr F. J. Bellenger, M.P., complained of an article in the *Sunday Express* published in December 1957 under the headline 'Socialist ex-Minister gives notice to quit to six tenants'. He said that some of the statements were inaccurate, but that he and the newspaper could not agree on a form of correction.

The Press Council found that the article was in part inaccurate and regretted that a correction had not been published. The Council suggested that Mr Bellenger should ask the newspaper to publish a letter from him pointing out that his agent had given notice to quit to three not six tenants, that it was the landlord's intention to negotiate new tenancies, but that following the publication of the article Mr Bellenger had changed his mind and decided to sell the property as it stood.

Mr Bellenger wrote the letter, but the *Sunday Express* refused to publish it because it was too long. The letter was eventually printed in the *Worksop Guardian* in order that it might be read by his constituents in the Bassetlaw Division. (1958/28–9)

SCOTTISH COUNCILLOR MISQUOTED

An article in the *Scottish Daily Express* contained the following passage: 'Highways Committee Convener, Councillor S., who shocked motorists on Wednesday with the announcement that the Corporation intends to "price" all-day parkers out of the city, used a Council car yesterday morning to take him to the Central Police Court. And he insisted that he was not anti-motorist simply because he is not a driver.' The Councillor denied the statement, and said that he drove a car. He asked the newspaper to retract the error.

The Managing Editor, Mr John E. Campbell, said that having a driving licence did not make the Councillor a motorist, and if he owned a car and drove regularly the newspaper would clarify the situation to its readers. A statement from another member of the staff of the newspaper was made in which he admitted an error in transcribing what the Councillor had said.

After hearing the statement the Press Council held that the newspaper had published an incorrect statement and should have corrected it when requested to do so. (1967)

REGRET BUT NO CORRECTION

The Secretary of the Amateur Swimming Association complained that an article in the *Daily Express* headlined 'Our angry swim kids plan showdown No. 2' had no foundation. All the members of the British team had signed a letter, stating the report 'in no way reflected the feelings of the team'.

The Editor, Mr Edward D. Pickering, had expressed his regret to the Secretary, but no correction was published.

The Press Council said that the article was admitted to be untrue in part, and the newspaper should have published a correction informing readers of a statement made by the Amateur Swimming Association. (1961/25)

'MINOR' AND 'GROSS' INACCURACIES

A father complained that a report in the Hull *Daily Mail* of the inquest on his son who had been killed in a road accident contained two gross in-accuracies which gave a totally wrong impression of his son's character.

The Editor declined to make a correction and apology or to send a personal apology to the father and informed the Press Council that even if 'quite minor inaccuracies *did* occur' he could not accept that they were 'gross' or could reasonably cause grievous distress to the boy's father and family.

> We recognise at all times [he wrote] our obligation to correct truly material errors where these occur in reports, and to express, in addition, regret where genuine damage or hurt results; but we must state quite firmly that we also consider it a duty to ourselves, as well as to news-papers, at large, to resist efforts to impose these when they are, in our opinion, inadequately based.

The Press Council held that the father and family were entitled to the correction and apology asked for, and it deplored the failure of the Editor of the Hull *Daily Mail* to publish a simple explanation. (1960/29)

For other cases where corrections should have been published see p. 116 (*Sunday Express*), concerning an incorrect quotation and headline, p. 117 (*Reynolds News*), incorrect facts, p. 121 (*Daily Sketch*), shortening a letter, p. 124 (*West London Observer*), mis-statement, p. 345 (*Queen*).

CORRECTION INADEQUATE WITHOUT APOLOGY

EASTER IN CYPRUS

The *Daily Mail* published a photograph of three Greek Orthodox priests conducting a religious service on a platform holding tripods of rifles with bayonets fixed; the caption said that while children were laying flowers in the streets of Cyprus to celebrate Easter, men went into the Orthodox churches to pray 'with guns strapped to their waists'. The headline to the article read: 'Not a cross, but guns . . . As Easter nears, priests thank God for independence'. The piled rifles were cited as a symbol of Greek Orthodox philosophy.

A reader complained that the publication was an attempt to blacken the name of the Greek Orthodox Church.

The Managing Editor of the newspaper, Mr E. V. Matthewman, said that because of an unforgivable oversight and failure to check the facts, the newspaper drew wrong conclusions from the picture. A reader's letter had been printed stating that the picture could not be an Easter service, because the Greek Orthodox Easter was not celebrated until a month after the publication. The picture depicted the commemoration of Greek Independence Day.

The Press Council held that, in view of the newspaper's acknowledgment of error, the reader's letter of correction should have been accompanied by an editorial footnote of apology. (1965/81–2)

FLUORIDATED WATER

The *Knutsford Guardian*, which was opposed to the fluoridation of water, reported that the late President Kennedy had refused to allow his children to drink fluoridated water.

Eight months later the newspaper published a letter which said the newspaper report about President Kennedy's attitude was completely untrue. The writer said she had obtained documentary evidence from the American Embassy and the American Dental Association that the President and his family drank the fluoridated water supplied to the White House. The letter was published with an editorial footnote stating that the newspaper's authority was 'a reputable Washington source'. The erroneous statement was not withdrawn, and no apology was made.

The Editor-in-Chief of the *Knutsford Guardian* group, Mr M. J. Trench, in reply to a complaint that reasonable efforts had not been made to check the facts, said that an extensive search had failed to reveal the source of the report. The letter of refutation had been published, and the editorial footnote implied that the denial was accepted. It was not normal practice for a newspaper correcting a mis-statement to include an apology when no one had been injured.

The Press Council said the editorial note was an inadequate form of correction, and censured the newspaper for not publishing a clear retraction of its erroneous claim with an expression of regret for having misled readers. (1964/72–3)

POLICE INSPECTOR SUSPENDED

The Chief Constable of Southend-on-Sea suspended one of his inspectors pending inquiries into the misuse of police petrol.

The *Daily Mail* in publishing the news added an inaccurate statement that the investigation concerned the alleged sale of police petrol to civilians. The newspaper published a correction, but the Chief Constable complained that it should have also published an apology.

The Press Council noted the immediate publication of a correction of its report, but was of the opinion that the *Daily Mail* should also have expressed its regret. (1957/25–6)

Other aspects of this case, concerning alleged intrusion, are dealt with on p. 265.

A FOOTBALLER PROTESTS

In an article headlined 'Five Players in Argyle Bust-up', the *Daily Herald* included the name of a professional footballer in the list of those alleged to be worried about their future and to be asking for a transfer. The statement was untrue as far as the professional player was concerned, and he asked that his denial should be published.

Ten days after publishing the article the *Daily Herald* published a paragraph under the heading 'R— Happy' saying that the player denied that he was unhappy with the club.

The Press Council deplored the way in which the player's complaint had been handled and the fact that ten days elapsed before any statement was published by the newspaper. The statement was inadequate, and the Press Council considered that a prompt retraction and an expression of regret should have been published. (1960/27)

PHARMACIES AND COSMETICS

An article in the *Daily Mail* headed 'Prescriptions for prosperity' stated that the Pharmaceutical Society had resolved by an overwhelming majority to confine the sale of pharmaceutical supplies to pharmacists, and to ban their sale in department stores and supermarkets.

Some days later the *Daily Mail* published a letter from a member of the Society which stated that the article might have created the impression that the Pharmaceutical Society intended to stop the sale of cosmetics at department stores, which was not so. The intention was to prevent the opening of a pharmacy within a supermarket, to allow new pharmacies to sell only cosmetic and photographic goods in addition to medicines, and to prevent existing pharmacies from adding additional non-pharmaceutical lines to their stock.

A complaint was made that the article was inaccurate. The complainant thought the newspaper should have published an apology as well as the letter of correction.

Mr E. V. Matthewman, the Managing Editor, said a genuine mistake had been made but the newspaper had published the letter.

The Press Council stated that the *Daily Mail* had acknowledged its error by publishing a letter of correction, but thought the letter should have been accompanied by an apology from the Editor. (1966/92)

Another case in which an apology was also necessary will be found on p. 279 (*Daily Sketch*). See also p. 343 (*Daily Record*) and p. 345 (*Daily Telegraph*).

CORRECTION AFTER PRESS COUNCIL INQUIRY

YOUNG LIBERALS CONFERENCE

A delegate of the conference of Young Liberals protested that the *Daily Mail*'s brief report of this event was misleading.

After investigation by the Press Council the newspaper published a correction. (1954/25–6)

A SELECT COMMITTEE REPORT

Mr George Jeger, M.P., complained that the *Daily Express* and the *Evening Standard* had wrongly interpreted the Report of a Select Committee on M.P.'s pay and expenses as being in favour of granting railway vouchers to the wives of members.

The newspapers stated that the wording of the Report was ambiguous, but told the Press Council that if they were supplied with an authoritative interpretation they would publish it.

The Chairman of the Select Committee, Mr Clement Davies, M.P., supplied a statement, and both newspapers published a correction. (1954/26–7)

FIRM INCORRECTLY DESCRIBED AS 'CHEMISTS'

The Pharmaceutical Society complained that the Swindon *Evening Advertiser* had incorrectly described a firm in a court case as 'chemists', and had refused to publish a correction drafted by the Society. This stated that the term 'chemist' could only be used in connection with the sale of goods by retail by a person whose name appeared in the statutory register of the Society, or by a corporate body which had appointed a pharmaceutical chemist as superintendent.

The Council informed the parties that in view of the position under the Pharmacy Acts, the correction should be published, with the addition of the words that 'the firm in question had informed the Press Council that they were acting as a drug store and not as chemists'. The Swindon *Evening Advertiser* duly published the Press Council statement in full. (1957/28)

POSITION AND SIZE OF A CORRECTION

AN INCONSPICUOUS CORRECTION

The Educational Institute of Scotland complained that the Glasgow *Sunday Post* had published in a prominent position an inaccurate statement that public money was being spent on sending Renfrewshire children on continental holidays. An editorial correction had been asked for, but the newspaper had only published in an inconspicuous position an extract from a letter signed 'Paisley Teacher' dealing with the point at issue.

The Institute stated that the newspaper had exposed to prejudice a section of teachers who were voluntarily and without payment giving their services in the interest of their pupils.

The Press Council was of the opinion that the newspaper did not print a reasonably prominent correction of a statement conspicuously made and likely to cause public prejudice, nor was the limited correction from the 'Paisley Teacher' accompanied by an editorial apology. The Council proceeded to lay down the principle quoted on page 188 at the beginning of this chapter. (1955/23–4, 44–6)

HEADMASTER'S SUSPENSION

A report in the *Scottish Daily Express* bore the heading 'Five hours' debate; 18 minutes' silence — then a burst of cheering signals 34–1 defeat of the Rector'.

The headline was said to be misleading, because the applause did not take place at the time of the vote but at a later stage when the Chairman was congratulated on the way he handled the meeting.

The report related to a meeting of the County Education Committee at which the headmaster of a school had been suspended.

A further complaint was that the front-page picture of the Chairman was described as having been taken after the headmaster had been told the decision, whereas it was in fact taken during the luncheon adjournment (this mistake was corrected on the following day).

The Press Council declared that the newspaper should have sought the reason for the applause rather than make an unfounded assumption, but the mistake would not have occurred if the Press had been allowed to remain when the vote was taken. The caption of the picture which, as the Editor admitted, gave an impression of gloating, should not have been published. The Council noted, however, that the correction was made the following day at the end of a further report on the same affair, and there could be few better positions for such a correction. (1960/32–3)

INQUEST REPORT — UNSATISFACTORY CORRECTION

In reporting the opening of an inquest on the death of a 73-year-old man who was killed when his bicycle was in collision with a sports car, the *Stafford Newsletter* under the heading 'Car dragged a man 70 feet' stated that the cyclist was dragged along under the car for 70 feet before it was able to stop.

At the resumed inquest the following week the verdict of accidental death was reported by the newspaper, and on another page the following paragraph appeared, headed 'Inquest report':

> In a report last week of the opening of an inquest it was stated that a cyclist was dragged 70 feet after a collision with a car. This should have read 27 feet. We regret the error and any distress caused to the people concerned.

Solicitors on behalf of the driver of the car complained of the original headline. No blame attached to the driver of the car and the newspaper had built up a headline story on facts which did not exist. Complaint was also made of the nature of the correction and the position in the paper divorced from the report of the case.

The Editor, Mr George Grimes, said that the driver of the car was not mentioned by name in the first report, and it was thought that it would be unfair to draw attention to him in the correction. For the same reason it was decided to put the correction on a separate page. There was no intention that the correction and expression of regret should be hidden.

The Press Council held that the correction was insufficient and upheld the complaint. (1966/93-5)

SIZE OF A CORRECTION

The *Daily Telegraph* published a story about wounded American marines having been executed after they had been ambushed by North Vietnamese troops. The following day the newspaper published a statement from the United States Military Command in Saigon which said that there was no evidence to substantiate the story.

A reader complained that the headlines of this article were less than half the height of those in the original report and only a fraction of the length; nor did it have the same prominence. The complainant contended that many readers who saw the original report would not notice the smaller correction.

The Press Council held that the correction published in the *Daily Telegraph* was sufficient. (1967)

IN WHAT EDITIONS CORRECTION SHOULD BE PUBLISHED

SMOKING IN OMNIBUSES

The Secretary of the Society of Non-Smokers complained that *The Times* had failed to publish a correction of an inaccurate report of a ruling given by the Ministry of Transport on smoking in omnibuses.

The Editor, Sir William Haley, admitted that the original report was faulty; at a later date a clarification in the earlier editions had been published, but this had to give way during the night to other news.

The Press Council expressed its regret that in view of the admittedly faulty nature of the original report, which had been published in a prominent position in the newspaper, arrangements had not been made for the clarification to appear in all editions instead of in the early ones only. (1960/30–1)

A GILES CARTOON

A cartoon by Giles depicted a country sub-post office with an unprepossessing postmistress knitting behind the counter on which was exhibited a notice 'Working to rule — G.P.O.' Standing at the counter were four old-age pensioners, and the caption read 'Calling me an idle old faggot won't get you your pension any faster'.

The National Federation of Sub-postmasters protested; the caption was particularly resented because sub-postmasters and sub-postmistresses were not taking part in the 'work-to-rule' action. Six days later the *Daily Express* published an official letter of correction in some, but not all, editions, and the Federation contended that it should have been printed in all editions in which the cartoon had appeared.

The Editor, Mr Roger Wood, accepted this, and said that the partial omission in this instance was caused by an error during the pressure of production. He had apologised to the Federation; Giles had drawn the cartoon in good humour and with no ill-feeling.

The Press Council found that the Editor was at fault in not ensuring that the correction of the error appeared in all editions. (1962/39–40)

HOAXER'S BOGUS INFORMATION

Through failure to check the authenticity of telephone information which proved to be bogus, the *Scottish Daily Express* reported that the Inverness branch of the National Union of Railwaymen was opposed to a proposed national one-day strike. In fact the branch was overwhelmingly in favour.

The information was published under the heading 'North rail men defy strike call'.

The District Council of the N.U.R. informed the newspaper of the mistake, but, although the Editor acknowledged the complaint and the fact that the newspaper had been misled, no correction was published. He told the N.U.R. that investigations were being made into the identity of the hoaxer. Five months later the Editor said the hoaxer had still not been traced.

The Editor, Mr Ian McColl, told the Press Council that there was apparent acceptance by the N.U.R. that the report had been published in good faith and that no further action was expected until the hoaxer had been identified. A correction had appeared in the *Scottish Sunday Express* the day after the publication in the *Scottish Daily Express*.

The Press Council decided that the reference to the matter in the *Scottish Sunday Express* only was not a sufficient retraction. (1963/47–8)

CORRECTION ADEQUATE WITHOUT APOLOGY

ERRONEOUS DEATH ANNOUNCEMENT

A man was erroneously reported in the gossip column of the *Daily Telegraph* to be dead. The following day a correction was published, and the columnist added: 'I am glad to say that, in fact, he is very much alive and perfectly fit.'

The man in question said he was horrified that the correction did not contain any expression of regret.

The Editor, Mr Maurice Green, stated the announcement was published in complete good faith and was corrected immediately they were informed of the inaccuracy. He regretted the omission of an apology.

The Press Council held that the newspaper had taken immediate and appropriate action to draw the attention of their readers to the error and, although the correction would have been better expressed with a note of regret, the important element of righting a wrong was achieved without delay. The complaint was rejected. (1965/85)

ALLEGED INACCURACY NOT SIGNIFICANT

An article in the *Daily Telegraph* reporting the Gallup Poll figures was alleged to be inaccurate on two points — the number of by-elections contested by Liberal candidates and the proportion of electors who had voted Liberal. The newspaper corrected the first point but contested the inaccuracy of the second.

The Press Council accepted the acknowledgment of the error, and expressed the view that it did not consider the percentage of Liberal votes cast to be of important relevance to the point of the article. (1962/48)

ELECTION RESULT ERROR

In reporting the results of elections to the Essex County Council the *Billericay Times* said that a candidate had won a seat by 2,000 votes, whereas the true majority was 200. The mistake was repeated in another page of the same edition.

A member of the public complained that the newspaper had been guilty of deliberate distortion, of failing to publish a correction and of political bias.

The Managing Editor admitted the error, which he said was due to a misunderstanding in a telephone message. In the next week's issue a letter from the defeated candidate had been published, calling attention to the error, and a special correction was also printed in the district edition which served the election area.

The Press Council decided that there had been no deliberate distortion of news. The error was adequately corrected by a letter in one publication and an apology in another. (1962/45)

A VICAR MISQUOTED

Princess Anne was in the congregation at St George's Church, Benenden, when the vicar preached a sermon in which he was reported in the *Daily Telegraph* as saying: 'There is an obsession with sex. You cannot read or hear anything, or go to any cinema, without it being brought in. Forget it. It is only a trifle.' Complaint was made that the report omitted from the end of the quotation the words 'compared with the search for the Kingdom of God'.

The complainant alleged that this kind of reporting undermined the values on which our quality as a nation depends.

The Managing Editor of the newspaper, Sir Colin Coote, stated that the reporter had a note of the sermon; it did not contain the remark about 'the Kingdom'. The reporter did not contend that the Vicar had not said this, but if he had, he did not hear it. There was no question of a deliberate omission. A corrected version of the sermon later appeared in the newspaper.

The *Observer* did not report the sermon, but in an introduction to an article on sex education quoted the remark, 'Forget it. It is a trifle.' In its next issue the newspaper published a letter from the vicar in which he stated the words he had in fact used.

A complaint was made that an editorial apology should have been appended to the vicar's letter.

The Press Council held that both the *Daily Telegraph* and the *Observer* publications were made in good faith with every reason to believe they were accurate, and when these were challenged both newspapers published corrected versions. (1964/37–8)

CHRISTMAS PARTIES

The Chairman of a firm in Gloucester complained of misrepresentation by the *Daily Mail* and of improper conduct by a reporter.

A news story stated that 'Workers at a Gloucester factory will be sacked on the spot if they drink alcohol at Christmas parties in the works. The warning of instant dismissal was sent out yesterday to 1,400 employees . . .'.

In fact the notice issued by the firm stated that the management was reluctant to interfere with established practice regarding Christmas parties for works and offices but found it necessary to decide that 'no alcoholic beverages of any nature whatever would be consumed in the works on December 23rd. Any employee disregarding this direction will be liable to instant dismissal'.

The Chairman complained that the *Daily Mail*'s wording of the notice was a misrepresentation, that the regret for the necessity to issue the edict was inaccurately paraphrased and that it was gross impropriety for any newspaper reporter to ring up a business establishment outside business hours and interview someone who chanced to answer the telephone.

The Managing Editor of the newspaper, Mr E. V. Matthewman, said that over-enthusiasm for the cause of road safety seemed to have led a normally reliable reporter to record the spirit of the decision more accurately than the precise way in which it was communicated. He denied that there was any impropriety in the interview with the member of the firm. An apology had been made to the Chairman, but an offer to publish a correction was declined.

The Press Council upheld the complaint of misrepresentation and inaccuracy, but said that these had been adequately dealt with by the

Editor's apology. The complaint of impropriety of asking an employee for his views was rejected. (1965/37–8)

RIGHT TO CORRECTION NOT ESTABLISHED

DENIAL OF ANTI-SEMITISM

The Board of Deputies of British Jews complained of an inaccurate report in the *News Chronicle* that the man Podola, later hanged for the murder of a London policeman, was 'of Polish-Jewish extraction'. No correction was published, nor was there any expression of regret for what was described as 'the justifiable resentment felt by the Anglo-Jewish community'.

The Editor of the *News Chronicle*, Mr N. S. Cursley, admitted that the paper had been misinformed, but the description was amended the following day as soon as the truth was known. The suggestion of anti-Semitism was resented.

The Press Council decided to take no action, and declared that there was no substance in the Board's implied suggestion that the publication of an admitted error showed anti-Semitic motives. (1960/25–6)

A LETTER TO THE QUEEN

The Secretary to the Council of Women's Kindred Societies was instructed to protest to the appropriate authorities at the inclusion in the Royal Command Variety Performance of a mission hall scene from 'Guys and Dolls'.

Mr John Gordon in the *Sunday Express* criticised the lady for writing personally to the Queen on the subject and also because, as he alleged, she was largely responsible for having the scene censored.

The lady said she had written to the Queen not in her personal capacity but as the Secretary of the Societies, and she complained that the newspaper had failed to publish a statement to this effect.

The Press Council in its adjudication said that on the fuller information it had, it could not ask the *Sunday Express* to publish a letter from the complainant. The Council also stated that the resolution passed by the Societies did not include an instruction for the Secretary to forward it to the Queen. Her complaint to the Press Council was gravely misleading because it omitted the essential point that she had complained to the Queen. In her letter to the Council and to the *Sunday Express* she stated she had only written to the Queen to convey loyal greetings. (1954/26)

EDITOR REFUSED TO WITHDRAW REPORT OF SPEECH

The *Shields Gazette* reported a speech at a political meeting in which allegations were made against four people including the complainant. The charges made were later withdrawn, but the Editor had refused to publish a statement in his newspaper. He gave his reasons for refusing the request to the Press Council which held that the report of the meeting was fair and that the action taken by the Editor was correct. The reasons were not divulged. (1959/24)

AN OBVIOUS SLIP

The *Yorkshire Evening Press* carried a news story which was headlined 'Trade Gap has Widened by £103 Millions'. The report included the sentence, 'The balance of trade, the crude gap between total exports and imports, widened to £103m. from £92m. in October'. Complaint was made about the absence of a correction or apology for the erroneous headline; readers would believe the headline, and not bother to read further or work out what the actual increase was.

The Editor-in-Chief of the paper, Mr G. R. Hardacre, said that most people would realise that the figure was a mistake, particularly as the correct statement was published in the report.

The Press Council decided that the slip in the heading was obvious and was not repeated in the article. Publication of a correction was a matter for the discretion of an editor. (1965/34)

REASONABLE OPPORTUNITY TO COMMENT

OPPORTUNITY FOR CORRECTION OFFERED

Must a newspaper, as a matter of principle, withhold publication of a statement by a responsible organisation on a matter of public interest, in order to give another public body contesting the accuracy of the statement time to consider what it wished to say in refutation? This was the issue when the

Winsford (Cheshire) Urban District Council complained of a report in the *Manchester Evening News*. The report stated that the Winsford Ratepayers' Association claimed that Manchester's overspill scheme at Winsford had failed and that Winsford Council was having to speed up demolition schemes to fill empty houses.

The Clerk of the Winsford Council said that when a reporter telephoned and invited his comments he had stated that parts of the statement were inaccurate, but he was not prepared to comment extemporarily. The reporter, however, had pointed out that the matter had to be published that day.

The Editor-in-Chief of the *Manchester Evening News*, Mr T. E. Henry, said that the Winsford Council had been told what the Ratepayers' Association had said, and the opportunity to reply was rejected. It was argued on behalf of the Winsford Council that a newspaper did not have the right to coerce anyone into giving an extempore comment over the telephone under the implied threat that otherwise information would be published irrespective of its truth or falsity.

Mr Henry replied that the newspaper had not been asked to publish a rebuttal which would have been done had the request been made.

The Press Council held that the *Manchester Evening News* had afforded the Winsford Council a reasonable opportunity to state for publication its view in reply to the statement of the Ratepayers' Association. The complaint was rejected. (1964/42–3)

12 Taste

CARTOONS

Taste is a quality most people claim for themselves and find lacking in others. It is difficult to define and varies in meaning according to the context. Taste is never static and what is acceptable today may not be so tomorrow. For the journalist taste has a negative connotation and describes something which on grounds of decency and propriety or because it unnecessarily causes distress should not be published.

Because opinions differ about what is suitable for publication offence will be taken by some at words, text, cartoons and pictures which others find unobjectionable. The change of the world of yesterday to the world of today is painful and difficult for those who yearn for standards that have been abandoned. Complaints of infringement of taste often merely signify a rigid resistance to change. Bernard Shaw thought so when he said that a man of taste is a man without originality or moral courage.

The Press Council made it clear from the outset that it would not use a nineteenth-century yardstick to judge the twentieth. In its first Annual Report the Council stated:

> Some of the critics probably hold that young persons ought to be shielded not merely against evil but against knowledge of evil. But how many people can hope to go through life without coming into close acquaintance from time to time with its sordid side? The grown up man and the grown up woman must know the perils against which they have to be on guard and against which they should guard children. A newspaper would be of little use to them as a moral guide if it gave only an idealised picture of life.

The following year the Council stated that it could not condone the vulgarity, triviality and sheer bad manners of some journals. Nevertheless the material conditions of human life, the Council pointed out, had altered more radically in the first half of the century than in all previous history, and with the new conditions had come unprecedented moral and social changes. Two world wars had shattered conventions, inhibitions and former standards of conduct. What would have shocked people at the beginning of the century was now accepted without question. A case in point was the public attitude towards divorce. Fifty years ago divorce involved social ostracism and virtual disqualification from political, professional and public advancement for both the guilty and the innocent party. The law, too, was stern in its judgment, restrictive in its remedies and unfair in its discrimination against women. In consequence the number of divorces did not amount to more than a few hundred each year.

The picture today is a very different one. The climate of public opinion has changed completely; divorce now carried no stigma; the former deterrents have ceased to operate; the grounds for divorce have been increased, and the sexes have equal rights before the law. The divorces granted each year are now counted not in hundreds but in tens of thousands.

The world the Press Council has to deal with is the world mirrored in the popular Press. There are many people who disapprove both of the changes taking place and of the newspapers that reflect them. In a letter to the *Daily Telegraph* in 1955, for instance, a noble lord wrote:

> For too long have we writhed under the excesses of the gutter Press. . . .
> No domestic privacy is safe from the attacks of these jackals. They pry
> into hospital wards and subject surgeons, engaged in the most critical
> cases, to third-degree interrogations. They exploit the grief of the
> bereaved in every tragedy. The pall-bearers of the coffin are shot at by
> the cameras of these ghouls, the discharged criminals are greeted at the
> prison gates with the searchlight of merciless publicity.

In the last analysis it is the public which controls what the Press publishes; the Press Council interprets public opinion in deciding what is permissible. An instance occurred after the trial at the Old Bailey in 1960 of the book *Lady Chatterley's Lover*. The *Spectator*, the *Guardian* and the *Observer* reported the 'four-letter' words in the novel on which the trial had largely turned. The Press Council issued a statement that the publication of these words was both objectionable and unnecessary. In general the Press, the Council added, had shown that a court case of this kind could be adequately and broadmindedly covered without debasing standards of decency. (1961/2, 32)

All three journals complained of discourteous treatment because the Press Council had not informed them that their case was to be considered and had condemned them unheard. The Council replied that there are occasions when newspapers fall short of the standards expected of them. The publication of the four-letter words could only have been the result of a deliberate editorial decision; the Council believed that it was a wrong decision and that it was the Council's duty to say so. The matter was too urgent for delay.

When challenged by the *Spectator* on the procedure it had adopted, the Press Council issued a further statement in which it said that no specific complaint had been lodged against the *Spectator* nor was there any issue of fact since it was not in dispute that the words had been published. In the circumstances, the Council said, there had been no necessity to. (1961/32–33)

Words which are forbidden today may be in colloquial use tomorrow and completely respectable the day afterwards. The Press Council considered the four-letter words were still forbidden and, despite all that had been said in their justification at the trial and afterwards, were still too offensive to public sensibilities to be suitable for publication in newspapers.

Frequently when an infringement of taste is alleged a strong case for and against the charge can be made. On the occasion of the Munich air crash, for instance, pictures showing the seriously injured members of the Manchester United football team lying in oxygen tents were regarded by some as a violation of privacy and in the worst taste; others thought the pictures were justified because they showed that in a hospital in another country the men were receiving devoted and expert care.

The responsibility of deciding whether or not to publish when a question of taste is involved is the editor's. The cases below are those where the editor's judgment has been challenged before the Press Council.

The reporting of unpleasant details in court proceedings is dealt with in Chapter 15.

TEXT

CALLOUS STATEMENT

The *People* published an article referring to a motor-car accident in which Don Manuel Casanova Carreras, Vice-President of London's Club

Taurino, met his death. The article commented: 'Pity it was not by a bull in the ring. Don Manuel would have been so proud. And so would the bull.'

Complaint was made that this comment on a distinguished journalist, war correspondent and former Civil Governor was inhuman.

The Editor of the *People*, Mr Stuart Campbell, said that the comment had been misinterpreted. It simply meant that Don Manuel, who was an enthusiastic supporter of the bullfight, would have preferred to have met his end in the bull ring rather than in an ordinary motor-car.

The Press Council held that the comment was callous and should not have been printed. (1962/46)

PATHETIC MENTAL CASE

The *Daily Mirror* published a report under the heading, 'Police chase nude and her dog in street'. The report described how a young woman stripped in public, ran along the street and was taken away by the police.

The complaint to the Press Council alleged that the report was cruel, unnecessary and increased the anguish of the girl and her family. It was obvious that mental illness was involved, and the Press should have the decency to ignore such cases.

Mr L. A. Lee Howard, the Editor of the *Daily Mirror*, said that the newspaper would not deliberately publish any story which might have a detrimental effect on anybody's mental state. Almost every news story might upset somebody. The girl had not been identified in the report.

The Press Council said that it could not lay down a general policy that cases of this kind should not be reported. The matter must be left to the discretion of the editor. In this case the girl's name had not been published. The complaint was rejected. (1965/94–5)

BLASPHEMOUS EXPRESSIONS

In a report in the *Sun* of an interview with Mr R. R. of the B.B.C., the reporter quoted him as using the expressions 'Christ! What do they mean?' and 'By God'.

A reader took exception and said the article was bound to give offence to every Christian reader. The Editorial Director of the *Sun*, Mr Sydney Jacobson, said that the intention of the article was to let Mr R. R. express himself in his own way, and this would not have been achieved if the newspaper had tried to censor his language.

The complainant replied that if Mr R. R. had used some obscene language the newspaper would not have printed it. The newspaper did have to censor the language of people interviewed. Mr Jacobson agreed, but did not accept that the words complained of were blasphemous in their context.

The Press Council regretted the use of the expression 'Christ! What do they mean?' in the report, believing that it lowered the standards of journalism. (1966/56–7)

FAITH AND GOOD FAITH

An advertisement in the births column of the *St Helen's Reporter* read 'CHRIST — to Mary and Joseph, at Nazareth, today (Saturday) 25th December, a son, Jesus. "Praise Be to God" '.

A complaint was made that the publication was in bad taste and that it was factually inaccurate.

On behalf of the newspaper, the point was made that the inter-denominational organisation responsible for the advertisement consisted of young people anxious to get the true meaning of Christmas over to the general public. The newspaper did not agree that it was in bad taste.

The Press Council held that while the advertisement was capable of being misunderstood, the Council was satisfied that it was tendered and published in good faith for a religious purpose, and rejected the complaint. (1966/102–3)

ADVICE TO THE UNDER-SIXTEENS

Two fourteen-year-old girls at boarding-school wrote to the teenage magazine *Marilyn* representing themselves to be fifteen and asking for advice on how they could get two boys who treated them as 'ordinary friends' to think more of them. In a written reply they were advised that each should squeeze the boy's hand tenderly, rest her head on his shoulder and hold her mouth up for a kiss.

The father of one of the girls complained that this sort of advice was 'designed to undermine morals' and that children below the age of sixteen should be protected, just as they were prevented from seeing X-certificate films in the cinema.

Mr Michael Butterworth, the Managing Editor, said the letter to the girls was reprehensible and indefensible and should never have been sent. Disciplinary action had already been taken.

The Press Council endorsed the views expressed and the action taken. (1962/49)

FIFTEEN-YEAR-OLD GIRL AND FOUR-LETTER WORD

'I shudder to think what depths the British Press would sink to if other organs were to follow your example', wrote a correspondent to the *Sunday Telegraph*. His complaint arose out of the publication in the newspaper of a letter from a fifteen-year-old girl which it was said glorified the use of an obscene word. The publication constituted nothing less, the complainant said than a wicked incitement to the young to throw every restraint to the wind and base their code of behaviour on the negation of all moral precepts.

The girl's letter said: 'And just what does Mrs Whitehouse think she is? A protector of poor innocent little children? Pooh! I am sure that half the children, in fact more, know that four-letter word.'

The letter continued: 'I hope the 21st century will not turn me into a fussy old —— who will try to put the clock back to the days when —— was not allowed to be said in public.'

The Editor, Mr Brian R. Roberts, denied that the publication of the letter was irresponsible. What the newspaper did was to demonstrate the climate which existed in a girl's public school. That surely was a matter of considerable public interest.

The Press Council held that the publication was a matter for editorial discretion and rejected the complaint. (1966/91–2)

HOSTILITY TO MINORITY GROUPS

The Rev. W. W. Simpson, General Secretary of the Council of Christians and Jews, called attention to the occasional appearance in children's papers of articles and pictures calculated to stimulate attitudes of prejudice and hostility to minority groups in juvenile minds. A particular case was a serialised pictorial version of *Oliver Twist*. The representation of Fagin,

Mr Simpson said, conformed exactly to the traditional caricature of 'the Jew' which was revived with such disastrous results in Nazi Germany.

Mr Simpson said it was no part of his council's intention to suggest the imposition of any kind of censorship or to discourage the reading of English classics in their proper perspective.

The Press Council agreed to give publicity to the letter. (1958/29)

PHOTOGRAPHS

INCIDENT AT CATHEDRAL CONSECRATION

During the consecration of Coventry Cathedral in 1962 the Lord Mayor, who was in the congregation behind the members of the Royal Family, fainted. A rota photographer, operating for all newspapers, took a picture of the incident showing the Lord Mayor slumped on the floor with his head resting on a chair.

Four national newspapers printed the picture, but the *Daily Express* was the only one reported to the Press Council. The complaint was that the picture was in bad taste and must have caused embarrassment and distress to the Lord Mayor.

The Editor of the *Daily Express*, Mr Roger Wood, maintained that the picture illustrated the most dramatic incident of the ceremony. The Press Council upheld the Editor and stated that the newspaper was fully entitled to publish the picture of an incident which had occurred during an important public event. (1963/32)

FANCY DRESS

The *Sunday Mirror* published a picture of a boy and a girl at a fancy dress parade at Carnoustie, Scotland. The boy, aged two, was wearing morning dress and a bowler hat and carrying an umbrella and a dispatch case on which was the name 'J. Profumo'. The girl, his three-year-old sister, was in a bikini with a towel draped over her shoulders. In the accompanying text she was said to represent Christine Keeler. The publication bore the heading: 'Now *was* this a good idea?'

The mother stated that it was just a joke, and the father said that nothing improper was intended; it was all light-hearted fun.

The article stated that critical letters had appeared in the local newspaper at Carnoustie, and that a Carnoustie Councillor and Minister had remarked that although the fancy dress was not in the best taste, no malice was intended, and the incident was good publicity for Carnoustie.

Complaint was made that the appearance of the children in public was bad enough, but the publication of the picture for all the world to see was revolting.

The Editor of the *Sunday Mirror*, Mr R. T. Payne, said he shared the general distaste at the idea of parading the children in public. His attitude was indicated in the headline and in the reference to local criticism. It was a matter of public interest that the influence of the Profumo case was spreading in this way.

The Press Council agreed that the incident and the publication of the photograph were in bad taste. The *Sunday Mirror* should have expressed its views in the text of the article, and not by publishing the photograph which served only to extend the offensiveness. (1964/53)

PICTURES SHOULD NOT CAUSE NEEDLESS DISTRESS

An official protest was made by Sir John Lang, Secretary of the Admiralty, on behalf of the Lords Commissioners of the Admiralty, at the publication of pictures of a Scimitar aircraft which crashed when being embarked in H.M.S. *Victorious*. Most of the national daily newspapers published photographs showing on a small scale the attempt made from a helicopter to free the pilot of the crashed aircraft before it sank, and the Admiralty had no objection to these photographs. The *Daily Herald*, *News Chronicle* and *Daily Sketch* published greatly enlarged pictures showing the pilot trapped in the cockpit accompanied by lurid headlines and captions.

The Lords Commissioners stated they were content to leave to the Press Council the questions of decency and taste arising from the publication of pictures which had been enlarged to draw attention to the situation of a man about to die a sudden horrible death. The pictures had caused deeply felt disgust in the Fleet, had added to the anguish of the relatives and friends of the dead pilot and caused distress and anxiety to the relatives and friends of all aircrew of the Fleet Air Arm. The Lords Commissioners hoped that the publication of similar material in the future would be discouraged.

In the *Daily Herald* the enlarged photograph carried a sub-heading reading: 'Doomed Plane lands on the Deck and then comes the Crash that Pilots Feared and Warned might happen.' The Admiralty said that the sub-heading was not supported by text nor by evidence, and was calculated to

H 2   L.T.P.C.

undermine the confidence of aircrew. In view of the special facilities accorded to the Press, the Lords Commissioners would have expected more consideration for naval sentiment in the treatment of the tragic accident. They were informing officers and men of the complaint to the Press Council.

The Editorial Manager of the *Daily Herald*, Mr A. Mellor, said the picture undoubtedly emphasised and dramatised the plight of the doomed pilot. The publication was a problem of taste, but he challenged the Admiralty's view that such pictures caused disgust in the Fleet and distress to the relatives. The evidence showed that the disgust occurred at Admiralty and senior officer level, not amongst the rank and file. The heading objected to was justified by material that had been cut for space reasons, and the *Daily Herald* regretted the deletion. If, however, the condition of a facility visit was that special treatment should be given, the Press would have to reconsider its attitude. Mr Mellor thought it astonishing that the Admiralty should circulate their complaint to the Navy after referring it to the Press Council, when it should have been regarded as *sub judice*.

The Chief Assistant Editor of the *News Chronicle*, Mr Colquhoun, denied that there was anything repellent in the picture they published. Particular care had been taken to avoid giving any grounds for complaint.

The Editor of the *Daily Sketch*, Mr Herbert Gunn, quoted from a speech he had made to the Institute of Journalists, in which he stated: 'In a long document of almost unparalleled pomposity, and in language redolent of the white walls of old England, the Lords of the Admiralty have reported the newspapers to the Press Council. I would like to know whether the Admiralty intend to send another signal when the Press Council has decided on their complaint.'

The substance of the adjudication of the Press Council was that the Council considered the pictures bore remarkable testimony to the spirit of the Navy, and the general effect of their publication was to increase the nation's admiration for brave men.

Whilst it is the function of newspapers to provide a true pictorial record of current events, the Council believed that they should take great care to ensure that the selection and presentation of photographs did not cause needless distress. The Press generally observed that standard on this occasion.

The *News Chronicle* and the *Daily Sketch* overemphasised the situation of the trapped pilot, but this did not deserve the severe criticism of the Admiralty.

The *Daily Herald*'s presentation showed a lack of humanity.

The Council asked that the statement should be circulated to the Fleet. (1959/17, 26–9)

COLOURING A WOUND

The *Sunday Times* was accused of 'cheap sensationalism' for superimposing red colouring on a black-and-white photograph of an African to give the impression of a bloodstain.

Mr Harold Evans, Joint Managing Editor of the newspaper, said that the picture was a genuine photograph of a news incident in which an African had been wounded. The caption supplied with the picture by a news agency stated that blood was streaming from a wound when the man was marched off to a police station after rioting in Salisbury, Rhodesia. The wound in the man's head could be clearly seen on the print, and it was common practice to overlay a single colour on monoprints. Far from being cheaply sensational the treatment of a print with a Kodatrace overlay had produced an accurate result.

The Press Council held that the publication of the picture and the use of the particular process was a matter for the Editor's discretion. The complaint was rejected. (1967)

PICTURE OF CHILDBIRTH

When the *Sun* published a photograph of the birth of a baby, a complainant objected to 'such a picture in such a visible part (or any part) of a daily newspaper where any of my young children cannot help but see it and be curious. I want to be the one to tell my children about childbirth, when I consider they are old enough to really understand the subject.'

The Editor of the *Sun*, Mr Sydney Jacobson, said that some readers had praised the picture not only for itself but for the help it gave them in explaining childbirth to their children. He added:

I considered possible objections to the picture very carefully before I decided to print it, since I knew it would be controversial. The conclusion I came to was that in an age of frankness, when the facts of birth are known to most children at an early age, when there is sex instruction at many schools and indeed the whole process of childbirth has been shown on television, we were justified in publishing this picture.

Four days after the publication the newspaper printed seventeen readers' letters. Eleven objected to the publication and six congratulated the Editor on his courage.

The Press Council held that the picture was entirely a question of taste and publication properly fell within the discretion of the Editor. (1965/77–8)

A HARMLESS PICTURE

A picture taken during the filming of *Cleopatra* depicting the assassination of Caesar was published in the *Daily Sketch* and was said by a complainant to cheapen life and encourage violence. The Press Council, however, decided that the picture was so theatrical as to be harmless, and it noted that the adjoining picture, showing 'Caesar' and one of his 'assassins' lunching together after the 'stabbing' removed any possible doubt about the intention of the feature. (1962/50)

A GRUESOME PICTURE

A picture in the *Exmouth Journal* showed the victim of a road accident being taken away in a coffin. The accompanying report described how the man was killed instantly and continued: 'It seems unlikely that one will ever see a car accident photograph that so completely conveys finality. We know it is shocking. But traffic accidents are shocking. We suspect this photograph may become a poster in a national road safety campaign.'

The man's wife and two daughters complained through solicitors of the publication of the picture, which they said was without their consent and before the burial of the deceased. The picture was particularly gruesome, depicting not only the smashed vehicle but also the coffin with the body partially revealed.

The Editor of the newspaper, Mr John F. Day, said in defence that the easy way out for any editor is never to run anything that might upset somebody. They had nothing to gain by publishing this stark photograph except the probability they could save some people from killing or mangling themselves or others during this particularly dangerous period when the roads were icy.

The Press Council held that the publication of a picture as gruesome as the one in question could not be justified on the grounds of assisting the road safety campaign, and upheld the complaint. (1966/83–4)

ROAD ACCIDENT — PICTURE OF DYING WOMAN

The *Surrey Mirror* was accused of a distressing lapse of taste in publishing the picture of a road accident which showed a woman victim lying in the road. The caption read: 'Badly injured in a collision in a car at Linkfield Corner . . . this pedestrian was rushed to Redhill Hospital by ambulance, with severe head injuries, and died next day. . . .'

The Managing Editor, Mr C. G. Gegg, told the Council that the newspaper's sole object in printing the photograph was to bring home to readers what no amount of reading of fatal accidents appeared to do, that all road users had a personal responsibility for the appalling loss of life on the roads. He expected the picture to shock the public conscience, and that was its object.

The Press Council considered that the publication of the photograph could not be justified on the ground of assisting the road safety campaign and upheld the complaint. (1966/84)

DEATH ON THE ROADS

A photograph taken after a road accident was published in the *Southern Evening Echo* under the heading, 'Two youths die on Andover's Black Saturday'. The caption read:

Only a matter of minutes before this picture was taken two North Tidworth youths were riding happily and carefree on their scooter. Now both of them lie dead on either side of the white line. . . . We publish this picture not to pander to the morbid, but to bring home once again the fact that the roads of Britain are becoming more and more dangerous and taking increasing toll of life.

The father of one of the boys said the picture had caused him and his family the greatest distress.

The Editor of the *Southern Evening Echo*, Mr Rodney Andrew, said they received hundreds of pictures of motor accidents and on this occasion decided to try to bring home to the reader the real meaning of the toll on the roads. That was the purpose and the only purpose of printing the picture.

The Press Council said that though the picture caused distress to the relatives and this was regrettable, nevertheless the motive which prompted publication was a perfectly proper one. (1966/52)

A PICTURE OF SIAMESE TWINS

A photograph appeared in the *People* of almost naked Siamese twins with a story reporting how a team of doctors had to decide whether to perform an operation. The babies were said to be 'incomplete twins', being fused from the waist down into a single body.

The complainant thought the photograph showed deplorable lack of public responsibility and deserved the heaviest condemnation. It was bound to cause mental anguish to mothers-to-be. The publication was a deplorable pandering to base instincts.

The Editor, Mr Stuart Campbell, said the complainant was the only one out of fifteen million readers to object. He thought it ridiculous to suppose that people accustomed to reading about Siamese twins and seeing live television pictures taken during serious operations would be shocked at a picture of two babies who were happy in spite of being malformed.

The Press Council held that the publication of the picture was a matter of taste within the discretion of the Editor, and rejected the complaint. (1966/82–3)

EXECUTION OF A TURKISH MINISTER

The *Sunday Telegraph* published a picture which showed the execution by hanging of a former Turkish minister. The Council said the publication was a matter of taste upon which it was impossible to lay down hard and fast rules. Such matters must be left to the discretion of editors. (1962/47)

TEARS AT A WEDDING

The *Daily Express* published a photograph of Miss Maureen Swanson, the actress, weeping at her wedding to Lord Ednam.

The Council held that the picture was not objectionable. (1962/47)

AN UNDESIRABLE PICTURE

The Salvation Army complained of a picture published in the *Daily Sketch* showing a two-year-old girl drinking from a bottle of stout.

The Press Council declared the publication as being against the public interest, since it was illegal to give alcoholic liquor to a child under five years of age except with a doctor's prescription or in an emergency.

The Council said that the picture should never have been taken and that pictures of this nature ought never to be published. (1956/35)

DISGUSTING OR ARTISTIC?

Complaint was made of a female study by Hatami, the distinguished French photographer, published in the *Sunday Mirror*. The complainant contended that impressionable youngsters had to be considered and that, if the female was to be portrayed, the pictures should be an inspiration, not a provocation.

The Editor, Mr Michael Christiansen, replied that the complainant was probably more shocked than the younger generation for whom he was concerned. In an age when sex instruction was given in many schools, and when the configuration of the human body was no longer a mystery, it was difficult to believe that any young person would be shocked, let alone corrupted, by the picture.

The Press Council held that the publication of the photograph was a matter of taste within the Editor's discretion. (1966/87)

A HUMAN TORCH

A picture published in the *Daily Mail* was described as 'obscene and objectionable' by a number of complainants. It showed a racing motor-car driver blazing like a human torch and was calculated, it was said, to cause distress to the relatives and friends of the victim and great upset to impressionable children.

The Editor, Mr Michael Randall, said he had the greatest sympathy for the victim, his relatives and friends, but it was essentially the accident that caused the distress, not the report and photograph. The motor-racing crash was not a private matter, but a public event before a paying audience and was legitimately exposed to newspaper reporting, broadcasting and television.

The objection to publication of the picture was equivalent to saying that the only accident that could be photographed was one in which no harm came to anybody and that only good news should be printed.

The newspaper published a selection of readers' letters objecting to the picture, and in an editorial footnote observed that pictures of war, starving children and victims of flood and earthquake were neither more or less horrifying than the picture of the crash. To ignore horror was not to avert it.

The Press Council said the picture was one of a grim public event before a paying audience, and it could properly be made a subject for public record. The complaint was rejected. (1966/84–5)

DEAD GIRL IN WRECKED AIRCRAFT

The *Sunday Mirror* published a picture of a dead girl hanging from a wrecked aircraft. Eighteen of the girl's friends and colleagues complained that they were shocked by the picture which they described as vulgar sensationalism. What effect it would have had on the girl's mother had she seen it was unimaginable.

The Editor, Mr Michael Christiansen, said that every tragedy inevitably caused grief to the relatives and friends of the victims, but it was the function of a newspaper to provide a pictorial record of current events. It was in the public interest that people should face the facts and realities of life and not try to escape them by closing their eyes.

The Press Council held that the picture was one that should not have been published because it caused unnecessary suffering and distress to relatives and friends and did not serve the public interest. (1966/85–6)

CARTOONS

THE QUEEN AND MR WILSON

An *Observer* cartoon depicted the Prime Minister before leaving for Rhodesia, kissing the hand of the Queen who was saying: 'Don't feel you need to fly back *each day* to report, Prime Minister.'

A reader complained the cartoon was discourteous to the Queen, and performed no service to Mr Wilson at a time of constitutional crisis, by its implication that substantial checks on the governing party in this country are tiresome and laughable.

The *Observer* informed the complainant that several letters protesting against the cartoon had been received, and one had been published with a footnote explaining the newspaper's view. The footnote read: 'Cartoons of royalty, including cartoons of reigning monarchs, have been published in this country for the last 200 years without diminution of the Royal Family's prestige. Certainly no unfriendliness was intended by Trog.'

Mr David Astor, Editor of the *Observer*, told the Press Council that the point of the cartoon was that Mr Wilson appeared to be consulting the Queen an unnecessary number of times about the Rhodesian crisis. This was a criticism of the Prime Minister, not of the Queen.

The Press Council held that the cartoon was not discourteous or offensive and rejected the complaint. (1966/81–2)

DUKE AND DUCHESS OF WINDSOR

A Trog cartoon in the *Observer*, published after the Duke of Windsor's eye operation, showed the Duke in dark glasses and a dressing-gown seated in a wheelchair in conversation with his wife. The Duchess was reported as saying '. . . and what she *didn't* seem to realise was that without me she wouldn't have *been* Queen.'

The Editor of the *Observer*, Mr David Astor, contended that the connection of the Duchess with the fact that Her Majesty is Queen was a proper point to make, but some people had gained the impression that the Duke's illness was being made a matter for satire. He regretted this accidental impression; he had published a letter of complaint.

The adjudication of the Press Council was that the cartoon was offensive and distasteful. The Council noted that the *Observer*, in publishing a strong criticism by a reader, had acknowledged receipt of other complaints. (1965/79)

PRESIDENT JOHNSON AND COLOUR PROBLEM

A cartoon by Cummings published in the *Daily Express* depicted President Johnson entangled in a large spiky tree representing coloured people, while near-by a man in blinkers described as 'M.P.s in favour of immigration' watered a crocus drawn with a face of a coloured person. The caption represented the President as saying: 'When ours was planted it looked like a crocus too.'

A complaint from Hertford College, Oxford, alleged: 'This cartoon distorts historical, political and social realities to express a view which is not merely in the lowest taste, but is a direct and calculated insult to coloured people both in Britain and America.' Other objections were also received.

The Editor of the *Daily Express*, Mr Robert Edwards, stated that to say the aim of the cartoon was to propagate racial unrest and bitterness was outrageous. It was contrary to the whole policy of the newspaper. The cartoon expressed the view that it would be folly to allow a situation in Britain akin to that in America, when control of immigration would enable our society to absorb people from the Commonwealth painlessly and on a basis of equality.

The Press Council rejected the complaint. (1965/80)

13 Royal Family: Right to Privacy

'You will I am sure readily agree that the Queen is entitled to expect that her family will attain the privacy at home which all other families are entitled to enjoy,' the Press Officer to the Queen, Commander (now Sir Richard) Colville wrote to the Press Council in 1955.

Scrupulous respect for the private lives of the members of the Royal Family has always been the aim of the Press Council. The Council recognises, however, the difficulty of reconciling the reasonable expectation of the Royal Family to privacy with the duty of the newspapers to meet the tremendous public interest in their activities and the desire for information not only about their official lives but also about their personal lives.

To say that the Queen is entitled to expect that she and her family should have the privacy at home which all other families are entitled to enjoy raised the question, the Press Council has said, whether a comparison of the Royal Family with other families is realistic. The private lives of public men and women, especially Royalty, have always been the subject of a natural curiosity. Everything that touches the Crown is of public interest, and there can be little escape from 'That fierce light which beats upon a throne'.

The newspapers are bound to record the movements of the Queen and the members of her family, but there are limits beyond which Royal tolerances should not be asked to go.

The Press Council tries to decide what these limits are, not only in regard to the way the news is obtained but also on the selection of items for publication.

Other cases involving the Royal Family will be found on pp. 48, 149 (*Daily Mirror*), 226, 227 (*Observer*).

The Council in 1956 made three suggestions for improving relations between the Palace and the Press, which were not all they should be.

1. The quality and supply of news and guidance from the Palace Secretariat should be improved.

2. Newspapers should refrain from tempting royal servants to break their contracts by offering large sums for their stories.

3. Royal news should at all times be handled with discretion.

MEMOIRS OF ROYAL SERVANTS

In 1954 Commander Colville challenged the Press Council on a ruling it gave in connection with the publication in the *Sunday Pictorial* of a series of articles by a former valet to the Duke of Edinburgh. The articles recounted the valet's experiences when he was in the service of the Duke; they covered the period of the Duke's honeymoon and of the trip with Princess Elizabeth to Kenya where she was when she learned that she had become the Queen on the death of her father King George VI.

A reader protested that to publish the revelations of a personal servant fell below the standards of journalism the Council was formed to maintain.

The Editor of the *Sunday Pictorial*, Mr Colin Valdar, said that he was satisfied with the authenticity of the material in the articles, which, in any event, was soon to be published as a book. None of the copy, he said, was derogatory to any of the persons mentioned.

The Press Council upheld the Editor. It had been the practice, the Council stated, for members of the staff at royal households to write their experiences, and no objection had generally been taken so long as intimate confidences were not betrayed or distress caused to members of the Royal Family. (1954/22, 37)

In a letter to the Press Council Commander Colville said that it had long been the custom that persons brought into contact by their work with the Sovereign or members of the Royal Family did not make their experiences the subject of books and articles. Because a small number broke the trust reposed in them did not change the fact that a trust existed. In recent years as an additional measure to ensure Royal privacy, a provision had been inserted in service contracts forbidding persons employed in the Royal Households to communicate to the Press information about the Queen or any member of the Royal Family acquired in the course of their employment.

Commander Colville's letter made it clear that the publication by a newspaper of the reminiscences of a former royal servant was regarded as aiding and abetting a breach of trust and possibly a breach of contract. The Press Council circulated the letter to the newspapers with a request that it should be seriously noted.

In 1956, some time after the publication of the articles by the Duke's valet, a series of articles by a former Deputy Comptroller of Supply to the Royal Family was published in the weekly magazine *Woman* under the headline, 'I shopped for our Royal Family'. There was no suggestion that the articles contained offensive or indiscreet material, but Commander Colville reminded the Press Council that the previous year the Council had requested all newspapers and periodicals to respect the privacy of the home life of the Queen and her family.

The Editor of *Woman*, Miss Mary Grieve, said that there was considerable precedent for the publication of recollections by those who have served the Royal Family. She believed that the readers of the magazine she edited were sincerely interested in the more personal and domestic life of the Royal Family and their affection for the Throne was largely sustained by an understanding of the home life of the Sovereign. The aim of the articles had been to achieve in broad terms an account of the ways by which the Royal Household had been adapted to the nation's changed life. She did not know whether the Queen's Press Secretary was complaining only about particular passages or whether he supported a ban on any information given to the Press about the personal activities of the Royal Family.

She did not think that the Council ever intended to support anything so restrictive on editorial freedom and discretion, nor did she suppose that the restrictive condition imposed on servants in the Royal Household could operate to make a breach of trust out of any information about the Royal Family that was communicated to a newspaper. She had taken care to inquire whether the former Deputy Comptroller had given any undertaking not to present his reminiscences for publication. He had assured Miss Grieve that he had not.

The Press Council said that while it accepted the assurance that no specific undertaking had been given not to publish reminiscences, the articles nevertheless infringed the spirit of the principles recently accepted by the Council.

Miss Grieve pursued the matter. She said she accepted with a sense of concern the Council's decision, but it left editors in some quandary. Since no definition was offered of the type of information that constituted an intrusion on the private life of the Sovereign, she was driven to the conclusion that the Council supported a policy of banning all statements by former servants that could in any way be related to the private lives of the Royal Family, without applying standards of taste and discretion in their judgment.

While she wished at all times to avoid causing the Queen and the Royal Family embarrassment she felt that any ruling which sought to raise a fence of silence round the Royal Family would not be in the lasting interest of the Sovereign. She suggested that the Council should review the whole problem.

The Council sent the letter to the Press Secretary, who expressed the view that publication of articles such as those in question, no matter what material they contained, infringed the Queen's privacy. (1956/23, 37–9)

Interest in the Royal Family is so intense that if newspapers cannot obtain information from official channels they would be forced to turn to unofficial ones. At the time the Press Council was established the Press Secretariat at the Palace, which had evolved over the years, had relations with the Press which were not very harmonious. In 1956 the Press Council drew attention to complaints by news editors that the Secretariat neither understood nor gave the news the Press wanted nor the necessary guidance on what was or what was not likely to become news. The Council recorded with regret that it would be lacking in candour if it pretended that dealings between the Press and the Press Secretariat in the Royal Household were always happy.

About the same time the *News Chronicle* declared, 'The fact remains that the present system is working badly. The British Royal Family are news — perhaps the most popular subject with the majority of the public. No paper can fail to report Royal news without failing its readers. It is high time the Press Department at the Palace recognised the truth of this truism.'

The Press Council invited editors and news editors to state in what respect they considered the Secretariat had not fulfilled expectations, to give specific instances and suggest how improvements could be made. A representative selection of replies was sent to Commander Colville, and the Council invited him to a meeting. The Commander accepted, and the meeting took place on 21 January 1958. There was a frank discussion of the problems on both sides, during which the Commander dealt with the criticism made by the editors and explained what was being done at the Palace to meet it. One of the principal complaints was that the Press Department was under-staffed. Command Colville told the Council that an additional secretary was to be appointed.

The meeting was a useful one and the hope was expressed that the contact established and the co-operation agreed upon would benefit the Palace and the Press.

A ROYAL ROMANCE

Press reports on the Royal Family have been the subject of complaints to the Press Council on a number of occasions both before and since that meeting. The newly born Council at its first meeting gave attention to a publication which caused considerable controversy. The names of Princess Margaret and Group-Captain Townsend were being linked, and there was much speculation about a possible marriage. The gossip was brought into the open by an announcement in the *Daily Mirror* that the newspaper would conduct a poll among its readers on whether the Princess should be allowed, if she so desired, to marry the Group-Captain. The propriety of the poll was as hotly debated as the possible marriage. Many people thought that the publicity given to such a personal matter was in the worst taste and a shameful intrusion into the private lives of the couple; others, on the other hand, welcomed the poll as an opportunity to express their affection and sympathy for the Princess or register their disapproval of the alliance according to the view they took.

The Press Council after considering what a complainant described as the 'grossly impertinent and unseemly speculations' made this announcement:

That this meeting of the Press Council, while conscious of the great interest of the public in the lives of members of the Royal Family, strongly deprecates as contrary to the best traditions of British journalism the holding by the *Daily Mirror* of a public poll in the matter of Princess Margaret and Group-Captain Townsend.   (1954/21–2)

Two years later the *Daily Mirror* published another front-page article headlined, 'Come on Margaret! Please make up your mind!' and 'For Pete's sake put him out of his misery'. The *Daily Mirror* later explained that the article was intended as a genial shout from the genial crowd. The newspaper took the view that it was nonsense to await an announcement from the Palace and cited the occasion when through the voluntary suppression of the news by the Press an astonished British public heard, when the silence was at length broken, of King Edward VIII's intention to marry Mrs Simpson although the public in every other country had known of it for some time. Affairs of state, such as the marriage of the Princess, the *Daily Mirror* said, were of vital public interest, and the public were entitled to know what was happening.

The Council disapproved of the headlines to the article, but nevertheless agreed there was much to be said for the *Daily Mirror*'s point of view. The Council recalled that after her return from the Caribbean some months previously a Sunday newspaper announced that the Princess had gone there to make up her mind whether she would or would not marry Group-Captain Townsend and thus renounce or retain her right of succession to the Throne.

When, following the Princess's return, the Group-Captain came here from Belgium and was in the Princess's company nearly every day until he left again, it was news, the Press Council said, which no paper could ignore. The situation was one which might involve Church and State, Crown and Constitution, and it was clearly the duty of the Press to keep the people informed day by day. The Council thought it right it said to mention these facts in order that some of the difficulties as well as some of the sins of the Press should be better understood. (1956/9–13)

The Princess did not marry the Group-Captain and when five years later she became engaged to marry Mr Anthony Armstrong-Jones she completely turned the tables on the Press. A statement announcing the engagement was issued on 26 February 1960 from Clarence House, the Princess's home. Publishing the news the next day under banner headlines the *Daily Mirror* described it as 'the announcement that surprised the world', which included Fleet Street. It transpired that the courtship had been going on for some time and had been conducted undetected under the eyes of Press men.

PRINCE CHARLES — REQUEST FOR PRIVACY

While the Press may often be an embarrassment to the Royal Family, the newspapers can be considerate where a reasonable request for restraint is made. Such an occasion occurred in 1955 when the Press Council was informed that the Queen and the Duke of Edinburgh had decided that Prince Charles had reached the age when he should take part in more grown-up educational pursuits with other children. This would involve the Prince attending school away from the Palace and visiting museums and other places of interest. The Queen and the Duke hoped he would be able to do so without constant publicity.

The Press Council notified the newspapers of the request and it was fully respected. (1955/15-16)

DUKE OF KENT'S 21ST BIRTHDAY PARTY

When the Duke of Kent became twenty-one his mother, the Duchess, gave a private party at her home at Coppins to celebrate the occasion.

A woman reporter of the *Daily Sketch* arrived at the front door and was shown by a footman to the ladies' cloakroom. He did not recognise her as an invited guest and reported her arrival to a lady-in-waiting who interviewed her. The reporter told her that she had forgotten her invitation, but that she was a personal friend of the Duke. The Duke was consulted, and as a result someone was sent to escort the reporter to the door. She turned and ran down a corridor but was caught and escorted off the premises by the police.

The next day the *Daily Sketch* published an article describing the reporter's visit including her arrival in the boot of a motor-car.

Two other uninvited freelance journalists who tried to attend the party were also escorted away.

The Queen's Press Secretary wrote to the Press Council saying that the Queen and the Duchess of Kent were seriously disturbed by these incidents. The letter proceeded to claim the right of privacy for the Royal Family in much the same terms as those quoted at the beginning of the chapter. On this occasion the Queen's Secretary said the family privacy was not only invaded in an improper manner, but the methods by which it was achieved bordered on deceit. Moreover the terms in which one of these incidents was reported did little to reduce the annoyance it caused. 'It is, perhaps, pertinent to note', the letter continued, 'that the Duchess of Kent especially authorised the issue of certain information concerning the private dinner party and subsequent dance, in order to provide newspapers and other publications with material regarding the Duke of Kent's 21st birthday.

The Press Council accepted the assurances of the Editors of two other newspapers that the two freelances were not representing their newspapers as they had alleged.

The Editor of the *Daily Sketch*, Mr Herbert Gunn, said that the Duke of Kent was so much a public figure and so prominent in the public eye that they had not fully appreciated the extent to which the party was a private one. He now realised he was wrong and expressed his apologies to the Queen and the Duchess of Kent.

The Press Council considered the Editor was guilty of violation of good manners by disregarding the Royal Family's wish to enjoy privacy in their own home. The Council said the apology expressed to the Queen and the Duchess should be repeated in the newspaper.

This was done. (1957/22–3, 31–2)

The better relations between the Palace Secretariat and Fleet Street established in 1958 have been reflected in the diminishing number of complaints against the Press. But invasion of Royal privacy, deliberate or inadvertent, is bound to recur from time to time.

PHOTOGRAPHERS TRESPASS IN A ROYAL PARK

In 1965 Commander (now Sir Richard) Colville, had occasion to write to the Press Council again. 'The Queen', he said, 'has noted with concern the attempts made by individual Press photographers over the past weeks to intrude on the privacy of Her Majesty and Her Royal Highness Princess Margaret, when they were using the grounds of Sunninghill Park for picnics and water-ski-ing.'

He went on to say that a number of photographs taken surreptitiously had appeared in the *Sunday Express* and the *People*. Some showed the Queen helping the Princess to don a water-ski-ing jacket, others showed Princess Margaret water-ski-ing and the Queen reclining on the ground.

On the Sunday when the Princess was again preparing to water-ski, a *Daily Express* photographer and a freelance photographer were escorted away by a forester, who discovered them hidden in the undergrowth with their cameras trained on the hut where the Princess was changing.

The Queen considers [Sir Richard continued] that behaviour of this sort, which has continued throughout the summer months, constitutes an unreasonable intrusion on the private lives of both Her Majesty and Her Royal Highness, and that the subsequent publication of photographs no longer justifiable even on the grounds of news interest, only encourages further abuse. It is Her Majesty's hope that the use of pictures taken under such circumstances may be discouraged, and that these activities will therefore become less profitable to the offending photographers.

The Queen was aware that the Press Council could not accept responsibility for the activities of freelance photographers, but she would nevertheless be grateful, Sir Richard Colville said, if the propriety of the photographers' actions could be examined and ruled upon by the Council.

The Great Pond, Sunninghill Park, lies in Crown lands east of Ascot Heath. A public footpath skirts part of the lake where Princess Margaret was ski-ing, and the question the Press Council had to determine was whether the photographs published in the newspapers could have been taken from the public footpath. Objection could hardly be sustained to a photograph taken from a place where the public was entitled to be and from there could have seen what the photographed showed.

The Editor of the *Sunday Express*, Mr John Junor, said that the pictures published in his newspaper came from a freelance photographer who had satisfied him that they had been taken from the public path. The photographer also told him that the Queen had even waved to people on the path. Mr Junor said he would not have published the pictures had he known that they were obtained by trespass.

Mr Stuart Campbell, the Editor of the *People*, also said that he had closely questioned the freelance photographer, and in the light of the assurance received he saw nothing objectionable in publishing a picture of what any member of the public could see from the footpath. Had he thought the photographs were taken surreptitiously and that the photographer was trespassing, he would have regarded the act as intrusion of an unpleasant kind.

The photographer denied that he was trespassing, and claimed that the background in the photographs was visible from numerous places on the footpath. He was invited to demonstrate to the Press Council how he had taken the pictures, but refused.

The Press Council thereupon invited the Manager of P.A.-Reuter Photos Ltd to nominate an independent photographer to make a test to determine whether the pictures could have been taken from the public path. An investigating party consisting of three members of the Press Council and representatives of the Crown Estates, the *Sunday Express* and the *People* was appointed by the Press Council and visited the site.

A careful examination was made of the area and the photographer took a number of test pictures with a telephoto lens. As a result he certified that, in his opinion, the pictures published in both newspapers could not have been taken from the public footpath whatever type of camera and lens were used.

The investigating committee concurred in the finding and were unanimously of the opinion that all but one of the pictures published were taken from within the private grounds.

Confirmation was provided by Mr Junor with a series of test photographs taken by the *Sunday Express* from the public footpath. The photographer of the challenged pictures took part in this test and the pictures were taken from the vantage point he claimed to have used. None of the pictures revealed a background comparable with the published pictures.

The Press Council found that the photographs published in the *Sunday Express* and the *People* were taken surreptitiously when the Queen and the Princess were clearly unaware that the pictures were being taken, and that the photographer was trespassing on the private grounds of Her Majesty at the time.

The Council was also satisfied that the photographer had deceived the Editors of the two newspapers and had led them to believe that the photographs were taken from a public footpath. Although the information was untrue it was accepted by the newspapers in good faith. Nevertheless, the Council said, editors must exercise care in publishing photographs of the Royal Family taken in circumstances which appeared to involve intrusion into their private lives.

The *Daily Express* photographer who was found in the Queen's private grounds was strongly censured.

A notable feature of the case was the great trouble and care taken to establish the facts. The charge was a serious one; it was of grave concern to the newspapers which had published the pictures; and for the photographer it involved his professional honour and integrity. The Council made searching inquiries uninfluenced by a sense of occasion, the source of the complaint or by what might have been regarded as a lack of co-operation on the part of the photographer.

Thoroughness of this kind in investigation must establish confidence in the Press Council's findings. (1965/3–8)

14 Intrusion and Invasion of Privacy

COMPLAINTS ARISING OUT OF COURT PROCEEDINGS

INVASION OF PRIVATE RESIDENCE

HOUNDING

I do not think it can be too strongly emphasised that in this country the Press has no right to go upon private property or into private places and intrude upon private people and into private rights, and that the standard of conduct and manners demanded of them is as high a standard as should be demanded of every citizen in a civilised community.

This passage is from a judgment by a High Court judge in a libel action (Lea *v.* Justice of the Peace Ltd and R. J. Ackford Ltd, *The Times*, 15 March 1947). The facts of the case were that a Bow Street magistrate had described the conduct of a young army officer who struck a Press photographer and stamped upon his camera as 'ungentlemanly' and 'cowardly'. The photographer had taken a flashlight photograph of the officer and his bride at their wedding reception in a private house which he had entered uninvited. The proceedings before the magistrate were for assault, and the officer was fined £10, ordered to pay £50 costs, and £135 for smashing the camera.

A legal journal reviewing the case stated that the magistrate's epithets 'ungentlemanly' and 'cowardly' exactly fitted the photographer. The result was the photographer sued the journal for libel. The Judge held that the remarks complained of were fair comment on a matter of public interest and gave judgment for the journal.

The judgment quoted above gives clear warning and a precise indication of the limitations journalists and photographers must observe in the course of their duties.

The law deals strictly with trespass to private property, even when no damage results, but gives no redress for the invasion of personal privacy, though it may cause immeasurable suffering and distress. Commenting on this anomalous situation, an American jurist once observed that the Englishman's home is his castle, but, while the courts will vigorously protect the closed front entrance, they leave the back door wide open to idle and prurient curiosity.

The question of legal protection for personal privacy has more than once been considered, but hitherto abandoned as impracticable.

The Porter Committee set up to review the law of defamation considered a suggestion that the law should be extended to bring the invasion of privacy under the scope of defamation. In their Report made in 1948 (Cmd. 7536, pars. 24–6) the Committee stated:

> The complaint which is summarised in the expression 'invasion of privacy' consists in the alleged practice upon the part of representatives of certain organs of the Press ... of intruding upon those who have suffered bereavement, or cross-questioning those who are related or otherwise incidentally connected with persons who have committed crimes or attained notoriety, and of publishing in any sensational form details of the private lives and affairs of such persons.

But the Committee was satisfied on the evidence of representatives of the journalists' profession, and by newspaper proprietors themselves, that the practice is one which is strongly deprecated by all reputable journalists and newspapers.

We think [their Report stated] that there are great difficulties in formulating an extended definition of criminal or civil libel which, while effective to restrain improper invasion of privacy, would not interfere with the due reporting of matters which are of public interest. It appears to us, however, that difficulties which confront this Committee should not form an obstacle to action by the Press itself or prevent it from dealing with the problem as one of internal discipline.

In 1949 the first Royal Commission had this to say:

We have given considerable thought to this suggestion, [that intrusion should be checked by legislation] but it would in our view be extremely difficult to devise legislation which would deal with the mischief effectively and be capable of enforcement. Methods of news-gathering which cause distress to private persons were condemned in 1937 by formal resolutions of both proprietors' and journalists' organisations, and we consider that it is for the profession itself to make this condemnation effective. The General Council of the Press could perform a valuable service by enunciating afresh the principles on which professional opinion is agreed and by drawing attention to cases in which they have been disregarded. (Cmd. 7700, par. 643)

Again in 1961 Lord Mancroft tried to introduce legislation 'to give every individual such further protection against invasion of his privacy as may be desirable for the maintenance of human dignity, while protecting the right of the public to be kept informed of all matters in which the public may be concerned.' He described the Bill as an extension of our age-old protection against eavesdropping 'Peeping Toms' and 'Paul Prys'. He drew attention to the law in America and cited a passage from a judgment of the Missouri Supreme Court (Barber *v.* Time Inc., 1942, 348 Mo. 1199):

The basis of the right of privacy is the right to be left alone.

'If the Court decides that the matter is outside the scope of proper public interest and that there is substantial evidence to show an unreasonable, unwarranted and offensive interference in another's private affairs, then the case is one to be submitted to a jury.'...

As long as 60 years ago in America it was believed, said Lord Mancroft, that legislation such as this would result in a flood of litigation. It was estimated that if a Right of Privacy Bill such as mine were to be passed into law it would have to be repealed for creating too much litigation. That particular Act has survived for nearly 60 years. Twenty

States in America now have the measure, or something roughly like it, and others are following.

Lord Mancroft said his Bill was designed to strike a balance between the essential freedom of the Press and the equally essential rights of the individual. He recognised the vital right of the Press to inform the public about matters which the public ought to know, and acknowledged that the field of legitimate news was a wide one.

In the end his efforts failed, not because of lack of sympathy and support for the purpose of the Bill, but because the difficulty of definition defeated efforts to draft legislation which would give an effective right of privacy without interfering with the legitimate freedom of the Press.

In 1965 a joint working party of representatives of Justice and of the British Committee of the International Press Institute drew attention to the same difficulty.

> We gave some consideration to the advisability of establishing an individual's right to privacy by legislation such as that advocated by Lord Mancroft which would give the aggrieved party a right of action. We felt, however, that legislation of this kind would impose an undue restriction on the proper activities of the Press. Moreover, the borderline between that which the public has a legitimate right to know, and that which constitutes an unnecessary intrusion on privacy, is in practice hard to define.

Lawyers and journalists, therefore, seem to have been in agreement that legislation was not the way to protect privacy and that the Porter Committee were right in their view that the problem was one of internal discipline for the Press itself Nevertheless feeling persists that some statutory protection from unreasonable interference is necessary.

In 1967 two private members' Bills came before Parliament with this purpose in view; the Law Commissioners were said to be studying the matter and it was also to be considered at a summer seminar at All Souls, Oxford. At their conference in Sweden in June 1967, the International Commission of Jurists referred to the United Nations covenant on civil and political rights and declared that the right to privacy being of paramount importance to human happiness, should be recognised as a fundamental right of mankind. They recommended that the right to privacy should be fully protected by law.

How the matter will develop in Great Britain remains to be seen. The difficulties of definition referred to in the debate on Lord Mancroft's Bill have still to be overcome and little will be gained and much may be lost if legislation to ensure the right of the individual to privacy results in restricting the liberty of the Press to conduct inquiries and publish information of legitimate public interest. Whether in the sphere of social behaviour preventive measures through legislation are justified or wise is a matter of controversy. The moral sanction can often be more effective than a legal one. There are many who feel strongly that the right to privacy is not a matter for the courts but rather for the Press Council, the guardian of the conscience of the Press.

A private individual has the right to be left alone and the invasion of his privacy is journalistically defensible only in special circumstances. 'It is the job of the Press', a distinguished editor said, 'to provide news, but not to poke and pry into things a person can rightfully and decently wish to keep to himself.' To invite a statement on the private affairs of a person whose name is before the public is not necessarily an infringement of privacy; to persist, pursue and attempt to coerce when a statement is refused becomes one. Intrusion begins where consent ends.

When dealing with complaints of infringement of privacy the Press Council considers such questions as whether the information sought was a matter of public interest; whether the conduct and methods employed by the reporter in obtaining it were legitimate and fair; whether the inquiries were made at a reasonable hour; whether the inquiries were made by newspaper representatives acting individually or collectively; whether their behaviour amounted to hounding, and so on. The public interest relied on as the justification for the enquiries must be a legitimate and proper interest and not merely an idle, prurient or morbid curiosity.

Often protests arise from the manner of the inquiries. If questions were put to distressed and bereaved persons on behalf of the Press as a whole, possibly no offence would be caused; it is when the questions are repeated over the telephone and on the doorstep by every newspaper in turn that the inquiries become intolerable. So, too, with photographs; a single photographer might be acceptable, but a barrage of flash-bulbs operated by a host of competing pressmen deeply resented.

In addition to the rulings of the Press Council the codes of the professional organisations offer some guidance on intrusion. The National Union of Journalists, for example, requires that in obtaining news or pictures, reporters and photographers should do nothing to cause pain or humiliation to bereaved and distressed people; the code of the Institute of Journalists declares that to obtain news or pictures by dishonest representation or any other form of dishonesty or by intimidation or undue intrusion on privacy is conduct discreditable to a journalist.

Conduct which at first sight may appear to be intrusion on persons at a time they are entitled to be left in peace, may in fact be justifiable despite the additional distress newspaper inquiries must inevitably cause. An instance was the case of Burgess and Maclean, the two Foreign Office officials who disappeared in 1952 and were suspected of having fled behind the Iron Curtain. Their defection was a tragedy for the relatives, and the interviews sought by the Press must have seemed callous and insensitive. But the disappearance of two men in possession of top secret information was a matter that concerned the security of the State and was of great public interest. The Press was justified in obtaining as much information as possible for the public. Again Press revelations about a private individual's connections with a public body may be a public service, see p. 78 (*People*).

In its first Annual Report the Press Council pointed out that the alleged invasion of private life was often raised by critics of the Press, but very few specific complaints had been made to the Council. Those were still early days, and in the years that followed further complaints have been made, but these do not amount to anything like the numbers generally believed. Bearing in mind the enormous number of interviews held and photographs taken every day of the year, all over the country by innumerable Press men attached to scores of newspapers; bearing in mind the ingenious modern techniques for obtaining long-distance pictures and listening into personal and private conversations, the number of complaints of intrusion has been surprisingly small; the number of complaints upheld even smaller.

Nevertheless the public continues to believe that intrusion is practised on a large scale. The belief largely explains why the image of the Press is so distorted. It also helps to explain the heavy damages awarded against newspapers in libel actions. Unfortunately the memory of a complaint of intrusion against a newspaper persists long after the newspaper has been exonerated of the charge.

Cases of intrusion upon the Royal Family are dealt with in the previous chapter, those concerning confidential occasions in Chapter 5, those concerning schools and hospitals in Chapters 20 and 21.

The other cases dealt with by the Press Council are as follows:

INTRUSION ON BEREAVEMENT

WIFE OF MURDERED BRITISH SERGEANT TELEPHONED

Within twenty-four hours of the murder of a British sergeant in Cyprus a representative of the *Daily Sketch* telephoned his wife in Nicosia. The War Office complained to the Press Council of what it described as a case of callous intrusion which had caused additional distress to the wife.

The Editor, Mr Herbert Gunn, informed the Council that there was a rigid office rule that there must be no intentional intrusion into private grief. When invited to appear before the Council he refused but asked the newspaper's legal adviser to appear. He continued to refuse when asked to bring any members of his staff who might be able to clear up the circumstances. He took the view, he said, that a journalist should be protected against unfair and possibly damaging cross-examination.

The Press Council regretted the unco-operative attitude of the Editor. Despite its 'rigid rule' the *Daily Sketch* had printed the interview. The Council held that the War Office had established a case of intrusion and recorded that the incident was damaging to the reputation of the British Press.

In its issue on the day after the adjudication, the newspaper described the criticism as unfair and unjust and said that the sergeant's wife had voluntarily stated that she had no grievance against the newspaper. Although the telephone call to Nicosia from the *Daily Sketch* had surprised her, it had given her the chance of letting the people at home know the conditions under which British servicemen and their families were living in Cyprus.

The wife then wrote to the Press Council, modifying her complaint, and the Editor asked the Council to reconsider its decision. But after considering the additional evidence, the Press Council still regarded the manner in which the woman was approached as callous intrusion into private grief. (1956/28, 40–2)

DUTCH AU PAIR GIRL MURDERED

In January 1958 *The Times* published a letter from Mr X commenting on the behaviour of 'a majority of the national daily newspapers' in connection with the murder of a Dutch *au pair* girl, Miss Y, in Essex. The letter contained a number of allegations, and asked whether such conduct was the sort of thing the Press Council was interested in.

As a result the Council interviewed Mr X and took statements from a number of witnesses including the Chief Constable of Essex. After consideration the Council reached the following conclusions:

1. Mr X complained that within five minutes of the murdered girl's family in Holland being told of her death reporters of British newspapers had swarmed into their flat and had even gone into the girl's bedroom.

In fact there was no British reporters present, and Mr X subsequently withdrew his statement that reporters had entered the girl's bedroom. The reporters present were Dutch, some acting for British newspapers. There was no evidence that they were callous, offensive or unscrupulous.

2. Mr X's statement that the English people who knew the family were subjected to a ceaseless stream of journalists proved on examination to mean that he and some others were asked whether they had any information about Miss Y.

3. Mr X said that a reporter threatened to make up some news if he did not give him any information, and that he did so.

In fact a story was not invented.

What happened was that a *Daily Mail* reporter had been told that a detective would meet Miss Y's father and sister when they arrived in England. A detective did call at Mr X's house where they were staying, but he spoke only to Mr X. The Council regretted the reporter assumed that the detective had questioned the father and sister without checking this.

4. Mr X alleged that, as he drove away after meeting the father and daughter at Harwich, there was a scramble to take photographs, and a queue of about five cars containing photographers followed them to his home. He stopped once to ask them for some consideration, but this spurred them on, and they went past one by one taking flashlight pictures as they passed.

The facts elicited were that photographers had not been allowed on the quay, and the reporters and photographers had congregated at a railway crossing. As Mr X's car passed photographs were taken. Five or six cars then followed him, and to this extent his complaint was fully justified. But the Council was unable to trace any photographer who took flashlight photographs when Mr X stopped and asked the photographers to desist.

5. Mr X said that a cameraman even wanted to photograph the father and daughter on the distressing occasion when they went to identify the dead girl's body.

The Council was unable to trace the photographer. At the inquest the father and daughter willingly posed for pictures, and afterwards Mr Y told Press representatives that he had been touched by the sympathy he had received.

6. Mr X further complained that when he reached home he found photographers in his garden. He told them they were trespassing and they left. The Editor of the *Daily Express* said one of his photographers took a picture of the relatives arriving at the house, but apologised and left at once when he was told he was on private property.

The Press Council found that while Mr X had failed to substantiate his charges made against the 'majority of the national daily newspapers', there was one case of serious inaccuracy in a report; there were also two episodes of badgering intrusion: the Press cars' pursuit of the family on the road from Harwich and the Press photographers' entry into the garden of Mr X's home. These matters were strongly condemned. (1958/20, 30)

CROYDON SCHOOLBOYS IN AIR CRASH

The widow of a schoolmaster killed in an air crash in Norway complained of intrusion by several reporters while she was waiting up for news of the aircraft which, at that time, was missing, and later by other reporters who called on her home after the fate of the airliner was known. She refused to give any information, and complained also that the reporters then asked her neighbours for information, which she considered to be inexcusable.

The complainant also objected to a photograph in the *Sunday Times* of one of her husband's pupils in the school laboratory. She said that the caption, 'The lost world of A.B.', was in extremely poor taste. A separate complaint about the picture was received from a parent of one of the schoolboys who had lost their lives.

In its adjudication, the Press Council said it appreciated that calls were made on the widow at a late hour, but at that time news was limited to the knowledge that the plane was missing. No doubt the newspapers felt that the complainant herself was anxiously awaiting information. On the issue of undesired personal publicity, the Council thought that in such circumstances it was inevitable that some details should be given of the lives and backgrounds of those involved, especially when they occupied public or semi-public positions. To avoid inaccuracy which itself can cause distress, the Press should be able to look for reasonable help in necessary inquiries. The *Sunday Times*'s explanation that its picture was an attempt to pay tribute to the people concerned was accepted. (1962/34–5)

CONSIDERATION FOR NEXT-OF-KIN

The Glasgow *Sunday Post* published a report that a man had been found dead in his room in an Egyptian hotel. A complaint was made that this was published before the widow had been informed, and that only the prompt action of the police had prevented her from learning of the death from the newspaper.

The Editor, Mr J. R. Martin, replied that the report was not published until the day after the news had been received, and he assumed that by this time the next-of-kin would have been informed.

The Press Council rejected the complaint, saying that although the Press should be considerate of the feelings of the next-of-kin, it could not lay down a general rule that a newspaper should not publish a report of a fatality with names until the Editor was satisfied that the next-of-kin had been informed. (1965/97)

A BEREAVED FATHER

The father of a young man killed in a road accident complained of the attitude of a Press agency representative and two women newspaper reporters of the *Hendon and Finchley Times* who called at his home after the tragedy. The agency reporter was said to have been insolent in his approach, and to have called three times in order to obtain a photograph of the son. On the third visit the father threatened to call the police.

The complainant said the family did not desire publicity and thought that this wish should have been respected. He also took exception to newspaper publication of photographs of the wrecked car.

The agency reporter explained that the third visit was made because the father was out on the first two occasions. He denied that he had been other than polite and sympathetic. The two women reporters also denied persisting in their inquiries when they found they were unwelcome.

A clergyman who was present when the agency reporter callled said that the reporter left quietly and politely when he told him that the father was not in a fit state to talk to him.

The Press Council expressed its sympathy for the tragic loss of the complainant's son. The incident, however, was a matter of public interest, and consequently Press inquiries and the publication of photographs of the damaged car were not unreasonable. The Council rejected the charge that the Press representatives were 'cruel' and was satisfied that this impression arose from the complainant's distress which was aggravated by the number of Press inquiries. (1964/70–2)

PRIVATE GRIEF

PRESIDENT KENNEDY

Complaints were made about the *Daily Telegraph*'s publication of a photograph of Mrs Kennedy taken at the graveside of the President three days after his burial. The picture was alleged to be an intrusion into private grief and in very bad taste.

The Managing Editor, Mr Colin Coote, said he felt that the occasion was one in which it was proper and right to publish the photograph.

The Press Council's finding was that the photograph was associated with an important historic event and that the *Daily Telegraph* was entitled to publish it. (1964/32)

TRAGEDY PHOTOGRAPHED

The *Western Mail* published a photograph of the wife and daughter of a man who had collapsed on a South Wales beach watching the vain efforts of St John Ambulance men to revive him. The picture was taken at a little distance and did not show the faces of the victim, his wife or daughter.

Complaint was made that the picture was likely to cause unnecessary distress to the relatives and that it was in bad taste.

12   L.T.P.C.

The Editor of the newspaper, Mr D. G. H. Rowlands, said that the picture had been carefully considered before publication. It conveyed an almost classic sense of tragedy, and, rather than being an intrusion on grief, it impelled the reader to share it.

The opinion of the Press Council was that the publication was not objectionable. (1964/34)

THE CHURCHILL FUNERAL

A member of the public complained of a picture taken at the funeral of Sir Winston Churchill showing the coffin on the shoulders of the bearers followed by members of the Churchill family. The caption to the picture read: 'The grief of the Churchills: handbag tightly clasped, the widow leads her son and daughter towards the train journey home'. It was contended that the sole purpose of the picture was to publicise something which was personal and private — a devoted widow's anguish.

The Editor of the *Sunday Times*, Mr C. D. Hamilton, said that far from publicising Lady Churchill's anguish, the picture showed her immense dignity. The occasion was one at which the public had a wish and a right to share.

The Press Council's adjudication was that no question of intrusion arose in the photograph of the family mourners at the State funeral. The complaint was rejected. (1965/92)

WEEPING MEN

Complaints were made about photographs published in the *Daily Mail* and the *Daily Sketch*. One of them showed two Belgian women dead on the roadside after being shot by United Nations troops in Katanga. Beside them were two men, one with his eyes bandaged and the other weeping in distress. Accompanying the picture in the *Daily Mail* was the comment that this was the price humanity would always pay for its folly in warfare; when those who did the shooting were the champions of peace it was much harder to bear.

A complaint of intrusion into private grief was made against the *Daily Mail*. Another complaint said that the presentation was hysterical and biased.

The Acting Editor of the *Daily Mail*, Mr Michael Randall, said it was right that the public should see such pictures. This one was deliberately captioned to drive home the tragic stupidity of events in Katanga.

The complaint against the *Daily Sketch*, which published a series of pictures of the incident, was that they were intended to create emotional feeling against the United Nations.

The Press Council decided that the newspapers were justified in publishing the pictures and captions to bring home to the public the horror of events in Katanga. The charges of intrusion into private grief and hysteria and biased reporting were rejected. (1963/57–8)

PICTURE OF DISTRESSED PARENTS

A man reported to Scotland Yard in response to a police announcement that he might be able to help them solve a murder mystery. Before doing so he telephoned the *Daily Express* to protest his innocence, which was subsequently proved. On the following day the newspaper published a photograph of the man's parents, and the Council was asked to say that such a picture 'of the anguish of the parents of an uncharged man' was 'a capitalisation of private unhappiness and utterly reprehensible and unjustifiable'.

The Acting Editor of the *Daily Express*, Mr Robert Edwards, maintained that it was perfectly proper to obtain the reaction of a man's parents, and they were entirely willing that the picture should be taken.

The Council held that although the relatives in this case had raised no objection to being photographed, newspapers should take great care to avoid exploitation of private unhappiness in the publication of such photographs. (1962/46)

SUICIDE VICTIM

In a report of the suicide of a man the *Daily Express* mentioned that the victim was due to appear in court on two charges of indecent assault.

A complaint was made that, although the report was accurate, it was unnecessary to publish the nature of the charges, which amounted to blatant disregard of the feelings of the dead man's relatives. The complainant was told by the *Daily Express* that the information was known in the district and had appeared in other newspapers, so there was no point in suppressing it. An alternative to publication was possible distortion of the facts in local gossip. In reply, the complainant claimed that few people knew the nature of the accusations, and even the widow was unaware of them.

The Editor of the *Daily Express*, Mr Robert Edwards, pointed out that this unawareness could apply at most only until the inquest. Although the *Daily Express* had no desire to cause unnecessary distress to families involved in tragedy, he could not feel it had fallen short of desired standards in its accurate summary.

In the Press Council's opinion, a brief statement of the charges was a necessary part of a balanced report of the tragedy. The complaint was rejected. (1964/57)

PRIVATE LIFE OF PERSONS IN THE PUBLIC EYE

CHAIRMAN OF THE LONDON COUNTY COUNCIL

The *South London Press* reported that Mr I. J. Hayward (later Sir Isaac Hayward), the Leader of the London County Council, was to be admitted to the London County Council Lodge of Freemasons. Members and leading officials of the London County Council regarded the report as an unwarranted intrusion into the private affairs of its members, and complained to the Press Council.

The Press Council did not agree that the report constituted intrusion. The admittance to membership of the Lodge of the Leader of the London County Council was of public interest, and there was no objection to the information being published. Public men were not more vulnerable to prying than private persons, but they must expect their actions to be noted outside their own intimate circles. (1955/20)

PICTURES OF FILM STARS

When the *Sunday Pictorial* published photographs of Mr Richard Burton and Miss Elizabeth Taylor — both at that time married to other people — holiday-making in bathing costumes in Italy, a complainant wrote: 'Is there no limit to the Press to publicise feeble, cheap sex drama?'

Mr R. T. Payne, the Editor, said he considered that the photographs were of news interest and that other publications had taken a similar view; but the Press Council deplored their publication. (1963/52)

PRINCESS BIRGITTA OF HOHENZOLLERN

The *Daily Express* published a picture of Princess Birgitta of Hohenzollern and Prince Johann Georg taken during their honeymoon in France. The Princess was lying face downward on a balcony of a private villa sunbathing, and her husband, stripped to the waist, was applying sunburn lotion to her back.

The Press Council upheld the complaint that the picture was distasteful and an unwarrantable intrusion into privacy. (1962/25)

DR BODKIN ADAMS

Dr Bodkin Adams, who had been acquitted of the murder of a patient in whose will he was a beneficiary, complained of persecution and intrusion by the *Daily Herald* in a series of reports of his friendship with a lady with whom he had spent a holiday in Madeira. The newspaper reported that they had occupied adjoining rooms.

He also complained of inaccuracy in this report and in another which had been followed by a correction and apology.

The Press Council held that the *Daily Herald* was seriously at fault in publishing the report. The complaint of persecution and intrusion was not, however, substantiated, more especially because the lady had given information voluntarily to the *Daily Herald* on more than one occasion. (1960/25)

MR JOHN OSBORNE

When Mr John Osborne, the playwright, moved into a new home in Sussex, a reader in Wales complained of a report which appeared in the *Daily Telegraph*. The report mentioned Mr Osborne's admission to the newspaper's representative that Mrs Penelope Gilliatt, whose husband was best man at Princess Margaret's wedding, was staying at the new house. The report also contained Mr Osborne's answers to questions by the reporter about Mrs Gilliatt's attitude to her husband, and of Mr Osborne's feelings towards his wife. The story described the comings and goings at the house and the collection of furniture at the London homes of both Mr Osborne and Mrs Gilliatt.

The complainant questioned the purpose of such an article, and asked whether the newspaper had any regard for the right of individuals to live their own lives.

No complaint was received from Mr Osborne or Mrs Gilliatt.

Sir Colin Coote, Managing Editor of the *Daily Telegraph*, said the occasion was one about which a considerable part of the reading public might legitimately expect to be informed.

The Press Council said that the article did not constitute an insult to the good name of the Press, as the complainant contended. The persons concerned had been very much in the public eye, and the newspaper properly regarded their activities as news. (1962/52)

CROWN PRINCESS BEATRIX OF HOLLAND

A *Daily Express* photograph of Crown Princess Beatrix of Holland with a male companion was said to be a gross intrusion into her private life. The caption to the picture read: 'Is this the man — A picture the Dutch people are still waiting to see?' Three other pictures were also published.

An engagement was rumoured at the time and the *Daily Express* carried the story of the royal romance as its front-page lead.

The Editor of the newspaper, Mr Robert Edwards, said that the picture had come into their hands at a time when there had been no official statement. The pictures were perfectly innocent, and he denied they constituted an intrusion.

The Press Council said there was no evidence of intrusion, and the complaint was rejected. (1965/93)

CHRISTINE KEELER

After the Court of Appeal had quashed the conviction and sentence of a man called 'Lucky' Gordon, the *Daily Sketch* published a news story headed: 'As M.P.s demand justice for Gordon, Christine says "I told no lies." ' The story told of Miss Keeler's return to her London flat, and gave her telephone number.

Through her solicitors, Miss Keeler said she realised she could not complain of the volume of publicity she had received, but the conduct of the newspaper in publishing her telephone number had no apparent reason except to add to the misery of her life. This seemed to have been done out of spite, because she refused to answer reporters' inquiries. A constant stream of abusive telephone calls had followed the publication.

Mr Howard French, the Editor of the *Daily Sketch*, denied the suggestion that the number was printed out of spite. It was included in the report because telephone calls were a focal point in the story. The consequence of giving the number had not been anticipated.

The Press Council held that the publication of the telephone number was objectionable, and the newspaper's action in doing so was deplored. (1965/97)

MISS KEELER'S WEDDING

Contrary to her expressed desire some newspapers gave Miss Christine Keeler's new name and address when reporting her marriage. A complaint was made to the Press Council that these details ought not to have been given; objection was also made to the use of the photographs obtained, it was suggested, by 'laying siege' to Miss Keeler's house. Blame was not attributed to specified newspaper representatives.

The Editors of the newspapers which did publish reports denied the allegation of harrying her. They maintained that Miss Keeler's marriage was a matter of public interest, and that she and her relatives voluntarily gave interviews.

Through her solicitors, Miss Keeler told the Council that she had hoped that her request that her husband's name should not be stated would be respected by the Press. From the Saturday afternoon on which her whereabouts were discovered until the following Monday afternoon, reporters and photographers were almost continuously outside her house. Repeated requests that she and her husband should pose for photographs were refused, but eventually photographers were asked whether they would go away if the couple walked from the house to their car without attempting to escape being photographed. One journalist to whom Miss Keeler gave an interview agreed not to disclose the couple's full identity and address. He was subsequently informed that this information had been obtained from another source by several newspapers, which he regarded as nullifying his own undertaking.

The Council was told that on the Sunday the number of Press men outside the house varied from eight to fifteen. In its adjudication, the Press Council said:

> It was inevitable that Miss Keeler's marriage should be reported as a matter of public interest, but her request that her name and address should not be published was a reasonable one. The Press Council regrets that this was either overlooked or disregarded by a number of newspaper editors. (1966/95)

PHYSICAL DISABILITY

The Secretary of the Guild of Dispensing Opticians wrote to the Press Council about an article in a daily newspaper which dealt with the wearing of contact lenses and named certain women who were known to use them. One of the persons named was extremely sensitive and was very distressed to see publicity given to a matter which she regarded as private. She had accused the dispensing opticians who made the lenses of disclosing the fact, an allegation which was denied.

The Secretary of the Guild did not ask the Council to investigate the case, but suggested that it might use its influence to remind the editorial staffs of newspapers that they should be particularly careful not to make gratuitous references to disabilities which might cause distress, concern and possible financial loss. (1957/29)

For two cases of hospital intrusion see p. 336, Munich Air Disaster; p. 338, Mr Aneurin Bevan; see also p. 330 (*Scottish Daily Express*).

PHOTOGRAPHS

INSIDE A FIRE STATION

Two *Daily Mirror* representatives called at Gravesend fire station to inquire about statements made in an anonymous letter complaining about excessive 'spit and polish' at the fire station. They were asked to wait for the return of the Station Officer, and while doing so they took photographs of the inside of the station without permission.

The Kent County Council complained about the conduct of the reporters, but the reporters said that on arrival at the station they had checked whether there was any substance in the anonymous letter with two firemen, and when they were asked to wait for the Station Officer, they went away and returned later. While waiting the photographer took some pictures.

The Press Council rejected the complaint. (1963/56)

PERMISSION TO PUBLISH REFUSED

A nineteen-year-old girl complained that the *Western Telegraph* had published a picture of her in a beauty series in spite of her refusal to give permission, and her repeated objections to publication. She said that she refused permission when told for what purpose the picture was wanted, but was told not to be so silly. When she said she would complain to the Press Council, the Editor told her that if she did he would take steps to recover any costs or expenses incurred by the newspaper.

The Editor, Mr Herbert A. Thomas, told the Press Council that the girl allowed herself to be photographed freely at a public function.

The Press Council upheld the complaint, saying that in the circumstances the publication of the photograph was wrong. The girl had personally informed the Editor that she objected to the photograph being published, and the Council censured the newspaper for its action and also for the terms of the Editor's reply to the complainant. (1965/78)

PHOTOGRAPH TAKEN WITHOUT PERMISSION

The *Scottish Daily Express* in a report of two young Scotsmen killed in an autostrada crash in Italy described the reception of the news by the fiancée of one of the victims. The other young man, the report stated, was the prospective fiancé of the first girl's friend, Miss S.C., who was to have flown out for the first girl's wedding, and herself become engaged.

The story was based upon an interview with Miss S.C.'s father in her absence. He denied that he had said that his daughter was engaged, or that she was to be engaged, when she flew out to Italy. Following the publication a reporter and photographer of the newspaper called on Miss S. C., who also denied that she was engaged. During the conversation the photographer surreptitiously took a picture of Miss S. C. and, in spite of her refusal to pose, it was published the following day with her name and caption 'Not getting engaged'. In an accompanying report her age, wrongly stated in the first report, was again wrongly stated, although the father, when he was interviewed, had given her correct age. The father's solicitors contended that the introduction of the daughter's name in the first news story was offensive and cynical, in view of the fact that the reporters had been told that her mother was dying.

The Editor, Mr Ian McColl, said that the father's statement about the girl's age was unknown to the reporter who was responsible for the second report, and he had innocently quoted the age as reported in the first story. The Editor regretted that the photographer took a picture of Miss S.C. without her knowledge, and that the newspaper had erred in stating that she was engaged. The case, however, was not treated sensationally, and the girl's father had not suggested to the reporters that their visits were an intrusion on private grief.

The Press Council held that the taking of a photograph of the girl in her home and publishing it after permission had been refused was indefensible. The newspaper was also at fault because of the inaccuracy of its first report of the girl's engagement and its failure to include the father's denial. The complaint was upheld. (1966/65–6)

Another case of a photograph being used without permission will be found on p. 102 (Glasgow *Daily Record*).

A QUEUE OF UNEMPLOYED

A picture published by the *Observer* showed a queue waiting in a local hall for unemployment pay. A complaint was made that men on the dole resented being photographed, and the picture constituted an intrusion into their privacy.

The Editor of the *Observer*, the Hon. David Astor, said the purpose of the picture was to illustrate an article dealing with the causes of the exceptional unemployment in Appledore and the efforts being made to relieve it. He did not wish to embarrass the unemployed, but contended that if the complaint was upheld no newspaper would be able to use pictures to draw attention to any kind of social distress for fear of causing embarrassment.

The Press Council held that the *Observer* was justified in publishing the picture. Note was taken of the fact that the individuals in the queue were not easily recognisable. (1964/34–5)

GAOLED FOOTBALLERS

The *Sheffield Telegraph* published photographs taken with a long-distance lens of three well-known footballers imprisoned for accepting bribes. The pictures showed the men playing football in the gaol compound. They were all clearly recognisable; the features of the other persons in the pictures had been obliterated.

The solicitors for one of the footballers complained that the publication was contrary to public policy. They were taken after the newspaper's photographer had been escorted off near-by Crown property. A probation officer said that the publication might hamper the men's chances of making good on their release from prison.

The Editor of the *Sheffield Telegraph*, Mr Michael Finlay, said in evidence that the football pitch was on the perimeter of the prison. When the reporter and photographer were told that a vegetable patch alongside the prison was Crown property, they moved to a point outside the gaol grounds and took pictures of something that was visible to any onlooker. He denied that the pictures could be prejudicial to the future of the men who were nationally known and who had figured in trials which had been given the utmost publicity. However, he agreed that the publication of identifiable pictures of persons in gaol was contrary to newspaper practice, and that the photographs in question were taken when the persons concerned were not aware of the fact. He denied that publication constituted persecution.

The Press Council condemned the publication of the photographs as a clear breach of Press standards. (1965/91–2)

DESECRATING GOD'S ACRE

Complaints were made about the behaviour of Press representatives at a country church whose Rector had attracted attention by declaring a religious curse on anyone in an adjoining village — of which he was also Rector — who gave false information to the Press or to the Bishop. One complaint was that the Press had debased and demeaned their profession by pestering the

Rector in his own churchyard on his way into the church to conduct Matins. Another complaint was that as the congregation left after the service a Press man again tried to photograph the Rector, an act described as desecrating God's acre.

Mr Robert Edwards, the Editor of the *Daily Express*, one of the newspapers concerned, said that, in the light of the publicity the Rector had attracted, his attitude was wholly unreasonable.

Complaints were also made of other incidents and reports, including an article in the *Western Daily Press* referring to the curse pronounced by the Rector and the efforts made by the reporter to interview him. The writer said his first attempt was at a Mothers' Union Meeting, but he was hustled out. The Rector complained that the statements were untrue, and that the reporter had forced his way into a private meeting. The reporter maintained that his account was completely factual.

In its adjudication, the Press Council said that the evidence in the case was confused. In regard to the incident before the morning service, the Council was not satisfied that it was apparent to the photographer, before he attempted to take a picture, that the Rector did not wish to be photographed. The Council saw no objection to the photograph taken after the service from outside the churchyard.

The complaint against the *Western Daily Press* was rejected. (1965/95–6)

A STOPPED WEDDING

A mother and her married daughter complained of an embarrassing and painful experience in connection with a report in the *Sunday Pictorial*.

A second daughter was involved in a wedding ceremony which was stopped in a church in Manchester. The girl was under twenty-one, and the family objected to her marriage to a young man who had been brought up in institutions. As the result of the objection to her marriage the daughter left home and the mother asked the *Sunday Pictorial*, which had published a picture of the daughter, where she could be found. She heard nothing until the eve of the wedding when a reporter arrived in Hull by car and offered to take her and other members of the family to Manchester so that they could object to the marriage. They were not given an opportunity to speak to the minister before the ceremony but were taken to the church just before the service began.

When the mother announced her objection the couple left the church and the mother was taken to the newspaper office. She said that she had been assured by the reporters that there would be nothing about the stopped wedding in the *Sunday Pictorial,* but in fact the following morning prominence was given to the report and to pictures, one taken inside the church.

The Editor, Mr Colin Valdar, said that the prospective bridegroom was wanted by the police and his arrest seemed certain to prevent the marriage ceremony. It was decided, in the circumstances, to do nothing to precipitate a dawn scene between the bride-to-be's family and the vicar over a wedding which police action anyway might prevent.

The Press Council's finding was that the newspaper did invite members of the family to go and stop the wedding and hoped in this way to obtain a sensational illustrated report. It had behaved improperly in providing no facilities for the family to see the vicar before the ceremony and had shown an indecent disregard for their feelings. (1957/23–4, 35–6)

For another case of photograph constituting intrusion see p. 331 (*Daily Mail*).

COMPLAINTS ARISING OUT OF COURT PROCEEDINGS

A CASE FROM THE COURT OF APPEAL

The Court of Appeal asked the Press Council to consider the conduct of photographers from the *Daily Express,* the *Daily Mail* and the *Daily Mirror* and of local correspondents from the *Daily Express* and *Daily Mail.*

On the same day that the Court of Appeal had granted the husband of a dissolved marriage limited access to his young daughter, the photographers and reporters had called on the child in the mother's absence. The mother complained of the action of the newspaper, and alleged that as a result of their visits the daughter, who had not seen her father since she was a baby, had been emotionally upset.

The Editors of the three papers agreed that photographs of the child should not have been taken without parental consent. They pointed out, however, that the photographers did not act by stealth, but tried to see the mother and in her absence photographed the child in the presence of her temporary guardian, and ostensibly with her permission. There did not seem to be any objection to making a courteous approach to the mother with a view to obtaining a picture.

The photographers had not told the child the reason for the pictures, and she was quite happy to pose for them. It was only later when a reporter called and told her of the Court's order that she became upset. The mother, in her evidence, referred to the blunt and callous way in which the news had been broken to the child.

Though none of the pictures appeared, the Press Council nevertheless held that the visits of the Press representatives to obtain pictures and information constituted intrusion into the family's private affairs, and it strongly condemned the newspapers responsible. (1964/36)

CUSTODY DECISION — BREAKING THE NEWS

A member of a Cambridge firm of solicitors complained that reporters from four London newspapers had ignored his request not to inform his client of the failure of a custody appeal in the Divorce Division until he had himself informed his client.

The Editor of the *Daily Express*, Mr Robert Edwards, one of the newspapers cited, said that his representatives were quite willing to co-operate in giving the solicitors reasonable time to contact their client, and they held up the story for more than two hours. The client appeared to be quite happy to be interviewed and photographed. The complainant agreed that no undertaking had been given other than that his request would be forwarded to the appropriate quarter.

The Press Council did not ask for replies from the other Editors concerned, and in its adjudication said that the reporters had acted properly in taking action to meet the solicitors' request. The Press may be expected to give careful consideration to any request by solicitors that they should be allowed time to break the news of a judgment which might cause distress to a client. But in this case the reporters had not interviewed the client before the solicitor arrived, and he did not make a clear request to break the news first. His client was quite willing to give interviews. (1965/56)

SOLICITORS REFUSE INFORMATION

A firm of solicitors complained of what it alleged to be unethical conduct by the *People*. The solicitors had refused to give a representative of the newspaper information about a client, and the newspaper then telephoned the client and endeavoured to obtain the information from her. The lady was embarrassed by the inquiry which was said to be an unwarranted intrusion into her privacy.

The Editor of the *People*, Mr Stuart Campbell, explained that the inquiries were to establish whether divorce proceedings had actually been started between the lady and her husband, because it was proposed to print an article about the husband, and he wished to safeguard himself against possible contempt of court. When the solicitors for the wife refused the information the newspaper contacted her.

The Press Council did not accept that it was always unethical for a reporter to seek information from a person whose solicitor has refused to give it. In the circumstances of this case, there was no intrusion by the *People*, and the complaint was rejected. (1965/93–4)

INVASION OF PRIVATE RESIDENCE

A CHIEF CONSTABLE PROTESTS

When the Chief Constable of Southend-on-Sea suspended one of his inspectors he made no mention of the matter to the Press. On being questioned by two journalists he issued a statement confirming the suspension and said that inquiries were being made about the misuse of police petrol. The *Daily Mail* published an inaccurate report, the subject of a complaint dealt with on p. 199.

A *News Chronicle* reporter called at the Chief Constable's house after being told that no further information was forthcoming and was reported to the Press Council by the Chief Constable for intrusion into his private residence.

The Press Council said that the reporter had conducted his inquiries in a courteous way and that it was not unreasonable to call at the Chief Constable's private residence.

The finding did not satisfy the Chief Constable, and he informed the Press Council that he had considered changing the arrangements for supplying information to the Press, but decided not to do so as it would be unfair to the local Press with whom he said he had no disagreement. (1957/25)

AN UNINVITED PHOTOGRAPHER

A woman photographer from the *Daily Mail* forced her way into a house when the front door was opened in answer to her call. She went into the lounge where a man who had witnessed the escape from Wandsworth Prison of one of the train robbers, was speaking to other Press representatives and took photographs of him. Her camera was seized but returned when she agreed to surrender the film.

The Editor of the *Daily Mail*, Mr Michael Randall, said she was angered by what appeared to be preferential treatment of other journalists. She regretted her action in forcing her way in.

The Press Council disapproved the conduct of the photographer, although it appreciated that she acted under a sense of irritation at what she regarded as cheque-book journalism. (1966/98–100)

For a case of invasion of place of business see p. 308 (*Daily Express*), for late telephone calls see p. 311 (*Daily Sketch, Daily Express*), and invasion of private practice see p. 345 (*Queen*).

HOUNDING

PARENTS OF CONVICTED MURDERER

The *Sunday Express* published an article giving the names of the parents of a convicted murderer with details of their emigration from this country including the name of the liner in which they were sailing and the date of arrival at its destination.

In reply to a protest the Assistant Editor said that 'The news which you mention was, I feel, quite suitable to present to the public and in fact we would be failing in our duty if we suppressed it.'

The Press Council did not share this view. It condemned the newspaper for hounding the parents and emphatically rejected the contention that there was a public duty to publish the story. (1959/21)

A TEN-YEAR-OLD SENTENCE

A social gossip story published in the *Sunday Express* in 1965 recalled a separation and a shooting incident in 1954 in which a peer was wounded and a woman assailant sent to gaol.

Complaint was made of the reference to a ten-year-old prison sentence and of what the peer described as an unwarrantable intrusion into the private lives of himself and his family; he considered it to be intentionally cruel and deliberate hounding by the Press.

The reporter contended that it was standard journalistic practice to bring in background information where this was considered relevant in reporting subsequent events.

Mr John Junor, the Editor of the *Sunday Express*, maintained that the separation of prominent people was legitimately a matter that might be reported and that it was permissible to recall items of news concerning the parties.

The Press Council considered it was wrong to refer to the shooting incident and the prison sentence passed more than ten years before. The newspaper was censured. (1966/42–3)

UNRELATED EVENTS — KILLER'S BROTHER

The father of a man hanged for murder complained to the Press Council that the *Evening News*, in reporting a police hunt for his younger son who had escaped from custody, published the story under the heading 'Hunt widens for Killer's Brother'. The father said that such reporting constituted hounding and was barbaric. It revived the suffering that he, his wife and family had suffered on another occasion.

The Editor of the *Evening News*, Mr C. Reginald Willis, said he considered the question to be one of taste. He had decided not to associate the brothers in future headlines.

The Press Council deplored the publication, and welcomed the Editor's decision to avoid future references to an unnecessary and hurtful association of unrelated events. (1964/69)

THE NURSE WHO RISKED HER LIFE

The attention of the Press Council was drawn to a leading article in the *Manchester Guardian*. It alleged that Sister Holland, who risked her life trying to rescue fifteen babies from a fire in a nursing home in Reading, had been unduly harassed by reporters. The article stated:

> Whether the offending reporters (and more important the news editors who instructed them) will be touched by the appeal for restraint is unfortunately in doubt, but it is good that they should know that most people feel that the hounding of people who happen to get 'into the news' can be carried too far. It is bringing newspapers into disrepute.

The Council wrote to the various newspaper proprietors' organisations expressing its concern at the allegation made against reporters in this article and expressed the hope that newspapers would do their best to avoid a repetition of such incidents.

The Newspaper Proprietors Association replied that it should have been given more evidence of such incidents than an article of opinion in a single newspaper. A copy of the Press Council's letter had, however, been circulated to its members. (1955/24–5)

A MODEL PRISONER

The *Daily Sketch* printed a report of the prompt recapture of two of four prisoners who escaped from Wormwood Scrubs Prison. Subsidiary to the main story was a news item headed: 'Scared girl flees from Britain'. It stated that a nineteen-year-old girl was leaving England for a hideout in Spain after months of living in terror of one of the two recaptured prisoners at whose trial she had given evidence. The report stated that she was in the house on the night a young married woman was raped by three named men who were subsequently convicted. The father of one of the named men complained that his son, who had been a model prisoner, was so upset by a newspaper reference to him that the prison welfare officer had mentioned to him his son's distress. The *Daily Sketch*, he said, was the only national newspaper to mention his son's name.

The Managing Editor of the newspaper, Mr Robert Johnston, said there was no intention to embarrass innocent parties. Facts previously published were used in the report only to the extent required to explain why the girl found it necessary to leave the country.

The Press Council in its ruling said that it would deplore the hounding of an ex-criminal and the dragging up of a man's past in an improper context, but a person convicted of a crime could not expect immunity from all subsequent journalistic reference. The father's name was not divulged by the Council. (1967)

For another case of hounding see p. 295 (*Sunday Dispatch, Croydon Times*).

15 Reports of Court Proceedings

Undoubtedly one of the most important services rendered by the Press is the publicity it focuses on the administration of justice.

The paramount importance of publicity to the maintenance of justice seems to have been recognised many centuries ago as is indicated by the following inscription from the tomb of Rekhmire, vizier to Tuthmosis III, King of Egypt in the XVIIIth dynasty (1580–1321 B.C.) quoted in the recent report (January 1967) of the American Newspaper Publishers' Association:

> Lo, whenever an administrator hears cases let there be publicity and let water and air report all that he may do. Lo, then his conduct is by no means unperceived. If he does anything (unseemly) and he is to blame he is not to be reinstalled on the authority of an acting official but men shall learn of it on the authority of his (proper) judge. . . .

In the course of the 1967 Riddell Lecture, Lord Denning, Master of the Rolls, stated that the presence of the Press in any court of justice was one of the foundations of British liberty; the Judge himself was on trial to see that he judged fairly.

A similar view was expressed in a 1966 American Judgment (Sheppard *v.* Maxwell, 384 U.S. 333) when the United States Supreme Court declared: 'The Press does not simply publish information about trials but guards against the miscarriage of justice by subjecting the police, prosecutors, and judicial processors to extensive public scrutiny and criticism.'

An example of how the vigilance of a reporter revealed an undesirable practice and how the publicity that followed caused the practice to be changed occurred in 1965. The reporter saw a man being escorted by a tipstaff from a room in the Royal Courts of Justice where a judge had been sitting *in camera*; he made inquiries and learned that the man had been sent to prison for contempt of court for not complying with a court order in a wardship case. A judge in such circumstances generally adjourns the case into open court so that the committal to prison can be made in public. But this was not essential, and under the Practice Rules the judge was entitled to make the committal order in chambers, that is to say while sitting in private without the public or the Press being present. The fact that a person could, under the existing procedure, be sent to prison in secret came as a shock to the public. Questions in Parliament revealed that the case was not an isolated one; the Attorney-General stated that in the previous twelve months thirteen applications for committal orders had been heard *in camera* and, of the four committals to prison, three were made *in camera*.

But for the alertness of the reporter the case would not have come to light. In the result the Rules of Court were changed and if a High Court judge sitting in chambers now decides to send a person to prison for contempt of court he must adjourn the case into open court and in the presence of the public and the Press state the person's name, the nature of the contempt and the length of the period of committal.

Reports of court proceedings are privileged, but only if the report is fair and accurate. The Press Council applies the same test of fairness and accuracy in determining whether a report of which complaint is made contravenes journalistic standards. Privilege is a question for the courts, ethics for the Council.

Although they operate in different spheres the work of the courts and the Press Council is often complementary. Acts of Parliament are drafted with precision, and the courts in giving effect to them must interpret them with equal precision. There is always an area adjoining the boundaries of the law in which good behaviour must be voluntary. It is in this area that the Press Council operates.

For example the Children and Young Persons Act, 1933, provides that no newspaper report of proceedings in a juvenile court shall reveal the name, address or school, or include any particulars calculated to lead to the identification of any child or young person concerned in those proceedings. In the cases that follow will be found instances where the Press Council dealt with reports that disclosed the identity of the juvenile or young person not in reporting court proceedings, which would have been a breach of the law, but in reports published before or after proceedings took place. The disclosure of the identity of the juvenile in such circumstances was not a breach of the law, but the Press Council regarded it as a breach of the spirit of the law and ethically reprehensible.

In other cases, which do not concern juveniles, the Council has held on ethical grounds that it is entirely wrong to disclose the names of victims of sex crimes and innocent relatives of persons convicted of criminal offences, even though the disclosure is not banned by the law.

Cases relating to persons who should not be identified are dealt with in Chapter 16. The cases that follow relate to occasions when the reporting of court proceedings gave rise to complaints to the Press Council.

IMPROPER REPORTS

ASSAULT UPON A GIRL OF ELEVEN

The Hull *Daily Mail* published a detailed report of a case of criminal assault upon a girl of eleven.

In a complaint to the Press Council the Hull Vigilance Association pointed out that the newspaper was the only local daily paper distributed in Hull and was in the nature of a family paper; the report was in the circumstances particularly unsuitable. As the accused had been committed for trial the Association wished, if possible, to prevent further publication of the details of the case.

The Editor stated that the case was one of considerable importance locally, and an unwelcome obligation had been put upon the local newspaper to report the proceedings notwithstanding that they were very unpleasant. Owing to the detail in which the Director of Public Prosecutions presented the case before the magistrates any report that aimed to be adequate could scarcely fail to be unpleasant. He admitted that certain terms and passages which had caused offence might have been omitted in the sub-editing, but said he was less in sympathy with the desire of the Hull Vigilance Association to prevent the report of future hearings of the case. If the Association meant only toning down the more frank details in future reports he would agree; if on the other hand the proposal was that future reports should be curtailed to the purely cursory to appease particular prejudices he could not agree, as this would amount to discriminative reporting.

The Press Council decided that the protest was fully justified. The newspaper had failed to observe the bounds of decency in publishing extensive details of the evidence. A special responsibility lay upon editors and sub-editors in handling proceedings for rape. That they should be reported, and in some cases reported at length, could not be disputed; it would be gravely to the detriment of the public interest, if, because of the nature of the offence, criminals of this type were spared the spotlight of publicity or those found not guilty deprived of the advertisement of their innocence. British newspapers had shown almost daily that such cases could be reported without going into unsavoury detail. The duty to report the general outline of the case did not entail a duty to repeat the abhorrent elements which if published could demoralise readers, particularly young people.

The Council added that these considerations were generally kept in mind by journalists, and the Council wished to endorse their correctness. (1955/18–19, 36–8)

UNNECESSARY ABHORRENT DETAILS

Two Ealing doctors complained that the report in the *Middlesex County*

Times of an Old Bailey hearing of a case in which four men were convicted of a series of gross offences against a young girl was offensive, unnecessary, unworthy of the Press and not in the public interest.

Mr C. R. Wallis, the Editor of the newspaper, Mr W. K. Hoenes, Editor-in-chief, said that, although the staff found it distasteful to report such cases, a newspaper would be lacking in its duty if it did not report all aspects of life in the area it served, There had been no deliberate exploitation of sex, but the contemporary society to which the report was presented would expect it to be dealt with in an adult manner.

The Press Council agreed that cases of this nature should be reported by newspapers as a matter of public interest. At the same time the Council felt that in this instance the detailed reporting in certain passages went beyond what was necessary to convey an adequate impression of the nature and seriousness of the case. It called the attention of the newspaper to its observations made in 1955 on the principles that should underlie the presentation of cases of an unsavoury nature (set out in the preceding case concerning the Hull *Daily Mail*). (1961/27–8)

The selection of cases for inclusion in the newspaper is a matter for the editor, but the choice should be made honestly and not for improper reasons. When the selection has been made no unfair discrimination should be made in the presentation of the facts.

IMPROPER OMISSION OF DEFENDANT'S NAME

The *Ashton-under-Lyne Reporter* was said to have omitted from the report of a case the name of a firm fined £40 for failure to provide a power press with adequate guards. This was the only case in the particular issue of the paper where the name of the defendant had been omitted. The point was conceded that the Editor was entitled to choose what he should report but, it was claimed, having made his choice he was morally bound to publish all the relevant particulars.

The Managing Editor, Mr Gerald Andrew, said the omission was an oversight and was regretted. Several appeals for suppression of the identity of people concerned in court cases were received every week, he said, but they were consistently rejected.

The Press Council stated the fact that this was the only omission of the name of a defendant in the specific issue of the newspaper would inevitably give rise to the suspicion that favouritism had been shown. The Council censured the newspaper for neglecting to give the name and failing to rectify the omission. (1964/76)

No newspaper relishes criticism from the bench. Nevertheless where this has been incurred journalistic standards require that the criticism should be published and not suppressed.

A JUDICIAL REBUKE

During the hearing of a divorce case at Leeds Assizes in 1965 the *Yorkshire Post* published a report of the evidence. In so doing it contravened the prohibition imposed by law against reporting evidence in such cases. On the day the report appeared, the Judge, Mr Justice Scarman, drew attention to the infringement of the law. He said that this was one of the rare divorce cases in which the publicity did no harm to the public or private interests concerned, but in the majority of cases harm could be done; this was the reason Parliament had passed legislation against reporting the evidence. The Judge added: 'I would ask the Press in Leeds and elsewhere to be particularly careful in divorce matters to observe the requirements of the Act.'

No report of the Judge's observations appeared in the *Yorkshire Post*, and the omission was reported to the Press Council.

The explanation given by the Editor, Mr K. Young, was that the judge's observations were addressed to the reporters in court and not to the public at large.

The Press Council held that although the newspaper's error was a technical breach, it should have published the Judge's remarks. (1965/54)

A QUESTION OF COURTESY

Should persons before the courts be referred to by their surname only in newspaper reports of the proceedings?

A schoolmaster prosecuted for beating a boy—on a private summons which was dismissed — complained that the report in the *Mansfield Chronicle-Advertiser* was biased; it presented him in a derogatory light and, while great prominence was given to the evidence of the boy which was challenged and disproved, little space was given to the evidence for the defence. He further complained that, although he had been addressed as 'Mr' by all in court,

K

the newspaper referred to him only by his surname. Anyone reading the report, he maintained, would get the impression that he was a sadistic bully.

The Editor said it was not possible to print a verbatim report, but the summary reported was both fair and accurate. The headline stated the charge was dismissed, and this was also made clear in the introduction. It was his newspaper's policy not to accord courtesy titles to anyone appearing before the court, on the ground that it was important that in the eyes of the law all men are equal.

The Press Council did not accept that the report was unfair or biased, but considered that as the schoolmaster was an unconvicted defendant the use of the term 'Mr' would have been appropriate. (1965/41–2)

AN UNCO-OPERATIVE EDITOR

The Town Clerk of Inverness wrote to the Press Council on behalf of the Inverness magistrates stating that two coal merchants had the same day been convicted by the Sheriff and each fined for selling coal underweight. One of the cases was fully reported in the *Highland Herald*, the other was not mentioned. The magistrates, the Town Clerk wrote, considered this apparent discrimination was unjust.

The Managing Editor of the *Highland Herald*, Mr Alastair Grant, told the Press Council that the editor of a newspaper had the right to use his own discretion as to what items of news he would publish in his paper. 'Fortunately,' he said, 'town clerks or town councils have quite definitely not the right to instruct him in the matter, nor, as you know, has the Press Council, and I resent this ill-advised attempt to do so . . . I do not propose to engage in any further correspondence on this matter.'

The Town Clerk said he was aware that the editor of a newspaper had the right to use his own discretion, but if the newspaper was publishing a report in the public interest then it was strange that it should record the conviction against only one party and not against the other fined for precisely the same offence.

The Editor had discriminated in the matter.

The Press Council passed the following resolution:

The Press Council regrets the attitude taken by the Managing Editor of the *Highland Herald*, Mr Alastair Grant, towards the Council's efforts to investigate a complaint. . . . On being invited to explain the apparent discrimination the Editor refused to do so, on the ground that it was for him alone to decide what to print. . . . The Press Council looks on this attempt to brush aside the complaint without a word of explanation as high handed, unworthy and a misuse of editorial power.

The Editor subsequently published a front-page article giving an explanation. The Press Council thereupon passed a further resolution regretting that the *Highland Herald* had published a misleading article in which it accused the Press Council of not appearing to have taken the trouble to verify the facts of the case. The Council stated the facts were that the Editor had refused an invitation to explain his apparent discrimination, would give no assistance in verifying the facts, and was thereupon told that the Press Council regarded his conduct as high-handed and unworthy. The newspaper now gave as its explanation the exigencies of space changing from week to week. 'The Press Council regrets that it has needed so much effort to get this explanation. It deplores the offensive manner in which the Editor has treated a proper request put by the Press Council in the interests of the Press as well as the public.' (1955/26–7, 47–9)

JURY DISCHARGED BECAUSE OF NEWSPAPER REPORT

During the trial of a case at Margate Quarter Sessions the Recorder called on all persons present in his court not to disclose an important fact to the jury which was out of court at the time.

The *Isle of Thanet Gazette* published this fact the following day while the case was in progress. The Recorder held that a fair trial had been prejudiced, discharged the jury and sent the accused men for trial to another Quarter Sessions. He referred the newspaper report to the Press Council, saying he did not feel that he need make any comment on the unfortunate affair, but he thought it right to leave it to the Council to take such action as might be deemed fit.

Mr E. T. Wenman, the Editor of the newspaper, tendered his apologies to the Recorder for the breach of confidence. Such an incident, he said, had never occurred before in his experience, and so far as his newspaper was concerned would never happen again. It had been a very sharp lesson to the whole of the reporting staff. The reporter was a young man whose attention had been distracted from what the Recorder had said.

The Council endorsed the complaint of the Recorder and noted the admission of error and the apology made. The Secretary to the Council was instructed to forward copies of the Recorder's letter to affiliated organisations.

In his covering letter to the affiliated organisations the Secretary drew attention to the paramount importance of the reporter's concentration on the proceedings of the court. The case had shown the need for direction to the inexperienced man. It also indicated the need for warning a young reporter that the indictment in the trial court may differ from the accusation preferred before an examining magistrate. Consequently, in the preparation of 'copy' it is dangerous to rely upon reports of what transpired in the lower court. (1961/34–5)

A ONE-SIDED REPORT

When a defendant in a magistrates' court reserves his defence and elects to go for trial, a newspaper is entitled to report the proceedings, even though serious allegations by the prosecution go unanswered. In such cases news editors must see that a full and fair summary of the defence is included in the report of the trial in the higher court.

The Press Council expressed this view in the adjudication of a complaint against the *South Wales Echo* in respect of its reports of a case at Petty Sessions and Quarter Sessions. The complainant alleged that the newspaper gave only statements made by the prosecution at the preliminary hearing without the modification that emerged in cross-examination. The report also stated that the defendant had been sent for trial giving the impression that the magistrate had deemed the case to be of such gravity that it should be dealt with by a higher court, when in fact the case was remitted for trial at the election of the accused.

The Sessions jury found the defendant not guilty on all counts, but the *Echo* report allocated fewer than forty words to the defendant's rebuttal of the allegations against him. The testimony of his six witnesses and his counsel's address were ignored, and no hint was given of the Recorder's observation that he was a man of unblemished character.

The Editor of the newspaper, Mr John H. Wiggins, admitted that his reporter did not attend the Petty Sessions hearing, but obtained the facts from the police officer. He regretted the inaccuracy in the statements that the defendant had been sent for trial. The report of the Quarter Sessions hearing, however, made it clear that he had been found not guilty.

The Press Council found that the newspaper to be seriously at fault in stating that the defendant was 'sent for trial' when in fact he had 'elected to go for trial'. The report of the subsequent trial ignored the evidence of six witnesses for the defence, and, while it reported briefly the case presented by prosecuting counsel, it gave not one word spoken by counsel for the defence. The report of the trial was inadequate, incomplete and unfair to the defendant. It fell much below the standards of balanced reporting. (1963/30–1)

DOUBLE CENSURE

A businessman chased and caught a car which was towing his own away. As a result three men were accused of being concerned in the theft.

Reporting the proceedings before the magistrates, the *Daily Mail* and the *Daily Sketch* stated that the three men towed away the car, although no evidence to justify this was given in court. When the case was tried at London Sessions one of the men was acquitted, but neither newspaper published this fact.

The man complained that, having informed the public that he had been accused of theft, the newspapers had a duty to correct their error and to record his acquittal at the Sessions. He had written to both Editors but did not receive a reply.

Mr Ingram, Deputy Editor of the *Daily Mail*, told the Council that no trace of the letter could be found; the Editor of the *Daily Sketch*, Mr Howard French, said that inquiries were made immediately after the receipt of the letter, but delay was occasioned by the absence on holiday of the reporters concerned.

The reporter who covered the proceedings for the *Daily Mail* and the news agencies at Sessions attended most of the hearing, but as the case was listed for the following day he left the court at 4 o'clock. Unexpectedly the case was finished that evening.

The Editor-in-Chief of the Press Association, Mr C. Jarvis, stated the case was a rare occasion on which human error had upset the operation of an effective system of covering cases.

Both the newspapers published a report of the man's acquittal when the Press Council called attention to the omission, but neither referred to the error in the report of the case in the magistrates' court.

The Press Council found that the court reporting, usually efficient, had broken down on this occasion with the result that the two newspapers failed to report the acquittal until their attention was later drawn to the matter. Both had also misreported the proceedings before the Justices and failed to publish a correction. The Council censured them for this and further censured the *Daily Sketch* for failing to express regret for the delay in reporting the acquittal. (1965/45–7)

DEFENCE NOT REPORTED

A youth complained that although actions against him and a friend were dismissed by Southend magistrates, the *Southend Standard* report of the hearing gave the points made for the prosecution but not a word of the successful rebuttal in defence.

The one-sided presentation of the facts amounted to a newspaper indictment of himself and his friend. When he complained to the Editor, he was told that the report was as fair as it could be made in all the circumstances because the evidence given by the youths and their witness was mostly inaudible.

The Editor, Mr K. H. Broadley, said that neither of the two senior reporters present could hear enough of the evidence to enable them to report any of it. There were repeated requests by the court that the witnesses should speak up. He felt justified in publishing the report as it was, because it seemed that dismissal of the accusations was based not so much on what the defendants said as on the inadequate evidence of the police.

The Press Council found that the report devoting considerable space to details of the prosecution but none to the defence was inadequate and unfair. In spite of hearing difficulties the newspaper should have included at least the gist of the defence which influenced the court in its decision to dismiss the charges. (1964/40)

IMPROPER THREATS TO
INFLUENCE REPORTS

An important declaration on the right of the Press to publish evidence given in open court was issued by the Council in May 1964. It arose out of statements made by defence counsel and the Chairman of the magistrates in two separate cases. The first of these was:

THE GREAT TRAIN ROBBERY

During the committal proceedings before the magistrates at Aylesbury in the Great Train Robbery case counsel for some of the defendants submitted to the magistrates that certain evidence tendered by the prosecution was inadmissible. The submission was rejected. Counsel then applied for the evidence to be heard *in camera*; this too was refused, but the Chairman of the magistrates asked the Press to exercise discretion and report only what was absolutely necessary.

After some of the disputed evidence had been given, defence counsel stated in open court that if any part of the evidence was reported by the Press, B.B.C. or television the matter would be referred to the Attorney-General with a view to proceedings for contempt of court on the ground that the report prejudiced a fair trial.

The threats made by counsel were referred to the Press Council.

The second case occurred in Oldham.

THE OLDHAM MAGISTRATES CASE

During committal proceedings in a case of considerable public interest involving charges of false pretences against men who were well known locally, counsel for one of the defendants asked for the hearing to be held *in camera* on the ground that he might at a later stage object to the admissibility of some of the evidence. The magistrates refused the request, but asked the Press not to report certain evidence, since there was doubt about its admissibility.

The *Oldham Evening Chronicle* in reporting what had taken place protested against what it called the attempt of the Bench to place on the shoulders of newspaper editors the burden of decisions which properly belonged to the court. Counsel for the defence alleged the comment constituted contempt of court. Some days later counsel objected to certain police evidence; the magistrates then decided to hear the evidence *in camera* and asked the Press not to print the police evidence already given at a previous hearing.

The case was also referred to the Press Council.

Having considered both cases the Press Council issued a statement the substance of which was:

1. It is a fundamental principle of British justice that subject to certain statutory restrictions, justice should be administered openly and in open court, and it is the duty as well as the right of the Press to publish full and fair reports of the proceedings.

2. As an alternative to the exercise by the court of a power to hear evidence in private judges and magistrates sometimes ask the Press not to publish evidence. Where such a request is made it should be complied with. The Council believed that judges and magistrates were conscious of the fundamental principle that justice must be done openly and did not make such requests except in the overriding interest of a fair trial.

3. A specific request is unnecessary in the case of a trial by jury where the evidence is given by witnesses or mentioned by counsel in the absence of the jury.

4. Requests of the kind made by the Chairman in the Great Train Robbery case that the Press should exercise discretion in reporting the evidence are quite impossible for the Press to comply with. A reporter cannot be expected to judge what should be reported and what should not.

5. The Press Council was ready to believe that counsel in making threats to the Press were acting out of a sense of duty to their clients, but in the interests of the freedom of the Press the Council had to express itself quite clearly. There was no authority whatever for the suggestion that newspapers which published what had taken place in open court, there being no ruling from the Bench to the contrary, could be punished for contempt of court. The further suggestion that the Press would be guilty of contempt unless it took steps which the court itself had not taken to ensure for the defendants what their counsel thought necessary for a fair trial and to remedy what he deemed to be the injustice done by the ruling of the court was, in the opinion of the Council, absurd. Editors and reporters should not be deterred by threats from the performance of their duty to the public.

6. The Council had expressed itself strongly because within a short time several such suggestions had been made by members of the Bar.

7. Nothing that the Council had said was intended to derogate from the right and duty of an editor or reporter to exercise his own discretion in refraining from reporting details of legal proceedings when the pain and distress that publicity might cause to an innocent individual outweighed the public interest. The only principle that could govern the use of this discretion was that it must be exercised always without fear or favour. The danger that

suppression might be ascribed to fear or to favouritism was sufficiently great and the need for publicity for legal proceedings so important that exceptions to the rule must be rare. (1964/13–16)

The Press Council statement appears in full in Appendix III.

REPORTS VINDICATED

A MAGISTRATE'S UNFAIR CRITICISM

This was a case not against a newspaper but of a complaint by a newspaper of unfair criticism directed at the local Press.

The case arose out of an article published in the *Guardian* on 28 December 1965.

The article described a case in which a man of good character and the father of a family had appeared before a local Bench on charges of shop-lifting. The man's wife had sent a letter to the Chairman of the Bench asking him to use his influence to keep any reference to the case out of the local newspapers for the sake of the children. The article, written by one of the magistrates concerned in the case, said that the Bench was unanimous in its desire to help a courageous woman.

> But how best to do so? We knew the local Press. To make such a re-quest for any omission could prove tantamount to seeking publicity. Their independence was jealously preserved. After discussion we de-cided to hand the letter over to the reporters without comment. In the event both papers went to town on the case. In one it was front-page news.

The 'local Press' was the *Sutton and Cheam Advertiser* and the *Sutton and Cheam Herald*. The article by the magistrate was referred to the Press Council by another newspaper.

The Press Council stated that justice was ordinarily administered in public because the importance of publicity outweighed the pain and distress that might be caused to individuals concerned. Publicity was generally regarded as part of the punishment a man of good character convicted in criminal proceedings had to bear. Judges not infrequently mentioned this fact as one they had taken into consideration as enabling them to deal with a convicted man more leniently than they would otherwise have done. Inevitably any

K 2   L.T.P.C.

punishment, whether it be publicity or imprisonment or even a substantial fine, must be felt by a man's wife and family.

Newspapers often received requests, some meritorious and others not, for suppression of details of criminal proceedings. They could not as a rule accede to them. If suppression were to be practised on a large scale, it would be an interference with the ordinary course of justice; it was for Parliament and not for the Press to define categories of cases such as proceedings in juvenile courts, to which publicity should not be given. If practised only occasionally it would lead to charges of unfair discrimination and would be open to abuse. Very exceptional circumstances could justify departure from every rule and the consideration of these must always be a matter for editorial discretion.

The Council repeated paragraph 7 of its declaration of May 1964 on the right of the Press to publish evidence given in open court which is set out on p. 282.

No responsible newspaper, the Press Council went on to say, could regard a request for suppression as a reason or as an excuse for giving greater publicity to an item of this sort than otherwise it would have merited. The passage quoted above from the magistrate's article clearly made this charge against two local papers, the *Sutton and Cheam Advertiser* and the *Sutton and Cheam Herald*. The passage was inaccurate and unfair both in what it said and in what it implied.

The *Advertiser* on page 5 had given no more space to the item than was necessary for a fair report. The *Herald* had given no report of the hearing at all. It was therefore inaccurate to say that, 'Both papers went to town on the case. In one it was front-page news'. On the point that the *Herald* carried no report at all of the hearing, the magistrate who was the writer of the article, by way of justification, referred the Council to a report in that newspaper of an earlier hearing of the same case three weeks before. As this was published before any request to the Press was made it was irrelevant to the suggestion that after receiving the request the newspaper 'went to town' on the case.

On the statement that 'to make a request for any omission could prove tantamount to seeking publicity', the magistrate said that the risk of a refusal seemed grave enough to deter the Bench from making the request. The Press Council commented that since there could be no risk involved in making a request if the only result was a refusal, this statement emphasised the view that the magistrate appeared unfortunately still to hold that the making of a request might result in greater publicity than would otherwise have been given to the news.

In support of this view the magistrate had cited to the Council two specific cases and a 'personal pre-war experience on a local paper, when any overt request that a matter should not receive publicity often carried with it the likelihood of refusal'. One of the two specific cases concerned a shoplifting offence in Wakefield. Neither this case nor the magistrate's experience on an unidentified local paper could justify the innuendo contained in the words 'We knew the local Press'. Nor was there any suggestion that there was any increased publicity resulting from the request, only that it was likely to be refused.

The other specific case concerned a report of shoplifting published in the *Sutton and Cheam Herald* on 26 November 1965 which the magistrate said was published after an informal request for omission made by a probation officer. Here again there appeared to be no suggestion of any increased publicity, and the Press Council had no fault to find with the way in which the Editor had exercised his discretion in reporting the case.

The Council considered that the statement quoted from the magistrate's article published in the *Guardian*, which would have been widely read as attributing to the local Press a standard of conduct far below that of a responsible newspaper, was quite unjustified. (1966)

LORD CHANCELLOR REFUSED TO APOLOGISE

The Editor of the *Wokingham Times* complained that the Lord Chancellor had refused to apologise for statements made on his behalf about a report published in the newspaper concerning a boy charged at the local juvenile court.

The matter was raised in the House of Commons, and it was stated that the Lord Chancellor considered that the report of the remarks made by the presiding magistrate was misleading because they were not published in full and were taken out of their proper context.

The Press Council examined the reporter's shorthand notes and decided that, although there was insufficient evidence on which to record a conclusive finding, the available evidence upheld the Editor's view that the report of the remarks made by the magistrate as far as it went was an accurate one. (1960/32)

16 Persons who should not be Named

JUVENILES IN JUVENILE COURTS

Under the law relating to juveniles, a newspaper may not in reporting juvenile court proceedings reveal the name, address, school or other particulars likely to identify a juvenile as being the person against whom the proceedings are taken or as being a witness in the proceedings; nor may pictures of such juveniles be published. The ban on identification will be dispensed with only if the court or the Secretary of State thinks that in a particular case the interests of justice require that it should be, and then only to the extent specified in the order.

The Press Council has made it clear in a number of cases that this protection against the disclosure of the names of juveniles must be observed in the spirit as well as in the letter. When, for instance, the *Rotherham Advertiser* published a report giving the name and the name of the school of a boy who was to appear in a juvenile court two days later in connection with the disappearance of a motor-cycle, the Press Council declared the publication violated the spirit of the law. (1959/24)

The following year the Council rejected a complaint that the *Harrow Observer and Gazette*, in reporting a case in the juvenile court, had given sufficient details to enable a boy to be identified, though his name had not been given. The Council held there was no positive identification but took the opportunity to remind Editors of the great care which should be exercised to observe the spirit as well as the letter of the law. (1960/27)

Some years later a father complained that a report in the *Crawley Courier* had identified his son by disclosing the name of the son's employer. The result had been that the boy's sister had been caused great misery at school.

The Press Council held that the newspaper was seriously at fault. (1964/58)

JUVENILES IN NON-JUVENILE COURTS

When a juvenile is involved in proceedings in a non-juvenile court, newspapers are not prohibited from publishing the name or other identifying particulars unless the court orders that they should not do so. Editors, however, sometimes find it difficult to decide whether they should publish names when there has been no order to the contrary.

Attention was focused on this situation when a young woman police officer of a society doing rescue work among children drew the attention of the Press Council to reports in some newspapers of a prosecution for rape in which the victim, a girl of fourteen, was named. No direction had been given by the court that the girl's name and address were not to be given. The point was made to the Press Council that had the girl been appearing in a juvenile court the newspapers would have been prohibited from naming her.

The Editors of the newspapers which had published her name, while generally agreeing that children should not suffer the odium of identification, said they were put in a difficult position when a court which had the power to stop publication of the name did not do so.

The Press Association was asked by the Press Council for details of their practice when reporting such cases. The Association replied that they considered it their duty to report the proceedings fully, including names and addresses of juvenile witnesses; they did not consider it right to operate a censorship on names where the court had made no order against their use. The Association left it to individual Editors to make their own decision.

The Press Council referred the matter to the Home Secretary, and drew his attention to the anomalous position. Protection against identification was based on the consideration of what was in the best interests of the juvenile. If these were best served by not publishing the name to the world, it was strange that the protection should to a large extent depend on the court in which the proceedings were heard. In non-juvenile courts, there was no procedure in operation under which a magistrate or judge made a decision before the hearing opened on whether to direct that reports should not reveal the name of a juvenile involved. Sometimes the matter was dealt with too late to prevent publication of names in the early edition; on other occasions the question was never brought to the notice of the court at all, and consequently no decision of any kind was given. The Press Council suggested to the Home Secretary that when the proceedings took place in a non-juvenile court, the court should consider at the outset of the hearing whether a direction should be given that names of juveniles should not be published.

The Home Secretary, Major Lloyd George, replied that he was in full agreement about the desirability of ensuring that the power of the court was operated as effectively as possible to ensure that child witnesses were protected and that reporters were in no doubt whether they might or might not publish identifying particulars. He promised to consider the position with senior officers of the police. (1955/33-4)

Early in 1956 he informed the Press Council that he had communicated with Clerks to the Justices, Chief Constables and Clerks of Assize and had urged that, in all proceedings in non-juvenile courts in which children and young persons were involved, the court should be reminded at the start of the hearing that it could give a direction prohibiting the publication of identifying particulars. Where a person was committed for trial, the Clerk to the Justices should enclose a statement with the depositions, indicating whether the examining justices had given a direction prohibiting identification of any child or young person concerned.

The Home Secretary's action was warmly welcomed by organisations concerned with the welfare of children.

The effect of the arrangement was to put the responsibility on the court for directing whether or not a newspaper should reveal the identity of any child or young person concerned in the proceedings in non-juvenile courts. If the court, having considered the facts, makes no order, an editor may name the juvenile without breaking the law or incurring the criticism of the Press Council, although he may of his own volition still decide to withhold the names.

A newspaper may unwittingly name a young person in circumstances where it would not have done so had it known all the facts or appreciated the consequences that would follow. For example, the London *Evening News* published the name, age and address of a girl under seventeen who was stated to have been dragged into an alley and assaulted. Five days later a man was accused of rape. The Press Council accepted the Editor's explanation that he was misinformed about the circumstances and did not know that a charge of rape was to be made in respect of the offence. The Council stressed the need for extreme care in identifying young persons involved in sexual offences. (1962/47-8)

JUVENILES — OTHER CIRCUMSTANCES

Newspaper reports unconnected with the Courts can sometimes have deplorable consequences for children.

COLOURED SCHOOLGIRL AND POETRY CONTEST

The case concerned a coloured schoolgirl who won a poetry contest and was invited to read her poem on a B.B.C. radio programme. This led to the discovery that the poem was not original.

The *Daily Mail* published a picture of the girl and gave her name and address. An interview with the girl and her mother was also reported and an account given of how the child had stood shamefaced while the head teacher exposed her before four hundred schoolmates. As a result of the publicity the child and her parents were subjected to threatening and offensive letters. To save her from further humiliation the girl was sent back to the West Indies and so parted from her family.

The Editor, Mr Michael Randall, pointed out that the report appeared in the *Daily Mail* after the child had been reprimanded before the school and the matter given widespread publicity by the B.B.C.

The Press Council in its adjudication said that no Editor could have foreseen the regrettable events which followed publication of the story. Nevertheless it had to be borne in mind that particulars which cannot be published in the case of a child involved in court proceedings are capable of causing harm even when related to less culpable action. The Council regretted that the child had been identified. (1964/53–4)

Two cases in which children were identified did not have the same immediate consequences. In one the child was still too young to appreciate the significance of the information published about her. Nevertheless, the publicity was considered to be in the worst taste. In the other, identification was likely to damage the child's future life. The circumstances of the two cases were:

A DOOMED CHILD

The *Daily Mail* published a photograph and disclosed the name, age and school of a six-year-old girl whom the doctors expected would die from a rare blood disease before she reached teenage.

The Editor, Mr William Hardcastle, did not seek to excuse the publication, but said the child's mother, a trained nurse, had consented to the publication and had allowed the child to appear on television on the day the story appeared.

The Press Council censured the newspaper for its callous article and photograph, but welcomed the Editor's admission of an error of judgment. (1962/36–7)

IDENTIFYING AN ILLEGITIMATE CHILD

An article in the *Sunday Pictorial* disclosed that a child whose name and photograph were published was illegitimate. In consequences, the child's history was revealed to her school companions.

The Editor, Mr Colin Valdar, stated that the question of the child's legitimacy was irrelevant to the report. No newspaper, he contended, would wish to distress a child by labelling it illegitimate.

The Press Council condemned the *Sunday Pictorial* for disclosing that the child was illegitimate and added that, although the Editor had declared that the inference of illegitimacy could not be drawn from what had been printed, the Council was of the opinion that the article could bear no other inference. (1956/33)

ADULTS WHO SHOULD NOT BE IDENTIFIED

The Press Council has held that there are occasions when even the names of adults should not be published.

AN OLD LAG

A case in question was that of a man who had spent two-thirds of his life in gaol, but had gone straight for ten years, and wished to thank those who had helped him. He asked the *People* to print a message, but said that he did not want his identity revealed. The newspaper printed an appropriate statement, but with it published a large photograph of the man and his dog.

The Editor, Mr Stuart Campbell, said the picture was ten years old and that the man and the dog had since altered in appearance.

The Press Council ruled that in publishing the photograph of an 'old lag' the newspaper had been guilty of a breach of faith.

Disclosure of the man's identity, however, had a happy ending in this case: he received many gifts from readers touched by the story. (1964/81–2)

REPROACH BY LORD CHIEF JUSTICE

The Court of Criminal Appeal had substituted a probation order for a sentence of preventive detention on a man whose former employer offered to re-employ him because he was confident that given a chance the man would be able to start a new life.

After the man was released on probation a reporter discovered where he was working. On going to the factory the reporter asked one of the workers whether he liked working with a man who had six previous convictions. The probationer's identity was, as a result, revealed; his position became impossible, and he had to be moved to another factory.

Lord Goddard, the Lord Chief Justice, sternly rebuked the reporter, telling him that what he had done was hitting a man when he was down. The court, he said, would not on this occasion take any action against him but hoped the Press itself would ensure that nothing similar happened again.

The Press Council endorsed the Lord Chief Justice's remarks and circulated his statement. In a letter of thanks to the Council, Lord Goddard said that his experience of the Press satisfied him that what had happened was out of character. (1959/18)

WOMAN WITNESS IDENTIFIED

A case was brought to the attention of the Press Council in which the name of a woman witness for the prosecution for attempted rape had been published, despite the fact that she had made a written request to the police that her name should not be disclosed.

The Council's inquiries established that her request had not been communicated to the magistrates during the hearing, and they had made no request on the subject to the Press.

The Council issued a statement emphasising that any request for the suppression of the name of a witness should be made to the magistrates at the opening of the case. It had little doubt that an editor in his discretion would carefully and sympathetically consider such an application if it was supported by the magistrates. (1957/28–9)

DISCLOSURE OF A SUPPRESSED NAME

The *Yorkshire Post* disclosed the identity of a young woman who had befriended a criminal, although judges of the Court of Criminal Appeal had refrained from doing so. A complaint was made that the newspaper had imperilled the chance of the man's redemption through the woman and their future happiness.

The couple had met just before the man was concerned in an armed robbery for which he was sentenced to ten years' imprisonment. The woman prevailed upon him to confess his crime, and the Court of Criminal Appeal halved his sentence because of her readiness to marry him. The newspaper, in its report of the appeal, stated that the girl's name was kept secret, but on the following day, under the heading, 'Hockey girl who loves a criminal', it revealed her name, employment, sporting distinctions and her father's occupation.

The *Yorkshire Post* published a letter of protest, with a footnote by the Editor stating that although the judges did not identify the woman, they did not make an order forbidding identification.

In its adjudication the Press Council said that in reports of this nature public curiosity is often aroused about unnamed persons. This, however, did not justify a newspaper ascertaining and publishing identifying particulars including, in this case, even the occupation of the father. The Council condemned the action of the *Yorkshire Post*, but took note of the fact that it had published a letter criticising the disclosure. (1962/39)

VICTIM'S NAME REVEALED

The *Kent Messenger*, in reporting that a young man had been sent to prison for an indecent assault on a local schoolteacher, disclosed the teacher's name.

The Editor, Mr H. R. Pratt Boorman, said the case was reported factually in his newspaper, but in accordance with an office ruling about cases of indecent assault, no details were given. Had the chairman of the bench requested that the name of the girl, who was not a juvenile, should not be used, the newspaper would not have mentioned it.

The Press Council's adjudication was that while it is impossible to lay down a generally applicable rule as to when the name of a person who has been indecently assaulted should or should not be reported, the Press Council considered that unless there are special circumstances, the name of the victim should not be published. In this case the Editor did not appear to have given any special consideration to the question. Had he done so, he would have found ample reason for omitting the name of the assaulted woman. (1965/71–2)

VICTIMS OF SEX CRIMES IDENTIFIED

A man was prosecuted for having raped three women and indecently assaulted another. The husband of one of them complained when *The Times* published the names and addresses of the victims. He said that no public interest was served by identifying the women. He and his wife were distressed by the report because it had destroyed their hope that the information could be kept from their sons.

The Editor of *The Times*, Sir William Haley, said that names were not printed where a request was made by the court that they should not be published. No request of this kind was made on this occasion. He agreed that they should not have been printed, and he had written a letter of regret to the husband.

The Press Council said the publication of the names and addresses of the women was a serious lapse, but it took note that the Editor had expressed deep regret. (1966/49)

SUICIDE AFTER IDENTITY REVEALED

An inquest was held in Staffordshire on a young man who had committed suicide after an affair with a married woman had ended. Although the woman's name and address were mentioned by a witness, none of the local reporters identified her in their reports. The coroner expressed the wish that the woman should not be identified.

She subsequently moved to a new address and was interviewed on behalf of the Birmingham *Sunday Mercury* but told the reporter she was anxious that no story should be published because of the effect on her children. Nevertheless a report was published under the heading, 'Mother of Six is

Trying to Forget', disclosed her name and address and recalled the inquest on the young man. As a result of the publication the woman committed suicide.

The Editor of the newspaper, Mr Frederick Whitehead, who was away on leave at the time the story was published, said the woman knew she was speaking to a reporter and that what she said might be published. He added: 'I feel all of us, in the light of subsequent happenings, feel that it would have been better if this story had not been used.'

The Press Council decided that the newspaper was gravely at fault in identifying the woman, following a request by the coroner that her name should not be divulged. The newspaper was also at fault in seeking out the woman at her new address, and in publishing the story it committed a grave violation of journalistic standards which deserved the strongest censure. (1959/17–18, 30–1)

INNOCENT RELATIVES

Another class of case which the Press Council has had to consider is that in which innocent relatives of criminals have been needlessly identified.

SEQUEL TO IDENTIFICATION

Complaint by the sister of a man convicted of murder who because of his age had been sentenced to be detained during Her Majesty's pleasure. At the time he was about to be released a *Sunday Dispatch* reporter interviewed the sister; she told him that she had two children at a local school and wished to avoid publicity. Nevertheless, the newspaper reported the brother's impending release and gave the sister's name and the district where she resided.

Following the publication of the report, the family's privacy was invaded by visits and telephone calls from other newspapers.

A report was also carried by the *Croydon Times*, which, in addition to the sister's address, also gave the address of the man's parents who had returned to England after having gone abroad.

Mr Herbert Gunn, Editor of the *Sunday Dispatch*, expressed regret and apologised to the sister. The Editor of the *Croydon Times* told the Press

Council that residents looked to the local paper for greater detail of a story relating to their area published in a mass-circulation newspaper. There was no intention to hound the relatives.

The Press Council ruled that:

1. The release of convicted murderers is a matter of public interest, but in reporting the release Editors should take special care to avoid identification of innocent relatives. The Editors of the two newspapers had failed in this duty.

2. The local newspaper was the more blameworthy for publishing the parents' address; the reason given by the newspaper that the residents in the specific area would expect a fuller story from the local newspaper was wholly indefensible.

3. Both newspapers had hounded the relatives and shown callous disregard for their feelings. (1961/30–1)

HEADMISTRESS IDENTIFIED

The *Stratford Express*, in reporting a charge of indecency against a well-known public man, stated that he had been living with a relative whom the newspaper identified as a former headmistress of a named school. Complaint was made to the Press Council that the identification was irrelevant and distressing both to the lady and a reputable institution, and showed a 'lack of humanity and ordinary consideration'.

The Editor-in-Chief, Mr Ivan W. Smith, said the lady's address was given on the charge sheet, and he thought this address and home background were of sufficient public interest to warrant publication.

The Press Council disagreed and strongly condemned the newspaper for identifying the relative, more particularly because of the prominent position she had formerly held in the field of education.

The Press Council again directed the attention to the harm caused by giving unnecessary publicity to innocent persons who are unconnected with such cases. (1963/31–2)

UNNECESSARY IDENTIFICATION

A complaint was made against the *Daily Mail* for its report of the same case. The Editor, Mr William Hardcastle, agreed that it was unfortunate when a family member was mentioned in an unpleasant case, but contended the information in this instance was brief, published without prominence and relevant to the man's background.

The Press Council stated that the name, address and professional status of the relative was unnecessary to the identification of the accused man in the public mind, and condemned the newspaper for giving it. (1963/39)

IDENTIFICATION BY PICTURE

The *Daily Express* published a picture of the wife of a convicted murderer, described by the judge in her action for divorce as a woman who had borne dreadful misfortunes with dignity. In an interview with the newspaper after the action, she was reported as saying that she was no longer Mrs ———, which was her married name; she said that she had adopted another name and lived in another town. The publication of the picture had revealed her identity.

Complaint was made that the point of the wife having changed her name to preserve her anonymity in her new life had been irreparably ruined by the newspaper's publication of her photograph. The judge had allowed her to write down her new name to avoid disclosing it when she gave evidence.

The Editor, Mr Robert Edwards, said the publication was accidental; the person responsible for the picture had not seen the story and the reference to the change of name.

The Press Council took note of the Editor's explanation, but once again drew the attention of editors to the need to exercise the greatest care to avoid unnecessary identification of innocent persons connected with criminals. (1964/55)

RELATIVES OF A SPY

After George Blake had been sentenced to forty-two years' imprisonment for spying, the *Sunday Telegraph* reproduced a copy of his marriage certificate. This gave the maiden name of his wife, her home address at the time of her marriage, and the name and professional capacity of her father. A Cambridge don complained that there was no legitimate news in the irrelevant associations of innocent people.

The Managing Editor of the newspaper, Mr Brian R. Roberts, contended that the marriage certificate contained information about Blake's environment that was relevant; that the certificate was a public document, and that any legitimate information about Blake was of great public interest.

The Press Council deprecated the publication, and said that it was not in the public interest to identify by this means persons connected by marriage with a convicted man. (1962/25)

UNNECESSARY HURTFUL PUBLICITY

The London *Evening News* published a picture described by the complainant as 'scandalous breaches of good taste.'

It was of the daughter of an English-born man who shot at the South African Prime Minister, Dr Verwoerd. The daughter's picture was published with a report of her father's suicide. The report stated that she had flown to the United States to marry a man who was specifically identified.

The Editor of the newspaper, Mr C. R. Willis, contended that a newspaper had the right to mention in retrospect matters which were common knowledge.

The Press Council held that the newspaper gave unnecessary and hurtful publicity to the daughter of the man who committed suicide by publishing her photograph with the report of his death, and by disclosing her coming marriage, and the name of the bridegroom. (1962/30)

FAMILY IDENTIFIED

The estranged wife of a man sentenced to death in New Zealand said in an interview in England that her eleven-year-old daughter had not seen her father since babyhood and she wished to keep the news from her. The *Daily Mail*, however, published enough information to enable neighbours to identify the family.

The Editor of the *Daily Mail*, Mr William Hardcastle, admitted that the publication was a lapse in taste, and an error of judgment that tended to occur from time to time in the conditions under which modern newspapers are produced.

The Press Council deprecated the publication and the identification that might result, but noted with satisfaction that the Editor had taken action to prevent a recurrence. (1962/27)

M.P. RELATED TO COURT-MARTIALLED OFFICER

The *Daily Express* and the *Daily Mirror* were accused of 'debased journalism' by reporting that a man accused at a court-martial was related to a Member of Parliament.

The Editor of the *Daily Mirror*, Mr L. A. Lee Howard, said each case had to be judged on its merits, and while in certain circumstances it would be wrong to mention a relationship, in this instance he did not think it was objectionable.

The Editor of the *Daily Express*, Mr Roger Wood, agreed with Mr Lee Howard and added that the defending officer had publicly referred to the accused's family background, and it was relevant to identify it.

The Press Council stated that it deprecated the unnecessary identification of relatives of persons accused of offences, but in this case no harm was done. (1963/48)

EXCEPTIONS — PERSONS WHO MAY BE NAMED

The Press Council had rejected complaints in a case where the Council took the view that in the particular circumstances the newspaper was justified in publishing names.

PUBLICITY INVITED

One case concerned a picture in the London *Evening News* of the wife and baby of a man accused of shooting at a bank official. It appeared with the report of the court proceedings. The Editor, Mr C. R. Willis, claimed that the wife invited publicity by openly appearing in court and giving evidence in defence of her husband.

The Press Council did not feel that the publication of the photograph was objectionable, as the newspaper had good reason to believe that the individual concerned was not averse to personal publicity. (1962/30)

'LONELY HEARTS'

The *Daily Express* published the names and addresses of persons referred to in a case in a German court. The case concerned a man who ran a 'lonely hearts' agency, and who was alleged to have used his wife's name to reply to offers of marriage made by men advertising for wives. Two letters from Englishmen were read in court, and the writers were identified. One of the men complained that he was not guilty of anything wrong, and the publication of his name and address was unnecessary and malicious.

The Editor, Mr Robert Edwards, said he regretted any embarrassment that might have been caused, but declared it was the duty of a newspaper to report court cases fairly and frankly.

The Press Council accepted the explanation and rejected the complaint. (1964/60)

ANONYMOUS BUYERS AT PUBLIC AUCTIONS

Many buyers at public auctions do not disclose their identity. Sometimes they buy through agents, sometimes they arrange with the auctioneers that their names shall not be made public. Should a newspaper discover the identity of one of these persons, has it an ethical duty to obtain the purchaser's permission for disclosure?

The Press Council had to consider the question when a person who had bought a house formerly belonging to a notable public figure brought the matter to the Council's attention.

The purchaser of the house agreed that the general public had a right to be at the sale, and to know the details of the property and the amount of the successful bid. He had taken particular care to preserve his anonymity, but a newspaper had disclosed his name. He considered the publication to be a violation of a sensible rule of estate agents and auctioneers that a purchaser's wish for secrecy would be respected.

The Editor said there was clearly public interest in the name of the buyer of a property which formerly belonged to a well-known person, and the purchase in public could not be regarded as a private transaction. A buyer had a right to try to keep his identity secret, but newspapers had an equal right to discover the name if they could.

The Press Council decided that there was no right to anonymity in the circumstances disclosed, but added that if a purchaser's name is obtained by improper means, the Council would consider a complaint. (1965/13)

FATHER OF A SPY

The *Evening Standard* published a photograph of the father of a Briton charged with spying for a foreign power.

A complaint was made that this added to the suffering and humiliation of the parents, and in this particular case reflected upon the clergy and was anti-clerical in its intention.

The Editor of the newspaper, Mr Charles Wintour, denied this, and said that the general background, including parentage and upbringing, of anyone who spied against his country must be of wide and legitimate interest.

The Press Council made the following adjudication: Although in a number of cases the Press Council has objected to the linking of innocent people with persons accused of criminal offences, it is felt, in this case, that the enormity of the charge made the particular identification permissible. (1963/62)

UNMARRIED MOTHERS

The organising secretary of the Manchester Diocesan Council for Moral Welfare Work asked for the views of the Council on the publication in local newspapers of names and addresses of parties concerned in affiliation cases. She said that the law expressly allowed this to be done, but in districts where such reports were made the illegitimate children suffered.

The Press Council said that no action on its part was called for, as this was a matter in which an editor must use his individual judgment. (1956/26)

HOMOSEXUALS

The Magistrates' Association informed the Press Council that it felt strongly that it would be desirable for newspaper reports to suppress the names and addresses of all persons under the age of thirty concerned in homosexual cases in order to protect them from the advances of older confirmed homosexuals.

The Council could not agree with the suggestion. (1956/26)

17 The Journalist and the Public

'Professionally the journalist ought to have no friends but his readers,' Lord Francis-Williams has said. 'He should regard himself as their representative and their voice, and in their interests he should be ready to affront, if need be, the whole forces of the Establishment.'

The journalist in the role of reporter is the representative of his newspaper in direct contact with the public. By his conduct he can advance or tarnish its good name, and even the image of the Press as a whole.

In a recent address to the students of Liverpool and Leeds Universities Mr Cecil King said that a journalist's most precious assets were spontaneity, intuition and a flair for news. Given talent and ability it was essential that the journalist should also have a sturdy physique. Much depended in journalism on sheer energy sustained over the years; the ability to work long hours and still be capable at the end of a long shift, when half the world was at rest, of doing first-class work with accuracy. These resources of energy were essential whether a man was a leader-writer, a specialist, a general reporter or an executive.

The journalist must also have the right temperament.

I would say, [said Mr King] that a good journalist has a match-winning temperament — a capacity for instant excitement is necessary, but it must be a controlled excitement, and this temperament can only be sustained by fervent interest in the job. Journalism demands irregular as well as long hours. It is necessary to work on public holidays and on Sundays. The domestic routine is often upset. It is necessary for the journalist to marry a woman of phlegmatic temperament who does not mind being left on her own at night, or being deserted for weeks or months when her husband is on a foreign assignment.

Journalism is clearly a hard taskmaster, but, while it does not confer any special privileges, it does provide the opportunity for valuable service in the public interest. In a leading article of 18 March 1963 *The Times* stated:

Journalists have no authority beyond that of other citizens. They do have in their hands an instrument which, when courageously and reasonably used, has so far proved in free societies to be the most effective in informing, in promoting discussion, in exposing error and malpractice and in preserving liberties.

Indispensable to the journalist is the goodwill of the public; if he alienates it, he will inevitably suffer frustration. Young reporters quickly learn this, and older ones relearned the lesson at the time of the Vassall case. During the debate in the House of Lords (29 May 1963) following the case, the Bishop of London (The Rt Rev. Dr Stopford) referred to the profession as being under a cloud, but said that the vast majority of the journalists in this country were men of great integrity and sincerity. They were feeling almost outcasts of society, hated and feared instead of respected. It was, he said, difficult to generalise about any particular profession, most of all journalism, for it was generalisation from a few instances that had so reduced the status of the profession as a whole. The journalist earned his living in conditions of exceptional difficulty, subjected to exceptional pressures, and the very conditions of his life divorced him in some way from society. There was very considerable and widespread public ignorance of the way in which the Press worked, and the bishop thought it should make its difficulties better known to the public.

The cloud the bishop spoke of was a passing one; nor was dejection of the journalists characteristic or chronic, and like the cloud soon passed. The bishop's remarks, however, reflected the low-water-mark to which relations between the Press and the public had sunk during the Vassall Inquiry and for some time afterwards. But at a time when journalists were suffering harsh criticism and hard knocks from every quarter, the bishop said in their defence:

> If I may just add my own personal testimony, I know very well — because I have experienced it so often — the co-operation, tact and integrity of very many journalists with whom I have had dealings both in provincial and national newspapers, whom I have never known to betray a confidence or fail to appreciate the delicacy of a particular situation.

People who are quoted in the Press frequently deny that they made a statement to a newspaper. Complaints generally arise because the reporter has neglected to reveal his identity and the newspaper he represents when interviewing a member of the public. Understandably people are annoyed when they discover that they have been denied the opportunity of refusing to comment for publication. The Press Council has also strongly condemned eavesdropping (see pp. 49–51).

A scoop may be a very gratifying achievement for a journalist, but it will have no value and less merit if it results from unethical methods. Misrepresentation and deceit used as a means of obtaining information is a cardinal offence and will vitiate a story based upon it. Nor should a journalist claim to have visited places when he has only telephoned (see p. 101, *Evening Standard*) or lived there for a week when he has merely paid a visit (see p. 103, *Daily Sketch*).

A task both difficult and disagreeable a journalist has from time to time to undertake, and one which involves him, generally unfairly in considerable criticism, is interviewing people who have been bereaved or are distressed by some tragic occurrence. Too readily the public regards such interviews as an indefensible intrusion on private grief, when in fact they may be justified in the public interest. Not all bereaved people resent being interviewed. Some welcome the publicity the occasion offers. Others find solace in being able to unburden themselves to a sympathetic listener. The manner and the circumstances will determine whether or not the interview is an infringement of privacy. Even when it is justified in the public interest an interview should not be pressed against the wish of the person interviewed. To persist in the face of refusal may change a permissible inquiry into an inexcusable intrusion. This matter is dealt with on p. 245 in Chapter 14.

The life of a journalist is hard and exacting, but it is also rewarding. 'The quality of journalism is made entirely by journalists,' said Mr Cecil King in his address to the universities. 'And upon the quality of journalism depends to a greater extent than we perhaps appreciate the quality of the public debate and so the quality of our public life.'

The whole of this book is to some extent concerned with the conduct of journalists, and cases which particularly affect the actions of individual reporters will be found in Chapters 14 (Intrusion), 20 (Schools), 21 (Hospitals and Doctors) and 25 (Cheque-Book Journalism).

Other cases follow here.

IDENTITY MUST BE DISCLOSED

REPORTER DID NOT REVEAL HIS OCCUPATION

The Chairman of the Isle of Islay's Tourist Board complained that the *Sunday Pictorial*, in an article about the encouragement of bird-watching on the island, had attributed to him a statement that he had not made, and had not subsequently withdrawn it. The reporter concerned, a free-lance, declared that he had spoken to the Chairman in a hotel bar and disclosed his newspaper interest, but the Chairman and a third person present said they understood that he was no longer following the occupation of a journalist.

The Press Council decided that there was no evidence that the journalist had disclosed that he was interviewing the complainant for the purpose of direct quotation in the Press, as he should have done. It was held that the complaint was justified. (1961/35)

PURPOSE OF VISIT NOT REVEALED

A humorous article by a reporter in the *Sunday Telegraph* led to a complaint that the method adopted by him in obtaining his information was unethical.

The complainant, the Managing Director of an office machinery company, said that the reporter purported to represent the S— Company, and that he visited his firm apparently to make inquiries about buying a machine called the Auto-Typist. He also objected to 'unnecessarily personal and offensive remarks about the figure and dress of a member of our staff who can be identified.'

The reporter, who was a director of the S— Company, acknowledged that he did not tell anyone on his visit that he might write an article about the Auto-Typist machine.

The Press Council held that he should have said that he intended to write a humorous article for the *Sunday Telegraph*. (1964/61)

COMPLAINANT WAS HARD OF HEARING

A news story in the *Sunday Express* was headed: 'Old comrades expel the member who went to a meeting at Munich. "Be friends with Germans" row splits submariners.'

The article stated that several members of Britain's 50-year-old Submarine Old Comrades' Association shocked their colleagues by announcing their decision to attend a meeting in Paris of the International Submarine Association.

Mr S., the secretary of the British Old Comrades' Association, was reported to have stated: 'We do not believe in fraternising with our former enemies. Any of our members who attend this meeting will not be representing the Old Comrades' Association.'

The report went on to state that a former Able Seaman who had attended a Munich meeting of the international body had been thrown out of the British association. Mr S. refused to discuss this case, and, when asked about a German holding membership of the British association, was reported as saying, 'No comment.'

Mr S. complained that he had not been interviewed by a *Sunday Express* reporter. He agreed that he was rung up by somebody 'representing an unidentified newspaper', who asked some questions and was told to write in.

Mr John Junor, Editor of the *Sunday Express*, said that the reporter had identified himself and his paper in the course of the conversation he had had with Mr S., and that Mr S. had been correctly quoted. The Chairman of the Association gave an account of a telephone conversation the reporter had had with him; he had taken exception to the reporter's attitude.

Both Mr S. and the reporter gave oral evidence to the Council. Mr S. wore a hearing-aid and required a number of the questions put to him to be repeated. He said that he did not know he had been speaking to someone from a newspaper until he read the story in the *Sunday Express*. He denied saying that the Association did not believe in fraternising with their enemies and nothing was said to him about a German being a member of the Association.

The reporter said that the remarks attributed to Mr S. were recorded in his notes; he had identified himself at the outset of his telephone conversation.

The Press Council found that the complainant was hard of hearing and there was therefore a possibility of misunderstanding. The Council was not satisfied, however, that he had been misrepresented and rejected the complaint. (1967)

UNETHICAL METHODS OF APPROACH

MISREPRESENTATION

The *Ilford Recorder* obtained an exclusive picture of a model of an architectural design for a new town centre after the Borough Council had refused to make one available until the official Press release. A woman purporting to speak on behalf of an unspecified firm of architects obtained the name of

L   L.T.P.C.

the model-makers by telephone from the architects of the centre. Two reporters then callled the model-makers and twice assured the manager that they had the architect's permission to photograph the model.

The Editor, Mr Ll. J. Sims, declared that publication of the picture was the result of journalistic resource in the face of a lack of understanding by officialdom of the needs of the Press in a matter of vital public interest. He had not given any undertaking to observe the official embargo on the plans, and he denied that the manager of the model factory had been deceived.

The Press Council acknowledged the importance to a local newspaper of publishing all available information as soon as possible, but held that the *Ilford Recorder* had not pursued its inquiries with complete frankness and was, therefore, at fault. (1962/43–4)

INTERVIEW AT SECURITY ESTABLISHMENT

Mr Frank Cousins' son, Michael, employed as a scientist at the Windscale Atomic Energy Establishment, complained of unwarranted and distasteful interference with his and his wife's private lives by a reporter and photographer of the *Daily Express*. The reporter tried unsuccessfully to interview him at his office. The two *Express* men then called at his private residence and when they found that his wife was not there they went to her place of employment. Mrs Cousins told them that she was not interested in talking to them. When she left the reporter pursued her asking questions all the time and finally offered her a lift home. Mr and Mrs Cousins regarded the offer as monstrous to the dignity of any woman. Mrs Cousins caught her bus, but on arriving at her destination the reporter was waiting and again approached her. She ran into a shop and asked for shelter. Mr Cousins was sent for and called for police protection. As he and his wife left the shop they were photographed as they ran. Later, while waiting for the police, Mr Cousins was again photographed by flash-light exposure.

The following day the *Daily Express* printed a front-page article which contained statements which Mr Cousins claimed were untrue and detrimental to him, as a person subject to the Official Secrets Act, and were a reflection upon his father. As a result of the article, Mr and Mrs Cousins were pestered by reporters from other newspapers. As a further result, Mr Cousins had been called before the senior management at Windscale.

The Editor of the *Daily Express,* Mr Edward D. Pickering, said the allegation of unwarranted and distasteful interference into the private lives of Mr and Mrs Cousins was regarded in the *Daily Express* as serious. The newspaper, having received information that Mr Michael Cousins was working at Windscale, did send a reporter and photographer to try to interview him, and they had called at the main gate of his place of employment. They went away when told he did not wish to speak to them.

The Editor apologised to Mr Cousins for the fact that as a result of the article he was questioned by the security staff. Mr Pickering confirmed that Mrs Cousins had been offered a lift, but his account of the reporter's attempt to interview her and of the circumstances in which the photographs were taken did not accord with the accounts given by Mr and Mrs Cousins.

The Press Council declared that Mr Cousins' employment was a matter of public interest, and that the *Daily Express* was therefore entitled to seek an interview with him. The Council deprecated the methods used when it became clear that neither Mr Cousins nor his wife were willing to be interviewed and deplored the attempt to interview Mr Cousins at his place of employment, which was a security establishment. (1961/26–7, 43–7)

TRICK ALLEGED

A reporter was alleged to have used a trick to try to obtain the telephone number of the wife of one of the convicted train robbers.

A firm of solicitors complained that, after they had told the *Daily Sketch* that they would not give the number, another reporter from the same newspaper had telephoned and, while waiting to speak to a partner, had asked a new office junior if she knew the telephone number.

The Managing Editor, Mr Robert Johnston, apologised to the firm for telephoning twice, but said the reporter was unaware that someone else had made the same inquiry earlier, and he did not know that the girl was a new office junior. Mr Johnston refuted the allegation of trickery.

The Press Council found that the representative of the *Daily Sketch* had openly stated his identity and the purpose of his call; the Council held that the complaint had not been substantiated. (1966/96–7)

ALLEGED POSE AS POLICE OFFICERS

A photographer from the *Daily Sketch* and a reporter from the *Sun* were alleged to have posed as police officers when they called on Mrs M. She said that when asked to produce their warrant cards they reluctantly admitted their true identity.

The reporter from the *Sun* said that two days before the visit he had seen Mrs M. at a magistrates' court. When he and the *Daily Sketch* photographer called at the house he told her: 'I am a reporter from the *Sun* and this is a colleague from the *Daily Sketch*.' He denied a suggestion that he had got into the house by false pretences.

The photographer confirmed this version of events. When asked by her for proof of identity he produced his National Union of Journalists card. He might have said that his 'Scotland Yard' pass was in for renewal. At no time did he say or suggest that he was a policeman. It would have been absurd for him to say so, as he obviously did not have the physical requirements.

The Press Council accepted the evidence of the two journalists, and the complaint was rejected. (1966/106)

MR SILVERMAN, M.P., COMPLAINS

Mr Sydney Silverman, who sponsored the Bill abolishing capital punishment, said that on the day three London policemen were killed an *Evening Standard* reporter telephoned his home. His son said that his father was not at home and, when asked where he could be contacted, replied that he did not know. Mr Silverman alleged that for the next five or ten minutes his son was badgered and pressed for information and was told his father would have to take the risk of the newspaper's comment in respect of the three policemen murdered 'all on account of him'. Mr Silverman complained of these unethical methods.

The newspaper did not in fact print any comment of this kind.

The reporter's account of the telephone conversation was that when he was asked why he wanted to speak to Mr Silverman he explained that since Mr Silverman's Bill had become law three police officers had been murdered and he wanted Mr Silverman's reaction.

Mr Silverman, when asked for a statement from his son, said he had related what his son had told him verbally and he saw no reason to ask him to repeat it in writing.

Eventually a written statement was sent to the Council, in which the son stated he was asked repeatedly where his father could be contacted; when he was unable to do so the caller said that Mr Silverman could not complain of what the newspaper might say, since three policemen had been slaughtered on the streets because of him. The caller seemed irritated and banged down the receiver. Mr Silverman's son agreed that the conversation lasted only a minute or two. Mr Silverman replied that he did not propose to offer any further comment, because he had come to the conclusion that what the reporter had said was said in a moment of irritation.

He was informed that an accusation had been made against the reporter and brought to his Editor's notice; the reporter had asked to be heard, and the Complaints Committee in strict fairness were bound to allow this.

The reporter told the Council that the only reference to the policemen was at the beginning of the telephone conversation when he said he wanted to get Mr Silverman's reaction. He was experienced in interviewing people and did not lose his temper.

The Press Council accepted the reporter's evidence and rejected the complaint. (1967)

See also p. 207 (*Daily Mail*).

LATE TELEPHONE CALLS

THE PROFUMO AFFAIR

At the height of the Profumo affair, it was rumoured that Mr Profumo and his wife had left London and gone to friends in Kent.

A *Daily Sketch* reporter made a telephone call at 12.30 a.m. to a lady with whom they were thought to be staying. He said he represented the *Daily Sketch*, and asked if Mr and Mrs Profumo were staying with her. She denied all knowledge of them, and subsequently complained to the Press Council that an inquiry at such an hour constituted an unwarrantable intrusion. She and her husband had been alarmed, thinking that some harm had befallen a member of the family.

The Editor of the *Daily Sketch*, Mr Howard French, said he realised the annoyance of a telephone call at that hour of the night, but the matter was of great importance, and there would have been grounds for an even more serious complaint if an unverified and incorrect report had been published.

The Press Council said that while it might be necessary to make inquiries late at night, the greatest care should be taken to avoid unnecessary disturbance. The facts disclosed in this case showed that the late hour call was unreasonable. (1964/32–3)

REPORTER'S INQUIRY

The Clerk of the Berkshire County Council complained that a *Daily Express* reporter telephoned him between 12.30 a.m. and 1 a.m., when he was asleep, in order to confirm a news report about the action that the Borough Council had taken requiring employees to hand over trading stamps received on the purchase of petrol for Council-owned motor-cars. He contended that while it was his duty as a public official to assist the Press, it was intolerable intrusion to be awakened in the middle of the night on a matter that was neither urgent nor important.

The Editor of the *Daily Express*, Mr Robert Edwards, said it did not seem to him to be an abuse to telephone a responsible official at such a time.

The Press Council reaffirmed its opinion on the need for newspapers to exercise the greatest care when making telephone calls late at night. On this occasion the Council did not think the matter was sufficiently important to justify the inquiry. (1964/35)

PRESS CONFERENCES

NON-JOURNALIST AT A PRESS CONFERENCE

At a Press conference given by Sir Toby Low, then Minister of State at the Board of Trade, Mr Cyril Lord, the textile company director, attended on behalf of the *Daily Express*. When asked for his credentials he produced a card saying, 'Cyril Lord, Staff Reporter, *Daily Express*'. The Manchester Branch of the National Union of Journalists complained that the *Daily Express* had sent someone who was not a journalist as a reporter to the Press conference.

Mr Edward D. Pickering, Managing Editor of the *Daily Express*, said that it was not the practice of the newspaper to send non-journalists as reporters to

Press conferences, and he had given instructions that there should be no repetition of the issue of credentials in this way.

In its decision, the Press Council held that the right of an Editor to send a representative who was not a member of the staff to a Press conference could not be challenged, particularly when a technical matter was under consideration, but the representative should not have been described as a staff reporter. (1957/27–8)

REPORTER NOT ALWAYS TO BLAME

A COMPLAINT FROM SCOTLAND

The Sheriff-Substitute of Roxburgh and Berwick complained that the *Scotsman* misreported him and then, on the strength of the reporter's notes, contradicted him in a footnote to a letter from him published in the newspaper.

The Editor said it was a common practice to 'blame it on the reporter'. Where, however, there was clear evidence to the contrary the blame should not be meekly accepted.

The Press Council expressed the view that the Editor had acted properly throughout, and there was no ground for complaint. (1955/28)

18 Reporting Crime

The reporting of crime covers reports of crimes committed as well as the reports of the criminal proceedings which follow. Some people take the view that the public, and particularly young people, should be shielded from the knowledge of the more sordid side of life, including crime of an unpleasant and violent character. Concealment, however, solves few problems, and if the Press was tempted to create a make-believe world by suppressing unpleasant facts it would not render a service to the community. But in fact there is no serious challenge to the right and duty of newspapers to bring crime, whatever its nature, fairly and squarely to the knowledge of the public.

Another type of crime reporting in recent years has been publication of the memoirs and confessions of notorious criminals. The demand for these articles gave rise to competitive bidding by the newspapers and resulted in the payment of large sums of money to persons whose only interest lay in the the crimes they had committed. These payments may not have been an inducement to the crimes committed, but they were a considerable consolation and compensation to criminals brought to justice.

So long as crime existed on a small scale it was of no great consequence if, for instance, highwaymen were represented as romantic figures ready to step a minuet with the pretty occupant of a plundered stagecoach. But in an age when criminals are ruthless, highly organised, and a major threat to the community, to glamorise crime and pay those who indulge in it large rewards for their memoirs is no longer tolerable, and the Press Council has taken a determined stand against the practice.

This aspect of crime reporting is dealt with in Chapter 25: Chequebook Journalism.

The law of England gives greater latitude than does the law of Scotland to the pre-trial reporting of crime. This is the result of the sterner view taken by the Scottish judges of what constitutes contempt of court. The English courts, of course, are no less concerned to ensure that there is no interference with the course of justice and that nothing is published that will prejudice the fair trial of a case. The limits on what can be reported when a crime has been committed become narrower when a person has been arrested and charged.

In reporting evidence in criminal proceedings newspapers have a defence of qualified privilege in the event of libel proceedings based on the report; qualified because the privilege depends on the report being a fair and accurate one.

There are also limitations on the reporting of criminal cases which the Press Council has held should be observed on ethical grounds. These are dealt with in Chapters 15 and 16 on Reporting Court Proceedings and Persons who should not be Named.

A statutory ban imposed by the Judicial Proceedings (Regulation of Reports) Act, 1926 on reports of judicial proceedings prevents publication of any indecent matter or indecent medical, surgical or physiological details calculated to injure public morals.

GLAMORISING WOMEN CRIMINALS

In 1954 the Archbishop of Canterbury, Dr (now Lord) Fisher, asked the Press Council to examine a complaint that there was an increasing tendency in a section of the Press to glamorise women released from prison and Borstal. He said that anything that frustrated the bringing back into good citizenship of these unfortunate people was to be deplored. Dr Fisher forwarded a memorandum from Miss H. L. Long, who was in charge of after-care work for released women prisoners, in which she gave illustrations of the type of publicity published in the newspapers after the discharge from prison of women whose only claim to notice was that they had committed some crime. Miss Long stated that she understood that articles dealing with the life-stories of ex-criminals enhanced the sales of newspapers, but she doubted whether the public realised the harmful effect on the prisoner herself, or the incentive it gave to others to commit crimes.

She quoted the following cases which concerned women for whom she was responsible:

A young woman was reprieved after being sentenced to death and in due course was discharged from prison. Immediately, two articles appeared in different newspapers purporting to be the story of her life, told in an emotional and sentimental strain; one paper included a highly glamorised photograph. She handed to Miss Long, as the person responsible for her after-care, the spate of letters she received, and asked her to deal with them. Miss Long was not surprised to see that the majority came from men only too obviously anxious to exploit an attractive young woman with a criminal record for immoral and criminal purposes. Some letters were from senti-mentalists of both sexes enclosing money, and there were a few genuine offers of employment. The result of this publicity was that the woman had to leave her home town and work elsewhere, but she became restless and unsettled.

Two years after her release an article appeared with a front-page photograph of three murderers, two of whom were men, and the young woman, sitting at a dinner table for four, being interviewed by a psychiatrist. The caption read: 'Should these people have been hanged?'

An ex-Borstal girl with a very bad record of larceny was discharged from prison after serving a sentence of corrective training. An article alleged to be descriptive of her life in prison was published. After that she did no work and imagined she would get a large sum from the newspapers for the story of her life.

A young woman with a record of fraud and larceny discharged from prison after serving a sentence of two years' imprisonment had an article published, giving details of her alleged failure to obtain honest employment after her release from prison. An extremely attractive photograph, bearing only a slight resemblance to the woman, appeared together with a leading article emphasising her sad plight and appealing to readers to give the young woman a chance. The usual avalanche of letters followed, and her old associates gathered round to share in the financial results. When Miss Long pointed out to her that the article contained very little that was true, her answer was: 'But the papers will believe anything!'

Miss Long said that while some of this publicity was no doubt well-intentioned, the effect was disastrous, for obtaining money without effort, whether from kindly sympathisers or from payment for articles in the Press, was the direct road to recidivism. This was not the worst feature, for the ex-prisoner basked in the sunshine of publicity and told the story of her life to anyone who was gullible enough to believe her. The mean fraud or sordid crime which earned her a sentence was ignored, and an ex-prisoner automatically became glamorous, charming and, of course, truthful. This made crime attractive to certain people, and it was quite common for Borstal girls and prisoners to state that they were writing the story of their life for publication. Those who genuinely intended to do well asked for nothing but merciful obscurity; for those who sought publicity it was only too evident that crime did pay.

The Press Council asked the Editors of the newspapers concerned for their comments. They agreed with Miss Long that it was wrong to glamorise criminals. The Editor of the *Daily Express*, Mr Arthur Christiansen, pointed out that the article in the *Daily Express*, the subject of the first complaint, related to the release of a woman imprisoned for life for murdering her husband, and so was news to be recorded; the newspaper had not disclosed the name the woman had adopted for her new life and she was, therefore, not prevented from dwelling in obscurity.

Mr Ainsworth, Editor of the *People*, said that there was nothing humorous about the second article mentioned in the memorandum. The photograph of the girl was posed so that she could not be identified, and she was not paid a large fee — a sum of £5.

In his reply, the Editor of the *News of the World*, Mr Reginald Cudlipp, said that it was not the policy of his newspaper to glamorise the criminal. 'The very fact that we emphasise the punishment in all our court reports indicates that we have the best interests of the public at heart.' He added that it was a pity that the girl written about in the third article in the complaint did not take advantage of the excellent opportunities that came her way as a result of the article.

The Editor of the *Sunday Pictorial*, Mr Colin Valdar, sent a formal acknowledgment but offered no comment.

After its investigation the Press Council wrote to the Archbishop stating that there was general support and sympathy with the views he had expressed. (1954/28–9, 45–8)

AN IRONIC REPORT

A story in the *Evening Standard* describing the arrest of an escaped prisoner was said by a barrister to be a 'glorification of criminal violence'. The Editor of the paper, Mr Charles Wintour, said that the account was clearly ironic in tone, and the Council upheld this contention. (1961/38)

A MURDERER'S STORY

When Sergeant Emmett-Dunne was convicted on a charge of murder by a court-martial in Germany, the *Sunday Pictorial* published a series of articles under the heading 'Emmett-Dunne's Own Story'.

The Council informed the complainant that his protest raised important issues which had been carefully considered. Such articles on much discussed crimes were a not uncommon feature, and the Council did not think it wrong to repeat the facts if the public were interested. But it would regard it as utterly wrong if articles signed by accused persons distorted the truth.

The Council felt that the headline 'I thought I had got away with it' lent an air of bravado to the convicted murderer, and the Council considered that such headlines should be avoided in the public interest. On the question of whether the supply of the articles to a newspaper was a breach of prison regulations, the Press Council held that this was a matter for the Home Secretary. (1956/34)

'I GOT AWAY WITH MURDER'

The Press Council received numerous complaints from members of the public who were concerned about articles written by Donald Hume which appeared in the *Sunday Pictorial* under the heading 'I Killed Setty and got away with Murder'. Hume had been acquitted of murder but found guilty of being an accessory after the fact to murder.

One of the letters received by the Press Council said that the article appealed to the 'jaded and unwholesome yearning for morbid sensationalism which should have no place in any Sunday newspaper. It is presented without editorial comment or criticism, and to the mind of a young person it might well appear as the glorification of a life of crime and dishonesty.'

Asked to comment on the letter, the Editor of the *Sunday Pictorial*, Mr Colin Valdar, rejected the suggestion that the publication without editorial comment of Hume's confession might appear as the glorification of a life of crime. The *Sunday Pictorial* had twice described his confession as appalling; the series challenged the public to face the issue of a man who tried to cheat justice; reference had also been made to Hume's 'chance of escaping from the torture of his ghastly secret' and to his 'nightmare of fear'.

The Editor added that when the Press published reports that a crime had occurred or that a man had been arrested, tried and sentenced, or had confessed to a crime, the allegation that the Press was automatically glorifying a life of crime was utterly insupportable. The fact that justice was not done in this case made the confession of greater, not lesser, public importance.

The suggestion that the confession should not have been printed at all, Mr Valdar said, was the least comprehensible criticism of all. The confession was news and disturbing news. It cleared up one of the greatest murder mysteries of the century. It completely vindicated the Scotland Yard men who had conducted the inquiry, and had the confession been made in court it would have been given the widest publicity.

On what possible grounds would it have been prudent or just for the *Sunday Pictorial* to suppress the news? Confessions normally appear simultaneously in all newspapers. This one, had it been made in court or immediately after the trial, would have been given the widest publicity, and no one would have suggested that its publication 'glorified' the guilty man. The argument that because the confession was made nine years later and to one newspaper only it should be suppressed did not justify serious consideration.

If Hume had issued his confession to a news agency and that news agency had distributed it to the Press as a whole it was undeniable that the Press as a whole would have published it.

The *Sunday Pictorial* appeared to be guilty of an offence which was traditionally considered by journalists to be the acme of enterprise — exclusivity.

The Press Council issued the following statement:

The Council, having considered numerous complaints from the public on the subject, strongly condemns the *Sunday Pictorial* articles by Donald Hume which appeared under the general heading 'I Killed Setty and got away with Murder'. The Council holds it to be against the public interest to give an atmosphere of successful crime to so sordid a story, or to allow criminals to justify or mitigate their crimes by romantic explanations which, never having been tested in a Court of Law, may or may not be true.   (1958/24, 36–8)

19 Treatment of Sex

The reporting of sex, like the reporting of crime, raises the question whether youthful readers should be protected from knowledge of squalor and violence. Should newspaper reports of sex matters be frank or reticent, as detailed as the law permits, or restricted to avoid shocking immature and unsophisticated minds?

The Press Council was confronted with these questions at its first meetings. 'The editor who knows his business', the First Annual Report declared, 'will draw a clear distinction between those reports with a sex element that may excite imitation of wrong conduct, and those in which the interest is scientific or at least arises from a healthy curiosity about the mysteries of human existence, the subject of so much classic literature'.

The Kinsey Report on sexual behaviour was being widely discussed at the time both in America and in England. Many protests were received by the Press Council from religious and other bodies on the way some newspapers were handling the Report. After considering these protests, the Council expressed its views in the following statement:

> This Council, while defending the right of the Press in the contemporary world to deal in an adult manner with matters of sex, is deeply concerned by the unwholesome exploitation of sex by certain

newspapers and periodicals. It places on record its view that such treatment is calculated to injure public morals especially because newspapers and periodicals are seen and read by young persons. It is also contrary to those standards of journalism which it is the Council's duty to maintain. The Council intends to keep this matter under review.

(1954/21)

The reporting of homosexual cases also gave rise to public complaints. In regard to these the Council were of the opinion that if the reports were carefully sub-edited they did a useful public service. To induce public ignorance of the problem was, the Council thought, a certain way of making it worse, and it was largely the publicity given to homosexual offences that led to the appointment of the Wolfenden Committee to review the law and treatment of persons convicted of these offences. (Cases arising from reports of court proceedings on rape and indecent assault are dealt with in Chapters 15 and 16.)

Some time later the Press Council was called upon to consider a proposal made by a member of the public that a Committee of Standards should be set up to deal with the 'growing competition in the exploitation of unpleasantness, particularly in the area of crime and sex'. The complainant also spoke of an alleged practice of introducing fictional material which bore little relation to the news.

The Press Council, in commenting on the proposal, referred to what it had said about the exploitation of sex in its statement above, and went on to say that while it was eager to improve the tone of the Press where necessary, and was ready to consider any detailed proposals, the Council could not be used as a substitute for the existing law on obscene and indecent publications, as the proposed Committee of Standards would involve.

The Council had given much thought to the methods it should adopt, and had expressed the view that it could only hope to establish a code of sound practice by its decisions on the specific cases brought before it. It would be much better, the Council considered, if instead of making vague charges against the Press without any specific instances of misdeeds, people who urged reform would restrict their complaints to specific cases which could be investigated. 'The Council does not believe in reform by general admonition. It believes that offences should be brought into the light, and, if necessary, censured.'

In 1960 the Council again published a forthright statement on the exploitation of sex, and denounced articles appearing in three London Sunday newspapers. It recalled its previous statements on the unwholesome exploitation of sex, and its declared intention to keep the matter under review. The Council said that it had considered the articles in the three newspapers dealing with the sexual adventures of persons connected with the stage and screen, who were named in the articles. A general improvement over the years in the treatment of sex in the Press had been registered and it was all the more to be deplored, therefore, that the newspapers in question should have permitted their standards to be debased to a level which was a disgrace to professional journalism.

The statement attracted considerable attention and received widespread public approval.

The public attitude to questions of sex can change rapidly and completely. This has happened on matters like birth control, abortion and homosexuality. The open discussion of these matters in the Press used to be considered improper, not only as contrary to good taste and morals, but, in the case of birth control, because of the deep religious feelings against it. Dr Marie Stopes, a pioneer of contraception, in her evidence to the First Royal Commission on the Press complained of the refusal of a number of newspapers to publish advertisements for her books and the clinics she conducted (1954/28). Birth control, like abortion and homosexuality, is now urgently debated in all its aspects in and out of the Press. The Press Council has dealt with the following cases:

CALL-GIRLS EXPOSED

A member of several welfare organisations complained about two articles in the *People* which dealt with the suppression of vice in London including the 'call-girl' system. The articles published the names and addresses of girls alleged to be prostitutes, which the complainant said was contrary to public morals.

The Editor of the *People*, Mr Ainsworth, said that apparently there was approval for exposing the organisers but not the girls, and presumably not the landlords who battened on them.

The Press Council said it realised that some harm might follow from such publications, but held that the exposure of vice by a newspaper was often a service to the community, and the publication of names and addresses may often be necessary for the exposure to be fully effective. (1955/28)

JUVENILE STRIP-TEASE PARTIES

The *Daily Herald* reported a statement made in a juvenile court that a thirteen-year-old girl had held strip-tease parties for her friends at her home when her parents were away. The heading of the story was: 'Striptease girl, 13, is mother-to-be'. A complaint was made that juvenile delinquency called for the utmost discretion, and scrupulous selection of material for publication, and that this report of a lamentable case of sexual precosity could not be justified on any grounds. The complaint condemned the headline as misleading, and the report as callous frivolity.

The Editor of the *Daily Herald*, Mr John Beavan, agreed that the matters revealed were shocking, but he believed that it was in the public interest to print them. The headlines were neither careless nor frivolous, and his view was that the complainant was really shocked not by the character of the report but by the facts of the case.

The Press Council held that the newspaper's treatment of the case was fair. It was a matter of serious interest to parents and the public. (1961/38)

ILLICIT SALE OF V.D. CURES

The *People* published a news story about do-it-yourself drug kits being sold to teenagers seeking a cure for venereal disease. A former chief pharmacist in the Prison Medical Service complained that the story was a scurrilous attack on the good name of pharmacists, and that teenagers who had not known that self-treatment for V.D. existed might be tempted to try it before facing the embarrassment of a clinic.

The newspaper report said that detectives were investigating 'a dangerous new drug traffic', and it included an interview with the Chairman of the local Health Committee in which he said that the traffic in drugs supplied by unscrupulous chemists was widely known amongst the medical profession in the Midlands. Three weeks later the *People* printed a letter from the Secretary of the Pharmaceutical Society saying that an investigation by the Society had shown that none of these drugs had originated from chemists.

The Editor of the *People*, Mr Stuart Campbell, said that the notion that a newspaper should not publish the disclosures of a person as well informed as the Chairman of the Local Health Committee, on the grounds that such information might corrupt teenagers, was nonsensical.

The Press Council held that the news report was a matter of public interest, and there was no objection to the report, which properly drew attention to the dangers of the traffic in drugs. The Council noted that the newspaper published the Pharmaceutical Society's statement on the outcome of its investigations. (1964/77–8)

EROTIC BOOKS LISTED

An article in the *Evening Standard* listed the titles and prices of various erotic books which were said to be freely on sale. The headline was 'Fanny Hill? She's a prude', and the story stated: 'Perhaps poor Fanny Hill is lucky not to be in such company. She would have been a prude by comparison.'

The President of the National Council of Women of Great Britain complained to the Press Council that it was deplorable and irresponsible that an article should deliberately provoke interest in and inform its readers of erotic books, some of which included perverse practices. The article read as though it were a deliberate advertisement for the books mentioned.

The Editor of the *Evening Standard*, Mr Charles Wintour, answered that it was desirable that the facts about the sale of erotic books should be widely known so that people could make up their own minds on whether this 'sleazy traffic' should be allowed to continue. Suppression of the details would have made the story too vague; there was no point in glossing over what was happening about the sale of 'this trash', and it was hoped that the story would provoke thought.

The Press Council held that the way in which the newspaper had handled the subject, especially the cataloguing of the titles and prices was regrettable, and likely to have the effect of stimulating the traffic in erotic books. (1965/87)

See also p. 272 (*Hull Daily Mail*) and p. 273 (*Middlesex County Times*).

20 Newspapers and the Schools

Teacher-pupil relations, examination results, school administration and other aspects of school life are of great public importance and public interest. Inevitably the Press takes an interest in these matters, and will report them particularly if circumstances make the occasion unusual.

Nevertheless certain responsibilities rest on the newspapers in regard to the manner in which they gather information and report the news. A school requires discipline, and the undermining of the authority of the teachers or the respect of the pupils for them makes discipline more difficult to maintain.

Many schools impose some uniformity in matters like dress, and this is sometimes resented by a difficult child or an unco-operative parent. A sensible teachers can generally handle a situation of this kind, but it can sometimes get out of hand and develop into national headline news. Some children will welcome the publicity and the opportunity a reporter's inquiries provide to make life more difficult for the teacher. In other cases Press reports can be harmful to the children themselves; for instance, disparaging comment on examination failures can discourage and and do great harm to those of immature years and sensitive nature.

Certain basic principles on the reporting of school affairs have been established by the Press Council. They are:

Reports should not be founded on the tittle-tattle of children.

If information about anything to do with a school is required it should be sought in the first place from a teacher — preferably the head teacher not from a pupil.

Reporters should not enter school property without permission.

Pupils should not be interviewed within the school precincts; trivial incidents should not be exaggerated.

The private lives of teachers should be respected.

'IRON-CURTAIN KIDS'

A story in the *People* described the success in the 11-plus examination of four Ukrainian boys and one Rumanian, who were described as 'a bunch of Iron-curtain kids'. The article referred to the Ukrainians as 'Russians' and classified pupils who did not obtain grammar school places as 'failures'.

The headmaster of the school said that the designation 'Iron-curtain kids' had done great harm by embarrassing the children; that the Ukrainians had felt insulted by being described as 'Russians', when in fact they were refugees from the Russians, and that it was wrong to describe children as 'failures' in an examination in which there was no pass-mark.

The Press Council regarded it as unfortunate that the *People* used the description, 'Iron-curtain kids', and also the term 'failures' in its reference to the 11-plus examination. (1962/47)

NO ONE PASSED THE 11-PLUS

When thirteen children of the island of Barra sat an examination for a senior secondary school, the *Scottish Sunday Express* published a news story headed '11-plus failures start island uproar'.

A complaint was made that the use of the term 'failures' was totally misleading, but the newspaper replied that although the term might not be technically accurate it described the feeling of a parent whose child did not obtain sufficient marks to warrant promotion to a senior secondary school. The Editor, Mr Archie Freedman, said nobody failed but some succeeded better than others.

The newspaper refused to publish another article in agreed terms, but gave a paragraph to say that one girl had since been allocated to a senior secondary school and that the Education Committee was satisfied with the headmaster.

The Press Council repeated the view it expressed in a similar case in the previous year that the use of the word 'failures' to describe children who were not selected to go to a senior secondary school was unfortunate. (1963/34–5)

PUBLIC DISQUIET

The *Scottish Daily Express* published a picture of 33 members of a school class, with a statement that every child in the picture had failed the 11-plus. The Educational Institute of Scotland complained that the picture and the article accompanying it constituted an unjustified criticism of the school and its teachers, and was inaccurate, as two of the pupils in the picture had been admitted to the High School.

The Editor, Mr Roger Wood, replied that the criticism of the teaching staff reported in the article came from the parents of all the children who had signed a petition seeking investigation of the school's teaching system. He admitted that two of the children were now in the High School, but said that one had been ill at the time of the examination and the other had been admitted after protests. He contended that it was the newspaper's duty to report the public disquiet.

The Press Council found that the story was a matter of public interest, and that it was fairly presented, except for the one inaccuracy referred to. This should have been corrected when attention was drawn to it. (1961/29)

DEMONSTRATIONS BY SCHOOLCHILDREN

Carlisle Education Committee complained about reports in three local and two national newspapers concerning two unrelated demonstrations by high school girls and secondary school boys.

The girls revolted against instructions to wear their berets in a particular way instead of individual styles. They invited Press representatives to come during the lunch hour and hear their views. Subsequently the headmistress saw the reporters and gave them her views.

The three local newspapers published her remarks. The headmistress later complained that the stories were exaggerated, that the reporters had not reported their presence to anyone in authority when they attended the school at the invitation of the 'insubordinate' girls, and that they had not told her that they had obtained statements from the girls.

The Council found that one local paper, the *Carlisle Journal* was guilty of great exaggeration, but that the reports in the *Cumberland News* and the *Cumberland Evening News* were moderately worded and fair, though the headmistress did not accept their estimate of the number of girls involved.

In the second case, two local papers, the *Cumberland Evening News* and the *Carlisle Journal*, and two nationals, the *Daily Express* and the *Daily Mirror*, reported a demonstration by boys who objected to a decision to merge their school with the local secondary girls' school. Newspaper estimates put the number of demonstrators at 200, but the Education Committee's complaint to the Press Council gave the number as only thirty. The boys, carrying banners and shouting slogans, marched to the girls' school when the Director of Education was visiting it.

The *Cumberland Evening News* and *Carlisle Journal* published apologies for inaccurate statements that the boys had refused to leave the grounds of the girls' school when told to do so, that the headmaster had kept in the school on the day of the demonstration and had stopped publication of the school magazine. The Editor-in-Chief of both newspapers, Col. J. L. Burgess, denied, however, allegations that reporters and photographers had incited the boys to demonstrate or had marshalled them for photographs.

The Press Council found that the complaints of exaggeration had some substance, but noted that the local papers had published retractions of certain statements at the headmaster's request. It rejected the complaint that reports in the *Daily Mirror* and the *Daily Express* were inaccurate. Press participation in marshalling the demonstrators had not been proved. The cameramen followed their normal practice of posing pictures. The event was of public interest, and the attendance of the Press was justified. (1963/54–5)

SCHOOL FIGHTS

The Hon. Secretary of the Lanarkshire Association of the Educational Institute of Scotland complained that the *Scottish Daily Express* had published a story about a fight between boys of two schools which carried the heading, 'Two are beaten up in School Gang Terror. Police are called in after boys injured in fight with belts.'

The Council held that this was an exaggerated version of a comparatively minor incident which was in no sense a case of 'gangster warfare'. (1959/25)

CHILDREN QUESTIONED ABOUT TEACHER

The headmaster of a Glasgow school complained about stories published in the *Scottish Daily Express* about a girl of fourteen sent home from school to get her nails cut. He alleged that a number of statements in the story were untrue; that a reporter attempted to intimidate him into making a statement for publication and that pupils had been questioned at the gates of the school. He also alleged intrusion into the private life of a teacher by visiting her at her home.

The headmaster denied that any girl was sent home or rebuked for the length of her fingernails.

The Press Council found that on several points there was a conflict of evidence, but the statement in the headline that the headmaster had sent the girl home was untrue and should have been corrected. The Council also found that reporters were seriously at fault in trying to elicit information from schoolchildren especially information relating to the personal habits of the teacher. This practice had been strongly condemned in the past, and the Council censured it again on this occasion. In favour of the newspaper the Council found that it published a statement from the headmaster that he and his staff took the strongest exception to the way the newspaper had dealt with the matter, and that a leader-page article supporting the cause of school discipline had been published. (1962/37–8)

SCHOOL CAPTAIN QUESTIONED

When a pupil was expelled from a High School in Edinburgh, the *Scottish Daily Mail* sent a reporter to the home of the school captain to obtain information.

In reply to a complaint from the Association of Headmasters in Senior Secondary Schools in Scotland, the Editor said that he felt that preliminary inquiries were necessary and that he should be free to decide whether to make them. But the Press Council held that the first check should have been with the headmaster. (1959/22–3)

CHILDREN QUESTIONED AT BUS-STOP

A reporter from the *Sun* approached some schoolchildren at a bus-stop, and inquired about information received from a parent that children at their school had been asked to write down the names of girls who might be stealing from the school.

The children told him that it had not happened in their class. The reporter then drove away.

The reporter told the Press Council that he only spoke to the children for about half a minute, and that there were some adults at the bus-stop. There was no attempt to influence the girls or do anything which would cause them embarrassment.

Mr Sydney Jacobson, Editorial Director of the *Sun*, agreed that where distress might be caused to a child, it was wrong to question one without the knowledge and consent of a parent. But he did not see any reason why this interview should cause embarrassment or distress.

In its adjudication, the Press Council said that the interviewing of children in these circumstances was regretted, and it drew attention to its previous condemnation of this practice. (1966/103–4)

PHOTOGRAPHS TAKEN IN SCHOOL HALL

The Kent Education Authority complained of an article and picture in the *Daily Mail*. A headmistress had refused permission for Press photographers to take photographs in the school examination room. But after the examination, representatives of the *Daily Mail* took a boy into the school and photographed him there.

The Press Council considered that the *Daily Mail* representatives were guilty of intrusion in interviewing a pupil inside the school, and also of taking photographs in a classroom despite the refusal of the headmistress. It added that the newspaper had incorrectly described the nature of the examination, a mistake which could have been avoided if full inquiries had been made. (1961/24)

STATE SCHOOL HYMNS

With a reader's letter criticising the singing in State schools of 'hymns that are often meaningless and sometimes downright fatuous' the *Sunday Telegraph* published a picture of a group of schoolchildren with an extract from the letter as a caption: 'They sing what we tell them. Not a single child in the school has a clue to what the words mean, but who cares?'

The headmaster of the Church of England junior mixed school in question complained that he had agreed to photographs being taken, but on the condition that they would not be used to attack religious education. He protested at the misrepresentation. The Editor, Mr Brian R. Roberts, apologised for the newspaper's error of judgment, but pointed out that the school was not in any way identified. He denied the misrepresentation, and said if an apology had been published it would have brought on the school a wide publicity which the headmaster doubtless wished to avoid.

The Press Council held that the newspaper had committed an error of judgment and upheld the complaint. (1966/67)

21 Hospitals and Doctors

As in the case of the schools, most of the complaints against the Press in relation to hospitals are of intrusion and of comment and conduct likely to disturb the routine procedure and efficient working of the hospital.

The Press Council quickly realised the importance of good relations with the medical profession and Hospital Management Committees and Hospital Boards. Discussions between representatives of the Press, led by the Chairman of the Press Council, and the medical profession resulted in an agreement in 1956 directed to promoting mutual confidence between the hospitals and the Press by the creation of good relations.

The agreement was concerned with the difficulties arising out of the confidential nature of the relationship between hospitals and doctors and their patients when Press inquiries are made about the condition of patients. Doctors may not normally give information about their patients. (An example of a permissible breach of confidence, concerning medical documents, will be found on page 46 (*Observer*).) For information to be divulged, not only is the consent of the patient required, and even where this is forthcoming, there may be good reasons why the information should not be given. Again relatives have to be considered, particularly in accident cases, to ensure as far as possible that they are notified before the Press.

The agreement with the medical profession was confirmed by the Press Council in May 1956 and circulated to the Press. It was commended to hospital authorities by the Ministry of Health, which had been represented at the preliminary discussions by observers.

Under the terms of the agreement information is not to be given to the Press without the patient's consent, and in special hospitals, such as mental hospitals and sanatoria, where the mere admission to the hospital implies the nature of the diagnosis, the doctor must satisfy himself that the information will not be prejudicial to the patient's interests. If the patient is too ill to consent, the consent of the nearest relative must be obtained.

In the case of well-known people, a brief indication of progress may be given, subject to the patient's consent.

In accident cases the Press is to be given the name and address of the patient as soon as possible, preferably after the relatives have been informed. Where, as in road, railway or air accidents, a number of people are injured, the need for the early publication of their names should be borne in mind in order to dispel anxiety about others.

The agreement also provides that all hospitals should ensure that an experienced and responsible officer is available at all times to answer Press inquiries and that Press representatives calling at hospitals should be able to produce documentary confirmation of their professional status. The agreement is reproduced in Appendix II.

In a great many hospitals, however, these arrangements did not produce the amicable co-operation which the newspapers hoped for. Suspicion and distrust steadily developed, and difficulty was experienced by many newspapers in obtaining information. The recommendation in the agreement that all hospitals should have an experienced officer to deal with inquiries was far from being observed.

The withholding of information about patients was not the only cause of strained relations. Exclusion of the Press from Regional Hospital Board meetings seemed to be becoming more widespread than was necessary or desirable in the public interest. The Press was not without blame for the deteriorating relations; newspapers were criticised for exaggerated and distorted reports and for their methods in obtaining information.

Distrust reached its climax in a case at a Midlands eye hospital where six patients suffered the loss of an eye through infection contracted in the operating theatre. The hospital made no announcement on the matter to the Press, and in consequence exaggerated rumours circulated and were not denied. (The case is dealt with on p. 339 below.)

The result of this case and reports received about others was that the Press Council drew the attention of the Minister of Health, Mr Kenneth Robinson to the fact that the arrangements made by hospitals for answering Press inquiries were not working well. Proper Press facilities were not provided, nor were experienced officers available to answer inquiries. Furthermore, the standard in the quality of information given to the Press varies considerably. The Press Council invited the Minister to stress once again the need for uniformity in the interpretation by hospitals of the 1956 recommendations.

The Minister did so and informed the Press Council that he had brought the points raised by the Council to the notice of senior lay and medical administrators throughout the hospital service and the Chairman of the Hospital Authorities. He had not only aimed at encouraging closer adherence to the arrangements recommended in 1956 and stressed the reasonable desire of the Press to be provided with information on matters of public interest, but had recommended further thought on the maintenance of good relations and mutual confidence. The Minister mentioned that, on occasions, the Press had published exaggerated or distorted reports based on unofficial sources, and used methods to obtain information that had given grounds for complaint. He asked the Press Council to foster co-operation by the Press in building up good relations.

But on the question of admission of the Press to meetings of hospital authorities Mr Robinson pointed out that the statutory right of admission to meetings of Regional Hospital Boards confirmed by the Public Bodies (Admission to Meetings) Act, 1960, did not cover meetings of Hospital Management Committees and Boards of Governors of Teaching Hospitals, and that Parliament had recently rejected proposals that the provision should be extended to them. The reason for this was that these bodies dicussed matters concerning individual patients and staff which ought not to be made public. The Minister felt that he must leave the procedure by which these bodies chose to conduct their business to their discretion.

The Press Council expressed its appreciation of the Minister's intervention.

The Council has dealt with the following cases.

HOSPITALS

MUNICH AIR DISASTER

In 1958 an airliner bringing home the Manchester United football team from a European Cup-Tie in Yugoslavia crashed when taking off from an icy runway after refuelling at Munich; eight members of the team and a number of distinguished sports journalists were killed. The Chief Executive of British European Airways, Mr (now Sir) Anthony Milward, visited the Rechts der Isar Hospital in Munich where the surviving victims were taken, and on his return wrote to *The Times* complaining of the horde of British cameramen gathered in the corridors of the hospital waiting for a chance to photograph them. He said that when he protested at the intrusion of some twenty cameramen the German doctor politely indicated that they were Mr Milward's own countrymen. To get them to leave the doctor had finally allowed them one photograph each of Mr Matt Busby, the team's manager, who was the main centre of interest. Mr Milward described the flash of camera bulbs as groups of photographers walked into the ward to photograph an unconscious man lying in a critical condition in an oxygen tent, and where three other men were also fighting for their lives.

Mr Milward's allegations of intrusion were strongly denied by the newspapers.

The Press Council made a thorough investigation of the charges. Mr Milward accepted an invitation to attend. A questionnaire was sent to Professor Maurer, the medical superintendent of the hospital; statements were taken from reporters, cameramen and witnesses on duty at the hospital.

In its adjudication, the Press Council stated that because of the international fame of the Manchester United football team the tragedy caused intense and widespread interest, and drew to Munich reporters and photographers from a number of nations. Though there were sharp differences of evidence, a fairly clear picture had emerged which enabled the Council to reach the following findings:

1. The British Press photographers were invited into the wards to take pictures and were given facilities for that purpose. None of them had forced his way into the wards. The charge of intrusion therefore failed.

2. Mr Milward was not aware of all the facts and had given a wrong impression in his letter to *The Times*.

3. The Press Council deplored the fact that so many people had assumed that Mr Milward's complaint was unanswerable and had at once blamed the Press; no distinction was made between indictment and conviction.

4. Flashlight photographs of the slightly-injured were not forbidden by the hospital authorities, provided the patients gave consent.

5. There was evidence that flashlights were used with the knowledge and presumably the approval of members of the medical staff.

6. As the number of Press, newsreel and television visitors of various countries increased, the situation became troublesome to the hospital, but the facilities could have been withdrawn at any time, and eventually were. It may have been a mistake to grant the facilities, but it was done from the kindest motives to show how well the Munich hospital was caring for sportsmen dear to the British public.

7. Professor Maurer willingly posed for photographs, which with other evidence indicated that he did not share Mr Milward's resentment.

8. The photographers, when they were allowed into the wards, did not abuse their privilege.

9. The general attitude of the British photographers was one of courtesy and co-operation with the medical staff's stipulations.

10. Whether some of the photographs in the British Press ought to have been published was a question of taste. Some papers printed photographs that others thought too harrowing.

The Press Council considered that as a general principle a photograph of a seriously injured person likely to cause needless distress and pain to relatives should not be printed.

Mr Milward was not satisfied with the finding that there had been no intrusion and invited the Press Council to publish certain evidence. The Council refused on the ground that the evidence was confidential; but stated that it saw no reason to alter a single word of its findings, which were based on exhaustive consideration of all the evidence. (1958/21–3, 33–5)

MR ANEURIN BEVAN

A complaint was made by the Labour Party about the conduct of Press representatives at the Royal Free Hospital while Mr Aneurin Bevan was gravely ill there. The charge against the reporters was that although they had been generally considerate in difficult conditions, attempts had been made to gain entry to Mr Bevan's room. The number of reporters and telephone calls, particularly after Mr Bevan's relapse, had seriously interfered with and sometimes almost completely disrupted the routine of the hospital. On two occasions journalists had penetrated into a ward near Mr Bevan's room and the inescapable inference was that they were bent on obtaining a sensational story. The newspapers had placed the collecting of news before reasonable considerations for the working of the hospital.

Statements were also made by Editors of the newspapers. These paid tribute to the courtesy and understanding of the hospital staff, but said that the arrangements made to deal with the Press were inadequate to bear the load suddenly thrust upon the hospital. There was a failure to understand the justifiable interest of the Press in obtaining information about the welfare of an important public figure.

The evidence revealed that on the day of Mr Bevan's operation, two reporters were near Mr Bevan's room; one was a girl from the *Daily Express* who asked for the sister-in-charge. She was told that no comment could be made about Mr Bevan. The other reporter was not identified. When the matron asked them to leave they apologised and did so.

On another occasion three reporters went to the deputy matron's office at her invitation. They were asked to leave the hospital and did so.

On a third occasion two reporters, one from the *Daily Telegraph* and the other from the *Daily Mail*, made their way to a general ward on the floor near to Mr Bevan's room. Their explanation was that they wished to obtain information from the nurse who was attending Mr Bevan.

The Press Council reached the following conclusions:

1. The administrative resources of the hospital were seriously over-strained by the volume of Press inquiries. This was due to the inadequate arrangements to meet the demand for news it was the duty of the Press to supply. The Press had a responsibility on such occasions to limit its inquiries as far as possible. But the Council recalled the terms of the agreement reached in 1956 by the medical profession and the Press relating to Press inquiries.

2. The reporters who made inquiries of the deputy matron and visited her room were not at fault, because permission had been given for the visit.

3. The Council regretted that some reporters thought it necessary to visit an upstairs ward in the hospital to pursue their inquiries. Undoubtedly they were at fault in doing so.

The Labour Party allegation that there had been unauthorised attempts to gain entry to Mr Bevan's room was misleading. It was not borne out by the evidence. (1961/22–3, 39–42)

SMALLPOX CASE

The *Evening Standard* commissioned a local news agency to obtain picture cover of a case of smallpox in Long Reach Isolation Hospital. The hospital authorities alleged that the photographer told the gate porter that he had permission to enter the hospital. The photographer denied this or that he had any intention of entering the hospital without permission.

The Editor of the *Evening Standard*, Mr Charles Wintour, admitted he had commissioned the picture, but disassociated himself from the means claimed to have been used in obtaining it.

The Press Council said there was a conflict of evidence about the instructions given to the photographer; it was clear, however, that before he visited the hospital permission for the visit had not been sought. The Council condemned the effort of the agency to obtain a picture of the smallpox patient in hospital. (1962/53)

THE HOSPITAL WAS NOT FRANK

Six patients at an eye hospital in the Midlands each lost an eye as the result of an infection contracted there, and the operating theatre was closed down.

M

The accepted practice of the Management Committee was not to volunteer information, and in consequence no announcement was made to the Press.   When the news leaked out a rumour began to circulate that five people had died. The rumour was officially denied, but eventually the hospital issued a statement through the Group Secretary giving the facts.

The Birmingham *Sunday Mercury* complained to the Press Council that it had been misled by the answers to inquiries made at the hospital, and had been given the impression that nothing was amiss.

The Editor of the newspaper, Mr Frederick Whitehead, said that an official 'deliberately misled' a newspaper reporter. Mr Whitehead maintained that the happenings at the hospital were a matter of grave public concern, and should have been disclosed to the Press at the earliest possible moment to allay harmful speculation. Comparatively junior hospital officials, he said, should not be encouraged to act as censors.

The hospital expressed regret to the Press Council that answers given by its spokesman to questions put to him by the newspaper should have caused incorrect inferences to be drawn.

The Press Council declared that if the hospital authorities had issued a statement on the occurrences at the eye hospital at an earlier stage, it would have avoided rumours spreading and enabled the Press to give accurate information to the public. In accordance with the spirit of the 1956 agreement between the medical profession and the Press, newspaper inquiries should have been answered frankly, and the Council regretted that this had not been done. (1965/99)

REPORTER DID NOT HAVE PERMISSION

Following the publication of a story in the *Daily Herald* under the heading 'Scandal of Ward E1 — Boy of 12 kept with 58 men for six months', the South-West Metropolitan Regional Hospital Board complained about the story and the way it had been obtained.

The hospital housed mental patients, and the boy in question was alleged to have been indecently assaulted.

In answer to the hospital's complaint that he had visited the ward without permission, the reporter said he had gone there in the company of the boy's father, who was a regular visitor.

The Press Council held that the reporter should have asked to see the

Medical Superintendent first and requested permission to visit the ward in which the boy was a patient. (1961/35–6, 48–9)

A DUKE IN HOSPITAL

The Duke of Norfolk complained that the *Daily Express* contained an inaccurate report of a brief stay he made as an in-patient at a London hospital.

The report stated that he had been visited by the Queen Mother. In fact she was visiting an old friend. A correction and apology were printed on the following day, but the Duke complained to the Press Council that such incidents did great harm to journalism.

The Press Council declared that while there was no evidence that the newspaper had knowingly published incorrect information, it was unfortunate that it did not pursue inquiries at the hospital in accordance with the procedure agreed by the medical profession and the Press. Had it done so it would have received from a senior official the information communicated to other newspapers.

The Council noted that the *Daily Express* had published a correction, the terms of which had been agreed with the Duke. (1960/28–9)

'OPEN DOOR' VISITING

The *Sunday Express* reported that many hospitals were finding it impossible to operate the 'open door' policy for visits, and cited instances of chaos in the wards resulting from the experiment.

A complaint was made that the writer failed to distinguish between visiting adults and visiting children. This was misleading because adult geriatric and child patients were medically and socially distinct; the newspaper story gave the impression that conditions for one group applied to all.

The Editor of the *Sunday Express*, Mr John Junor, said the report was directed only to problems of unrestricted visiting, and was not a comprehensive investigation of the subject of hospital visiting.

The Press Council held that although the *Sunday Express* report on hospital visiting did not distinguish between different categories of patients, it was not incorrect or biased. (1963/43)

REPORTER SAID HE HAD AN APPOINTMENT

In a national newspaper story a woman was said to have described how witches met and tried to invoke powers to do good. A photograph showed her robed, standing in an attitude of supplication.

The following day the *South London Press* published a report to the effect that the residents of the rest home conducted by the woman were surprised to learn she was a witch.

A reporter from the newspaper was permitted to speak to the patients by stating he had obtained her permission to do so. His report implied a personal interview with the woman, but in fact the remarks attributed to her had been taken from the national newspaper report. The reporter assured the staff at the home that he would see her before his report was published, but he did not do so. Other newspapers had respected her wishes that the name and the address of the home should not be disclosed.

The Editor of the *South London Press*, Mr Eric Kinton, said that it did not occur to him that, after all the national publicity she had received, the lady in question would try to keep from her patients her association with witchcraft.

The News Editor also said that had he known of her strong objection to the link, he would have respected her request to suppress the name of her rest home.

The reporter admitted that he had been allowed to speak to the patients on the understanding that the lady who ran the rest home would see his report before it was published, but said that when he telephoned the story to the newspaper, he had placed an embargo on it until he had obtained permission to use it. This was denied by the person who took the dictation.

The Press Council censured the newspaper for publication of the article and the reporter for falsely representing that he had permission to interview residents in the rest home and failing to make it clear to his newspaper that the report was subject to an embargo until it had been cleared for publication. (1964/75–6)

NURSE REFUSED LEAVE TO GET MARRIED

A story in the *Northern Echo* gave publicity to the story of a student nurse at Bishop Auckland General Hospital who was refused a day's leave to get married because she was due to attend classes. In its leader column, the newspaper commented that in refusing to discuss the matter, the Matron of the hospital seemed to be doing her best to give the impression that she was a 'dragon'. It asked whether, perhaps, it was all a stunt to encourage more young women to take up nursing as a career.

The Hospital Management Committee told the newspaper that the nurse in question had had ample opportunity to arrange her private affairs to avoid any conflict with her course of study, and asked for the statement to be printed in verbatim in a similar position in the leader column as the original story entitled 'Permission to Wed'. Otherwise the statement should not be published. Thr newspaper refused, and the Hospital Management Committee complained to the Press Council.

The Editor of the *Northern Echo*, Mr Harold Evans, told the Press Council that no official comment could be obtained from the Matron or the hospital authorities. What seemed to be in issue was the right of a newspaper to comment on a public service unfavourably.

The Press Council said that the leader was fair comment expressing a view that could reasonably be held. The Editor was not under an obligation to print the reply in the editorial column, and the complaint was rejected. (1966/38–9)

'A CAMPAIGN OF VILIFICATION'

An article in the Glasgow *Daily Record* criticising a local hospital's maternity unit was described as 'a campaign of vilification and irresponsibility against a hospital' in a complaint by the Hospitals Board. After investigation, Mr Alex Little, the Editor-in-Chief, admitted serious errors, and wrote to the Board offering to print a correction which retracted a statement that some women had their babies in the corridors; clarified a point about deliveries on hospital trolleys and made clear why a woman who lost one of her babies left hospital the next day. The Board did not reply to his letter, but complained to the Press Council that the correction was most unsatisfactory. They felt that the newspaper should make it clear that the wole contribhution was totally inaccurate. The Editor, not getting a reply to his offer, decided to publish the correction and apology as drafted.

The Press Council deplored the publication of an article which was admitted to contain serious errors, but noted that the Editor published a correction and apology when the facts were brought to his attention. (1964/70)

HOSPITAL UNFAIRLY CRITICISED

An article in the *People* involving criticism of hospital authorities was the subject of a complaint by the Leicester No. 1 Hospital Management Committee. It criticised the doctors for leaving a young girl to make a decision about whether her husband, who was in hospital and a 'hopeless, pathetic wreck' after an accident, should be nursed by his mother or herself. The hospital told the Press Council that so far from leaving it to her, they had done all they could to persuade her to leave her husband in hospital. The hospital view was that the interests of the wife had been sacrificed to the provision of a sensational article. The Press Council held that the article should never have been published because it misrepresented the facts and reflected unfairly on the hospital authorities. (1963/46–7)

NEW-BORN BABY DISCHARGED FROM HOSPITAL

When the *Sunday Pictorial* published a story under the heading '4-Hour Baby sent out of Hospital', the Chairman of the hospital complained that the report suggested lack of care by the hospital, and that two reporters had obtained access to the maternity ward by trespass.

The Press Council investigated and found that the newspaper had been told of the discharge by the father of the child. It held that his complaint to the newspaper was a matter of public interest and that the Editor was entitled to publish it, especially as the newspaper gave prominence at the same time to the hospital's statement on the subject, and to its assurance that the health of the mother and baby was not endangered by the early discharge from the maternity ward. It was unfortunate that the reporters making the investigation chose to visit the maternity ward before making inquiries at the administrative office. (1959/20)

DOCTORS

DOCTOR'S NAME DISCLOSED AGAINST HIS WILL

A few days after a twenty-one-year-old Welsh boxer collapsed and died in a London ring the *Daily Telegraph* recorded that a doctor whom they named and identified by his practice had said he had examined the boxer ten days before the fight and had refused him a fitness certificate. The edition sold in the town where the doctor was practising identified him, though the London edition did not.

The doctor had informed all newspapermen who called him by telephone that he would speak only on the understanding that his name was not mentioned. He complained of a gross breach of faith.

The Editor of the *Daily Telegraph*, Mr Maurice Green, expressed regret, but said the news desk understood that the doctor had been interviewed for television and thought that his name would inevitably be published elsewhere.

The Press Council held that it was clearly wrong to have published the name of the doctor in the circumstances disclosed. It noted that the Editor had apologised. (1965/52)

GYNAECOLOGISTS AND THEIR PATIENTS

A complaint was made about an article in the *Queen* entitled 'The Smart Gynaecologists', on the grounds that it was professionally embarrassing to the gynaecologists, and because it falsely stated, amongst other things, that one of them offered his patients a stiff drink after a consultation. The article seemed to assume that the relationship between a gynaecologist and his patients was a suitable subject for publicity. The gynaecologists maintained that no principle of freedom of the Press necessitated such intrusion into the affairs of private individuals.

The Editor-in-Chief of the *Queen*, Mr Jocelyn Stevens, said that only one of the fourteen gynaecologists mentioned in the article had complained, and the complaint related to the statement that he offered drinks to patients after consultations; this the Editor said he could prove to be true. Had the gynaecologist in question suffered damage he could have taken legal action. The Editor did not think the matter had anything whatever to do with the Press Council.

The Council, in its adjudication, stated that the article was deplorable. The disclaimer and apology that the practitioners had asked for were reasonable and should have been published. (1962/33, 78)

22 The Press and the Police

Crime is the business of the police. But crime is news, of public interest, and the public is entitled to be informed about it. In the normal gathering of the news and in the course of legitimate inquiries reporters frequently obtain information which enables fraud, corruption and vice to be exposed in the newspapers and the police to bring those involved to justice.

'It is one of the professional tasks of newspapers to unmask the fraudulent and the scandalous', Mr Justice Lawton told the jury in his summing up in a case against footballers involved in bribery charges. The judge went on to say that it was in the public interest that newspapers should do so; it was a task they had done time and time again in their long history.

The case was an outstanding example of an exposure based on a painstaking investigation by a national newspaper. The criminal authorities might never have been able to launch a successful prosecution without the assistance received from the Press.

The Royal Commission on the Police had no doubt of the value of good relations between the Press and the police. Its Report of 1962 stated that the Press was an important intermediary between the police and the public and that it had a useful part to play in helping the police; the police, for their part, could render a reciprocal service by taking the Press into their confidence and making available information the public should be given.

Indeed, the police and the Press have a common purpose — the maintenance of law and order and the safeguarding of public liberties against lawbreakers of every kind. Good relations between the police and Press were not only desirable in themselves, but necessary because they contributed to the greater efficiency of both bodies. It was no exaggeration to say, the Willink Commission on the Police stated, that the police could not carry out their task of maintaining law and order without the support and confidence of the people; the public interest therefore required that the people should have confidence in the police, and any unfair or inaccurate reporting which tended to undermine that confidence could do nothing but harm. There was, therefore, a clear need for liaison between the police and the Press.

The Commission was satisfied on the evidence it heard that the Press was aware of its responsibilities towards the police and discharged them properly. There was no general lack of sympathy, on the contrary the Press was always ready to applaud the police whenever the occasion occurred and to report prominently the not infrequent instances of bravery.

A number of witnesses told the Commission that the newspapers, because of inaccurate and distorted reporting of police news, were partly responsible for the deterioration of relations that had occurred between the police and the public. The Commission realised, however, that the erring policeman, like the defaulting parson or schoolteacher, was 'news'; stories of the prosecution and conviction of policemen were frequently given prominence. But the Press had a duty to report the news accurately, and if it was sometimes unfavourable to the police the Press could not be blamed. Indeed, the prominence given to such cases demonstrated the anxiety of Chief Constables to maintain high standards of discipline. Occasions did occur, however, when the news was distorted and inaccurately reported, particularly in headlines.

The Press Council had been invited by the Commission to give evidence but explained that it could be of limited assistance as it had no direct contact with the police and its function was mainly to investigate complaints. Nevertheless an informal meeting did take place between the Chairman of the Council and Sir Henry Willink, the Chairman of the Commission, when it was agreed that the Council would investigate three cases of alleged biased and misleading newspaper reports about the police and a complaint about

M 2   L.T.P.C.

the reporting of a memorandum presented to the Commission by the Law Society.

In one of the three cases the Chief Constable concerned withdrew his complaint; in another the complainant refused to take part in the investigation. In the third, seven national dailies were cited. A dossier of evidence amounting to approximately 12,000 words was sifted by the Council; four of the newspapers and a Chief Constable were held blameworthy for some factors; on other points there was a conflict of evidence and the Council was unable to reach a decision.

The complaint of the reporting of the Law Society memorandum involved four national newspapers. The reports in three of them, the Press Council decided, were neither unfair nor unbalanced; fault, however, was found with the headlines in three instances. The Law Society had paid generous tribute to the integrity and ability of the police, but alleged there were isolated cases in which police conduct fell short of the usual high standard. Three of the newspapers printed headlines which singled out in sensational terms the criticism of police behaviour, but gave no hint of the Law Society's tribute. One headline, for example, read: 'Solicitors Say Police Fake Evidence'.

The four cases were selected by the Commission from a substantial number brought to its attention by the police as instances in which the Press was said to have acted irresponsibly in reporting police activities. 'We do not think on the evidence that this charge has been substantiated,' the Commission declared. Much of the police criticism of the Press, the Commission said, was the result of the isolation of the police from the rest of the community, which inclined them to be over-sensitive to criticism. If the police helped the Press to publish fair and accurate news about their activities, they would help themselves by ensuring that people understood what they did and why they did it.

It was not enough for the police to understand the requirements of the Press; the Press had also to understand that the police worked under difficulties and could not always communicate information of news value to the Press; to do so could prejudice subsequent judicial proceedings. For example, in the case of Podola, subsequently hanged for the murder of a policeman, the police were accused in Parliament and the Press of unnecessary violence when making the arrest. Police repudiation of the allegation was not possible at the time, because the circumstances of the arrest were likely to be important at the trial. Journalists should remember that the police are often given information in confidence which they are not at liberty to divulge and should not be expected to do so.

The Commission stated that relations were sometimes strained by the number of Press representatives detailed for a particular task. There would be better co-operation if the Press limited the number of reporters and photographers covering an incident. It was irritating if representatives from the national Press, the Press Association, local news agencies, the B.B.C. and I.T.V. came at different times; it was almost inevitable that some would be told to go away if important work was not to be impeded. Photographers jostling one another and the police in an effort to get a dramatic picture could not complain if they fell foul of the police and were kept away from the scene altogether.

The Commission endorsed and commended to the police the suggestions made by the National Union of Journalists for developing good relations with the Press.

1. Recognised times should be arranged for Press men to make routine calls at police stations.

2. Information officers should be appointed.

3. The communication of information to the Press should be speeded up.

4. Officers in charge of the investigations of major crimes should hold Press conferences.

5. Off the record conferences should be held, where necessary, to give the Press background information. (Cmnd. 1728, par. 404.)

The Commission believed that these recommendations formed the basis for developing good working relations with the Press.

Comparatively few cases have come before the Press Council, and one of them, concerning a Chief Constable and two newspapers, has already been dealt with on pp. 198 (*Daily Mail*) and 265 (*News Chronicle*).

ROUGH TREATMENT OF REPORTERS

When two of the Manchester United footballers who had survived the Munich air-crash arrived back from Germany a crowd gathered at Liverpool Street Station to greet them. A Press Officer of British Railways obtained the players' consent for reporters to interview and photograph them, but when the players left their compartment railway police and porters pushed the journalists and well-wishers violently to one side.

The Editor of the *Star*, Mr Ralph McCarthy, referred the matter to the Press Council. The Council obtained statements from the journalists and photographers who were on duty, and from the General Manager of the Eastern Region of British Railways who, however, felt unable to comply with the Council's request for written statements from the police inspector and Public Relations Officer of British Railways who had been present.

In its adjudication, the Press Council held that the railway police were at fault in dealing roughly with Press representatives, who were attempting to carry out their duties in accordance with prior arrangements made with a British Railways Public Relations Officer. (1958/23)

POLICE ASK NEWSPAPER FOR INFORMATION

After two members of the Nottingham C.I.D. visited the offices of the *Nottingham Evening Post*, the Nottingham branch of the National Union of Journalists protested to the Press Council.

The police had received an anonymous letter about a proposed demonstration in favour of nuclear disarmament which, it was felt, might result in a breach of the peace. A C.I.D. officer asked for the co-operation of the newspaper in supplying information, but this was not forthcoming.

A week later, the officer returned to the office with a detective-sergeant, and suggested to a member of the staff who handled 'letters to the Editor' that where there was a possible security background the journalists might be prepared to disclose the identity of writers of letters who wished them to be published under pen-names. The request was refused.

The Press Council felt that the police must be at liberty to make inquiries in newspaper offices, as elsewhere. But in the case before it, the Council considered that it was improper for a request to have been made for a journalist to act as an informer in the supply of general information. (1960/26)

POLICEMAN USED PRESS-CARD

During the hearing of a case at Bow Street Magistrates' Court concerning a West End Club, it was stated in evidence that a police witness had described himself as a journalist and had carried a Press identity card.

The Press Council at once took the matter up with the Chief Commissioner of Police, who agreed that the police officer did describe himself as a journalist and did carry a Press identity card, which in fact he had no occasion to produce. The Press Council said that the incident was likely to discredit the Metropolitan and City Police identification card system.

The Chief Commissioner replied that the card was not one which had been issued or purported to be issued by him, and that he did not think any real harm was done by this means of concealing the identity of a police officer. But he appreciated the Press Council's anxiety, and had given instructions that this particular subterfuge should not be used in future. (1958/26)

APPOINTMENT OF CHIEF CONSTABLE

When the Blackpool Council was considering candidates for the post of Chief Constable, the *Sunday Graphic* published an article containing references to possible candidates. As a result the Town Clerk asked the Press Council to endorse the local authority's view that comments upon the merits of men who might or might not be in competition with others for a vacant post was 'most improper and irresponsible'.

The Editor, Mr Alan Hall, replied that although he would publish corrections on matters of fact, he felt bound to reserve the right to comment on the filling of public appointments.

The Press Council informed the Blackpool Council that it could not support an objection to the article in general; and as the *Sunday Graphic* had apologised for certain inaccuracies, and had published a letter from the Town Clerk, it did not consider that further action was called for. (1959/19)

23 Reporting Politics and Political Parties

The desire for publicity and rivalry for electoral support have the effect of sharpening the sensibilities of candidates and political parties to Press reports, particularly at election times.

The Press Council has had to deal with a number of complaints of alleged unfair reporting and failure to report the views of candidates and the policy of the party to which they belong.

The legal restrictions on the extent to which newspapers can be partisan at election times is mainly regulated by the Representation of the People Act, 1949. The Press Council is concerned rather with the standards of fair reporting, and to ensure that political bias does not cause distortion of facts.

The nature of the Press Council's function in the field of elections and politics can be gleaned from the Report of the First Royal Commission. The Commission regarded it as axiomatic that a newspaper purporting to record and discuss public affairs should record them truthfully. A newspaper is entitled to express what opinions it pleases, but opinions should be advocated without suppressing or distorting the relevant facts. Adherence to a political party can be made plain by its opinion columns, but should not be expressed by the colouring given to the news. Inevitably, and quite legitimately, the newspaper's politics will affect its judgment of the relative interest of news items.

Party and political bias in the selection of news can result in suppression of facts which ought to be known, just as a quotation out of context from an important speech may reduce the report of the speech to a travesty. The consistent selection of items of news which support a newspaper's own policy, and the omission of those that do not, can, the Commission pointed out, produce in the minds of readers an impression totally divorced from the truth, although every statement of fact preserves the most meticulous accuracy.

The Press Council will not hinder the free expression of opinion, but complaints of excessive bias, misrepresentation or distortion, whether calculated or inadvertent can raise questions of ethical standards.

Minority parties and candidates representing them sometimes complain that they are ignored altogether or are inadequately reported. Newspapers, however, are concerned with the publication of the news, and as a rule there is more news than there is room for in the newspaper. The Editor's paramount right to decide what goes into the newspaper is accepted by the Press Council. Minority political groups and politicians have no automatic right to space and their views are only likely to attract the consideration of an editor if, in his judgment, they are news. In making up his mind he will doubtless have regard to the interest these views have for the readers of the newspaper.

Some cases concerning politics have been dealt with elsewhere, for instance page 164 (*Sunday Express*).

The remaining cases considered by the Press Council are as follows.

PRESS COMMENT AT ELECTION TIMES

The Torquay Trades Council objected to leading articles in the Torquay *Herald Express* by 'The Idler' published during the 1955 General Election. The Trades Council considered that the articles constituted a grave abuse of the impartiality of the British Press at election times. The feature, it was complained, 'exercised undue influence on the electorate when it was necessary for the national and provincial Press to present news without comment, in order that the country's political judgment might be fairly decided.'

The Editor, Mr Reginald A. Colwill, said that the newspaper always aimed to be scrupulously fair towards all political parties in its presentation of news. But it retained to itself the right of expressing any opinion in articles which were apart from actual news. Its correspondence columns were open to all shades of opinion.

The Press Council said that the articles did not go beyond the accepted rights of a newspaper to comment on matters of public importance, whether local or national. (1955/27)

DISTORTION AND BIAS ALLEGED

A Labour candidate in a by-election complained that *The Times*'s reports of his campaign were distorted, and contained mis-statements of fact and were so presented as to give a disparaging overall picture. He said that his letter to *The Times* had not been published. The Editor, Sir William Haley, said that the letter had accused the newspaper of having made statements that had not, in fact, been made. He thought that the candidate had misunderstood the reporter's function, which was not to take sides but to report. There was no desire to malign the candidate, and no reasonable person reading what *The Times* printed could think it had done so.

The Press Council decided that the candidate had not substantiated his complaint. (1961/32)

ELECTION CANDIDATE MISREPRESENTED

An independent candidate in the 1964 election complained that the *Western Daily Press* published extracts from his eve-of-poll statement which, being out of context, altered its meaning and damaged him electorally.

The Press Council was told that the candidate's remarks were cut for space reasons, as were those of other candidates, but the Council upheld the complaint on the grounds that the condensation had resulted in unintentional misrepresentation. (1965/36–7)

PARLIAMENTARY PRIVILEGE

An unusual case arose out of a breach of Parliamentary privilege.

The facts were that during a period of petrol rationing, the Editor of the *Romford Recorder* published an article under the heading 'M.P.s too kind to themselves'. The House of Commons Committee of Privileges held that the headline was a contempt of the House, but not of such a nature as to make it necessary to take further action.

The Editor complained to the Press Council that he had been condemned unheard, and drew attention to the danger of restrictions on the Press and public freedom of speech.

The Press Council pointed out that the House of Commons has extremely wide powers in matters of breach of privilege. A libel reflecting on the proceedings of the House is a violation of its rights and privileges, on the ground that it tends to obstruct the House in the performance of its functions by diminishing the respect due to it. On this occasion the Committee of Privileges had obviously decided that although there had been a breach, it did not tend directly to obstruct or impede the House in the performance of its functions, but indirectly tended to do so by bringing the House into odium, contempt or ridicule. The Committee was acting within its recognised powers in reaching its decisions.

As to the complaint that the Editor was condemned unheard, the Press Council drew attention to a passage in Erskine May, the recognised authority on Parliamentary procedure:

> It has been objected that to adjudge that the offence has been committed before hearing the accused party is a very serious deviation from the common course of criminal justice. As, however, the question whether the writing is defamatory can, in most cases, be determined from the terms of the document without recourse to extrinsic evidence, and as the falsity of the libel is not an essential element of the offence, if the defamatory character of the writing is apparent on its face, no explanation which might be offered could alter the decision of the House on that point, though it might materially influence the House in deciding what punishment, if any, to inflict. . . .

The Press Council stated that as the Committee had decided that the heading 'M.P.s too kind to themselves' was a contempt of the House, the case obviously fell within the category of those in which there was held to be no need for extrinsic evidence or scope for argument. The Council did not think that the Editor of the *Romford Recorder* had been unfairly treated. (1957/8, 33–4)

M.P.'S EXCLUSIVE ARTICLE

After allegations against the Governor of Barlinnie prison in a Parliamentary debate, Mr W. Reid, M.P., made a tour of the prison. The visit attracted considerable public interest in the light of the Commons statements and an official investigation.

A Clydebank journalist complained that after the tour Mr Reid ignored the reporters and photographers of all newspapers except the *Scottish Daily Express*, in which an exclusive article by him appeared the following day. The journalist suggested it was wrong for a Member of Parliament to make a public statement on a matter of public interest exclusively to one newspaper. He had been taken to the gaol in a *Daily Express* motor-car and was hurried away afterwards in the same car.

Mr Reid commented that he had been quite willing to talk to representatives of other newspapers but he had not been asked. It was generally known, he added, that he would be going back to London by train that night, but no one had troubled to approach him at the station.

The Editor, Mr Roger Wood, said that in accordance with normal newspaper practice, Mr Reid had been invited to contribute a special article, which he agreed to do, and that at his request a car had been provided by the newspaper for his convenience. No other newspaper reporters had questioned him after leaving the prison.

In view of Mr Reid's statement, the Press Council decided not to take any action. (1961/33)

COMMUNIST CLAIM TO SPACE

The twelve Communist candidates in the 1965 Leeds municipal elections wrote to the Editor of the *Yorkshire Evening Post* protesting that during the election, although numerous articles were published about the policies and personalities of Conservative, Labour and Liberal candidates, and eve-of-the-poll statements from leaders of the parties were given, nothing at all was published about the Communist candidates and their policy. The candidates contended that their exclusion was an act of calculated political prejudice. Subsequently they complained to the Press Council.

The Secretary of the Leeds Area Committee of the Communist Party contended that while the newspaper had a right to put forward its editorial views, its news columns should show some sense of balance during an election period.

The Editor, Mr A. H. Woodward, replied that it was neither the duty nor the intention of the newspaper to propagate Communism. But if it were felt that Communist activities were of interest to a substantial number of readers, the newspaper would aim to give these readers the news. In fact, only a tiny fraction of readers were interested, and the Communists had been given the space to which they were entitled on this basis. He further argued that the Press Council ought not to be used as an instrument by any political party to exert pressure upon an editor to print any particular views. If this could be done, any candidate or group of candidates, no matter how outrageous their views, could claim the right to have their opinions printed irrespective of whether there was any public interest in what they said.

The Press Council held that there was no obligation on an Editor to publish news of candidates which, in his judgment, would not be of interest to readers. (1965/80-1)

ELECTION DISCRIMINATION DENIED

A Belfast councillor complained to the Press Council that he had lost votes in an election for the Northern Ireland Parliament because the *Irish News* denied him the use of its columns both editorially and for advertising. He said that he was given one editorial write-up, and one advertisement was published. But he claimed that when a second advertisement was submitted it was refused, and his supporters picketed the newspaper offices as a protest. He admitted that the newspaper had published a statement that the copy for the advertisement was not refused, but that it had been offered at 11.45 p.m., and that he had been requested to bring it back during normal office hours. No evidence was offered that the advertisement was resubmitted.

The Press Council found no evidence of discrimination by the newspaper against the councillor. (1963/50-1)

'SMEAR CAMPAIGN'

When a Member of Parliament married a member of the Moral Rearmament movement, of which he was also a member, the executive of his local constituency association recommended to the association that its support for him should be withdrawn.

The *Scottish Daily Express* described the executive's decision as 'monstrous persecution' and a 'mediaeval witch-hunt'. Subsequently, the local association rejected the advice of its executive, and confirmed support for the sitting member.

A woman member of the executive complained to the Press Council that she and her husband had been subjected to a 'smear campaign', and to bitter and malicious abuse, by the *Scottish Daily Express*. She submitted eleven cuttings from the newspaper and three from other newspapers to substantiate her charge.

The Press Council ruled that in a political and religious controversy which aroused strong emotions the newspaper took one side and the complainant the other. The references to the complainant and her husband in the *Scottish Daily Express* were within the admissible limits of political controversy. (1963/53)

RESOLUTIONS AGAINST NATIONALISATION

The *Birmingham Post* reported that two resolutions against nationalisation had been submitted to the Transport and General Workers' Union national conference, under the headline, 'Union urged: "Halt State Ownership" '. A complaint was made that the report did not mention the twenty-odd resolutions in favour of nationalisation, which were also on the agenda; this, it was alleged, was 'a deliberate attempt to create a different impression in the mind of the reader than that given by the whole truth'.

Examination of the official list of conference resolutions showed that of the 27 resolutions on nationalisation none was against it. Two called for the delay in the extension of nationalisation, two suggested improvements, and the remaining 23 favoured extension unequivocally.

The Joint-Deputy-Editor, Mr W. Stevens, said that the story was based on an agency contribution. One would have expected more nationalisation to be advocated at the conference, but that there should be two motions advocating a delay was unexpected and highly newsworthy. He added that the comments by the Industrial Correspondent which followed the news story put the whole matter in perspective.

The Press Council found that the report was misleading. It should have included reference to the fact that there were 23 motions tabled favouring an extension of nationalisation whereas only a few urged temporary delay. (1964/38)

COUNCILLOR POSES IN BUBBLE-BATH

The *Daily Express* published a large picture of a forty-seven year old mother of four children, a Conservative member of the Leamington Borough Council, posing in a bubble-bath. The story quoted her as saying that it was meant to be an 'eye-catcher to advertise Leamington as a Spa town', and that her political opponents claimed it was meant to be a vote catcher. The local Conservative agent was reported as 'pleased' and to have said: 'I am sure many of our supporters will be immensely relieved to find that it is in fact the Liberal bubble that has been burst by all this.'

The agent complained that he had been wrongly quoted, and that the inaccuracy was causing him embarrassment. His remarks had been taken down in longhand and were read back to him at the time. What appeared in the newspaper was inaccurate, and he wanted it to be known that he had nothing to do with the photograph, which was not an election stunt. He had treated the whole matter light-heartedly at the time of the interview.

The reporter who had written the story stood by the quoted statements. The Editor of the *Daily Express*, Mr Robert Edwards, produced the page of the reporter's notebook on which the interview was recorded; it showed that the quotation published was substantially that indicated in the note.

The Press Council rejected the complaint that the agent's remarks were inaccurately reported. It added that his attitude might have been more clearly stated to have been 'light-hearted' rather than 'pleased'. (1964/39)

MUNICIPAL ELECTION COMPLAINT

Sutton Coldfield Labour Party complained that the *Sutton Coldfield News* had discriminated against the party during the 1965 municipal election campaign. The Secretary of the party said that there had been a lack of coverage for the party's policy. When he complained he had been assured that coverage would be given to the policy pamphlet in the next issue. It was not given, and the Editor explained that the other two parties had bought space, and there was no room for the Labour Party item.

The Secretary said that this suggested that political news items were likely to be excluded in the interests of commercialism, and that to ensure coverage a party must buy space in a newspaper.

The Editor-in-Chief, Mr W. J. Webb, replied that the Sutton Coldfield Labour Party apparently thought that local newspapers had to give equal space to each party. Local news value was the sole criterion in deciding what went in the newspaper. A story about the Labour policy statement had appeared.

The Editor of the newspaper, Mr A. S. Hale, said that, as his newspaper did not print manifestoes as such, he had used the letter which had been sent to him with the manifesto. He could not think of anything he had said which could have given the impression that the fact that the other parties had bought space was a reason why he could not print Labour Party news.

The Press Council rejected the complaint, saying that there was no unfair discrimination against the Labour Party. (1966/37)

SHOULD MINISTERS BE PAID FOR ARTICLES?

In its 1965 Annual Report the Press Council noted that the Prime Minister had been asked in the House of Commons what rules he had laid down, and what directions he had given, to Ministers of the Crown, regarding acceptance of offers to contribute paid articles in public periodicals or to appear on television.

Mr Wilson had replied that there had been no change in the long established policy that Ministers should not practise journalism. A Minister was not debarred from writing articles or letters to newspapers to supplement other methods of informing the public of the work of his department. He should not accept payment for such articles, but Ministers had discretion to accept payment for appearances in television programmes if it was clear that they were speaking in a private capacity. (1965/26)

In a news story about a book by the former Member for Smethwick, the *Daily Express* stated that Hansard showed that during the debate on the Queen's speech on 3 October 1964, the Prime Minister, Mr Wilson, said that 'the Smethwick Conservatives can have the satisfaction of having topped the poll and of having sent here as their Member one who, until a further General Election restores him to oblivion, will serve his term here as a Parliamentary leper'.

In fact, the record stated that Mr Wilson in addressing the Leader of the Opposition, Sir Alec Douglas-Home, in reference to the Member for Smethwick said:

> Does he now intend to take him to his bosom? Will the Conservative Whip be extended to him, because if he does accept him as a colleague he will make this clear; he will betray the principles which not only his party but the nation have hitherto had the right to proclaim. And if he does not, if he takes what I think is the right course, and what, I am sure, the country will think is the right course, the Smethwick Conservatives [*Interruption*] — hon. Members opposite will have to listen now — if, as I say, the right hon. Gentleman takes what I am sure the country would regard as the right course, the Smethwick Conservatives can have the satisfaction of having topped the poll, and of having sent here as their Member one who, until a further General Election restores him to oblivion, will serve his term here as a Parliamentary leper.

The complainant to the Press Council alleged that the newspaper had been guilty of dishonesty and of slanting facts for political spite; the word 'if' was all-important, and what the Prime Minister said was if — and only if — Sir Alec took the action of not accepting the Member would the Member be a 'Parliamentary leper'.

The Editor, Mr Derek Marks, said that he had heard Mr Wilson's speech and was in no doubt what the Prime Minister meant. He drew attention to an Opposition motion which expressed regret at the description 'Parliamentary leper' and of the Prime Minister's refusal to withdraw the expression. Mr Marks contended that it was not merely the exact words that were used, but the manner and circumstances in which they were used, which determined the sense of what they meant. He denied that the summary given in the *Daily Express* gave a false impression.

The Press Council found that the question was whether the sense of the passage in Hansard was that the Prime Minister was calling the Member for Smethwick a Parliamentary leper or whether he was saying that if the Leader of the Opposition disowned the Member he would be a Parliamentary leper. The *Daily Express* was certainly entitled to take the first view, but not to omit from the quotation the phrase relied on in support of the second view. The effect of the omission was to leave the reader with a wrong impression, and to this extent the article was misleading. (1966/68–70)

CANDIDATE'S NAME OMITTED FROM CONSTITUENCY LIST

The *Birmingham Planet*, in an 'Election Guide' published on 24 March 1966 as part of a normal issue and containing details of the candidates for the Birmingham divisions, stated: 'Miss S. W., who again faces Sir E. B. in Handsworth, has a straight fight on her hands this time. Councillor W. L., the Liberal who made it a three-cornered fight at the last election, has departed to Ladywood and pastures new . . .'.

In its next issue published on 31 March the newspaper published a paragraph, headed 'Three-Cornered', which read: 'There is a three-cornered fight in Handsworth at this General Election — and it is not a straight fight between Labour and Conservative as reported in last week's *Planet*. The third candidate is Mr J. H., of the Union Movement.'

Mr J. H. told the Press Council that months before the election he had notified the *Birmingham Planet* of his adoption, and in the following months the newspaper was supplied with details of his pre-election activities. When he was nominated on 16 March two other Birmingham newspapers reported the fact, but not the *Birmingham Planet*.

When the *Planet* the following week again ignored his candidature and suggested there were two candidates only, he protested. The newspaper published a three-line correction in an obscure position in its polling day issue, too late to be seen by the majority of its reader voters.

Mr J. H. contended that the publication of the false and misleading statement that there was to be a straight fight as compared with a three-cornered one at the last election was calculated to create the impression that he was not a candidate and to prejudice his electoral chances.

The Editor of the newspaper, Mr M. H. Guy, said that an error had been made through an oversight by the writer of the article. It was the newspaper's intention to publish a fair summary of the election news; it denied the intention to publish information likely to prevent the election of Mr H. or to secure the election of any of his opponents. As soon as the error was pointed out by Mr J. H. an apology was tendered, and the correction published on polling day was the earliest possible occasion this could be done. In any case the newspaper after closure of nominations did not indicate that there would be a straight fight between Labour and Conservative; reference to Mr J. H. had been made in previous issues.

The Press Council held that the newspaper failed in its duty to the electors of the constituency by omitting the name of a candidate who had been validly nominated while publishing the names of two other candidates. (1967)

24 Advertisers and Advertisements

ADVERTISEMENTS AND PUBLICITY FOR NEWSPAPERS AND PERIODICALS

Because of the large part advertising revenue plays in the economy of a newspaper, there is a widely held belief that advertisers can and do exert an influence on editorial policy. Editors are said to be subject to direct pressure from advertisers and to indirect pressure through their own advertising departments to avoid publishing anything detrimental to advertisers' interests.

Both the 1947–9 and the 1961–2 Commissions examined the suggestion that improper pressures were exerted by advertisers, and both came to the same conclusions.

A newspaper depended on advertisements for about half its revenue, the 1949 Report stated, and therefore had a considerable inducement to adopt a tone which would cause advertisers to regard it as a good advertising medium; this view, however, overlooked the fact that sales revenue and advertisement revenue depended on pleasing the readers and possessing their confidence; no newspaper would wish to prejudice its independence in the eyes of its readers by becoming subservient to its advertisers. In evidence to the Commission the Advertising Association put the point succinctly: 'An editor who thinks more of his advertisers than of his readers will soon have neither advertisers nor readers to think of.'

An advertiser seeks the highest return on his money in terms of response to his advertisement, and to ensure this advertising agencies make exhaustive studies both of readership and of spending. But if the newspaper needs the advertiser, the advertiser also needs the newspaper. To the newspaper the individual advertiser is one among scores, but to the advertiser the newspaper may be one among only two or three. This was true not only of individual advertisers but of whole industries, and no industry contributed enough to the advertising revenue of the Press to be able to hold it to ransom.

The Shawcross Commission was satisfied that the dominant consideration in placing advertisements was without doubt the commercial advantage of the advertiser and not the political inclination or editorial policy of the publication.

The conclusions reached by both Royal Commissioners were:

1. Individual advertisers occasionally sought to influence the policy of a newspaper or to obtain the omission or insertion of particular news items. Any attempt by an advertiser to do so was to be condemned, but such attempts were infrequent and unsuccessful.

2. There was no evidence of concerted pressure by advertisers to induce newspapers to adopt a particular policy.

3. So long as newspapers do not pay without advertising revenue a newspaper may well think twice before it adopts any policy which is likely to reduce advertisers' demands for its space. The type of advertising a newspaper gets will depend on the character of its readership and to that extent on its own policy. If, however, owing to the paper's policy readership decreases, advertising revenue will also decrease.

4. A newspaper which is not very strong financially will probably avoid taking a line detrimental to the advertisers' interests unless by so doing it can increase its interest to the public. If, for instance, people are not interested in attacks on brewers the paper will not make them; if they are, it will.

5. A newspaper which is strong financially or able to command a market which advertisers are anxious to reach, is under no necessity to have regard to the interests of advertisers where those interests conflict with its own policy. (Cmd. 7700, par. 527; Cmnd. 1811, par. 276.)

As long as newspapers are sold to the public for less than they cost to produce they will need a supplementary source of income, and the sale of space to advertisers, both Commissions thought, was one of the least harmful. The income to be feared was that which came from a concealed source and was earned by the sale of the editorial columns. Revenue received from a known source in payment for a recognised commercial service stood on an entirely different footing. Its receipt created a relationship both remote and impersonal and laid newspapers open to no more influence than they were able to resist. The publication of advertisements should not be regarded as a departure under pressure of economic necessity from the proper function of a newspaper. It is an essential part of the service which the newspaper renders to the community, valuable alike to commerce and industry and to the general public.

It emerged, therefore, from the investigation of the Royal Commissions that the direct influence of advertisers on the policy of newspapers is negligible and that dependence on advertising does not involve any interference with the accurate presentation of news and the free expression of opinion. 'We have no evidence at all that advertisers are able to influence the treatment of public questions in the Press,' the 1949 Commission declared. 'On the contrary, we are convinced that the Press is alert to any such demands by advertisers and ready on all occasions to repulse them.'

The dependence of newspapers on advertising for their viability was vividly illustrated at the close of 1966, as the economic squeeze began to take effect. The Royal Commissions on the Press had pointed out that as long as newspapers were sold for less than they cost they needed the prop of advertising not only to make a profit but to remain solvent. Since advertising revenues comprise 50 to 70 per cent of a newspaper's income, a cut in the amount of advertising available is a serious matter for the newspaper. It is estimated that economies made by industrial companies and commercial houses resulted in cuts in advertising expenditure ranging from 10 per cent to over 80 per cent in October 1966, compared with the same month last year.

Although the circulation of the *Guardian* over the year increased by 10,000 copies, the effect of the reduced advertising was to create, in the words of Mr Laurence Scott, the Chairman and Managing Director, a 'serious financial position'. He informed the printing and editorial unions on 6 December that production costs had to be cut by a quarter, amounting to £500,000 by the end of the month, if the newspaper was to continue to be printed in London as well as in Manchester.

Other newspapers were also expected to be in difficulty unless a reduction in production costs was made.

In its first Annual Report the Press Council put on record to the credit of the Press and by way of a commentary on the allegation that the Press is under the influence of advertisers the great publicity given to reports associating cigarette-smoking and lung cancer, irrespective of the fact that the tobacco industry is a lucrative source of revenue to newspapers, and spends hundreds of thousands of pounds in advertising.

In contrast to allegations that newspapers are subject to pressure from advertisers, allegations that newspapers sometimes refused unreasonably to accept advertisements from would-be advertisers were investigated by the first Royal Commission. They considered it entirely wrong for a newspaper to boycott a particular advertiser arbitrarily and for personal reasons. The refusal of all advertisements of a particular class was a different matter. A newspaper had a right to refuse advertisements of any kind which were contrary to its standards or might be objectionable to its readers. The right, however, ought not to be excercised arbitrarily.

Nevertheless, cases have come before the Press Council of alleged attempts to influence the policy of a newspaper by the threat to withhold or by actually withdrawing advertisements. One such case was the termination by West End theatre managers of their advertising in the *Observer* because they disapproved of a particular feature containing brief reviews of performances advertised. Another was a threat by an important advertiser to discipline a journalist whose articles he disliked by reporting him to his editor. The notable fact is the small number of complaints of this kind that have been made to the Press Council.

The editor's decision on which advertisements are acceptable is final, but it should not be exercised capriciously or unfairly. The exclusion of an advertisement out of spite is an abuse of authority, but an editor will not be criticised by the Council for a decision honestly arrived at, even if his reason for rejecting an advertisement is wrong; for instance where the advertisement is refused because it was mistakenly believed to infringe the law'

Space to advertise on behalf of a cause should not be refused merely because the cause in unpopular or controversial. This view was endorsed by the Press Council when a complaint was made against *The Times* for giving space to an advertisement by the South African Government explaining the apartheid policy. Some years earlier, however, the same newspaper had refused advertisements from Dr Marie Stopes for her books on birth control, and the Press Council had upheld the newspaper's right to do so.

Editorial and advertising matter must be clearly distinguishable. This has been emphasised by the Press Council on more than one occasion. The reason, of course, is that readers should not be led to mistake the propaganda of an advertiser for the considered opinion of a responsible newspaper.

The Press Council has also adjudicated upon newspapers' own advertisements and publicitiy and censured those considered misleading or in bad taste.

The cases dealt with follow.

ADVERTISING IN THE PRESS

ADVERTISER'S RIGHT TO STATE A CASE

In 1962 a number of newspapers carried advertisements on behalf of the South African Government.

A complainant stated that all the national newspapers had carried the same advertisement, but he pursued his case only against *The Times*. He contended that it was not proper for a newspaper, even allowing for the usual puff by the advertiser, to publish an advertisement which was untrue and misleading as this one was. If it was wrong to publish a news story known to be false, it was equally wrong to publish false information for a fee in the form of an advertisement.

He further claimed that it was improper for a newspaper to publish an advertisement that was not only false, but which also aided and abetted a policy condemned throughout the world as a breach of obligations under the United Nations Charter. It was analogous to publishing an advertisement from the Hitler Government which falsely described and justified German Jewish policy.

The Editor of *The Times*, Sir William Haley, maintained that the South African Government should be allowed to use the media of the Press to further its policies. The newspapers of this country, he said, had not hesitated to state in the most forthright terms what they thought about South African Government policy. This was particularly true of *The Times*, which, in fairness, had also published letters and statements contradicting its views. Should the South African Government wish to take space to state its case it would be improper for British newspapers to refuse it the right to do so.

If an advertisement contained statements demonstrably untrue *The Times* would refuse to accept it, but this was not such a case. The advertisement put the facts in the most favourable light, and the South African Government, like any other advertiser, was perfectly entitled to do this. *The Times*, in its editorial and advertising columns had always preserved the right of others to state their case whether it agreed with them or not.

The Press Council considered that the advertisement was rightly regarded by *The Times* as a statement of a case which the advertiser was entitled to make, and it rejected the complaint. (1962/41–2, 74–5)

EDITORIAL AND ADVERTISING MATTER SHOULD BE DISTINGUISHABLE

The Chairman of the Anti-Apartheid Movement complained that a four-page illustrated article entitled 'Blueprint for South West Africa' published in the *Weekend Telegraph* misled people into thinking that they were reading the views of a responsible newspaper, when they were, in fact, reading the propaganda of a government agency. Although the first page of the feature bore the words 'This article has been provided by the South African Information Service', the general impression given was that it was an ordinary article in the newspaper.

The Editor, Mr John Anstey, acknowledged that the feature was an advertisement, but said that this was apparent as it was quite different in lay-out and typographical headline treatment from that used by the newspaper editorially.

The Press Council decided against the newspaper, and ruled that there had been a clear breach of the principle that a proper distinction should be made between editorial and advertising matter. (1965/89–90)

COMPLAINT ADMITTED

A complaint was made about a supplement published by the *Guardian* containing editorial and advertising matter, alleged to be presented in such a manner that the ordinary reader could not distinguish between the two.

The supplement was headed 'Man-Made Fibres', and below were the words 'A Guardian survey of the industry and its influence on the textiles in use'. The text overprinted an illustration of a pair of stockings which was part of an advertisement appearing on the page.

The Editor of the *Guardian*, Mr Alastair Hetherington, agreed that the complaint was justified.

The Press Council said that a mistake had been made, but noted that the Editor had expressed regret. (1965/88–9)

HOLIDAY SUPPLEMENT

A country newspaper, the *Bucks Herald*, published a four-page holiday travel supplement in the newspaper's usual style of presentation, with illustrated articles surrounded by display advertisements. On the front page a panel stated that the supplement was issued by a travel company.

A reader complained that as the supplement appeared in the guise of editorial matter it was misleading because of the difficulty in distinguishing between editorial and advertising matter. The Editor, Mr Gareth Harry, contended that the supplement was clearly an advertising feature, and that it made no pretence of being more than an extension of the display advertising.

The Press Council stated that newspapers should take great care in the publication of advertisements to distinguish between the editorial content and the matter supplied by advertisers. In this case the Council believed it reasonable to suppose that most readers of the newspaper would have understood that the editorial text of the holiday supplement was supplied and paid for by the advertiser. (1964/62)

IMPROPER PRESSURE BY ADVERTISERS

In 1959 the *Observer* began publishing at monthly intervals a 'Quick Theatre Guide' as a service to readers. The Society of West-End Theatre Managers objected to the periodic repetition of adverse criticism which was based on performances seen by the critic at a much earlier date.

After the Guide had run for some time the Theatre Managers withdrew their advertisements, and the *Observer* responded by publishing the Guide weekly instead of monthly. The Editor, the Hon. David Astor, complained that the withdrawal of their advertisements constituted an improper attempt to put pressure on the newspaper. The objection of the Theatre Managers that the Guide was unfair was, the Editor said, unfounded. The newspaper's critic saw each production every three months, and contentious ones more often; furthermore the Theatre Managers had been asked to notify any changes in cast or production which materially affected the performance so that the critic should see it again.

The Press Council held that an advertiser had a clear right to withdraw his advertisement from the newspaper, but the general withdrawal in this case was an attempt to influence editorial policy which the Council deprecated. The Council also thought that the 'Quick Theatre Guide' should be based on recent visits to the theatres. (1963/32–4)

IMPROPER THREAT

A branch of the National Union of Journalists brought to the attention of the Press Council the case of one of its members who contributed articles to the *Stage* reviewing Tyne-Tees Television programmes.

The programme director of Tyne-Tees Television, which advertised in the *Stage*, complained to the journalist about some of his articles, and threatened to 'raise Hell' and have him removed. He admitted that he had lost his temper, and said that when he did complain to the Editor his complaint was of ill-formed, inaccurate and prejudiced reporting; he had not requested the journalist's dismissal.

The editor of the television section of the *Stage* told the journalist not to send any more copy until relations with the advertiser were restored. He had no complaint about the journalist's ability, but he had been informed by various people that he appeared to be prejudiced against television. Some time later he wrote to the journalist saying he had received information which shocked him and he invited the journalist to resume his contributions.

The Press Council stated that it was gravely disturbed by the complaint, but the official had made a full apology. It accepted his assurance that he had made no request that the journalist should be dismissed, and that he would have considered a request of this kind improper. The Press Council also noted with satisfaction the offer by the editor of the television section of the *Stage* to reinstate the journalist as a contributor. (1960/27–8, 39–40)

DISCRETION OF THE EDITOR TO ACCEPT OR REJECT

The North Devon branch of the Campaign for Nuclear Disarmament advertised each week in its local newspaper the *North Devon Journal-Herald*, quoting a statement by a prominent public figure. In due course the newspaper informed the branch that no more quotation-type advertisements would be accepted on the ground that the accuracy of the quotation could not easily be checked.

The Press Council held that, while it is very desirable that in a free Press space should be found for minority views, the editor must have discretion as to what news and advertisements will be published. In this case there was no criticism of the way the editor exercised his discretion. (1964/62–3)

COACH TOUR OF BATTLEFIELD

The *Glasgow Herald* refused to publish an advertisement that seats were vacant in a privately hired bus for a tour of the 1914–18 battlefields on the ground that it was illegal to advertise to the public seats in a privately hired coach. While this was the position in Britain, the coach was to be chartered on the Continent where the legal prohibition did not apply.

The Press Council held that the newspaper believed at the time of rejection of the advertisement that publication would have been illegal. This was a sufficient reason for rejecting it. (1965/90)

C.N.D. ADVERTISEMENT REFUSED

The *Southend Standard* refused to accept an advertisement from the local branch of the Campaign for Nuclear Disarmament. The reason given was the undesirability of advertising an organisation which incited people to break the law.

The newspaper was informed that the C.N.D. did not advocate civil disobedience and was a separate body from the Committee of 100, which did. The Editor was of the opinion, however, that so many people were associated with both organisations that it was difficult to judge the true position.

The Press Council ruled that the acceptance of advertising was a matter within the discretion of the Editor. (1963/62–3)

VARIATION OF AN ADVERTISEMENT

A firm of printers complained that when they wished to advertise a vacancy for a compositor the *Leicester Mercury* informed them that the advertisement could not be accepted unless a reference to profit-sharing, one of the attractions of the job, was deleted.

The Editor explained that there was an acute shortage of compositors in the industry, and the newspaper wished to prevent a competitive kind of race in regard to terms offered to induce men to leave one firm for another.

The firm protested that this was an unjustifiable interference with the mobility of labour and the decision whether or not a worker should be encouraged to go to another job was not one for the newspaper.

The Press Council ruled that while it is the prerogative of a newspaper editor to accept or refuse advertisements, the conditional acceptance in this case was objectionable because the deletion was required in the interest of the newspaper. (1962/26)

PROPORTION OF ADVERTISING TO EDITORIAL MATTER

What proportion of advertising to editorial matter should a local newspaper contain? The question was raised in a complaint against the *Inverness Courier*, a bi-weekly journal. It was alleged that, in a particular issue when there was no lack of local news, the newspaper contained approximately one page of news out of twelve, the rest being devoted to advertisements; this made the journal more an advertising medium than a newspaper.

The Editor, Miss Evelyn Barron, said that the advertisements were unsolicited, and twelve pages was the biggest paper they could produce. Advertisers could not be dictated to about the dates of their advertisements, and they nearly all insisted on Fridays. The news omitted on a Friday generally appeared on the following Tuesday if it was not of a ephemeral nature.

Miss Barron told the Press Council that she had no knowledge of any general understanding that advertising should not exceed 60 per cent of the contents of a newspaper. Such a restriction on a weekly or bi-weekly newspaper was completely unrealistic.

Both the Scottish Newspaper Society and the Scottish Newspaper Proprietors Association corroborated her statement that they knew of no agreement in Scotland that newspapers should carry any particular proportion of news.

The position in England is that the Post Office requirements for registration as a newspaper include the rule that the advertisement content shall not exceed $66\frac{2}{3}$ per cent.

The Press Council's adjudication was that the *Inverness Courier* customarily published a large proportion of advertisements in its Friday issue. The fact was well known to readers. The complaint was rejected. (1966/97–8)

COMPANY SHARE QUOTATIONS

In a letter for publication in the *Guardian* the Chairman of a company stated that the fact that normally respected British newspapers were influenced by payment for the insertion of news items was not known to the general public.

He said that some years ago the price of his company's shares was sufficiently newsworthy to warrant inclusion seven days a week in a well-known daily and a Sunday newspaper. Since then his company had grown in size. Despite this it had been presented with an ultimatum that either it paid for continuance of the quotation or it would be omitted. Other firms had been added to the public list because they paid. There was no indication whatsoever that the published daily list was in fact in whole or in part paid advertising.

The writer went on to say that it appeared undeniable that items deemed to be newsworthy were inserted or withheld according to whether those interested in publication were willing to pay. This was not in the public interest.

The complainant conceded that the ultimate decision of newsworthiness was the Editor's, but the decision was now taken according to whether the payment was made.

The newspapers in question were the *Daily Telegraph* and *Sunday Telegraph*. Their Advertisement Directors had sent out a circular stating that a comprehensive fee of £100 per annum for each item for entry in both papers would be made to help cover the cost of Stock Exchange information.

The Editor of the *Daily Telegraph*, Mr Maurice Green, said that, while all news was a service, some news was a service only to sections of readers. The shares of the complainant's company were still of some marginal news value, but with increased costs quotation became unjustifiable and uneconomic without some financial contribution from the company.

The Editor of the *Sunday Telegraph* associated himself with Mr Green.

The Press Council at first held that the question of newspaper charges for publication of company share quotations was a commercial question and not one that involved newspaper ethics. Later the Council reconsidered the matter and came to the conclusion that there might be a danger that quotation would be taken as an expression of editorial opinion on the merits of the shares. Newspapers were therefore recommended to append a note that quotations might be included on payment of a fee. (1966/19)

CAMPAIGNING AND ADVERTISEMENTS

The *Manchester City News*, a weekly newspaper, published a series of articles under the heading 'Café Scandal' stating that the newspaper, shocked and disgusted by the filthy standards and poor food of many eating places in Manchester, had decided that it would expose the racketeering in the catering trade. At the same time it intended to publish reports of those good eating places where clean food might be had at fair prices.

Side by side with this campaign, caterers in Manchester received a letter from the proprietors of the newspaper which said that they were sure that reputable caterers would desire to support the newspaper's efforts by taking advertising space in the newspaper. This caused the caterers to think that the campaign on the café scandal was not as disinterested as readers of the newspaper might be led to believe.

The Secretary of their association drew the matter to the attention of the Press Council and inquired whether this was an example of newspaper practice of which the Council would wish to be kept informed.

The newspaper denied the attempt to link its campaign in any way with advertising.

The Press Council expressed the opinion that the association of advertisement canvassing with a critical editorial campaign might be liable to give rise to inferences which it would be desirable to avoid as contrary to accepted standards of journalism. (1954/27, 40–3)

NEWS VALUE — THE TEST OF PUBLICITY

The National Trotting Association of Great Britain wrote to the Sports Editor of the *Bognor Regis Post* giving details of three trotting race meetings and enclosing a Press pass. A reply arrived from the advertising manager which stated that it was not the custom to cover events unless they were advertised and suggesting that advertisement space should be taken.

The Press Council expressed the view that reports of events should be given space according to their news value as judged by the editor.

The Editor of the newspaper subsequently wrote stating that a slip in phraseology on the part of its advertisement manager had given an entirely wrong impression, and that editorial policy was, and always had been, to cover all events of news value in the district irrespective of whether they were advertised or not. (1954/27–8)

AN UNFAIR AND MISLEADING ADVERTISEMENT

The *West Lancashire Evening Gazette*, Blackpool, devoted two feature pages to the re-opening after modernisation of a local hotel. The feature consisted of an illustrated write-up with surrounding advertisements contributed by firms which had participated in the modernisation.

A firm of printers which had participated was not invited to share in the feature. Instead a large display advertisement for another firm of printers, a subsidiary of the newspaper, was inserted. The advertisement did not claim that this firm had any connection with the modernisation.

A representative of the printers who had participated complained that his firm was deprived of the credit for their work and the advertisement suggested that the other firm had done the hotel's printing. A credit had been published by way of amends, but it incorrectly named the firm and did not include its address or telephone number.

The Advertisement Manager of the *West Lancashire Evening Gazette*, Mr John F. Grime, told the Council that as they ran a separate general printing works advertisements from competitive firms were not sought. The advertisement from their own printing firm was inserted because there was a vacant space.

The Editor, Mr J. Favell Grime, said that they had tried to redress the grievance by publishing an advertisement for the hotel free of charge in which the services of the participating printers were acknowledged. He denied any intention to mislead or deceive.

The Press Council deplored the unethical conduct of the newspaper in inserting their own printing department's advertisement in the feature, when they were well aware that another printing firm had undertaken the hotel printing. (1966/107)

ESTATE AGENT AND POLITICAL PROPAGANDA

Should an estate agent's newspaper advertisements include political propaganda matter?

Complaint was made of a series of property advertisements inserted in the *Observer* by an estate agent. The advertisements referred to gifts to the Save the Children Fund and mentioned that Americans were embarrassed about their little victims. The article continued: 'As Ky their much loved

"Meaningful" S. Vietnam protégé is an open admirer of A. Hitler, why don't they set up Gas and Incinerator Chambers as a final solution; the original manufacturers are still in business in Germany.'

The Editor of the *Observer*, the Hon. David Astor said that for many years it had been the agent's practice to include highly provocative and tendentious political statements in his advertisements. The Press which claimed freedom for themselves must extend the same freedom to their advertisers. Censorship was exercised only in those cases where the advertiser's claims were fraudulent, libellous or offended against good taste.

Mr Astor suggested the political utterances in the article were so far-fetched as to be self-defeating. The complainant urged that the advertisement was an unwarranted attack on the Americans and that it was unethical to include it in a so-called advertisement.

In the following issue of the *Observer* the estate agent's advertisement space began with a letter from the complainant.

The Press Council consulted the Advertising Standards Authority and was told that the Code of Advertising Practice required that advertisements should not be misleading about the product or service advertised and that they should be truthful. The present instance was a borderline case.

Mr Astor in further answer said that the right of an individual to be able to buy space in a newspaper for the purpose of stating political views was clearly very important. The fact that the estate agent used the space he bought to sell houses did not affect the principle.

The Press Council held that the acceptance of advertisements of the type of the one in question is a matter for the editor's discretion. The complaint was rejected. (1967)

PRESS PLACARDS AND POSTERS

A MISLEADING POSTER

The day after the marriage of the Duke of Kent and Miss Katherine Worsley, a resident of Bournemouth saw a contents bill outside the local newsagent's shop which read 'Hundreds killed at York wedding'. The resident was greatly shocked and complained to the Press Council of a gross example of bad taste in advertising.

The newsagent told the Council he had had so many complaints, after exhibiting the poster for half a day, that he withdrew it.

The poster was issued by *Reveille*, the weekly periodical. Mr A. Clarkson, the Editor, stated it was the policy of the paper to publish informative articles of a historical nature. *Reveille* did not contain news reports, so nobody could regard the contents bill as recording news. Had such a disaster occurred at the Duke of Kent's wedding people could not have failed to hear about it.

The Council expressed the opinion that the contents bill was open to misconception, and that the public complaints about it were justified. (1962/27–8)

MISLEADING PLACARD

A *Daily Sketch* placard bore the announcement 'Holiday Travel Allowance Shock'.

Complaint was made that the announcement was a misrepresentation. It was inspired by a speech made by the Chancellor of the Exchequer in opening the Boat Show at Earls Court. Since, however, Mr Callaghan's speech contained no reference to the holiday allowance the 'shock' referred to was non-existent.

The explanation by the *Daily Sketch* was that the bill was written and sent out at a time when their information was that the Chancellor was likely to follow up his speech with some form of restriction. Instead the Chancellor issued a denial of any such intention. Some of the bills were then recalled.

The complainant maintained that newspapers have a great responsibility to ensure that only the truth is published, and on this occasion there had been a breach of public trust.

The Managing Editor, Mr Robert Johnston, regretted that the bill implied something more than was contained in the story and said the newspaper's bill writing system had been tightened up.

The Press Council held that the *Daily Sketch* placard was misleading and upheld the complaint. (1966/104–5)

CONTENTS BILL GAVE WRONG IMPRESSION

The *Evening Standard* announced on a contents bill 'British Rail Colour Special'. As a result of the poster the complainant, a railway enthusiast, bought a copy of the newspaper, but discovered that the supplement was an advertisement for the Southern Region of British Rail. He contended that it was unethical to mislead readers into thinking that the newspaper contained something of special interest on the lines of a colour supplement.

The Editor, Mr Charles Wintour, said that the contents bill announcement was a fair description of a lot of useful information about the service available on British Rail and therefore had genuine news value. Six thousand readers had applied for the free map advertised in the feature.

The Press Council held that the contents bill gave a wrong impression and upheld the complaint. (1966/105–6)

NO OBJECTION TO CONTENTS BILL

An *Evening Standard* contents poster reading 'The Queen escapes death crash' was complained about on the ground that it was untrue and designed to 'catch pennies'. The complainant argued that as no crash took place, the Queen could not have escaped something that did not happen.

The Editor of the newspaper told the Press Council that the available evidence at the time the poster was written pointed to the Queen having had a narrow escape.

The Press Council said that although the bill was inaccurate in its reference to a crash involving death, no serious objection could be taken having regard to the knowledge available at the time it was written and the limited space available on a contents bill. (1961/33)

'MINISTER SHOT DOWN'

An *Evening News* placard stated 'Minister shot down'. The complainant said he had immediately bought a copy of the newspaper, but discovered that the minister referred to was the Laotian Foreign Minister. He suggested that this was not of the importance to the British people that was suggested by the newspaper's contents bill.

The Editor, Mr C. Reginald Willis, replied that the news was held to be so important that it was the lead story in the early editions, and remained a major inside page lead for the rest of the day. The situation in the particular country justified the treatment, and there was no intention of misleading.

The Press Council rejected the complaint. (1963/61)

ADVERTISEMENTS AND PUBLICITY FOR NEWSPAPERS AND PERIODICALS

A DEPLORABLE ADVERTISEMENT

An advertisement issued by *Time and Tide* and published in the *Daily Telegraph* and the *Guardian* was designed to publicise an article entitled 'How to go Mad'.

The advertisement consisted mainly of the shadowy face of an apparently demented person and carried the caption 'Ten to one you will go mad'. At the foot of the advertisement was the following statement:

> One person in every ten suffers from mental illness some time in our lives. 41 % of all the hospital beds in Britain are filled with mental patients. Madness can knock on any door. But it seldom does so dramatically. The staring Bedlam picture is far from the facts. But what ARE the facts? What treatment is available? What does it cost? How long does it take? Does it cure?

The article, it was claimed, was giving facts that should be known about a major social problem. Complaint was made that the advertisement outraged the normal social canons of responsibility, and was likely to do untold harm to people suffering from a fear of madness.

The Managing Editor of the *Daily Telegraph*, Mr Colin R. Coote, said that the advertisement was regarded as a gimmick to call attention to an important topic. Mr Alastair Hetherington of the *Guardian* stated that the advertisement had been published with some misgivings; both Editors said they had taken action to prevent a repetition.

The Rev. T. W. Beaumont, on behalf of *Time and Tide*, said the advertisement was certainly calculated to alarm members of the public, in order to combat the widespread and extremely dangerous apathy and ignorance over mental illness. If none but public authorities were to be allowed to awaken the public from their inertia on some matters he had no defence. He was sure, however, that the Council would grant that individual organs of the Press ought to be allowed this freedom. The caption, 'Ten to one you will go mad', was an error for which he was sorry.

The Council deplored the publication of the advertisement because it publicised the subject of mental illness in a disturbing and sensational way. (1961/36, 50–2)

ARTICLE ADVERTISED BUT NOT PUBLISHED

When the *Observer* failed to publish a feature it had advertised, a complaint was made that the omission was 'a flagrant, reprehensible breach of faith with the public, virtually amounting to obtaining money by false pretences and misrepresentation.'

The newspaper said that the mistake was an outcome of human error, which was unique in their experience. The Press Council accepted the explanation. (1962/53)

QUESTIONABLE PUBLICITY

The cover of the magazine *Queen* announced: 'Your own cut-out Courrèges.' A woman purchased the magazine because she understood the announcement to mean that the journal was offering a ready-to-sew outfit at a special price, a common practice among women's journals. What in fact the magazine contained was a cut-out paper dolly and pictures of clothing to fit it.

The Editor, Mr Jocelyn Stevens, told the Press Council that he did not consider the cover announcement in any way constituted a shabby practice to attract customers as the disappointed purchaser had described it. If she had previously read the magazine she would know it was not the practice to make free offers.

The Press Council ruled that the description on the cover of the magazine was capable of misleading readers and said the complaint was justified. (1965/90–1)

NEWSPAPER COMPETITION

The *News of the World* promoted a competition in connection with which they announced that they had chartered the *Queen Mary*, something nobody had ever done before, and that the winners would be taken for a cruise. Every passenger who sailed in her would be the guest of the newspaper.

A woman who had successfully completed the competition was told that there were more winners than berths and that only entrants offering the best suggestions for a weekly article would get tickets. Readers were then invited to enter another contest run by another company for one hundred berths on the same cruise. When complaint was made about this, the Editor said the competition advertised 1000 berths, and that was the number available.

In a statement to the Press Council, Mr S. W. Somerfield, the Editor, said that the newspaper contracted with the Cunard Line to take 1200 berths, and those not required to meet their obligations to readers were made available for another competition.

The Press Council having investigated the details of the newspaper's competition and the terms of all the announcements made about it found that readers were not misled, and that the *News of the World* had fulfilled its obligations. (1966/100–1)

TELEVISION ANNOUNCEMENT

On the Saturday following the assassination of President Kennedy, a director of the Daily Mirror Group announced on commercial television that the *Sunday Mirror* had received the latest and happiest family pictures of the President and his son. Overnight they had become the most moving pictures of all time. He said they would appear the following morning in the *Sunday Mirror*.

A complaint was made to the Press Council that the *Sunday Mirror* had used the President's assassination for advertisement purposes. The television announcement was alleged to be tactless, tasteless and an affront to common decency.

The Editor of the *Sunday Mirror*, Mr R. T. Payne, said that the pictures were purchased before the President's death for their great interest, and after the assassination they had become an eloquent commentary on the personal and family aspects of the tragedy. If it was right to publish the pictures, a right which he suggested could not be challenged, it was surely equally permissible to announce the intention of doing so.

The Press Council held that there was no objection to the television announcement drawing attention to the photographs which were of wide interest, more particularly because of the tragic circumstances. (1964/54–5)

25　Cheque-Book Journalism

A series of sensational espionage cases culminated in October 1962 with the trial and conviction of William John Christopher Vassall, a clerical officer in the Admiralty. His sentence of eighteen years' imprisonment did not match the twenty years the Krogers received, the twenty-five years given to Lonsdale or the forty-two years imposed on Blake; nevertheless the Vassall case caused greater shock to the public and had wider repercussions than did the others.

When the major spies had been rounded up and steps taken to eliminate weaknesses revealed in the security arrangements, a reassured nation began to relax. The reassurance, however, was short-lived. On an autumn evening only some eighteen months after Blake and the others had been jailed, Vassall was arrested as he left his office in Whitehall. The public learned that for nearly eight years he had operated undetected as an agent for the Russian Secret Service, first in the British Embassy in Moscow and for the six years before his arrest in the heart of the Admiralty itself.

Anger at his treachery was aggravated by a series of articles, purchased for a substantial sum, entitled 'Why I betrayed my country' which appeared in the *Sunday Pictorial*. The publication of the memoirs of notorious people had become a common newspaper practice, but the growing public resentment now expressed itself with vehemence against a practice that made it possible for a traitor to flaunt his treachery and to make a handsome profit from doing so.

The Vassall exposure in the latter part of 1962 was a prelude to the dramatic and incredible year that followed. Relations between the Press and Parliament and between the Press and the public deteriorated to a deplorably low level. The Government was stung to anger by what it considered an abdication of responsibility by the Press; writs for libel were served on national newspapers on behalf of a minister of the Crown and by a former minister forced to resign his office because of vile insinuations about him. Two journalists were sent to prison for refusing to disclose information considered essential in the national interest and a third just escaped a similar fate. The public was shocked by scandals involving people in high and not so high places and resented the detail in which the newspapers reported these matters.

The inquiry into the Vassall affair by the Radcliffe Tribunal opened at the beginning of 1963, and it soon became clear that the honour and integrity of the Press was as much on trial as that of ministers, civil servants and security officers. The Press emerged in a far from favourable light. Its image was further tarnished by the coverage given to events connected with the names of the former Secretary of State for War, Mr J. D. Profumo, Miss Christine Keeler and Dr Stephen Ward. Much unfounded gossip circulated and malicious rumours multiplied. An unnamed cabinet minister was said to be the unidentified man in an improper photograph which featured in a society divorce suit; another unnamed member of the cabinet was alleged to be the masked and naked waiter who served the scantily dressed guests at smart West End dinner parties. The Press was blamed for the impression created that public life had become corrupt and public morals decadent.

In the debate in the Commons on the Vassall Report on 7 May 1963, the Leader of the Opposition, Mr Harold Wilson, said:

> There is one code of conduct which should be rapidly applied either voluntarily or in some other way, that the Press should be bound to stop this odious practice of buying for large sums the memoirs of convicted

criminals. It has long been the practice in the procedure of this country that no one can make a profit out of a proven crime. This ought to be stopped, along with the undignified scramble in court, if a man is found guilty, as journalists jostle one another in their efforts to buy his memoirs.

In the House of Lords Viscount Hailsham, Lord President of the Council, replying to a question on 4 July, said that the Government deplored the publication of memoirs which lent glamour to crime or to vice and catered for an unhealthy interest in them. The Government, he added, would welcome any consideration that the Press Council felt able to give to the matter.

In response to this invitation the Press Council on 24 September issued a statement in which the Council said that it had received complaints about the conduct of the Press in the reports, articles and illustrations on the trial of Stephen Ward and the activities of Miss Christine Keeler and their associates; there had also been many public expressions of criticism. The complaints had covered not only the detailed reporting of the court proceedings involving publication of a great deal of evidence dealing with immorality and vice, but also, in the words of Lord Shawcross, 'the publicising of pimps, prostitutes and perverts in highly-paid interviews or feature articles.'

Some of the complaints had specifically referred to the publication of the confessions of Christine Keeler in the *News of the World*. The advertising of these articles in other newspapers had also been criticised.

Throughout many of the views expressed by people who had complained ran the feeling that the very large financial rewards paid for articles on immorality and vice had the effect of glamorising people who indulged in a life of this kind and of tempting young people to follow their example.

The Press Council pointed out that it was important to recognise that there were two distinct problems: (1) the reporting of news, and (2) its elaboration in memoirs and other articles. It was the responsibility of the Press in the public interest to record what was going on, and the extensive reporting of the court proceedings in the Ward case in the majority of newspapers was not only justified but necessary, however much the facts revealed may have shocked or dismayed many people.

Newspapers could not ignore matters of this kind because of the risk that such reports might be read by young people but had to deal with adult questions in an adult manner. This did not mean that newspapers should publish in detail matter which could be regarded as offensive. The Press had shown in the past that vice and sex cases could be adequately reported without going into excessive detail.

The Press Council had informed the Editor of the *News of the World*, Mr Stafford Somerfield, of the specific criticism of his newspaper, and published the following observations made by him:

The Christine Keeler story was news. No newspaper had failed to recognise this. The only difference between the *News of the World* and other newspapers was that the *News of the World* was the first to publish material with an authentic basis. In order to provide the facts the newspaper had had to pay.

The complaints against the *News of the World* appeared to be mainly directed to the profits which accrued to unworthy persons to capitalise their notoriety. Such criticism might in particular cases be perfectly valid, but when directed to the *News of the World* in this instance was clearly misconceived. Did anyone suggest that the Christine Keeler story should have been suppressed? A healthy society demanded exposure, however sordid, in the context of recent events.

Nothing published in the *News of the World* by way of comment had sought to disguise as virtue that which was vicious. But, in the belief that the public was entitled to know what was going on, and to know authentically, the newspaper had discharged a prime duty by giving the news.

A prodigious and mounting readership tacitly acknowledged the rights of the course the *News of the World* had followed.

The Press Council accepted that there was an element of news in stories of the kind, but rejected the argument that in this case any newspaper had a responsibility in the public interest to publish them. The Council recognised that in the competitive world of the Press the publication of personal stories, even though objectionable to some people, might be legitimate and of public interest, but in the Council's opinion there were few things today which were doing more to discredit the Press as a whole than the memoirs of immoral or criminal people.

The Press Council made the following adjudication on the issues raised:

1. The excessive reporting of court proceedings in the Ward case was justified as news of exceptional interest and public concern. Nevertheless, some intimate details should have been omitted.

2. In their presentation, headlines and photographs, a number of newspapers gave excessive prominence to and thus glamorised the people concerned in the prostitution and vice revealed in this case. This was strongly condemned.

3. The Council deplored, as it had done on previous occasions, the publication of personal stories and feature articles of an unsavoury nature where the public interest did not require it, and it urged Editors and managements of newspapers to discuss what arrangements could be made to avoid publication of material of that sort.

4. The action of the *News of the World* in paying £23,000 for the confessions of Christine Keeler, and publishing in those articles details of her sordid life story, was particularly damaging to the morals of young people. By so exploiting vice and sex for commercial reward the *News of the World* had done a disservice both to public welfare and to the Press. (1964/17–19)

THE DENNING REPORT

Following the resignation of the Secretary of State for War, Mr J. D. Profumo, the Prime Minister, Mr Macmillan asked Lord Denning, the Master of the Rolls, to undertake an inquiry to consider whether the national security had been endangered by the circumstances leading to Mr Profumo's resignation.

In his report Lord Denning expressed the hope that ministers and others who had been contemplating proceedings for defamation in respect of rumours about them would not now pursue them. Some people thought that the rumours were a symptom of a decline in the integrity of the public life of the country. 'I do not believe this to be true', Lord Denning declared, and he concluded his report with the following observations:

> Scandalous information about well-known people has become a marketable commodity. True or false, actual or invented, it can be sold. The greater the scandal, the higher the price it commands. If supported by photographs or letters, real or imaginary, all the better. Often enough the sellers profess to have been themselves participants in discreditable conduct which they seek to exploit. Intermediaries move in, ready to assist the sale and ensure the highest prices. The story improves with the telling. It is offered to those newspapers — there are only a few of them — who deal in this commodity. They vie with one another to buy it.

Each is afraid the other will get it first. So they buy it on the chance that it will turn out profitable. Sometimes it is no use to them. It is palpably false. At other times it is credible. But even so, they dare not publish the whole of the information. The law of libel and the rules of contempt of court exert an effective restraint. They publish what they can, but there remains a substantial part which is not fit for publication. This unpublished part goes around by word of mouth. It does not stop in Fleet Street. It goes to Westminster. It crosses the Channel, even the Atlantic, and back again, swelling all the time. Yet without the original purchase, it might never have got started on its way.

When such deplorable consequences are seen to ensue, the one thing that is clear is that something should be done to stop the trafficking in scandal for reward. The machinery is ready to hand. There is a new Press Council already in being.

(Official Report, 1963, pars. 341–2)

A RETURN TO RESPONSIBILITY

The hostility and bitterness towards the Press which had been mounting for some years reached its peak as a result of the events of 1962 and 1963. Respect for the Press, if its rights and duties were to be recognised, had to be restored. In a leading article of 18 March 1963 *The Times* declared that the lesson of recent events was that the only people who could preserve the freedom of the Press were the journalists themselves. It was mistaken escapism to believe the responsibility could be concentrated in a Press Council.

The *Guardian*, on the other hand, on 20 March expressed the opinion that a stronger Press Council was an obvious remedy, a Press Council with an independent Chairman and members drawn from outside the newspaper industry as recommended by the Ross Commission in 1949 and more recently by the Shawcross Commission in 1962. Such a Council could consider essential questions of conduct affecting every newspaper. Some of these questions were:

What limits should be set to payment for information whether from company directors, trade union officials or charladies?

Is it proper to pay criminals or call-girls for their memoirs?

Is it legitimate to represent unverified hearsay as fact?

When is it in the public interest to give details about crimes that stimulate imitation?

On 20 June 1963 the *Daily Mirror* published a statement on behalf of itself and five associated newspapers, the *Daily Herald*, the *Daily Record*, the *People*, the *Sunday Mirror* and the *Sunday Mail*, a statement of policy these newspapers would observe. The statement quoted from a speech by Lord Shawcross made two days previously when he referred to the publication of highly-paid interviews and feature articles by worthless people and asked:

> Is it a useful thing from the point of view of the community to pay large sums of money for these so-called memoirs, generally written up by some ghost writer, of criminals however sensational their crimes, of prostitutes however degraded, of adulterers however notorious in café society?

What is difficult for the Press to decide, said the *Daily Mirror*, is when a matter of salacious interest is also of national importance. The Profumo case had increased the difficulty.

The newspaper went on to welcome the recently made decision of the Press Council to appoint an independent Chairman. This would strengthen the Council's influence, but it should not be thought that any Press Council, however constituted, could solve with the stroke of a pen or a public rebuke the problems which those who conduct newspapers had to face urgently day by day.

It would be unwise, the *Daily Mirror* said, for the Press to lay down inexorable rules about what it would or would not publish. A mealy-mouthed Press would be grossly inadequate, and could make no claim to serve the public at a time when the Government itself was a shambles and the fabric of society had been loosened by a major political scandal. If the Press has satisfied itself that democracy, or the basis of the British way of life, or the public interest, was at stake it should go the whole hog.

'This conceded, this duty fulfilled, the Daily Mirror Group of newspapers agrees with Lord Shawcross that pimps, prostitutes and perverts should not profit from their notoriety and degradation'.

Even before its reconstitution under an independent Chairman, the Press

Council had begun an inquiry into 'cheque-book journalism'. After the events of 1963 it seemed certain that unless the Press Council did something about the publication of unsavoury articles Parliament would. The Council put out an interim statement, summarised above, in September of that year while it proceeded to investigate the subject in greater depth.

Not all transactions involving the payment of large sums for feature articles and interviews are morally objectionable; those that are vary in degree and reason for being so, as the following cases dealt with by the Press Council show:

A GLASGOW MURDER

A man with a criminal record was accused of the murder of a Glasgow taxi-driver. The jury brought in a verdict of 'Not proven'. When the accused left the court he was mobbed by reporters waiting to interview him. In the free-for-all that followed, representatives of the newspaper which had purchased his story bundled him into a motor-car and drove to a hideaway.

The Press Council examined statements from seven Scottish Editors; four supported the traditional right to purchase a story deemed to be of interest, the others opposed the practice.

The Press Council was unable to say whether the strong-arm men present or the journalists were responsible for the disgraceful scene outside the Court, but regarded the incident as deplorable and a lowering of journalistic conduct. The Council condemned the methods used. (1963/56–7)

A PROTEST FROM BRISTOL

A case of another kind related to a young husband who obtained his discharge from the Army on compassionate grounds. The *Bristol Evening Post* interviewed the couple and published a news story. The following day a Bristol morning publication sent a reporter and photographer to do a follow-up story, but the couple said they were under contract to a national newspaper and refused to have pictures taken.

Complaint was made that the matter was an example of cheque-book journalism and was contrary to journalistic ethics. The objection was to the exclusive acquisition of information and its denial to other newspapers.

The Editor of the Bristol publication said that by such methods a wealthy national newspaper could go into any city or town and deny the local newspaper the right to publish a local news story. He regarded cheque-book journalism as a shabby unconstructive practice.

The Editor of the national newspaper concerned said that he was always willing to make reasonable sharing arrangements with local newspapers where the material was of particular interest to their readers.

THE SOUTHEND-ON-SEA QUADS

In another case the *Daily Express* acquired the exclusive rights to photograph quads born at Southend-on-Sea. The *Daily Express* offered the local newspapers pictures of the quads on condition that they published an acknowledgement. The local Press was not prepared to do so.

The *Southend-on-Sea Pictorial* published the following statement:

> While publishing this story of Southend's quads, we feel an explanation is due to our readers for the absence of a picture. Exclusive rights to take pictures of the babies have been purchased by the *Daily Express* and, in spite of protests, they insist on extending their embargo on photographs to the local Press. They are prepared to supply pictures, but only on condition the *Express* is given credit for them in an acknowledgment line. This we are not prepared to do, feeling strongly that the behaviour of the *Express* constitutes an unwarranted interference with the liberty of a local newspaper to do its work in its own area in its own way.

EXCLUSIVE PUBLICATION RIGHTS

Cases of this kind give rise to the following questions:

1. Should a dividing line be drawn between payment for exclusive use of general news material and the purchase of signed feature articles, an accepted form of newspaper enterprise?

2. Should the practice of purchasing exclusive rights in news and photographs be discontinued as contrary to the public interest, on the ground that it restricts the dissemination of news, puts a false value on news and lowers the status of the Press and the standards of journalism?

3. Is an attempt to deny a member of the public the right to sell and a newspaper the right to buy the exclusive news and photographs an un-

warrantable interference with the freedom of the individual and a threat to legitimate newspaper enterprise?

4. If interference with the right of a newspaper to make an agreement with a willing seller of information is a curb on legitimate newspaper enterprise, and an interference with the right of an individual to dispose of his possessions in an advantageous manner should not newspapers recognise that agreements for exclusive rights tend to stem the free flow of news and avoid abuse by limiting the occasions for them?

WHAT IS 'CHEQUE-BOOK JOURNALISM'?

Opinions differ on the meaning of 'cheque-book journalism'. To some the term connotes the purchase of memoirs of notorious people; others understand it as the exercise of the power of the purse to deny competitive journals legitimate access to general matters of public interest. The fact is, however, that a person has a right to sell what is his; this may take the form of information which another wishes to buy. If *The Times* is entitled to buy the story of the conquest of Everest or of Sir Frances Chichester's lone voyage round the world, why should not some other newspapers be entitled to buy similar rights in the memoirs of a criminal? If the distinction lies not in the purchase but in the publication of the material, there is a need for guidance on what may be bought but may not be published.

The Press Council sought the views of the Press on the matter generally.

VIEWS OF THE NEWSPAPERS AND THE PROFESSION

One national newspaper thought that the most effective curb on the exploitation of vice and sex for commercial reward was the cumulative effect of public opinion. The skill of Parliamentary draftsmanship would be defeated in any attempt to write acceptable law on such a matter, and the fewer restrictions there were on the printed word the better. To say that as long as this sort of journalism helped to sell newspapers all influence would be impotent against it, was to underestimate the powers of public opinion and the sensitivity of journalists.

Another national journal agreed that legislation was obnoxious and that the right way to deal with the matter was by means of a code of conduct developed through the Press Council. There were limitations, however, to what the Council could do; it could not do more than establish a working definition of what was and what was not acceptable.

A large publishing house took the view that it would not be possible or prudent for newspapers to agree on an all-round condemnation of a form of newspaper activity which could not be precisely defined. Hard and fast rules would have the immediate effect of a veto on legitimate enterprise. It was 'cheque-book journalism' as well as enterprise for one newspaper to outbid another for an important series of articles. It was 'cheque-book journalism' for newspaper A to lure talent from newspaper B by offering a higher salary. The publication of an exclusive picture of particular merit was obviously the result of 'cheque-book journalism'. Any blanket prohibition of 'cheque-book journalism' of this type would impose a crushing restriction on the freedom and individuality of newspapers, and the result would be deadly sameness throughout the Press. The decision on what should and what should not be bought for publication was the responsibility of a newspaper's editor and management.

One of the professional bodies stated that 'cheque-book journalism' was a modern idiom which had been employed as a disparaging term, yet the words simply meant a payment for features, information, news and pictures, a practice as old as journalism itself. This could be a defensible, indeed an essential part of newspaper production in respect of memoirs or other material against which no criticism could fairly be made. What was deplored was trafficking in scandal as a salable commodity. Offering money for information tempted the unscrupulous into exaggeration and falsehood. The dilemma lay in finding a solution to a problem which was largely one of taste and ethical standards; the content and source of the material were considerations in determining whether it was objectionable. Of equal complexity was the abuse of the system of payment for the material. It was a matter for concern that sources of news and pictures of legitimate interest were being closed to all but the highest bidder. The freedom to collect news was an essential part of the freedom of the Press, and journalists could not discharge their duty to the public if they imposed upon each other restrictions against which they would rise in wrath if they were imposed from outside.

Other professional bodies condemned the publication of unsavoury memoirs, although on occasion publication might be justified as informing the public of aspects of life it was entitled to know about. The view that 'pimps, prostitutes and perverts should not benefit from their notoriety and degradation' would have prevented the publication in newspapers of Oscar Wilde's *De Profundis* and other works of merit. Exclusivity involved a threat to less affluent newspapers, and encouraged the public always to expect to be paid for interview and photographs.

THE PRESS COUNCIL'S ANALYSIS 1965

After studying these observations the Press Council in 1965 published a statement of its own views.

It contained a reference to the statement issued by the Council in 1963 on unsavoury memoirs. The Press Council on that occasion, the 1965 statement declared, had not hesitated to condemn the glamorisation of vice and the rewarding of criminals, which were the aspects of cheque-book journalism that made the biggest impact on the public. The Press Council was heartened to note that since its outspoken comments on the Christine Keeler memoirs in 1963 there had been a marked improvement in the standards of newspaper approach to matters of this kind.

The Council said that it could not provide an all-embracing definition of cheque-book journalism. The facets of the subject were so varied that each case had to be considered on its own facts and circumstances. The term 'cheque-book journalism' was of recent introduction into colloquial language; it was difficult to define, and, like 'democracy' and 'progress', could convey a different meaning whenever it was used; the term was wide enough to cover the cost of entertaining a contact to luncheon to the payment of thousands of pounds for the discreditable memoirs of a notorious person.

Many people used the term by way of opprobrium solely in regard to special articles or interviews on vice or immorality by notorieties of the moment, but this did not represent the full scope of cheque-book journalism. Fundamentally it was the power of the purse, a power which if misused could give a wealthy newspaper an unfair advantage over its less opulent rivals.

Normally the critic of cheque-book journalism had in mind the purchase of news or views from non-journalists. There was, however, nothing inherently wrong in the purchase of knowledge from a willing seller, and a person of standing had no greater right to benefit himself financially by the sale of autobiographical matter than a rogue.

The Council proceeded to state the objections to some aspects of cheque-book journalism. They were three in number:

1. The exercise of the power of the purse to deny competitors legitimate access to news or facts that the public ought to know was against the public interest. The public interest was not necessarily the national interest. A news event could be trivial, considered nationally, but might be of great importance to the public of a given provincial area. People who relied primarily upon their town or country newspapers for their local news could be deprived of the news by its exclusive purchase by an outside newspaper. It was difficult to say when exclusive rights were objectionable; each case had to be judged on its own merits.

2. The quest for specially purchased stories which tended to lead to unseemly conduct. Cases like the street fracas between journalists of rival newspapers trying to interview the man discharged after the Glasgow murder trial brought the Press into discredit.

3. The steps sometimes taken to ensure that a person whose information has been purchased should not be in a position to divulge it to rival newspapers, a form of action known as 'body-snatching'.

The Press Council's statement drew attention to the function of newspapers sometimes overlooked by critics. The Press had a responsibility to the community to record what was going on, and it would not be discharging its duty if it ignored matters of public consequence simply because they were unpleasant. Objection arose when these matters were reported in excessive detail and resulted in pandering to the baser elements in man's nature. The claim that a large section of the population demanded this sort of journalism was no excuse for providing it.

The Council unhesitatingly condemned as immoral the practice of financially rewarding criminals for the disclosure of their criminal practices for the public entertainment. A wrongdoer should not benefit by his offences against society. The prospect of publicity and reward for criminal activities could be a vivid and compelling inducement to some people.

The Press Council expressed some reservation about the publication of revelations by convicted spies. Many people regarded them as criminals, but only in respect of the country they injured; when they spied for their own country they were regarded as heroes by their compatriots. The publication in Britain of the memoirs of the foreign spy could be beneficial in exposing weaknesses in the nation's security. On the whole, however, the Press

Council felt that it was contrary to public welfare to reward criminals, whether they were vicious or treasonable.

The Council stated that it would keep the subject of cheque-book journalism under consideration and issue its views on cases reported to it.

The 1965 statement is reproduced in Appendix IV.

The case of Donald Hume's memoirs is dealt with in Chapter 18, p. 318 (*Sunday Pictorial*).

26 Cases Outside the Ambit of the Press Council

RADIO AND TELEVISION
OTHER CASES

The scope of the Press Council's jurisdiction is determined by the objects set out in the constitution. The Council confines itself to matters within the scope of these objects and those it conceived to be within range of the Council's responsibility.

The following cases raised issues which the Council decided were outside its jurisdiction:

RADIO AND TELEVISION

The Council will deal only with complaints against the Press and not those against other media such as radio and television. This was made clear when complaints were made against Pressmen based on a B.B.C. television broadcast. The B.B.C. televised the arrival of Mr Greville Wynne at Northolt Airport following his release from a prison in Russia and the news conference he gave. The airport pictures showed him seated in a chair with one or two interviewers near him and a number of newspapermen ranged behind him. Complaint was made of the conduct of the Pressmen which was described as 'disgraceful' and 'heartless'; they were referred to as 'a horde of vultures' and 'callous brutes'. In particular, exception was taken to a question put to Mr Wynne about what was the first thing he said to his wife.

The B.B.C. provided the Council with a re-run of the television broadcast and a script of the recorded conversation. It was explained that Mr Wynne answered questions put by reporters when he landed. After a private telephone conversation with his wife he went to a specially prepared studio for the conference, which was televised.

The picture showed that the newspapermen ranged behind Mr Wynne did not move from their allotted positions, and that they did not conduct the interview, nor did any of them ask the specific question to which objection had been taken. The Council also observed that Mr Wynne was not pressed by any questioner when he said he did not wish to answer a question, that he was courteously addressed as 'Sir' and did not once ask that questioning should cease. Mr Wynne told the Council that he made no personal complaint.

The Press Council's adjudication was: The desirability or otherwise of a conference being arranged for the benefit of television on the arrival of Mr Greville Wynne does not come within the ambit of the Press Council. Nor has the Press Council any jurisdiction in the matter of interviews for media other than the Press. So far as the conduct of the Press at Northolt was concerned the Press Council had no fault to find. (1965/82–3)

OTHER CASES

ETHICS NOT LAW

The Press Council deals with questions of journalistic conduct not with questions of law. Even where a complaint is one within the competence of the Council it will defer dealing with it if civil or criminal proceedings have been started, or are imminent, relating to the matter complained of.

An instance of the Press Council delaying an inquiry because of the possibility of legal proceedings occurred at the time of the Moors Murder Trial at Chester Assizes. In the course of the trial a witness for the prosecution under cross-examination stated that he was in receipt of a weekly payment from a Sunday newspaper to which he was under contract for his story. The weekly payments made by the newspaper were in part payment of the purchase price. He was asked if under the agreement he would have a very large sum in a certain eventuality. He said that he would, and agreed that he had a vested interest in the conviction of the accused. As a result of these answers the Judge, addressing the Attorney-General, who appeared for the Crown, said that there seemed to have been a gross interference with the course of justice; he asked the Attorney-General to inquire into the matter and take such action as was desirable. The Attorney said that he would do so. The occasion is dealt with more fully on pp. 448–57.

The purchase of a story of this kind also engaged the attention of the Press Council as a possible infringement of ethical standards and the Council issued the following notice:

> The Council has asked the newspaper concerned to furnish a statement, but, in conformity with its practice, will not consider the ethical aspect until the legal implications, if any, have been resolved.

So, too, where libel proceedings have been or are likely to be initiated against a newspaper, the Press Council will defer consideration of a complaint arising out of the publication until the legal proceedings have been disposed of.

SUPPRESSION OF THE PRESS

The function and primary purpose of the Press Council is the maintenance not the suppression of the freedom of the Press. A polite intimation of this was given to Portuguese students at Oxford when they complained of unfair and false reports about Portugal published in the *Guardian* and the editorial comment that 'Britain should extricate herself from ties with Portugal until a civilised government comes to power there'. The students called on the Council to stop the English Press from launching further insulting attacks on the Portuguese people.

The Secretary of the Council told the students that it was not possible for the Council to take action of this kind. In Britain there was freedom of the Press, and no one could dictate to a newspaper editor what he should or should not publish. He advised them to make a reasoned protest to the newspaper in the form of a letter for publication. (1961/8)

PAST HISTORY

The Council was asked to investigate criticism made in the House of Lords and the Commons of alleged inaccuracies in an article by Mr Arthur

Koestler in the *Observer* on hanging. Lord Mancroft on behalf of the Government accepted without reservation Mr Koestler's assurance that he had not deliberately omitted from the article a material part of the instructions to prison governors on information to be given after executions. The Press Council said that this was satisfactory, but it would have been better still if the Government's withdrawal of its imputation had been more emphatic.

The Council, however, refused to inquire into the contradictory statements which had been made many years before concerning the execution of Mrs Thompson.

The Council did not consider that its duties required it to investigate ancient rumours when Members of Parliament by the use of question and answer had failed to establish their truth. (1956/31)

JOURNALISTIC STANDARDS

The Press Council will not act as arbiter in settling local disputes. The Council will investigate an alleged breach of journalistic standards, but will not intervene where no question of this kind is involved. Where, for instance, a newspaper of one political complexion expresses a particular opinion and a newspaper of a different complexion expresses a view precisely the opposite, it is clear that both cannot be correct. Nevertheless both newspapers have the undoubted right to speak their minds and, so long as they do so fairly and honestly, the Council will not sit in judgment to decide which point of view is right.

CONTEMPT OF COURT

The Press Council was asked by Yiewsley and West Drayton Urban District Council to say whether the *Middlesex Advertiser and County Gazette* had been guilty of contempt of court in publishing comments on the decision of its Public Health Committee to take court proceedings against the owner of a local industry. Powers had been delegated to the Committee to take such action in the name of the District Council.

The Editor of the newspaper, Mr H. W. Tilley, said that he was unaware that the Committee had power to initiate legal proceedings and was under the impression that their decision was subject to ratification by the parent Council.

The Press Council took counsel's opinion and was advised that the comments published in the newspaper were capable of constituting contempt of court, although counsel did not think that a court would hold that the particular publication was of a kind likely to interfere with the course of justice.

The Press Council decided that the question of contempt of court was not one for its jurisdiction. (1962/51–2, 76–7)

PART THREE

The Council
Speaks for the Press

27 Monopolies and Mergers

The terms of reference of both Royal Commissions had called for an inquiry into the economics of the Press. In 1947 as in 1961 the reasons for the decline in the number of independent newspapers were not difficult to diagnose, but the problem of arresting the decline proved an intractable one. A number of suggestions were made to the Shawcross Commission which involved discriminatory controls on the mass-circulation newspapers and the Commission was not prepared to recommend this.

Hardly had the Shawcross Commission presented its Report in 1962 than the alarm was sounded again. In 1964 five evening newspapers closed down causing a drastic reduction in the range of the news service available in the provinces. Glasgow remained the only city in Great Britain outside London with more than one evening newspaper. In Parliament the Prime Minister, Sir Alec Douglas-Home, was asked what proposals he had for implementing the recommendations of the Shawcross Commission in regard to the formation of a Press Amalgamations Court. Had he studied the resolution passed by the National Executive Council of the National Union of Journalists and the concern expressed over the closure of these five newspapers and the imminent closure of a sixth? The Prime Minister replied that he shared the general concern; the Government was considering the recommendation of an Amalgamations Court but the proposal presented serious difficulties

The Shawcross Commission had recommended that the Court should consist of judges of the High Court and of the Court of Session and lay members appointed on the recommendation of the Lord Chancellor after consultation with the Trades Union Congress and the Press Council. It was to have a Registrar, and the pattern would be the same as under the Restrictive Trade Practices Act, 1956; the Registrar might well be the same official.

The function of the Amalgamations Court would be to scrutinise transactions involving the purchase of newspaper titles or of controlling interests in companies which, directly or indirectly through subsidiaries, owned newspapers. The scheme was to be limited to daily and Sunday newspapers, and a transaction would be required to be investigated only if the purchaser controlled weekly sales of daily or Sunday newspapers of more than three million copies either before or as the result of the transaction. The Tribunal would grant consent to a transaction only if it were deemed to be in the public interest.

The Shawcross Report stated that there was more than one view of the question whether the public interest was actually injured by the degree of concentration of ownership and control of newspapers existing at a particular time. The 1949 Report had recommended that steps should be taken to ensure that significant developments in the size and organisation of Press undertakings were brought prominently before the public. It had further recommended that the Press Council should undertake the task of conveying this information to the public, a proposal that the Shawcross Commission later also approved. In accordance with the recommendation the constitution incorporated as one of the objects of the Press Council the study of developments in the Press which tended towards greater concentration or monopoly. Had this object been fulfilled, the Shawcross Commission declared, much of their inquiry would have been unnecessary, and public awareness of possible developments might indeed, of itself, have modified the course which those developments actually took.

The potential danger to the public interest of further concentration of ownership and control of newspapers by amalgamations was, the Shawcross Commission said, beyond doubt. The question that arose was whether the public could continue to rely for the proper satisfaction of their varied needs on a system which enabled large undertakings to expand their control over the Press irrespective of whether they misused the powers thus obtained or not. Expansionist tendencies could lead to results which would be beyond tolerance in a free society. One newspaper company in its evidence to the Commission said, taking the matter to its extreme, if one man came to own all the newspapers in the United Kingdom, and conditions were such that no one else could successfully establish a rival newspaper, then the nation would be in real peril. The Commission reached the conclusion that the potential danger of deliberately contrived concentrations of ownership could not be dismissed, and that some means should be sought to protect the public against this. But concentration of ownership and control could arise not only from amalgamations but also from the closing of publications for purely economic reasons, and no remedies designed to restrict the extension of proprietary rights could prevent a reduction in the number of independent publications through the excess of deaths over births.

The Commission thought it would be wrong to place a statutory limit on the circulation of a newspaper or on the total circulation of a group of newspapers. The growth of a newspaper's circulation depended on its attractiveness to readers, and a restriction of circulation would be a restriction on the readers' choice. The freedom of the Press involved not only a freedom to publish but also a freedom of choice of a newspaper to read. The Commission were also opposed to a statutory limit to the number of publications which could be owned by one individual or one undertaking.

While there was a case for legislation to enable future extension of group ownership to be scrutinised, there should be no wholesale prohibition of all future amalgamations or expansions. No public interest was served by preventing a merger such as occurred in the case of the *News Chronicle* with the *Daily Mail*, when the newspaper taken over would have gone out of existence in any event. There were, however, other cases where amalgamation could be contrary to the public interest, such for instance, the acquisition of Odhams Press Limited by the Daily Mirror Group, where the company taken over could have survived economically on its own. The merger was decided wholly by the financial interests of the shareholders who were not, as such, concerned with the public interest.

PARLIAMENT DECIDES

The Wilson Government which succeeded Sir Alec Douglas-Home's also had reservations about the Shawcross Report. It did not accept the recommendation of a judicial body because it did not think, as the President of the Board of Trade, Mr Jay put it, that freedom of speech, the free expression of opinion and the public interest were justiciable issues. The Government, however, did not intend to evade the 'awkward and prickly' subject of newspaper mergers. It was no use disguising the fact, Mr Jay said, that Press amalgamations had threatened and still might threaten the freedom and variety of the expression of opinion and perhaps even the unbiased presentation of news. Instead of the suggested Amalgamations Court the Government had decided to give additional powers to the Board of Trade to refer proposed mergers to the Monopolies Commission. But the issues raised by newspaper mergers were so different from those in the normal take-over bid that a special panel of individuals would be added to the Commission for this particular form of inquiry.

In the course of his speech on the second reading of the Monopolies and Mergers Bill when he introduced it in March 1965 Mr Jay said:

> It has also seemed to me, as one who has been a working journalist for over twenty years or so, that this is perhaps the field where there exists potentially an insidious threat to real democracy in this country. It raises far different and wider issues than the economic consequences of ordinary business mergers, but I think it is reasonable to infer from the report of the Royal Commission on the Press on the one hand and, on the other, from the public disquiet at the time, for instance, of the disappearance of the *News Chronicle* and the *Star*, the swallowing up of Odhams and the extinction of the *Daily Herald*, that many people are anxious whether the business forces making for amalgamations in the newspaper world might not one day imperil our liberties, though, thank goodness, there are plenty of discordant voices raised in the Press at the present time which we can all hear.

THE PRESS COUNCIL'S VIEW

When the Bill was before Parliament the Press Council issued a statement defining its attitude. In the statement the Council said that it had studied the Bill and observed that the proposals sought to control newspaper mergers of a certain size. From time to time the Press Council itself had expressed concern about the trend towards the increased concentration of ownership, coupled with the reduction in the number of newspapers, but had not been able to advance any curative scheme which did not interfere with the essential freedom of the Press.

In an age of powerful financial groupings it was too much, the Council declared, to expect the Press to remain unaffected by an almost universal tendency. The Press, however, differed from an industry engaged in the production of commodities. It had in its keeping one of the cherished liberties of the British people, and if concentration of ownership restricted dissemination of news and opinions to fewer and fewer journals, the freedom of the Press was thereby endangered.

The Press Council said that it would welcome a just solution of the problem, but would be neglectful of its duty if it did not call attention to the fact that the freedom of the Press could be in issue in the proposals incorporated in the Bill. Because this freedom went to the very roots of British democracy the Press Council earnestly entreated all parties of the House to place this important matter above doctrinaire considerations. The freedom of the Press was not merely the right to publish but the right to read what is published, a privilege to be exercised, at will, by all. The common people had fought and died for this right.

The Press Council did not oppose the provisions of the Bill but offered the following observations for consideration:

> The freedom of the British Press and its reputation in the world are largely founded on the absence of special Press laws which allow exercise of Government control. The penal effect of Clause 8 of the Bill would effectively make the measure Britain's first Press law.
>
> The law allows any man to establish his own newspaper at will, and this by inference confers the right of disposal in equal measure, provided that the action does not impede.
>
> The definition of 'public interest' and the guiding principles to be kept in mind by the Monopolies Commission in considering proposed Press mergers will be important. The Council drew special attention to the observations of the Shawcross Commission on these points.
>
> The additional members to be appointed to the Commission to deal with cases of newspaper ownership should be people who are aware of the special problems of the newspaper industry.

The statement concluded by saying that the Press Council would keep the closest watch on any procedures which might infringe the freedom of the Press. (1965/130–1)

The Government refused to give way on the penal clause in the Bill. The reason given was that the divesting procedure proposed for other industries was inapplicable to newspapers because newspapers are very different from other businesses. An industrial merger could be unscrambled but a newspaper destroyed by a merger could not be restored. A deterrent, which in a sense protected the freedom of the Press, to prevent newspapers being taken over and suppressed inevitably had to be more severe.

The guiding principles, given in the Shawcross Report, to which the Press Council called the attention of the Government related to questions to be considered in deciding whether a particular transaction was in the public interest. Under the recommendations of the Shawcross Report an applicant would obtain Board of Trade consent for a merger transaction if he were able to convince the relevant tribunal (now the Monopolies Commission) of one of the following facts:

(*a*) That the newspaper to be acquired was not likely to continue in production unless sold to a purchaser prepared to continue it and no other offer had been made involving the continued publication and the payment of a reasonable price having regard to the value of the property. If there is a possibility of continued publication it is important to save a newspaper even if it can only be done by increasing the potential influence of a large undertaking.

(*b*) That the economies or increased efficiency to be achieved by a joint control of all the newspapers which would be controlled by the applicant group of newspapers would probably secure the continued publication of all these newspapers, some of which would otherwise be likely to be stopped. For instance, this might happen when an evening newspaper is purchased to support a morning newspaper.

(*c*) That having regard to the specialised character and readership of the newspaper to be acquired the transaction would be likely to affect the accurate presentation of news and the free expression of opinion.

(*d*) That the transaction would leave the aggregate circulation of newspapers controlled by the vendor greater than that controlled by the purchaser. There is no overriding public interest in preventing the diminution of a greater Press empire even if it meant increasing the size of a smaller one. (Cmnd. 1811, par. 348.)

The Monopolies and Mergers Act received the Royal Assent on 5 August 1965. The influence of the Shawcross Report is manifest in section 8, which provides that the transfer of a newspaper to a proprietor whose newspapers have an average daily circulation amounting with that of the newspaper concerned to 500,000 or more copies shall be unlawful and void unless the transfer is made with the written conditional or unconditional consent of the Board of Trade, following a report on the matter from the Monopolies Commission. The Board of Trade, however, if satisfied that the newspaper concerned is not economic as a going concern and as a separate newspaper, may consent to the transfer without a report from the Commission. But in such a case the Board of Trade must also be satisfied either that the newspaper is not intended to continue as a separate newspaper or, if it is so to continue, the case is one of urgency. Consent without a report from the Commission being required may also be given if the average circulation of the newspaper to be transferred is not more than 25,000 a day. The Board may from time to time vary the circulation figures.

Where an application for consent to a transfer is referred to the Monopolies Commission for investigation and report the Commission shall report whether or not in all the circumstances the transfer of the newspaper may be expected to operate against the public interest, taking into account all relevant circumstances and having regard to the need for accurate presentation of news and free expression of opinion.

The transfer of a newspaper without the consent of the Board of Trade, where consent is necessary, is a criminal offence punishable on indictment by imprisonment up to two years or by fine or both.

THE TIMES MERGER

The first reference to the Monopolies Commission under section 8 of the Act was an application for the merger of *The Times* and the *Sunday Times*.

The facts established by the Commission which made its Report on 15 December 1966 were that the Times Publishing Company had for several years past been concerned at the unsatisfactory performance of *The Times* from a commercial point of view. Its circulation had been almost static for the four years 1961–5 and about 70 per cent of its circulation was concentrated in London and South-East England. Additional capital was required to meet major technological changes in printing methods, the use of colour, the desirability of regional printing in order to improve sales performance and to cover the high cost of production.

Trading profits, in spite of a partial recovery in 1964, had tended fairly steadily downwards since 1960, and, as a step towards making itself commercially secure, *The Times* needed a sharp rise in readership in order to attract more advertising.

On 3 May 1966 changes were made in the lay-out, one of the changes being printing the news on the front page. These measures resulted in a 17

O2   L.T.P.C.

per cent increase of circulation, but the cost of the publicity campaign caused an excess of costs over revenue from the increased circulation. The Times Publishing Company decided that a substantial and successful newspaper was required as a partner to bring to *The Times* the ability to raise money, modern management skills and additional readers. Readership would need to be raised from 250,000 to a net sale of 400,000–500,000 copies daily. To this end an expenditure of £2,000,000 to £3,000,000 for expansion and development was required over a period of years and an immediate infusion of new techniques, research and marketing skills was necessary. Before turning to the Thomson Organisation, the Times Publishing Company explored the possibility of joining forces with other quality newspapers, namely, the *Guardian*, the *Observer*, and the *Financial Times*. None of these offered a solution to its problem. Eventually discussions were opened with the Thomson Organisation, which led to the formulation of the proposals which were the subject of the investigation by the Commission.

Under the proposed merger a new company would be formed to publish *The Times* and the *Sunday Times* as a seven-day-a-week newspaper operation. The name of the new company would be Times Newspapers Limited, to which the goodwill, copyright and business of the existing *Times* and *Sunday Times* would be transferred from the Times Publishing Company and the Thomson Organisation respectively. Mr Denis Hamilton, a former Editor of the *Sunday Times*, would be appointed as first Editor-in-Chief of the two newspapers. The Editor-in-Chief and the Editors of *The Times* and the *Sunday Times* would be appointed by, and could only be removed by, the Board. Each of the two Editors, in consultation with the Editor-in-Chief, would be responsible for the day-to-day running of his newspaper. Each would make his own decisions on matters of opinion on leading articles and each newspaper would continue to take separately its own lines of policy.

The day-to-day business management of Times Newspapers Limited would be in the hands of an informal executive committee of which Mr Hamilton as Editor-in-Chief would be Chairman. The constitution of a committee would be a matter for the Editor-in-Chief, but it would probably consist of the directors with executive responsibility, the two Editors, and the senior management in charge of departments (*e.g.* marketing and advertising).

Mr Hamilton assured the Monopolies Commission that the two Editors would be responsible for the editorial opinions of the two newspapers and that they would be free to put forward opposing views. He also assured the Commission that he would make it clear to the two Editors on appointment that they would be expected to take full responsibility for the editorial policy of their papers.

Lord Thomson endorsed Mr Hamilton's assurance on the independence of the two Editors and the view he had expressed that an Editor did not form opinions as it were in a vacuum, but was bound to be influenced by the views of other members of the editorial team who were expert on particular subjects, and by the views of the Editor-in-Chief.

Sir William Haley, Chairman designate of Times Newspapers, also assured the Commission that it would be his intention that the two Editors should retain their independence; he would regard the establishment of the independence of the Editors as his major task. Ultimately, however, the independence of the Editor must depend upon the strength of character of the individual who held that office.

The roles of the Editors and the Editor-in-Chief, and their relationship with the proprietors, were a matter of concern to most witnesses who gave evidence to the Commission. Many were doubtful whether a satisfactory relationship could be established between an editor and editor-in-chief; experience elsewhere suggested that the editor-in-chief would emerge as the effective editor. Nothing was more damaging to a newspaper than an attempt to run its policies by a committee. Some witnesses thought that the Editor-in-Chief's attitude could hardly avoid being influenced by the commercial wishes of the proprietor. The Editor-in-Chief would then be likely to use his influence with the Editor to adopt a policy of moderation, and in consequence it would be much more difficult for the Editor to pursue a vigorous independent line on a major aspect of national policy.

The Commission considered that the title of Editor-in-Chief was bound to create doubts as to the genuine independence of the two Editors and to diminish their status and authority in the eyes of their staffs and of the public. Lord Thomson recognised the force of this argument, but took the view that since it had been announced publicly, to change the title which Mr Hamilton would bear in the new company would create difficulty for him at that stage of bringing the two newspapers into a single company. An attempt would be made to persuade the Board to change the title of the post to Editorial Director when Mr Hamilton vacated it.

The general aim of the proposed merger, the Monopolies Commission reported, was to make *The Times* more attractive to its readers and substantially to increase the volume of advertising carried. News coverage would be extended and cultural interests developed. *The Times* would also be kept in the forefront on technological development. Lord Thomson and his son told the Commission they would consider that they had a national duty to maintain the prestige of *The Times*, and that they would not allow quality to suffer in order to save money.

The first question to which the Commission addressed itself was the role of *The Times* and whether there was anything that distinguished it from other quality newspapers and the extent to which it was regarded at home and overseas as the voice of Britain. The opinions of witnesses varied substantially about this. Some regarded *The Times* as a national institution which should be preserved inviolate; others took the view that it had long since lost any special role (pars. 101–2).

The Commission also had to consider whether the transfer of *The Times* would affect its independence in the sense not merely freedom from proprietorial interference in editorial policy but freedom from subservience to a political party and from commercial pressures. The evidence of witnesses on the other hand was that no newspaper could be truly independent unless it was commercially sound. Most of them took the view that marriage of *The Times* with another newspaper was inevitable and some considered that no more suitable partner than The Thomson Organisation was likely to appear.

Opposition to a merger with Thomson interests was mainly on four grounds:

(1) It would put too much power in the hands of the Thomson Organisation.

(2) It was undesirable that a newspaper with the reputation of *The Times* for independence and objectivity should become associated with any newspaper chain.

(3) Although commercial soundness was the only guarantee of independence, too great a preoccupation with profitability was likely to make a newspaper more concerned with pleasing its customers than undertaking its task as a leader of opinion.

(4) The Thomson Organisation had substantial interests outside the newspaper industry, and the editorial staff could not disregard these interests; where there was a conflict, news might be suppressed or opinion distorted.

The conclusions reached by the Commission were that in the face of the losses anticipated and of the need for capital for the development of *The Times*, the Times Publishing Company could not continue to publish *The Times* without some outside assistance. While the market for quality newspapers was growing, the circulation of *The Times* remained static. With its present circulation *The Times* would have difficulty in attracting enough advertising revenue to enable it to stand on its own.

The Commission had no hesitation in concluding that the proposed link with the *Sunday Times* offered a good prospect of keeping *The Times* in being. It did not follow that *The Times* could not be preserved by other means, but there was no alternative in sight offering as firm grounds for confidence as the proposal under review.

On the question whether the public interest might suffer as a result of the proposed transfer, the Commission said there were three questions to be considered:

(i) Whether the transfer would cause an excessive concentration of newspaper power;

(ii) Whether there would be a threat to the survival of other newspapers;

(iii) Whether changes in the nature of *The Times* were likely to result which would rob it of the quality which made its preservation a matter of public interest.

The Report of the Commission pointed out that the transfer of *The Times* would be the addition of an important vehicle of opinion and a material increase in the power of The Thomson Organisation; it would also constitute a continuation of the movements towards concentration in the ownership of the Press which must ultimately tend to stifle the expression of variety of opinion. The Commission stated that The Thomson Organisation had given its editors a great deal of freedom and although there was no guarantee that its successors would continue this policy, nevertheless the transfer of *The Times* to a company with such a policy involved little risk, certainly less than would the transfer of a proprietor who regarded newspapers as vehicles for his own views. Accordingly the Commission did not consider that the proposed transfer would lead to an undue concentration of newspaper power (pars. 161–2).

The concentration of newspaper and other interests might not only afford power to control the expression of opinion but might also bring commercial and financial power. If *The Times* were preserved only at the cost of losing one or more other newspapers, the public could suffer as much as by its loss.

If it was to be made commercially successful it would have to compete for readers and if it was supported by the marketing skill and strength of The Organisation, it would compete very strongly for advertisers. Some newspapers were already financially weak and competition from *The Times* could add to their difficulties, but the Commission concluded that the consequences of the transfer would not of themselves be sufficient to kill any newspaper which would otherwise have survived, They did not think, therefore, that the prospect of increased competition was a reason for objecting to the transfer or for placing any restraint on its ability to compete (pars. 164–8).

The Commission stated that the evidence of the witnesses showed that the proposed transfer had aroused apprehensions for the public interest and their own investigations indicated that these apprehensions were not groundless. If *The Times* came under the control of the Thomson Organisation, commercial considerations would play a greater part than they had in the past. But the survival of *The Times* would be assured, and the public would continue to be offered a good and in some respects an improved newspaper. In matters of editorial opinion there was reasonable assurance that it would continue to speak with a separate voice, although it would no longer be the same voice or the same *Times* as in the past. The combination of *The Times* and the *Sunday Times*, backed by the commercial strength of the Thomson Organisation, would present formidable competition to the other quality newspapers, some of which already faced a difficult future.

> But [the Commission concluded] we think that neither this increase in competitive strength nor the increase in concentration of newspaper ownership which would result from the proposed transfer is, of itself, cause for concern. Taking into account all the relevant circumstances and having regard to the need for accurate presentation of news and free expression of opinion, we conclude that the proposed transfer of *The Times* and the *Sunday Times* to a newspaper proprietor may be expected not to operate against the public interest.

One member of the Commission dissented from the conclusions of the other seven. He regarded the merger as a significant step in the direction of monopoly control of the quality national newspapers. While he accepted the assurances in relation to the independence of the Editors of *The Times* and the *Sunday Times* and the maintenance of the separate identities of the two newspapers given by Lord Thomson and Mr Hamilton, he regretted that they were not accompanied by a readiness to change immediately the title of 'Editor-in-Chief' of the two newspapers. The merger would give effective control of *The Times* and the *Sunday Times* not to the individuals who gave assurances but to a body corporate whose future views and policies might well differ from those of its present Directors. The risk of change in this case seemed greater than usual in that the body concerned had widespread and diverse interests outside the publication of newspapers. For these reasons he thought that the proposed merger might operate against the public interest unless the Board of Trade obtained as a condition of consent to the merger that the personal assurances given to the Commission were reinforced by a formal undertaking given by the Thomson Organisation.

On 21 December 1966 the President of the Board of Trade, Mr Douglas Jay, informed the House that he had received the Report of the Monopolies Commission. The Commission had reached the decision that the proposed transfer would not operate against the public interest.

'I accept its conclusion,' said Mr Jay, 'and have accordingly given my consent to the proposed transfer.'

He went on to state that the Thomson Organisation had formally confirmed to him the personal assurance given by Lord Thomson to the Monopolies Commission about the preservation and the separate identities of *The Times* and the *Sunday Times* and the maintenance of the independence of their Editors.

Lord Devlin gave evidence to the Monopolies Commission on behalf of the Press Council. In their Report the Commission expressed their indebtedness to the Press Council for help with statistical and other information given in connection with the inquiry.

28 How the Council Serves the Press

A UNITED PROFESSION

The First Royal Commission thought it remarkable that although a number of organisations existed to represent sectional interests within the Press there was none representing the Press as a whole. No one body was concerned to maintain either the freedom of the Press or the integrity on which its reputation depended; no single organisation expressed the common interest in these things of the men who shared the responsibility for the character of the Press. This was the more surprising because those engaged in newspaper production were acutely aware of the Press as an entity and were jealous for its independence and its reputation. Yet the Press had taken fewer steps to safeguard its standards of performance than perhaps any other institution of comparable importance.

If the Press was to develop in the right direction from the point of view both of society and of those concerned for its own standing and reputation, it needed to foster those tendencies which made for integrity and for a sense of responsibility to the public.

The relationship between practitioner and client in other professions is a direct one; in journalism the relationship is between the newspaper and the reader, and the responsibility is shared by all who shape the newspaper and its personality — proprietor, manager, editor and working journalists. Nevertheless, a line between the proprietorial and administrative side on the one hand and working journalist on the other is sharply drawn; proprietors and managers who are not working journalists are excluded from full membership of the professional organisations of journalists.

The Commission did not consider that the relationship between the proprietor as employer and the working journalist as employee rendered such action impracticable; on the contrary there was sufficient common ground between them to warrant the belief that progress could be sought in building up standards common to both and not in assuming perpetual conflict. By sharing responsibility proprietors, managers and working journalists would come to regard themselves as members of a single profession with the means of formulating a common conception of reputable professional conduct. An organisation to weld the various interests together was needed, and this was what it was intended the Press Council should be. It would unite the profession, safeguard its traditions, interpret its aspirations, and eradicate discreditable practices. The Press Council would give the Press an official voice. Instead of being a number of constituent organisations as it was the Press would become a new entity with a real status.

This conception was embodied in the constitution, one of the objects of the Council being to make representations on appropriate occasions to the Government, organs of the United Nations, and to Press organisations abroad. As the Press Council grew in strength and prestige its recognition was more widely accepted and its authority more firmly established. Complaints in Parliament about the conduct of the Press came to be regarded by the Government as matters for the Council. Government departments and other organisations, official and unofficial, at home and abroad, have come to regard the Council as the authority on matters relating to the Press. Tribunals conducting official inquiries turned to it for the views of the Press. The Press Council has given evidence to the Royal Commissions on the Press (1961–2), the Police and on the Tribunals of Inquiry; it gave evidence to the Tucker Committee, the Departmental Committee appointed by the Home Secretary to report on committal proceedings. As the representative of the Press, the Council has expressed its view on proposed legislation arising out of the Report of the Tucker Committee and on the Bill relating to Monopolies and Mergers. On behalf of the Press it has negotiated closer liaison with the Public Relations Office at the Palace in improving the flow of information on the activities of the Royal Family and has had discussions with the Minister of Health and medical authorities for a better news service from the hospitals. Most recently it has on behalf of the Press made a Declaration of Principle on the purchase of stories from persons likely to be witnesses in criminal cases and the publication of unsavoury feature articles generally.

CUSTODIAN OF ITS GOOD NAME

As the custodian of the honour of the Press, the Council deals not only with complaints of journalistic offences but will without waiting for a specific accusation take the initiative when in its view, newspapers fall short of the standards expected of them. An instance occurred following the prosecution of *Lady Chatterley's Lover* when several newspapers published the 'four-letter words' used in the novel. The Council recorded its opinion that the use of the words in the newspapers was objectionable and unnecessary.

On another occasion as a result of the detailed reporting of the activities of Miss Christine Keeler and of the evidence given at the trial of Stephen Ward the Press Council warned newspapers of the harm being done to the good name of the Press by the excessive publication of sordid particulars. The Council developed the theme in a later memorandum relating to what is called 'cheque-book journalism'. The Council sought to make it clear that no curb on reporting the news was involved, but pointed out that there was a basic distinction between reporting the news and the elaboration of the news by unsavoury memoirs and other articles of a similar character.

GUARDIAN OF ITS RIGHTS

As guardian of the Press the Council watches developments which overtly or latently threaten the rights of the Press. A case in point followed the publication of the Report of the Vassall tribunal. The Press Council met in special session to consider the implications of the Report for the Press. A statement the Council subsequently issued declared that, while the Press had the right and indeed the duty to investigate and comment on matters concerning national security, the Council condemned the publication in some news-papers of false information and damaging innuendoes based on nothing more than conjecture, assumption, and speculation. Such reports were a serious lowering of the standards of a responsible Press. But the Council went on to express its deep anxiety about the severe penalties of imprisonment imposed on two reporters for declining to depart from the journalistic code of honour to respect confidences. It was vital that newspapers which depended so much on confidential information should continue to be in a position to investigate and ventilate matters of public importance. The Council expressed the belief that there should be a re-examination of the rules which governed contempt of court, especially in relation to Tribunals of Inquiry. (1963/20)

In its evidence to the Royal Commission on Tribunals of Inquiry in 1966 the Press Council reiterated the concern expressed on the dilemma of conscience in which reporters were put during the Vassall Inquiry and which ended in their imprisonment for refusing to depart from the journalist's code of honour to respect confidences. In the case of a journalist the obligation of secrecy was one that the public interest as well as his own professional code required him to observe. It was universally accepted as necessary to the process of democracy that there should be a well-informed Press able to comment critically on public affairs. Recognising this, members of the public would talk freely to a journalist on the understanding not merely that he did not disclose the source of his information, but often also that he did not print the information at all. It was the factual knowledge that a journalist obtained in this way that enabled him to comment fairly and intelligently.

The Council expressed the hope in the course of its evidence that the Royal Commission would not consider the matter simply in relation to the circumstances of the Vassall Inquiry. The question was not merely whether the public interest demanded that the threat of imprisonment should be used to quash conscientious objections. The further question involved was whether, in the long run, it was in the public interest that objectors should be forced to give way. For the sake of information, which it was possible might be of only peripheral value in a particular inquiry, a principle was breached; and, because of the breach, public men would become afraid to make use of the power of the Press in the way in which it should be used — in letting light into places that would otherwise be kept dark.

During the committal proceedings at Aylesbury in the Great Mail Train Robbery case, counsel for the defence threatened the Press that if certain evidence considered prejudicial to the accused was published, contempt proceedings would be taken. A similar threat was made by counsel in another case which came before the Magistrates at Oldham. The Press Council reviewed both cases and issued a forthright and vigorous statement on the right of the Press to report the evidence given in court. The two cases are dealt with in Chapter 15, p. 28.

At the time of the Aberfan disaster, the Attorney-General in a statement in the House of Commons made after the appointment of a Tribunal of Inquiry, gave a warning that further comments on the disaster might be followed by proceedings for contempt of court. The impression was created that the Government was attempting to silence all comment. The Press protested indignantly. The Press Council questioned the validity of the Attorney-General's statement and declared that intrusion into the domain of free speech by ill-defined threats of legal proceedings was harmful to the conduct of public affairs in a free society.

The matter is dealt with in greater detail in Chapter 30.

PROTECTOR OF ITS FREEDOM

'Our liberty depends in freedom of the Press and that cannot be limited without being lost' said Thomas Jefferson, one of the founding fathers and third President of the United States. So strongly did he believe in a free Press that he declared that were it left to him to decide whether the United States should have a government without newspapers or newspapers without a government, he would not hesitate for a moment to decide in favour of the newspapers.

There is often a tendency on the part of those who govern and of the governed to regard freedom of the Press as a mere catch phrase. But if the Press ceased to be free so, too, would the people. As Jefferson realised, Press freedom is the guarantee of all freedoms. Yet despite their purported support for the freedom of the Press, there are those who are not reluctant to urge statutory controls and restrictions on the Press as the debates in Parliament show. The same is equally true of local authorities and other organisations responsible for administering public funds. While on particular occasions there may be good reason for sitting in private, often the passion for secrecy results in unwarranted exclusion of the Press from meetings.

The Press Council has shown itself watchful for any challenge to the freedom of the Press, however indirect or concealed it may be; where it detects a challenge the Council is swift and vigorous to expose it. The history of the Press Council is, indeed, largely the history of its defence of Press freedom.

Two instances illustrate the range of the Press Council's interest.

LOCAL AUTHORITIES

In its first Annual Report, 1954, the Council commented that relations between the Press and local authorities were a subject of continuing difficulty, because too much public business was done in private to the detriment of the interests of the ratepayers.

Journalists had long wanted to see the Local Government (Admission of the Press to Meetings) Act of 1908 which gave the Press the legal right to be present at local authority meetings amended and brought up to date. Since that measure came into effect many new authorities had come into existence, including administrative tribunals and bodies to deal with nationalised industries and institutions, and it was generally felt that their activities should be reported. Many did co-operate with the Press, but others in varying degrees were hostile to the admission of reporters to their meetings. The various organisations of the Press had for a good many years tried to have the law amended, and a conference of these organisations had drawn up proposals to secure the right to report more freely the proceedings of authorities that spent public money. The Press Council stated that it was the one body that could now claim to speak for all sections of the Press and that its influence would be important when a Bill incorporating these proposals was introduced into Parliament.

Under the 1908 Act the Press had the right, except where temporarily excluded by resolution in the public interest, to attend and report local authority meetings, but the local authority by going into committee could still exclude the Press, and projects involving large public funds were often debated and decided in secret. Not much progress was made in getting the law amended until the printing dispute in 1959 brought matters to a head. Several city councils declared that emergency editions of newspapers affected by the dispute were 'black' and decided by going into committee to exclude the Press and to exclude reporters from meetings of various committees to which they customarily had access; instructions were given to the Medical Officer of Health, the Fire Brigade and waterworks officials to refuse information concerning their departments; schoolteachers were forbidden to invite the local Press to prize-givings and sports days; newspapers were banned from public libraries. Nottingham City Council excluded the Press, but not the B.B.C., from meetings on the grounds that the B.B.C. was the public, but the Press was not.

This discrimination against the Press gave rise to protests from many quarters; the Press Council passed the following emergency resolution:

The General Council of the Press condemns the action of those local authorities, which, during the present dispute in the printing industry, have excluded journalists from their proceedings. The Council regards such action as a gross violation of the right of the subject to be kept informed of the proceedings of his elected representatives.

Before the strike, while the Press was pressing for more liberal treatment, the Minister of Housing and Local Government, Mr Henry Brooke, expressed the view that the enlargement of Press rights to report meetings of local authorities would be better resolved by goodwill among the parties than by further legislation, but he had warned that, if these consultations did not result in a satisfactory solution of the difficulties, he would have no hesitation in recommending the Government to introduce legislation. Following the action taken by the Leeds Corporation during the printing strike of withholding news from the Press, the Minister, through the Permanent Secretary of his department, wrote to the Town Clerk that he had had a number of complaints about the exclusion of the Press, including one that Press representatives were required to leave a meeting when members of the public and representatives of the B.B.C. were allowed to remain. The Minister reminded the Council that the Press was entitled to be present at meetings under the 1908 Act unless the nature of the business made exclusion advisable in the public interest, and that the Press could not lawfully be excluded for any other reason. The Press on this occasion had been excluded for reasons not connected with the confidential nature of the business, but solely because of the printing dispute. The Minister had no doubt that the action of the Council was contrary to the spirit of the Act and to the principles which local authorities should observe in their relations with the Press. He was wholly out of sympathy with any council which deprived local electors of the opportunity of informing themselves from Press reports about Council business; he was also out of sympathy with any local authority which took sides in an industrial dispute.

The Permanent Secretary went on to state that the Minister believed that the great majority of local authorities recognised their responsibility to keep the public fully informed at all times, but there were exceptions, and he had made it plain in Parliament that he would not be content until all local authorities gave full facilities to the Press. He had also said he would not hesitate to propose amending legislation if this proved necessary. It had been his hope that all could be brought to observe a proper code in this matter without the need for new legislation. He was, therefore, gravely concerned that some local authorities had taken action during the printing dispute which suggested that they attached little importance to keeping the electorate informed. He might be forced to conclude that the object which he had in view and which he was sure was shared by the great majority of responsible local government opinion, could be secured only by imposing new statutory obligations and a new procedure for enforcement on all local authorities.

The Minister sent a copy of the letter to the Press for publication.

The new legislation foreshadowed in this letter was introduced as a Private Member's Bill. It had the blessing of the Government and became law as The Public Bodies (Admission to Meetings) Act, 1960. Under this Act any meeting of a local authority or any other body exercising public functions to which the Act applied (the list was set out in the Schedule to the Act) was to be open to the public. The public could be excluded from meetings only when publicity would be prejudicial to the public interest by reason of the confidential nature of the business. Reasonable facilities for reporting the proceedings of meetings open to the public were to be afforded to the Press.

ATTEMPTED CENSORSHIP

From time to time attempts are made to narrow the coverage of the Press. An example was the attempt by a Private Member's Bill to introduce legislation to prevent the publication of the contents of wills of deceased persons. The Press Council strongly opposed it. It was argued against the Bill that a will on which probate had been granted was a public document and as such could be inspected by anyone. Interest in how much money a man had left was legitimate, and to enforce silence on this subject would be against the public interest. The publication of wills yielded valuable public information about the distribution of wealth, and the Press Council contended that the circumstances did not call for the censorship proposed. No progress was made with the Bill.

A BAN ON PRESS REPORTS — THE TUCKER COMMITTEE

The purpose of proceedings known as committal proceedings is to enable the examining justices to establish whether the evidence of an offence to be tried on indictment is sufficient to put the accused upon trial by jury. Although the proceedings safeguard the accused against committal on a frivolous or malicious prosecution, and give him details of the evidence he will have to face at the trial, the proceedings have been much criticised on the ground that they are time-wasting, unnecessary and indeed prejudicial. As a rule only the prosecution case is heard during the committal proceedings, the case for the defence is generally reserved until the trial; the risk of prejudice is further increased by the possibility that evidence admitted by the magistrates may be excluded by the trial judge, or, as in the case of Dr Bodkin Adams, evidence of a highly prejudicial character presented by the prosecution at the commital proceedings may not be tendered at the trial.

The Byrne Committee in Depositions in 1949 expressed the view that committal proceedings before examining magistrates were no mere formality. But many people disagreed with this view and considered that committal proceedings were in fact a formality and a very wasteful one.

In 1957 the Home Secretary, Mr R. A. Butler, set up a Departmental Committee presided over by Lord Tucker 'to consider whether proceedings before examining justices should continue to take place in open court, and if so, whether it is necessary or desirable that any restriction should be placed on the publication of reports of such proceedings'.

The inquiry had its origin in the trial at the Central Criminal Court of Dr Bodkin Adams for the murder of one of his patients. The doctor was acquitted, but there was a general uneasiness that the verdict might have gone the other way because of the prejudicial effect on the jury of evidence given on behalf of the prosecution before the examining magistrates, but not at the trial, of the circumstances in which two other patients of the doctor had died.

In his summing up to the jury at the trial the presiding Judge expressed the opinion that it would have been wiser if the magistrates had decided to sit in private, as they could have done. In a case which had aroused widespread discussion it was inevitable, said the Judge, that reports should appear in the Press and be read by people who subsequently had to serve on the jury. He also pointed out that proceedings before the magistrates might be quite different from the proceedings as they subsequently emerged at the trial.

The Tucker Committee was not concerned with the merits of committal proceedings; by its terms of reference the Committee's inquiry was confined to the consideration of the possible dangers of pre-trial publicity.

The possibility that the publication of court proceedings might be restricted immediately put the Press and the Press Council on the alert. From the outset the Press Council took the view that if proceedings are held in open court the Press has the right and duty to report them. It is one thing for magistrates to sit in private where there is a danger that the publication of evidence prior to trial may prejudice the defence; it is quite another thing to suppress publication where the court sits in public. An informed public is a necessity if justice is to be properly administered, and the public can only be informed on the conduct of judicial proceedings if the Press is able to report them.

The evidence given to the Tucker Committee by representatives of Press organisations and by journalists was almost unanimous in its opposition to any change in the existing law.

In a memorandum to the Committee the Press Council made the following points:

(1) The contentions that preliminary hearings ought to be in private were based on inadequate knowledge of the working of justice. The opening of the case before the magistrates checked rumour and gossip.

(2) At the preliminary hearing the accused learned of the charges that he had to face.

(3) Those who wished to curb Press reports were nevertheless ready to admit the public to the court. This was an inadequate and often misleading way of reporting by word of mouth.

(4) The Press Council did not think that reading a report of the magistrates' hearing would permanently prejudice someone who later served as a juryman in the case; faith in trial by jury rested upon the approved ability of juries to respond to the direction of the judge to come to their verdict on the evidence, disregarding whatever they might have heard and read elsewhere.

(5) The work of the justices should be done with the full knowledge of the public.

(6) Magistrates have power to hear evidence in private but except for special reasons all stages in the committtal proceedings should be conducted in open court with all its powerful safeguards.

After hearing evidence from many sources, the Tucker Committee agreed that there were formidable objections to examining justices sitting *in camera*. It was not possible to establish that trials were prejudiced by reports of committal proceedings but there was a widespread belief that they were. The Committee recommended that newspaper reports of committal proceedings should be restricted to particulars of the name of the accused, the charge and the decision of the court. (Cmnd, 479, pars. 70, 71.)

No immediate action was taken on the recommendation, but in January 1965 the Home Secretary, Mr Frank Soskice, stated that the Government had decided that reports of committal proceedings should be restricted in the manner recommended by the Tucker Committee.

The announcement caused the Press Council to re-examine the whole question. The Council's views given to the Tucker Committee had been put forward by the old Press Council when Sir Linton Andrews was Chairman. The views now expressed by the new Council were no less disapproving.

The statement put out by the Press Council after the Home Secretary's announcement recalled the terms of reference of the Tucker Committee, the nature of its recommendations and the fact that the Press Council had given evidence in support of the view that the law and practice in committal proceedings should remain unaltered, and went on to say that, notwithstanding the authority and reasoning of the Tucker Report, the Council remained of the same opinion. The Council acknowledged that there were weighty arguments in favour of the view that committal proceedings should in certain circumstances be held in whole or in part in private and that the fair trial of an accused person must always be the paramount consideration. But the Council believed that judicial proceedings, especially committal proceedings, should always be held in public unless that should be contrary to the ends of justice in a particular case. The Council said that it would not repeat the arguments and evidence it had laid before the Tucker Committee, but wished to make it clear that it was very much concerned where a restriction on Press reporting was contemplated.

The Council then referred to the passage in the Tucker Report which said 'it is a serious matter to fetter the freedom of the Press to report what is done in public by a public body'. The Committee's decision to recommend a breach of this fundamental principle was, the Council said, based upon a misunderstanding of the nature of publicity in a modern society and of the functions of the Press in relation to it.

The Tucker Committee itself had recognised the need for publicity, and the Council recalled this extract from their Report:

There are weighty objections to committal proceedings being generally held in camera:

(*a*) There is a general distaste for the idea of justice being administered in a court of law behind locked doors.

(*b*) If examining justices were to dismiss a charge when sitting in camera, it might be suspected that some favouritism had been shown to the accused.

(*c*) There might be suspicion that the conduct of proceedings did not come up to the normal high standards of magistrates' courts.

The Press Council contended that it was unreal to suppose that any of these objections could be successfully overcome simply by admitting members of the public to the proceedings as it was proposed to do. In the ordinary unsensational case the public might not even be present. In the exceptional case the court might be crowded with sensation-seekers, but they would not be people qualified to detect signs of favouritism or judicial misbehaviour or to do anything about it if they did. The only way in which suspicion could be effectively dispelled was if it was known that there were present throughout trained reporters with the experience to criticise where criticism was needed and with organs of publicity at their disposal in which criticism would be effectively expressed. To admit members of the public, but to deny all facilities to the newspapers, was to mistake the forms of publicity for the substance.

The Press Council went on to say that the function of the Press was to provide the public with up-to-date news, not events that happened long before. It was hardly to be expected that a newspaper would find space at the end of the trial or when the accused was discharged to publish a report of the committal proceedings to bring to light instances of judicial misbehaviour.

In the few cases in which the justices refused to commit, and the percentage was extremely small, a newspaper would in theory be able to publish a full report at once. It was at least doubtful, however, whether editors would send reporters to cover committal proceedings when there was only a very remote chance that a contemporaneous report could be used.

The Tucker Report, the Press Council said, was bad in principle and in practice and did not meet realistically the weighty objections the report itself set forth to committal proceedings being generally held *in camera*.

Copies of the statements were sent to all Members of Parliament.

As a result of these a change of mind on the part of the Government appears to have occurred. Replying to a Parliamentary Question on 29 April

1966 the Home Secretary, Mr Roy Jenkins, said that he wished to give further consideration to the whole question of committal proceedings before introducing legislation; he denied the suggestion that he was yielding to Press pressure in not adopting the Tucker recommendations at once. Some months later, on 12 December, during a debate on the Criminal Justice Bill the Government proposed to submit to Parliament, Mr Jenkins said:

> I considered carefully whether it would be possible to sweep away committal proceedings completely, but this, I became convinced, would not be right. No one ought to be put on trial at assizes or quarter sessions — and perhaps spend about six weeks in custody awaiting this — without some preliminary judicial investigation. In certain cases, also, it is a real advantage to the defence to have the evidence sifted at this stage. Furthermore, a decision has to be made as to whether or not bail should be granted. For all these reasons we cannot get rid of committal proceedings entirely. But we can greatly restrict their role. What I propose is that the prosecution, if they do not desire committal proceedings, will serve on the accused copies of the statements of the prosecution witnesses. If, having seen the statements, the accused does not wish any of the witnesses to be called to give evidence orally, he will be brought before the justices and committed for trial on the basis of the written statements and in much curtailed proceedings.
>
> If either the prosecution or the defence wish witnesses to be called at this stage, they can be called, but only the witnesses who are specifically requested, so that the proceedings will still remain substantially simplified. If these proposals are put into effect I believe that only a small proportion of witnesses would have to give oral evidence at the committal stage, and that we would produce a substantially streamlined but equally just judicial system. The saving of police time should be considerable.
>
> I have also had to consider what should be the rule in the new circumstances about the reporting of committal proceedings. The Tucker Committee, which reported as long ago as 1958, recommended that there should be a ban, somewhat similar to that which has applied for 40 years to the reporting of evidence in divorce cases. It is easy to understand some of the reasons for this. In a sensational case like the Moors Murder the public are served up with the revolting details twice over. In other cases the defence might be harmed by the difficulty, after a well-publicised preliminary hearing, of finding an unprejudiced jury.

In other cases substantial damage might be done to a man's reputation by the publication of an uncontested prosecution case and not corrected by the less interesting news, six weeks later, of his acquittal. To balance against these considerations there is the natural repugnance of most of us for court proceedings not being fully publicised.

The new rules will create a new situation. In many committal proceedings there will be no evidence to report. For the remainder I think the fairest arrangement is that the defence should always be given the right to opt for publicity, but that if they do not do so there should be a restriction on reports of more than the bare details of committal proceedings until the trial has been completed. In this way I think the main purpose of the Tucker recommendations can be achieved without any measurable restrictions of the rights of Press or public.

At the end of 1966 the Criminal Justice Bill was laid before Parliament.

In accordance with the recommendations of the Tucker Committee, Clause 3 of the Bill made it unlawful to publish or broadcast reports of committal proceedings beyond the bare facts of the committal until the case had been finally disposed of either by the examining justices or by the court of trial. If, however, the accused applied for the removal of the restriction, the court could make an order allowing a full report.

Subject to this the only matters that could be contained in a report of committal proceedings were:

(a) The identity of the court and the names of the examining justices.

(b) The names, addresses and occupations of the parties and witnesses, and the ages of the defendant and witnesses.

(c) The nature of the offence with which the defendant was charged.

(d) The names of Counsel and Solicitors engaged in the proceedings.

(e) Any decision of the court to commit the defendant.

(f) The charge and the court to which the defendant was committed.

(g) In the event of committal proceedings being adjourned the date and place to which they are adjourned.

(h) Any arrangements as to bail.

(i) Whether legal aid was granted to the defendant.

If the report of the proceedings goes beyond these limitations the proprietor, editor or publisher of the newspaper is to be liable on summary conviction to a fine not exceeding £500.

On 23 January 1967 the Home Secretary, Mr Roy Jenkins, met a deputation of the newspaper proprietors, editors and journalists, who objected to the provisions. The deputation stated that the restrictions of court reporting would operate against the public interest and would create difficulties for those concerned in newspaper production. The Home Secretary said he would consider the objection.

On 16 March the Press Council itself put out a statement which trenchantly criticised the Bill. In the statement the Council said that having considered the substantial amendment of procedure in the committal of defendants for trial and the restrictions imposed on Press reporting provided by the Criminal Justice Bill the Council saw no reason to depart from its earlier criticism of the Tucker Committee's Report.

The Council's statement went on to condemn unequivocally the provision that allowed the public to attend committal proceedings but denied newspapers the right to publish other than a formal record of committal or adjournment. The illogical association of acceptance of the principle that justice shall be administered in public with a restriction that confined knowledge of what was done to the few members of the community who could afford the time to attend the court made a mockery of the principle it was professed to support. The absurdity of the provision was heightened by the fact that whereas newspaper proprietors, editors and publishers responsible for a published report of a committal hearing unauthorised by the Bill would be liable to a heavy fine, any member of the public could go away from the court and talk freely about what was said and done without danger of prosecution. Apparently he could relate his version of the proceedings to a public meeting with the same immunity.

The dangers of rumour and distortion of fact that could arise from this state of affairs, the Council declared, ought not to need emphasis. The Press Council would continue to protest against mock publicity where it related to legal proceedings or anything else.

The only alternative mode of procedure, if the Government was determined not to allow newspaper publication of evidence given in committal proceedings, was to hold the pre-trial processes *in camera*; there was, however, widespread public distaste for the administration of justice behind closed doors and general recognition of dangers of maladministration inherent in the practice. In making the choice between publicity and secrecy, and there was no defensible half-way stage, particular regard should be paid to the categorical statement by the Tucker Committee that it was not possible to establish either that trials were prejudiced by newspaper reports of committal proceedings or that they were not. This basic fact revealed clearly that the cause of justice did not require fundamental alteration in procedure, even though personal convenience and financial considerations might make it attractive.

The consequential difficulties in newspaper reporting that the proposed legislation would cause were considerable. The Press Council took its stand on the level of the ordinary citizen in a free country whose concern it was to see that the ends of justice were served by adequate public provision of knowledge of what the nation's judiciary was doing in his name.

At the time this book went to press, it appeared unlikely that the Government would yield to the opposition of the Press Council and refrain from giving statutory effect to the recommendations of the Tucker Committee.

However, the Home Secretary, perhaps to mollify the critics, said in the course of a speech on 1 July 1967 that he was thinking of abolishing committal proceedings altogether. Mr Jenkins pointed out that at present these proceedings were necessary in England, otherwise the decision of whether someone should stand trial on indictment would be left solely to the Police. He went on to say 'Perhaps a different system of prosecution, more akin to that prevailing in Scotland where the decision to prosecute rests with an independent prosecutor, could be applied with profit to England as well.' He had no yet reached any decision on the point but he intended to see that a thorough study was made of the possible relevance of the Scottish system to English law.

It has often been said in justification of the publication of committal proceedings that publication may assist an accused person by bringing forward new evidence. Concrete examples are few but, by a coincidence, in May 1967, while the controversial provision in the Criminal Justice Bill for banning the publication of these proceedings was still under consideration, a case did occur.

A man arrested for attacking and robbing a hospital nurse was picked out at an identification parade; he was committed for trial on a charge of robbery with violence.

When he appeared for trial at Leeds Assizes, counsel for the prosecution told the Judge, Mr Justice Howard, that as a result of the publication of the committal proceedings a man had come forward and confessed to the crime; he said that he did not want someone else to suffer for what he had done. The

Police, after investigating the confession, were satisfied the wrong man had been charged.

On the direction of the Judge, the jury found the accused not guilty.

GUIDE, ADVISER AND ALLY

Guidance on journalistic standards, advice on matters germane to the Press and active support in combat to maintain a free Press, are some of the variety of ways the Press Council serves the Press. In the final analysis, the influence and authority of the Press Council depend on the trust, goodwill and respect it inspires in the Press. The miscellaneous services rendered by the Council promote and follow from harmonious relations.

The Annual Reports record the adjudications of the Council, review the debates in Parliament relating to the Press, call attention to important legal decision and generally give information and valuable advice. Some instances follow.

TWO IMPORTANT JUDGMENTS

In the 1960 Annual Report attention was called to two important cases.

One was a cause of contempt of court in Scotland; it arose out of the publication in the *Scottish Daily Mail* of a picture of a man detained by the police in connection with the murder of a girl; the picture was accompanied by a report of interviews with the relatives and friends of the accused and of the murdered girl. The Press Council published this extract from the judgment of the Lord Justice-General (Lord Clyde):

> The Press in this country is free, free, in particular, fairly to report anything in open court when a trial takes place, free to publicise anything that is said or done by a judge or a counsel or a witness, or by the jury at that trial. For in doing so the Press is performing a genuine public service in enabling the public to see for themselves whether justice is being done. The high standard of discrimination and fairness with which this work has been done by responsible Scottish newspapers has made it unnecessary for our Courts to lay down rules in this matter. We have been content to rely on their honour, their good sense and their discrimination. But freedom does not mean licence, and the freedom which the Press rightly enjoys carries its own responsibilities. If freedom is abused, and if the content of a newspaper is such as to be likely to

endanger the prospects of a fair and impartial trial in Scotland, then it is the duty of this Court, and it has always been recognised to be the duty of this Court, to take cognisance of it and to punish the wrong that such conduct involves.

The other case was an action for defamation against *The Times* in respect of an alleged libel contained in a report of the trial in Switzerland of a British subject for the murder of a Swiss citizen. The action was a test case on the outcome of which depended whether actions against a number of other English newspapers which had carried similar reports of the trial would be proceeded with. The question of law raised by the case was whether privilege attached to a fair and accurate report published in English newspapers of a case tried in a foreign court. The statutory privilege under the Defamation Act, 1952, did not extend to proceedings in a foreign court, but the judge held that the case created a legitimate and proper 'interest' to the public, as distinct from an 'idle curiosity', and the report of the trial was therefore privileged at common law.

CROWN COPYRIGHT

The Press Council sought clarification of an official announcement and published the result of its inquiries in the Annual Report for the benefit of the Press related to the question of Crown copyright, a subject generally dealt with by section 39 of the Copyright Act, 1956.

Crown copyright is vested in the Controller of Her Majesty's Stationery Office, and permission to reproduce from official material may be given only by him or by departments to which delegated authority has been given. The practice with regard to Crown copyright is indicated in a Treasury circular dated 9 January 1958 which divides Government publications into a number of classes, the first three of which were

(1) Bills and Acts of Parliament, Statutory Rules and Orders and Statutory Instruments.

(2) Other Parliamentary papers including reports of Select Committees of both Houses and papers laid before Parliament by statute and by command.

(3) The official report of the House of Lords and House of Commons (Hansard).

On 5 March 1965 an announcement appeared in the *London Gazette* of a revision in the terms of paragraph 5 of the 1958 circular. The revised paragraph was in the following terms:

It is in the public interest that the information contained in publications falling in the first three classes should be diffused as widely as possible, and legal rights of the Crown in respect of copyright in them will not normally be enforced. But all Crown rights in respect of them are reserved, and will be asserted in cases considered by the Controller of Her Majesty's Stationery Office as exceptional — for example, in the case of reproduction of any part of any publication in these classes in undesirable contexts, or reproduction of the whole or a substantial part of any such publication, either as a separate document or as a major part of another work, in such a way as to result in a significant loss to public funds. Copies of Acts of Parliament, Statutory Rules and Orders and Statutory Instruments other than those reproduced by or by the order of the Stationery Office, must not purport to be published by authority. Applicants desiring to make reproductions from the Official Report of Parliamentary Debates (Hansard) should be warned that any person or body publishing unofficial reports of proceedings in Parliament, even though they are verbatim reports of speeches as reported in the Official Report, may not enjoy, in proceedings for defamation, privilege as extensive as that enjoyed by the Official Report. Reproductions from the Official Report in connection with advertising are not permitted.

The Press Council thought that comparatively few newspapers would be likely to possess copies of the 1958 circular; it therefore asked the Controller of the Stationery Office for clarification of the 1965 amendment.

The Controller said that the amendment did not represent any change of policy. In the three classes of publications specified above the Crown would permit normal newspaper quotation without the need for prior permission, but the reproduction of the whole or a substantial portion of a Crown copyright publication in a way that would result in a significant loss in public funds would not be allowed without consent.

The rights of the Crown in the three classes mentioned had never been allowed to lapse, but previous Treasury statements had not indicated the type of circumstances in which the enforcement might be pursued. The point was brought to focus by a national newspaper's reproduction in full of the Denning Report, for which a four-figure fee had been paid, and by a provincial daily's printing of a substantial section of another Report without prior permission. It was estimated that both these publications affected the sale of the official publication and so resulted in a loss to public funds.

The Controller further explained that the principle of charging fees for special reproduction of Crown copyright publications had been practised for many years, but, in the absence of the emphasis now given by the new paragraph 5 of the circular, there had been an impression in some quarters that these fees were not payable in respect of the classes mentioned.

In assessing fees it was the practice of the Controller's department to base them on the value of the material to the applicant and the extent to which private reproduction would affect revenue from sales of an official publication. The Controller had complete discretion to waive or reduce fees in appropriate circumstances. The revised instruction would not alter this practice.

29 The Moors Murder Trial — Press Council's Declaration of Principle

'Is not this a matter which requires investigation? No doubt, Mr Attorney, you will see that this is done.'

Mr Justice Fenton Atkinson interrupted the cross-examination of David Smith, the principal witness for the prosecution at the trial of Ian Brady and Myra Hindley in what came to be known as the Moors Murder case, to put this question to the Attorney-General, leading for the prosecution.

'I can assure my lord,' the Attorney-General replied, 'that the investigation will take place immediately and most thoroughly.'

'And you will consider what action, if any, is desirable,' the judge added. 'It seems to be a gross interference with the course of justice.'

The murders with which Brady, who was twenty-seven, and Hindley, twenty-three, were charged were of a peculiarly brutal and gruesome nature. The bodies of two of the victims, a girl of ten and a boy of twelve had been buried on the moors; the body of the third victim, a youth aged seventeen, which was discovered in the house occupied by the accused, was intended, it was believed, for burial there, too.

The judge's intervention occurred when it emerged from the cross-examination of Smith, an eye-witness to the murder of the youth, that Smith was under contract to a newspaper for a series of articles about the crime. Under the agreement he was to be paid £1000 for his story and in addition was to participate in the syndication rights. The newspaper had paid the expenses of a trip to France for Smith and his wife; it was paying his hotel expenses during the trial, and a sum of £15 a week, the payments were to be set off against the lump sum he was to receive.

Counsel suggested to Smith that if Brady and Hindley were acquitted the value of his story would be greatly reduced and asked:

'You have a vested financial interest in their conviction?'

'Yes, sir,' Smith replied.

Asked the name of the newspaper to which he was under agreement Smith refused to give it. He said that many reporters had called at his flat before the trial, usually leaving their cards and a five-pound-note. (No evidence in corroboration of this was given.) Smith, who was eighteen, admitted that he had discussed with Brady an armed robbery of a bank that he had agreed to take part in and had even been keeping watch on a certain bank to this end. He also admitted that he had previous convictions for violence.

When Smith refused to identify the newspaper which had purchased his story, the *News of the World* the same day issued the following statement:

> The unidentified newspaper mentioned in the Moors Trial was in fact the *News of the World*. This information was immediately given to the Attorney-General by us early this afternoon.

Some days later the Press Council made the following announcement:

> The Press Council has taken cognizance of statements made during the hearing of the Moors Murder Trial at Chester Assizes, about a witness's alleged financial arrangement with a newspaper.
>
> The Council has asked the newspaper concerned to furnish a statement, but in conformity with its practice will not consider the ethical aspect until the legal implications, if any, have been resolved.

No further reference was made in court during the trial to the agreement made with the *News of the World* by the witness Smith; the Attorney-General subsequently told Parliament that he had decided not to proceed against the newspaper for contempt, because he was satisfied that an interference with the course of justice had not occurred.

This was the conclusion reached by the judge also. In his summing up to the jury Mr Justice Fenton Atkinson said: 'I do not think it is suggested that the substance of his [Smith's] evidence has been substantially affected by this extraordinary arrangement with this newspaper.'

In the House of Commons on 12 May the Attorney-General answered a number of questions on the matter. Mr Gresham Cooke asked him if he would instruct the Director of Public Prosecutions to bring proceedings against the newspapers which made payments to witnesses for articles and stories, in view of the fact that such payments have the effect of suborning witnesses.

The Attorney-General replied:

There is no evidence that the testimony of any witnesses in the murder trial was affected by the payments in question. After careful considera-tion I have decided not to take proceedings in respect of the newspaper concerned. However, the practice of paying witnesses for information about the subject matter of the trial and interviewing them about that information before they give evidence does give rise to serious problems in relation to the administration of justice. Accordingly, the Govern-ment proposes to examine these problems with a view to making such changes in the law as may prove necessary.

In a supplementary question, Mr Gresham Cooke asked Sir Elwyn whether he was aware that many people thought that practices of the nature evidenced in the Moors Trial should be stamped on very hard because of the belief that payments to witnesses in criminal trials where the sums were bigger if convictions were secured might influence the evidence given.

The Attorney-General said that he was aware of the public concern and shared it himself. He did not, however, accept the suggestion that in this particular case a bigger sum was offered in the event of a conviction. It would be unfair to the newspaper concerned to allow the suggestion to remain unchallenged.

In replying to a question from another member the Attorney-General said that one of the matters he had had to consider was whether under the agree-ment the witness in the Moors case was to receive payment only in the event of a particular result of the trial. This did not appear to have been the case. The factor which decided him not to take proceedings was the knowledge that the evidence of the witness Smith and the evidence of his wife had not been affected by the payments made by the newspaper.

Mr Grimond asked the Attorney-General to bear in mind when con-sidering any changes in the law that might be necessary that responsibility must lie on the proprietors and owners of newspapers and not be sloughed off on to editors and newspapermen.

Sir Elwyn agreed and said it was essential that in this country there should be no trial by newspaper and that the fountain of justice should not be polluted by external pressures.

Mr Carlisle asked whether the important point was not so much whether payment was contingent on the result as whether or not the witness thought that it was.

Sir Elwyn replied that it seemed to him that the process of questioning a witness at length before he gave evidence at the trial had possibilities of grave impropriety for the proper conduct of the trial. He concluded:

> I am grateful that these questions and opinions that have been expressed in the House have underlined the importance of the matter. I hope that, even before any Government action is taken, Fleet Street will now put its house in order.

The statement of the Attorney-General that he proposed to introduce legislation to deal with the practice of newspapers paying witnesses for information was a plain warning to the Press that the Government was in earnest. However the invitation to the Press to put its house in order, suggested that if it did so Government action might not be necessary. If this was a correct interpretation of his remarks the choice left to the Press was whether it would discontinue an indefensible practice voluntarily or under compulsion.

When the Moors trial ended the Press Council considered the conduct of the newspaper as it had announced it would. The purchase of Smith's story by the *News of the World* appeared to be a case of cheque-book journalism of the kind the Council had condemned in 1963. Since the agreement with Smith might have influenced his evidence there was a question whether the agreement did not also constitute contempt of court. This was a question of law and one for the court to decide. Whatever the judge and the Attorney-General may have thought about the ethics of the agreement, they were only directly concerned to ascertain whether its effect was likely to prejudice the fair trial of the accused.

The danger of legislation of the kind the Attorney-General had threatened was that it might not be confined to preventing newspapers having dealings with witnesses before they gave their evidence. The opportunity might be taken of new legislation to provide a stricter control over what could be published in the Press and to create a kind of censorship which many critics of the Press had been demanding for years.

In any case the Attorney-General's statement in the Commons on 12 May calling on Fleet Streeet to put its house in order was taken very seriously by the Press Council. Lord Devlin went to see the Prime Minister and the Attorney-General.

The Lord Chancellor, Lord Gardiner, informed the House of Lords some days later (25 May) that Lord Devlin had said when he met the Prime Minister that he recognised that what happened in the Moors case was a matter of great gravity which called for urgent consideration and that the Press Council would consider it from that point of view. Lord Gardiner went on to state his own view that it was obviously wrong for a witness to be paid money by a newspaper, or for a newspaper to agree to pay money under circumstances in which the probability was that the money would not be payable unless there was a conviction.

The Press Council thought that the best way to meet the concern of the Government would be to give assurances in the form of a declaration of principle in respect of practices that were indisputably repugnant. If the declaration was to have any weight the Council had to have the support of the Press and be able to satisfy the Government that the Press would honour the declaration.

A committee of the Council was appointed to draft the declaration. When it had done so Lord Devlin sent copies to the Editors of all the national newspapers and through the President of the Guild of Newspaper Editors to representative editors of provincial publications with a covering letter asking editors for their views on the draft and inviting them to attend a meeting of the Drafting Committee if they wished to discuss any particular point.

The draft declaration was widely drawn and dealt with three matters: (1) the payment of witnesses in criminal proceedings for information for a story; (2) the questioning of witnesses about their evidence before they gave it; (3) the publication of personal and feature stories of an unsavoury nature.

From the comments and suggestions made by editors the declaration gradually took shape in the form it was finally published. Some of the observations made on the proposal to ban payment of witnesses were:

A ban of this kind till the end of the trial was extreme. A differentiation should be made between a proper inquiry and a practice everyone wanted to stop.

Reporters should have a right to question eye-witnesses before legal proceedings began, even though the people questioned would probably be witnesses in subsequent proceedings.

The ban should apply not to a person 'likely' to be a witness, but only to a person 'subpoenaed' to be one.

One newspaper made the point that no ban of any kind was required. Everybody deplored an attempt to subvert the course of justice by the payment of money to witnesses, but the law of contempt of court enabled cases of this kind to be dealt with, and legislation was not needed.

Points made by editors on the subject of questioning witnesses about their evidence before they gave it in court were:

It is often necessary for newspapers to prepare background information for publication after the case has ended. This is reasonable newspaper practice in the interest of the public and may often entail informal interviews with people who will be witnesses, generally prosecution witnesses. Questions to these witnesses on background are unlikely to influence their evidence.

The ban would stop the kind of character study of the Moors Murder psychopaths presented in certain newspapers after the trial, based on interviewing the witnesses.

The ban should not prevent the publication of a story which exposes a racket or illegal practice which could lead to a criminal prosecution.

One editor cited the case of the kennelmaid who had been paid for information in a dog-doping case which eventually led to the prosecution and conviction of the men she accused. It was clear when she was paid that she would be a key witness in the event of the exposure leading to criminal proceedings.

A similar case quoted by another editor was the case of the bribed footballers who were prosecuted and convicted as the result of a story published in the *People* which the newspaper purchased from the man at the centre of the scandal.

These exposures, it was argued, would not have been possible if payment to potential witnesses had not been possible as the draft declaration proposed.

Another editor pointed out that over recent years there had been a number of occasions when newspapers had made payments or offers of payments in the pursuit of legitimate inquiries which would be ruled out if the payment of witnesses was banned without reservation.

Other points were that the interests of justice might require witnesses to be questioned between committal and trial, where, for example, a newspaper believed a wrong man had been identified or there had been perjury at the committal proceedings.

What was the position of a newspaper which wished to make inquiries while minor proceedings were going on about other and more serious matters.

The Press should be able to talk to witnesses in the same way as other members of the public. An interview might bring additional facts to light which would assist the course of justice.

There was more difficulty on the third subject of the declaration, the publication of personal and feature stories of an unsavoury nature. Some of the observations by editors on this were:

The intention was admirable, but blanket prohibitions were to be deprecated.

Censorship of any kind should be opposed. If a ban on unsavoury publications was applied it should be so worded as to be clear that the public interest was the dominant consideration and would override the ban.

What was 'unsavoury' and what constituted 'the public interest' were difficult to define. They were questions upon which editorial judgment must be freely exercisable; this was the very basis of the freedom of the Press.

A newspaper's job, like that of a camera, was to reflect the society in which we live, warts and all. The editor making the point went on to state that he would prefer to have more freedom than was implicit in the proposed declaration, but to be subject, as now, to the censure of the Press Council and to the penalties of the law if he misconstrued his duty.

Another editor was of the opinion that the proposed declaration should be confined to those matters which arose during the Moors Trial and should not be extended to include unrelated aspects of Press conduct. The matter which concerned Parliament, the public, and the Press Council was the paying and questioning of witnesses actually involved in criminal proceedings. The Press Council should not try to restrict in advance the judgment of editors as to what they might or might not buy or publish. These were matters for the judgment and integrity of editors.

A study of the declaration in the form it finally took will show the points made by the editors on the original draft and the safeguards they considered necessary have been largely incorporated. The complete declaration is set out in Appendix V. The ban on the practices now declared contrary to approved journalistic conduct in the following terms:

1. No payment or offer of payment should be made by a newspaper to any person known or reasonably expected to be a witness in criminal proceedings already begun in exchange for any story or information in connection with the proceedings until they have been concluded.

2. No witness in committal proceedings should be questioned on behalf of any newspaper about the subject matter of his evidence until the trial has been concluded.

3. No payment should be made for feature articles to persons engaged in crime or other notorious misbehaviour where the public interest does not warrant it; as the Council has previously declared, it deplores publication of personal articles of an unsavoury nature by persons who have been concerned in criminal acts or vicious conduct.

A reasonable latitude to question witnesses is preserved by the provisions that: 'The Council does not intend that the principles enunciated shall preclude reasonable contemporaneous inquiries in relation to the commission of crime when these are carried out with due regard to the administration of justice.'

In regard to the ban on payments to persons engaged in crime and other notorious behaviour, reservation was made where it is necessary in the public interest. The Council realised that it was not possible to lay down rigid and arbitrary rules. The Declaration stated: 'No code can cover every case. Satisfactory observance of the principles must depend upon the discretion and sense of responsibility of editors and newspaper proprietors.'

Finally the Declaration put on record that it had been prepared in consultation with newspaper editors, and it acknowledged the wide support given by them to the broad principles it contained.

The Declaration of Principle when published was greeted with virtually unanimous approval by the Press. The amendments made disposed of most of the doubts and objections previously expressed. Uneasiness still persisted in regard to the restriction on 'articles of an unsavoury nature', and one or two newspapers while generally welcoming the declaration and associating themselves with it made reservations on this subject. The *Daily Sketch*, for instance, declared that 'this newspaper reserves the right to obtain the personal story of any person where we believe it is in the public interest to do so.'

The *News of the World* regretted that the Council should impose a general restriction in advance on the judgment of editors as to what they might or might not publish. This was another step on the road to censorship. 'The public interest demands that matters which are criminal, vicious and unsavoury should be exposed and not concealed. The greater the evil, the greater the need for exposure.'

The value of the declaration will largely depend upon the spirit in which it is interpreted. One editor has said that he favours any reasonable influences that are brought to bear on newspapers to prevent excesses, but thinks that over-rigid statements of principle can sometimes infringe upon the legitimate functions of the Press. On the other hand, a newspaper may seek to circumvent the declaration by trying to justify the publication of an unsavoury story on the ground that it is in the public interest to do so.

In a leading article on 28 July the *Sun* said that the great merit of the new code was that it was a voluntarily accepted code, compiled with the aid of national newspaper editors. The article went on to state that the declaration placed restraints upon Press freedom, but they were restraints which responsible newspapers would regard as reasonable in their own interests and the interests of justice.

The declaration of principle is undoubtedly a major event in the history and development of the Press Council. It is important for what it says, for the circumstances which gave rise to it and for the purpose it was directed to achieve. Once again the Press chose voluntary restraint rather than legislative control.

Lord Devlin has said that the Council is the creature of the Press. This did not mean that there should be no public criticism of the Council. It would be a pity, however, if the natural inclination to take up the editorial pen as the weapon nearest to hand led to the belief that this was the only way in which editors and journalists could help to shape the policies of the Council.

The Declaration of Principle was the result of a more direct consultation and collaboration between the Council and the Press than had at any time previously been achieved. It demonstrated the increasing confidence of the Press in its Council and the growing stature and authority of the Council itself.

The Government has not indicated whether it regards the declaration of principle as meeting its request that the Press should put its house in order and whether the assurance of voluntary restraint is accepted in place of the compulsory restraint by the legislation previously threatened. Some indication, however, of the Government's view of the matter was given in a message the Attorney-General sent to the High Court Journalists' Association on the occasion of its annual dinner on 1 December 1966. In it he expressed pleasure at the Press Council's declaration of principle and said the question of newspaper payments to witnesses in court cases was a problem that the Press itself should tackle.

The Press Council has made no further statement on the arrangement made by the *News of the World* with the witness in the Moors murder case which was the occurrence that led to the consultations between the Council and the Press and ultimately to the Declaration of Principle. The Press Council doubtless considered the principles enumerated in the Declaration on the payment and questioning of witnesses disposed of the case.

The *News of the World* in a leading article following the publication of the Declaration stated that it had reservations on point 3, but considered that the Press Council had rendered a service to newspapers generally in laying down a code of conduct in relation to criminal proceedings.

30 Aberfan — The Attorney-General Warns the Press

Shortly after school started on the morning of Friday, 21 October 1966, the coal-tip overhanging Aberfan collapsed and avalanched into the village engulfing the junior school and a number of other buildings. 144 people were killed of whom 116 were children between the ages of eight and ten.

On the night of the disaster the Prime Minister, Mr Wilson, flew to the scene and promised 'a most high-level independent inquiry'. During the weekend it was announced from Downing Street that the inquiry would be in public, that the headquarters of the inquiry would be in Merthyr Tydfil and that it would open as soon as arrangements could be completed; it was also announced that Lord Justice Edmund Davies had been invited and had agreed to conduct the inquiry. The Lord Justice was born at Mountain Ash about two miles from Aberfan and knew the Aberfan colliery and coalfields intimately from boyhood and through his professional career; until he became a High Court Judge he had served as Recorder of Merthyr, Swansea and Cardiff. His appointment as Chairman of the inquiry was intended to reassure the Welsh people that it would be thorough.

Over the weekend a stunned and shocked nation was given a detailed coverage of the disaster by Press, radio and television. The public learned that warnings given two years previously that the tip was unsafe and was a serious menace to the school had gone unheeded.

Some of the reporting from the scene of the disaster was described as quite improper and ghoulish. Lord Robens, Chairman of the National Coal Board, protested in particular at the television interviewing. Much of the material put out by Press and television, he said, was informative and restrained, but occasionally the very worst form of callous reporting broke through with a jarring and hideous note. Often, he alleged, there was a cruel attempt to make a public spectacle of private grief. He did not think that live interviews with the sufferers should have been permitted. Families who had lost children were brought before the cameras, and microphones were thrust before them while they were still numbed and broken by shock.

Both the B.B.C. and Independent Television rejected Lord Robens's criticism; minor lapses of taste there may have been, but generally the public appreciated the completeness of the information given. The Controller of Programmes for B.B.C. Television, Mr Huw Wheldon, said: 'The nation wanted to know, and had the right to know, what was happening. It wanted even in some measure to share the storm of grief that was descending on the valley, or, if there was to be any hope, to share that hope. Our job was to respond as truly and directly as we could to that challenge . . .'. Mr Wheldon went on to say that it was cruel and inaccurate to impute cheap motives to an operation which may well have been raw and fragmentary but which was carried out by people who were as deeply moved as anybody else by the situation in which they found themselves. A similar view was expressed by I.T.V.: 'Our aim', said Lord Hill, Chairman of the Independent Television Authority, 'has been to give a true picture of what happened. We would have been guilty of falsifying events if we had tried to prevent the reality from coming through.'

Sir Miles Thomas, Chairman of the Development Corporation for Wales, also disagreed that the disaster had been dealt with in a sensational manner. In his opinion it had been described by Press, radio and television 'with deep feeling and great sincerity of reporting'.

THE TRIBUNAL OF INQUIRY

On Monday, 24 October, the Secretary of State for Wales, Mr Cledwyn Hughes, informed the Commons that, following a discussion he had had with Lord Justice Davies, Parliament would be asked for the inquiry to be conducted under the Tribunals of Inquiry (Evidence) Act, 1921.

On 25 October the House approved a motion moved by the Prime Minister, 'That it is expedient that a Tribunal be established for inquiring into a definite matter of urgent public importance, viz. the causes of, and all the circumstances relating to, the disaster at Aberfan, Merthyr Tydfil, on Friday the 21st October, 1966.'

A resolution in the same terms was moved by the Minister without

Portfolio, Lord Champion, in the House of Lords the same day and agreed to.

The following day the names of the other two members of the Tribunal to sit with Lord Justice Davies were announced.

THE ATTORNEY-GENERAL'S STATEMENT

This was the situation when the Attorney-General made a statement in the House of Commons which was to cause a storm of protest in the Press. The statement was made on 27 October, a week, after the disaster and two days after the establishment of the Tribunal of Inquiry to investigate the causes of the disaster; it was as follows:

> The Tribunal having been established with wide terms of reference, it is highly undesirable that any comments should be made either in the Press or on the radio or on television on matters which it will be the express function of the Tribunal to investigate.
>
> Apart from their manifest undesirability, such comments may have legal consequences which are, perhaps, not at present appreciated. Just as comments on the subject of a pending trial may constitute contempt of court, so, also, the Tribunal would have to consider whether such comments amounted to such an interference with their highly important task as to necessitate the Chairman certifying that it called for an investigation by the High Court as to whether there had been contempt of the Tribunal. The possible consequences call for no elaboration by me.
>
> I should like to add that I am authorised by Lord Justice Davies, the Chairman of the Tribunal, to say that all who have relevant information will be afforded the fullest opportunity of submitting this to the Tribunal.

He added in reply to questions that there was danger in examination of potential witnesses on television and in the Press when the best means of ventilating opinion and passing on information was now by communication with the Tribunal itself.

The reaction in Parliament to the statement perhaps gave the Attorney-General an indication of its probable reception outside the House, but even so he must have been astonished at the intensity of the indignation.

In Parliament Sir John Hobson, a former Attorney-General, asked Sir

Elwyn to reconsider whether his statement did not go too far. An attempt should not be made to stifle comment of every sort by Press and public because comment of a reasonable kind might very well lead to a new line of inquiry by the Tribunal.

Mr A. W. Lyon, M.P., a supporter of the Government, asked whether the Attorney-General was aware that his announcement would be received by many inside and outside the legal profession with great regret. The whole pattern of events over recent years had been to limit the area of contempt of court and where a jury was not involved the kind of comment that might be made in the Press or television was unlikely to sway those who had to make a decision. In the case of a judge and two assessors of outstanding merit the law of contempt should surely not be extended still further.

Mr Gordon Walker, the former Labour Secretary for Foreign Affairs, invited the Attorney-General to draw a distinction between actual questioning on television of possible witnesses and general enlightened discussion and argument, including such discussion on television and in the Press about the broad nature of the events.

The Press interpreted the Attorney-General's statement as an attempt to gag it and to stifle comment. The threat of contempt proceedings against those who disregarded the warning given was particularly resented. The statement was not a carelessly worded extempore one; the Attorney-General had read what was clearly a carefully prepared and considered announcement. The timing as much as the wording was unfortunate. In the highly-charged atmosphere that prevailed a Government statement relating to the disaster capable of being misunderstood was bound to create suspicion about the Government's motive.

THE PRESS COUNCIL'S CONCERN

The reaction of the Press Council was immediate. The Attorney-General made his statement in the Commons on the Thursday afternoon; on the Friday morning the Press Council declared that it viewed 'with alarm' what the Attorney-General had said.

The Press Council's statement continued:

When a great disaster occurs the public has a right to hear about it at once from the lips of those concerned. Discussion about its nature and cause cannot be stifled until after a tribunal of inquiry has issued its definitive report. Reasoned discussion and comment will assist rather than impede the task of the Tribunal.

There can be no objection to a reminder to editors of the need for exercising discretion and to the undesirability of attempting to prejudge in any way the issues before the Tribunal. Likewise, reporters can be reminded that in getting stories and information from those who may be called as witnesses they must exercise the greatest care not to colour the evidence that may be given, but the intrusion into the domain of free speech of ill-defined threats of legal proceedings is harmful to the proper conduct of public affairs in a free society.

A few extracts from the newspapers will illustrate the feelings of the Press:

In an editorial the *Daily Express* declared: 'It is intolerable that Ministers should threaten the use of legal processes that might limit the search for truth.'

Thr *Daily Mail* was prepared to accept that the statement was legally correct, but considered it politically mistaken.

The *Sun* said that the hints given on behalf of the Government following the hostile reaction that the Attorney's statement was not threatening but just a friendly warning was not good enough. The Prime Minister himself should issue a statement making it plain that the Government had no intention of trying to invoke the law on contempt in order to prevent free speech and comment. No responsible newspaper or television programme would interview prospective witnesses in a manner that would hamper the Tribunal's work.

The *Times* after saying that there was no precedent for the Attorney's warning and precious little authority for it went on to say:

'Sir Elwyn Jones' statement is basically an attempt to extend the law of contempt at a time when the legal profession itself believes it should be limited even more strictly.'

The *Sunday Times* made the point that without Press investigations the Inquiry would have had great difficulty in discovering essential facts.

The most defiant challenge to the Attorney-General came from the *Sunday Telegraph*:

'He has brought his high office into the contempt from which he egregiously sought to protect the Aberfan Tribunal, and his statement should in turn be treated with the contempt which it deserves. If he disagrees with this verdict let him bring a test case.'

So strongly had the Attorney-General's statement been attacked in the Press and by the professional bodies — the National Union of Journalists, the Institute of Journalists, the Newspaper Society, the British Committee of the International Press Institute all made their protest — that the Government could not ignore the general and widespread resentment. Moreover during the weekend following the statement the leader of the Opposition, Mr Heath, in a speech at Scarborough, described it as the arbitrary act of an authoritarian government and said that it not only threatened the freedom of the Press but the freedom of everybody.

On 1 November in the House of Commons, the Prime Minister replied to the criticism. He repudiated suggestions that the statement of the Attorney-General was made for political and party political reasons and described these suggestions as 'a gross and contemptible slur upon him'.

The Prime Minister reminded the House that a Tribunal had been established clothed with all the powers of a judicial inquiry. Since it was the desire of the House, the public, the Press, television and radio that the Tribunal should get at the truth, it was vital that nothing should be done which in any way weakened its power to do this. The statement of the Attorney-General was made with Lord Justice Edmund Davies' knowledge and approval, and there was good reason for it.

The Prime Minister went on to say that on the night of the disaster the great majority of Press reporters and also those of television and radio did their duty with great responsibility and consideration. But certain television interviews had involved cross-examination of potential witnesses of a kind so searching that they appeared to be seeking to do the work of the Tribunal.

Statements describing action taken or actions which should have been taken were matters to be elucidated by the Tribunal. Once statements had been elicited by television interviewers under non-judicial procedures, they were on record in a form which could hinder the Tribunal's ability to get at the truth.

Those who imputed unworthy motives to the Attorney-General, Mr Wilson said, disregarded the precedent of a previous Tribunal set up to investigate the submarine *Thetis* disaster in 1939 when the then Prime Minister, Mr Neville Chamberlain, after moving the resolution to establish the Tribunal, said that he earnestly deprecated in any form or in any conditions, any speculation of what happened now that a court had been set up to investigate the circumstances. He hoped that whatever people may have thought and said in the past they would say no more about it until the Tribunal reported.

The Prime Minister went on to say that from the earliest days of these Tribunals the House took the view that having established a court with full judicial powers it could not discuss any matter within the competence of the Tribunal. If Parliament restrained its own functions once a case was *sub judice*, the Attorney-General was abundantly justified in acting as he did, so that others outside the House were advised of the legal position.

The Lord Chancellor, Lord Gardiner, made the same statement in the House of Lords as the Prime Minister had made in the Commons.

Lord Harlech asked the Lord Chancellor whether the television interviews complained of had not all taken place before the Tribunal was set up and whether the Attorney-General's statement was not clumsily worded and guaranteed to give the maximum affront to the Press, radio and television.

Lord Gardiner replied that the Prime Minister had promised an inquiry on the Friday. On the Monday in the B.B.C. '24 Hours' programme a man described as knowing more about the behaviour and nature of coal-tips than anyone was severely cross-examined about their danger unless regularly inspected. What was a man likely to do, the Lord Chancellor asked, when he came before the Tribunal with the knowledge that millions of people had already heard him make an important statement which he subsequently realised was erroneous?

The interview ended, Lord Gardiner said, by the interviewer looking straight at the camera and saying: 'Now I have, as a young journalist, attended and reported several public inquiries into pit disasters and disasters involving men working under ground. And in nearly every case I have to report to you that, when grief had safely abated, the final report was a frustrating exercise in official "whitewashing".' This was a deliberate attack on the *bona fides* of the Tribunal.

Lord Gardiner went on to say that some of the statements in the Press plainly meant that, because there was a Labour Government and because the National Coal Board was a nationalised industry, in some improper way they were going to try to secure that there would be a 'whitewashing' Report. The Attorney-General was not only justified in saying what he did, but it was high time somebody reminded the newspapers and television what the law was and that the law of contempt of court applied equally to a Tribunal and to a law court.

Despite the statements by the Prime Minister and the Lord Chancellor, the Attorney-General's statement continued to be regarded as a threat to the newspapers, to responsible comment and to freedom of speech.

If the mischief aimed at was the effect a television interview might have on a potential Tribunal witness in committing him to statements made under cross-examination by television interviewers, the right time for the Attorney's warning would have been after the Prime Minister had announced on the night of the disaster that there would be an inquiry. But the Attorney-General's statement was not made until a week later, by which time the television interviews had stopped and comment was restrained as a result of the realisation that the disaster was *sub judice* following the establishment of the Tribunal. The mind of the newspapers was reflected in comment in one of them: 'As if anybody needs lecturing or advice at this particular time on this particular subject'.

Lord Dilhorne, a former Lord Chancellor, in a feature article (*Daily Express* 4 November 1966) described the Prime Minister's defence of the Attorney-General as a skilful irrelevance. The Attorney-General had said that comments on matters to be investigated were highly undesirable, but he had not stopped there. He had gone on to make threats. Lord Dilhorne pointed out that the courts had refused applications to commit for contempt where the object was merely to stifle comment.

Other newspapers pointed out that if the reasoning of the Prime Minister and the Attorney-General was correct it would be possible for a Government wishing to suppress discussion in the Press on a matter embarrassing to it to do so simply by setting up a Tribunal of Inquiry.

The speed with which the Press Council acted on the Attorney-General's statement demonstrated its watchfulness for any threat, real or potential, to the freedom of the Press. The hostility of the newspapers might be considered predictable, because they were directly affected. The Press Council on the other hand, although the official representative of the Press, also includes representatives of the Public, and in consequence speaks with enhanced authority. The declaration by the Press Council that 'the intrusion into the domain of free speech of ill-defined threats of legal proceedings is harmful to the proper conduct of public affairs in a free society' could not be lightly regarded.

Aberfan will be remembered as the scene of an appalling disaster. It will also be remembered in the history of the Press Council as the occasion when the Council in the name of the freedom of the Press and of freedom of speech challenged the validity of a Government pronouncement.

The Attorney-General has indicated that he will on a suitable occasion elucidate his statement. Until then uncertainty on the legal position will persist. The uncertainty is whether the law of contempt of court applies equally to a court of law and a tribunal established under the 1921 Act.

The tribunal itself has been given no power by the 1921 Act to commit for contempt. It has power to order a witness to attend and to answer questions and must have some sanction in case of disobedience. Disobedience by the witness amounts to contempt in the face of the court and, though the tribunal cannot itself commit, it can certify to the High Court that an offence has been committed, and the High Court can punish the offender on the evidence of the tribunal based on its own knowledge.

But what is the position in regard to the other type of contempt committed by comment outside the court which is alleged to influence the course of justice?

A trial by a court ends in a verdict or judgment; an inquiry by a tribunal in a report to Parliament. If through prejudicial comment a judgment or verdict is influenced a miscarriage of justice may occur and may be difficult to rectify. For this reason where the administration of justice is concerned the public interest in a fair trial must prevail over the public interest in free speech.

In the case of a tribunal, on the other hand, if its inquiry is influenced by Press comment the worst that can happen is that Parliament is misinformed. Undesirable though this obviously is, it is not grounds for silencing the Press.

Furthermore there is a serious procedural difficulty where a tribunal is concerned in respect of outside contempt which does not arise where the contempt is in the face of the court. The tribunal cannot certify outside contempt without evidence, as it can when the contempt is in the face of the court and therefore within its knowledge. The High Court will have to repeat the investigation and possibly reach a different conclusion on the evidence.

For other reasons, too, it is problematic whether the 1921 Act provides a sanction for anything other than contempt in the face of the court.

The Attorney-General's statement has been interpreted as meaning that any comment on the Aberfan disaster was not only undesirable but punishable. It is common belief that where a matter is *sub judice* all comment is prohibited, but that is not so. What is prohibited is comment that is intended or calculated to interfere with the impartiality of the Court. A tribunal is not bound by the rules of evidence and can have regard to any material worth considering. Tribunals have found newspaper articles sometimes suggest a useful line of investigation. The members might certify that they were influenced by sensible comment, but they would hardly wish to punish that.

31 Summing Up

We believe that among men of repute in the Press, whether proprietors, editors or other journalists, there is a considerable measure of agreement on what constitutes sound professional practice. We should like to see the General Council express and extend that agreement, safeguard the traditions and interpret the aspirations of the profession and use its influence to eradicate discreditable practices.

Such was the faith of the first Royal Commission, such the purpose for which the Press Council was to be established.

The faith of the Royal Commission was to prove more justified than the apprehension with which the proposed Council was viewed by the Press. The misgivings related to the means by which the objectives of the Council were to be achieved. However excellent the motives might be, a Press Council designed to supervise the conduct of the Press and sit in judgment on what was published in the newspaper would, it was believed, inevitably become an intolerable censorship. The Press found the restrictions imposed by the law irksome enough, and it had no desire to add others of its own creation.

Not surprisingly, therefore, a complete lack of enthusiasm greeted the recommendation of the Commission. Indeed lack of enthusiasm described the most favourable state of mind towards the proposed Council; majority opinion ranged from disapproval to open hostility. When at length the Press agreed to establish the Council it did so at pistol-point as the alternative to having one imposed upon it by statute.

THE THREE PHASES OF THE COUNCIL'S HISTORY

The history of the Press Council falls into three phases. The first can be described as the period of resistance and lasted from 1948 to 1953; the second covered the years 1953 to 1963, the period when the Council consisted entirely of Press representatives; the third phase is the present era, which began in 1963 when the Council was reconstituted under an independent Chairman and with representatives of the public.

During the first phase newspaper proprietors and journalistic organisations met spasmodically, ostensibly in compliance with the will of Parliament to set up the Council recommended by the Royal Commission, in reality to avoid doing so as long as possible. 'To a newspaper Press which had enjoyed absolute freedom from restriction and special taxation for something like a century', said Mr George Murray, the third Chairman, 'the appointment of a body to safeguard its liberties by curbing its excesses was a startling innovation.'

The Press held out for four years, but then, as the result of a move in Parliament to establish a Press Council by legislation, the proprietors and journalists decided that a Council of their own making was preferable to one imposed on them, and a constitution was drafted and agreed without further delay.

The Press submitted under duress, but the surrender was not complete. The Royal Commission had recommended that the Chairman of the Press Council should be someone outside the newspaper industry and that membership should include a percentage of lay members to gain the confidence and support of the public. The recommendation was not accepted, and the Council created by the Press was confined to representatives of the Press. Mr Murray described the Council as one that stood halfway between the kind of control preached by some extremists and the continued absence of supervision which most newspapers would have preferred. It was not unreasonable, he thought, and the founders obviously agreed with him, that journalsm with its long immunity from interference of any kind should take a cautious first step towards an unaccustomed regulation. The founders settled on a compromise and so made a typically British approach to the problem.

Once the Press Council had been established its members accepted the challenge to make it work. Lord Astor of Hever, Colonel Astor as he then was, chief proprietor of *The Times*, agreed to be the Council's first Chairman. His personality and prestige proved of great value in getting a tentative and uncertain project launched. Unfortunately his term was a short one, and to the genuine regret of all his colleagues he was obliged to resign for reasons of health after only one year of office. During that time he made the Council's purpose clear and gave direction to its work. The aim, as he saw it, was the defence of the freedom of the Press by combating abuses which brought it into disrepute. The Press had to be free, but it had also to be trustworthy. The Council's appeal would be to conscience and fair play. However the belief remained strong that an organisation few wanted would collapse and many hoped that it would.

Mr Linton (later Sir Linton) Andrews, Editor of the *Yorkshire Post*, succeeded Lord Astor as Chairman. Both these gentlemen and Mr George Murray, the third and last of the newspapermen to occupy the Chair, were highly respected in their profession; all three used their best endeavours to realise the principles for which the Council stood. The Council had need of such men during the years of its infancy.

A debate on the Press in the House of Commons on 17 May 1957 on the performance of the Press Council to date reflected a considerable difference of views. Some members thought that the Council had had no influence one way or the other, some believed that it would never have any influence so long as it could not impose sanctions; others thought that the Council had done very well in the short time it had been in existence; some said that they could not subscribe to the satisfaction the Press Council felt about its own achievement.

The Joint Under-Secretary of State for the Home Office, Mr J. E. Simon (now Sir Jocelyn, President of the Probate, Divorce and Admiralty Division) was the Government speaker. He dealt with the question of sanctions and said that if the Council was given 'teeth' a big inroad would be made on the freedom of the Press. In a free Press there was bound to be a reflection of the tastes of the community at large; the most fruitful approach to the improvement of standards was through the advance in the general education of the readership of the Press. The Press was a vital institution in a free society; its health was of great importance to the social life of the community, and its health would be injured rather than promoted by an attempt to influence it by Government action.

In 1960, seven years after the Council was founded, those who bore the burden of making it work stated that the Council's authority would be strengthened if the 'quality newspapers' took a more active part in its work. A number of newspapers were critical, as they were entitled to be. Criticism, the Council conceded, was the function of newspapers and must normally be divorced from any responsibility for the actions of bodies criticised. When, however, the organisation under review was so intimately concerned with the Press, collaboration could be more helpful and effective than constructive criticism.

Despite the lack of support from sections of the Press the Annual Reports began to show a growing confidence of the Council in itself. The early fiasco many expected had not occurred. Many still scoffed at the Council's efforts and thought that it was unnecessary and pretentious, but it was undoubtedly gaining ground both with the Press and the public.

Sir Linton Andrews resigned as Chairman of the Council in 1959 and was succeeded by Mr George Murray, a director of Associated Newspapers Limited. When the Shawcross Report recommended that the Press should be given a time limit within which voluntarily to establish the kind of Council the 1949 Commission had suggested and that if this was not done Parliament should take the matter in hand, Mr Murray realised that the Press Council could no longer hold out. His last service to the old Council was to prepare the way for the new one with its independent Chairman and lay members. He did so the more readily because the Press Council, he said, could not have a better leader at a time of troubled relations between the Press and the public than the new independent Chairman Lord Devlin, 'a brilliant judge and one of our most distinguished public men'.

Mr Murray's retirement marked the completion of the first decade of the Council's existence. 'It is not often that time provides so neat a conjunction,' Mr Murray wrote in a valedictory message. Had he been asked, he said, what had been the Council's greatest achievement he would have answered, 'We survived.' The Council had survived despite the predictions of opponents, sceptics and pessimists that it would have nothing to do; that it would be submerged in complaints, that it would be ruined by damages awarded against it in lawsuits. By its mere survival the Council had accustomed newspaper editors to the existence of a body constantly on the watch to see that they maintained the standards expected of a decent and responsible Press. The old Council was able to pass on to the new Council a name and an organisation which had won acceptance by the newspapers and the people.

Nevertheless, a large section of the Press remained unreconciled to the idea of a Press Council or, if there had to be one, to a Council as it was then constituted. The public, too, continued to regard the Council as a buffer against well-founded charges of newspaper misconduct. The Chairman of a large newspaper group, which had stood aloof, was firmly of the opinion that until an independent chairman, unconnected with the Press, was appointed, one whose judgment would command the confidence of the public and who would have the strength of character to resign rather than condone disgraceful conduct on the part of a newspaper, the Council would never be really effective.

The third phase of its history began when the Press Council was at last constituted as the two Royal Commissions had recommended. Under its first independent Chairman, Lord Devlin, and with its representatives of the public, the new Press Council held its first meeting on 14 January 1964.

SIX ESSENTIAL FACTORS

In an address to the Annual Conference of the Commonwealth Press Union some three years later Lord Devlin stated that there were six factors which he believed to be essential to the creation and proper working of a Press Council. They were:

1. A general acceptance by the Press itself that the Press Council was a desirable thing to have.

2. An acceptance by the Government of the country concerned that the Press has a constitutional part to play in the formation and expression of opinion.

3. The existence of standards of conduct to which the Press conforms. This did not necessarily mean a written code; it did mean that the individual journalist could not decide for himself the standards he chose to observe.

4. Acceptance by newspapers of the obligation to publish adjudications of the Press Council against themselves.

5. The public should be represented.

6. The Council must not be merely a tribunal which convicts or acquits. It should also stand for the freedom and rights of the Press.

REPRESENTATIVES OF THE PUBLIC

The first Royal Commission believed that members from outside the newspaper industry would broaden the basis of the Council and increase its authority. The Press was part of the nation's political machinery, and since the public had a deep interest in the independence and integrity of the Press it was desirable that the interest should be recognised by seeking the co-operation of the public in the work of the Council.

The Press, however, when the first constitution was drafted, approached the task in chauvinistic mood. The advice of the Royal Commission was rejected and the attitude adopted that the Press was equally capable of managing its own affairs without outside assistance as the other professions. If representatives of the public were admitted, so it was thought, they were bound to form and vote as a bloc against the professional members. No provision was, therefore, made in the Constitution for their inclusion, and the first Press Council consisted entirely of Press men.

The appointment of an independent Chairman and the inclusion of independent members disposes of the jibe that the Press Council was just a body of journalists concerned to protect and exonerate their colleagues against charges of violation of journalistic standards. The jibe was unjust, but the fact that many people believed it was an additional reason for removing the cause of criticism. It is significant that in the year that followed the admission of public representatives the number of complaints against newspapers rose by forty-three per cent; the assumption that this was due to the increased confidence of the public following the admission of lay members to the Council was not an unreasonable one. The participation of members of the public in the work of the Council in adjudicating complaints demonstrated to the public that the Press is not the sole judge in its own cause; their presence also ensures that the reaction of ordinary members of the public to a complaint will be registered in Council.

Lord Devlin has said that to describe the representation of the public on the Council as essential might perhaps be an overstatement; nevertheless he believed that it was very important and desirable that the public should be represented. The Press helped to form and express public opinion, and its standards should take public opinion into account. The Press is free because the public wants it to be free, and the public is therefore concerned in the way in which the freedom is exercised. This concern could be and is adequately expressed through a minority membership which offers no threat of domination. A Council on which the public is represented can assert the rights and duties of the Press with greater authority than could a purely professional body; professional men can easily fall into the error of judging complaints against themselves too narrowly.

The expectation that members of the public would form and vote as a bloc against the representatives of the Press has not been borne out in practice. The lay members take part in discussions as individuals, and their incorporation has caused no breach of continuity.

THE PRESS AND THE COUNCIL

Apart from dwindling pockets of resistance the Press Council is now generally accepted and supported by the Press. The antagonism of the early years
was due to various reasons — fear that the Council would restrict editorial
freedom; a cynical disbelief that newspapers sitting in judgment on friends
and rivals could act with impartiality; the sincerely held belief that any form
of control, even of a voluntary kind, was contrary to the freedom of the
Press.

As the years passed antagonism receded and since the reconstruction of
of the Council has given way to a growing confidence in the Council. The
Press has come to realise that the Council is not the threat they had first
believed it to be; on the contrary they found that it is a powerful ally in
combating threatened encroachment on Press freedom. The expected
censorship has not occurred, nor has there been any display of authoritarian
methods; complaints are patiently judged and the balance held fairly between
the Press and the public. The Council has shown that it is something more
than a tribunal which 'convicts and acquits'. Opposition and indifference
have subsided; newspapers previously critical are now collaborating.

THE JOURNALISTIC CODE

The British, it has been said, have an inherent distaste for the written word.
They have an unwritten constitution in regard to the government of their
country; the system of law under which they live, the Common Law, is of
immemorial antiquity but likewise unwritten. The ethical code of the Press
is yet another example of the preference for the unwritten commitment.

When the Press Council was established one of its members described it as
a court of honour without a code to administer. This was not entirely
correct. The professional bodies had their own code of conduct, and,
although there was no written set of rules which could be described as the
ethical code of the Press, there were certain principles tacitly acknowledged and observed by journalists as the unwritten ethics of their profession.

These were the principles the Press Council proceeded to declare and
apply in much the same way as the courts of law declare and apply the
Common Law. The 'case law' of the Press as based on the adjudication by
the Press Council of complaints made against newspapers. The ajudications

of the Press Council, like the judgments of the courts, declare the principle applicable to the facts of the particular case, but provides invaluable guidance on the principles to be observed in cases of a similar kind. Gradually the Press Council is formulating a conception of reputable professional conduct by censuring undesirable journalistic conduct.

The 1966 Declaration of Principle of the Press Council stated that no code could cover every case. Satisfactory observance of the principles must depend upon the discretion and sense of responsibility of editors and newspaper proprietors. The advantage of an unwritten code is its flexibility and adaptability to the changing circumstances and problems that inevitably accompany the passage of time.

ARE SANCTIONS NECESSARY?

The Royal Commission had to consider the question whether to recommend that the Press Council should be established by Statute, as was the General Medical Council, or by the voluntary action of the Press.

The Commission was told in evidence that a sense of responsibility in the Press could only be achieved by putting behind professional standards a sanction sufficiently strong to deter journalists from violating them. This would have involved setting up either a Registration Council with power to keep a roll of qualified journalists and the power to strike off for professional misconduct; alternatively the creation of a single professional association embracing all staff journalists, with power to expel. These methods could only have been worked by turning journalism into a closed profession. The Royal Commission thought that this would have been disastrous. If a voluntary organisation could be made to work it would have great advantages and in the end this was the method that Commission recommended. The Press Council would not have power to control entry into the profession, a power which characterised the statutory professional bodies, but would depend for its effectiveness on its moral authority, not on sanctions.

When those who urged strong-arm discipline realised that the Press Council was to have no power of punishment they immediately assumed that it would have no authority. A reprimand, however severe, was they said no substitute for a penalty that would punish and deter. A Press Council without 'teeth' was a Council that could be defied with impunity.

The critics completely underestimated the strength and effectiveness of the Council's censure. The obligation and moral duty of a newspaper to publish an adjudication of the Council against itself had the effect of reinforcing the Council's condemnation with the condemnation of the public which the publicity ensured. Nothing can be more disparaging and unwelcome to a newspaper which values its good name than to be obliged to publish to its readers a judgment of the Press Council that it has infringed journalistic standards.

The answer, therefore, to the question whether sanctions are necessary, is that they are not and the Press Council has proved it. Sanctions of a punitive nature would be as repugnant to the Council as they appeared to the Royal Commission.

The role of the Press Council is that of educator not inquisitor; its method is persuasion not force; its weapon is publicity not punishment; its appeal is to conscience and fair play. In a free Press sanctions would be an incongruity.

IS THE COUNCIL SUCCEEDING?

The appointment of an independent Chairman and the inclusion of lay members on the Council when it was reconstituted in 1963 reconciled newspapers which had previously withheld their support; the confidence of the public in the Council was increased and the Council was, in consequence, immeasurably strengthened. Without the support of the Press as a whole the 1966 Declaration of Principle would hardly have been possible or have much value; without lay members the Council could not have spoken with the weight and authority the combined backing of Press and public gave it when it criticised the Attorney-General's warning to the Press at the time of the Aberfan disaster.

The Press Council is manifestly restoring the relations between the Press and the public which had been so seriously damaged by the events associated with the names Vassall, Profumo, Keeler and Ward. It has virtually dissipated the apprehension its creation caused in newspaper circles. The most obdurate critics are coming to realise that the Council is pursuing a policy both constructive and in the best interests of the Press. The days when the Council's survival was in doubt have been left behind and it has now taken firm root. It has the advantage of commanding the aid of the six factors its Chairman, Lord Devlin, said were essential to the proper working of a Press

Council. If these considerations are indicative of success then the Press Council is succeeding.

Success is also confirmed by the practical test of comparing the Press as it is today with the Press as it was when the Press Council came into existence. The comparison shows an impressive change in the tone and the content of the newspapers particularly of the popular Press. More space is now devoted to the news, the treatment of current affairs is more mature, social and moral problems are discussed with more frankness and generally there is a greater seriousness and sense of responsibility. The improvement may be largely due to the demand of a more educated readership; the Press itself has made its contribution by encouraging the trend and catering for higher intellectual levels. But some credit is also undoubtedly due to the influence of the Press Council for the better standards displayed.

The growing repute in which the Council is held by the public and the respect it commands with the Press further demonstrate that the Council is consolidating its position and authority by its own merits. Recognition of the place it holds in the life of the nation is not confined to Great Britain; great interest in the Council has spread to many other countries. Many distinguished newspapermen, diplomats, lawyers, university professors, politicians and government officials from all parts of the world visit the Council's headquarters each year to study its purpose and methods. Not without interest is the fact that many of the Council's visitors are the guests of the Foreign Office and the Commonwealth Relations Office.

FUTURE OUTLOOK

Since its establishment fourteen years ago the Press Council after an uncertain start advanced with growing confidence guided by its lengthening experience. Now firmly established the Council appears destined to become an institution of constitutional and national importance. It speaks with the authority of the profession behind it and is listened to as the authentic voice of the Press.

To enable it to fulfil its disciplinary function the Council has been entrusted by the Press with the power of condemnation, a power that must be exercised with responsibility and restraint. Lord Devlin has given this caution:

As the Press Council becomes more and more firmly established, it will have to watch more and more carefully the use of this power and

Q   L.T.P.C.

see that it is never employed to interfere with the proper editorial discretion over what is printed and what is not. This discretion is essential to Press freedom.

As a result of the Shawcross Report the Press Council can in future be expected to give more attention than it has done to the economic problems that confront the newspaper industry. The Report stated that the Council had devoted itself almost exclusively to professional standards; it had not taken advantage of being a body that represented the Press as a whole to enlarge public knowledge of the problems the Press had to face. The Shawcross Commission recommended that in addition to giving greater publicity and statistical information about developments that tended towards concentration or monopoly in the Press as its constitution required the Council to do, it should also scrutinise and publicise changes in the ownership, control and growth of Press undertakings having the same tendency. The information would increase the knowledge of developments which were of concern to the citizens of a free country. The Press Council's Annual Reports are now giving more information of this kind and doubtless will give even more in future.

If the information the Commission thought the Council should make available is to be really complete, the Council may consider restoring an object previously contained in the constitution but dropped through lack of resources — the promotion of research. A department of specialists devoted to the study of the economic problems confronting the Press might prove of great value in keeping trends constantly under revue

For the Press to be free and to represent every point of view something like the number of newspapers existing at the time of the Shawcross Commission was believed to be necessary. Nevertheless the Commission gave warning that the future effect of the various economic pressures caused grave anxiety. To the pressures operating in 1962 from an overall decline in circulation of the national and Sunday newspapers have been added those caused by the economic squeeze in 1966, the fall in advertising revenue in particular.

Even so the public was quite unprepared for the shock caused by the announcement towards the end of 1966 that two of the best-known quality newspapers were in serious financial difficulty; one was *The Times,* the other the *Guardian. The Times* had come to be regarded as a national institution and Lord Thomson's take-over bid was likened by Lord Arran in a debate in the House of Lords on 25 January 1967 to a take-over of the Royal Navy by Mr Onassis. In the case of the *Guardian* Mr Laurence Scott, the Chairman and Managing Director, said that unless an annual economy of £500,000 could be effected in production costs, the newspaper would have to cease production in London.

Worse still was to come. Early in 1967 the contents of the Report of the Economist Intelligence Unit was disclosed to the public. The Report followed a survey commissioned in 1965 by the General Board for the National Newspaper Industry, the brief being to carry out a comprehensive factual survey of the structure and operation of the industry with a view to making recommendations which would lead to increased efficiency.

The Report of the E.I.U. was described by Lord Thomson as 'a devastating indictment of Fleet Street'. The view reflected in the Report was that the industry as a whole was likely to face a very difficult period over the next five years. Of the eighteen years studied in depth during the survey the Report concluded that probably only nine could be reasonably certain of making a profit. If the present cost structure remained unchanged it was likely that in the next five years one quality daily newspaper, two popular daily newspapers and one quality Sunday newspaper would be forced to cease production.

The outlook, however, is not entirely one of deep gloom, and the hard times the Press is enduring could give way to the realisation of great expectations.

The beginning of the year 1967 saw the industry on the threshold of a technological revolution. The Technical Manager of the *Financial Times*, Mr Walter Partridge, has said that newspaper proprietors who have to re-equip their printing works to provide for future growth find the pace at which new techniques are becoming available little short of alarming. Until recently the choice between one basic printing method and another was easy. Only letterpress rotaries could print fast enough for big circulation dailies, but developments in offset printing showed this was becoming the best method for small circulation provincial and weekly papers. He went on to say that a new generation of big capacity, high-speed offset presses with built-in colour facilities was now being designed, and it was possible that this method of printing would overtake letterpress for the majority of newspapers before the end of the 1970s.

Computer typesetting is already very well established in the United States and is being adopted elsewhere; in Japan printed news-sheets have been delivered by transmitting news direct from a news centre to a receiver installed in the customer's home.

Speaking in a debate in the House of Commons on 8 February 1967 the Minister without Portfolio, Mr Gordon Walker, said that the critical challenge that seemed to be facing the industry and on which its whole future depended, was that there was a combination of an over-manned industry facing technological change. He went on to state that all sections of the Press must realise that it was in effect on public trial and that in modern conditions the Press depended upon public judgment. If it did things which public opinion would not easily bear, such as allowing great newspapers to disappear, or treated itself too much like a commodity without realising that newspapers must be run with social, political and responsible purposes, in the end it would suffer in public esteem and a steady decline in circulation would follow.

The question the future will decide is whether managements, the Joint Board and the Press Council by their separate and combined efforts will restore the Press to a sound financial state and ensure the diversity of opinion which is the essence of freedom. On the achievement of this depend the tens of thousands who constitute the industry and earn their living from it; on its achievement also depends the democratic freedom of the community. 'I am convinced', Lord Shawcross has said, and his view is one with which few will disagree, 'that the continued existence of a free Press is something which is absolutely vital to the continuance of a healthy democratic society in this country'.

The 1949 Royal Commission declared that the British Press is inferior to none in the world. The aim of the Press Council is to keep it so by preserving its freedom and ensuring that the highest professional and commercial standards are maintained.

Appendices

Appendices

Appendix I

PRESS COUNCIL: ARTICLES OF CONSTITUTION

Articles of Constitution of The Press Council approved by the Newspaper Proprietors Association Ltd., The Newspaper Society, The Scottish Daily Newspaper Society, Scottish Newspaper Proprietors' Association, The Institute of Journalists, the National Union of Journalists and The Guild of British Newspaper Editors hereinafter referred to as the constituent bodies.

I. FOUNDATION

The Press Council, hereinafter called the Council, is voluntarily constituted on and from the first day of July, 1953, by the Organisations named in the preamble hereto in the designation 'The General Council of the Press'. The Council revokes that style and title on and from the first day of July, 1963, but accepts responsibility for all acts performed by The General Council of the Press as though they had been done by The Press Council.

2. OBJECTS

The Objects of the Council are:
  (i) To preserve the established freedom of the British Press.
 (ii) To maintain the character of the British Press in accordance with the highest professional and commercial standards.
(iii) To consider complaints about the conduct of the Press or the conduct of persons and organisations towards the Press; to deal with these complaints in whatever manner might seem practical and appropriate and record resultant action.
 (iv) To keep under review developments likely to restrict the supply of information of public interest and importance.
  (v) To report publicly on developments that may tend towards greater concentration or monopoly in the Press (including changes in

ownership, control and growth of Press undertakings) and to publish statistical information relating thereto.

(vi) To make representations on appropriate occasions to the Government, organs of the United Nations and to Press organisations abroad.

(vii) To publish periodical reports recording the Council's work and to review, from time to time, developments in the Press and the factors affecting them.

3. MEMBERSHIP

The Council shall consist of:

(i) A Chairman who shall be a person otherwise unconnected with the Press.

(ii) Twenty members nominated by the following bodies in the proportions indicated:

The Newspaper Proprietors Association Ltd.	5
At least two of whom shall be editorial — as distinct from managerial — nominees	
The Newspaper Society	3
At least one of whom shall be an editorial nominee	
The Periodical Proprietors Association Ltd., including one editorial nominee	2
The Scottish Daily Newspaper Society	1
Scottish Newspaper Proprietors' Association	1
The Guild of British Newspaper Editors	2
The National Union of Journalists	4
The Institute of Journalists	2

(iii) Representatives of the Public who shall not exceed 20 per cent of the Council's total membership entitled to vote 5

(iv) Additionally each constituent body may nominate one of its officials to attend meetings of the Council in a consultative capacity. Such nominees may speak but not vote. Constituent bodies may change these nominees by giving seven days' notice to the secretary of the Council.

4. METHODS OF APPOINTMENT

(i) The Chairman shall be invited to accept office on such terms as shall be agreed mutually by him and the Council.

(ii) Members nominated within the provisions of clause 3 (ii) shall be persons who, at the time of appointment, are full-time directors of newspapers, periodicals, news agencies supplying a daily service of news to newspapers in Great Britain and/or overseas OR full-time editorial or managerial employees on the staffs of such organisations. Editorial qualification shall extend to include also full-time professional freelance journalists regularly engaged in supplying news and/or articles to recognised newspapers, periodicals or news agencies. A member ceasing to be so qualified shall notify the secretary or acting secretary of the Council in writing within one calendar month and his membership shall terminate within three calendar months.

(iii) Representatives of the Public co-opted to the Council shall be chosen by the chairman and other members of the Council in consultation. These representatives shall rank equal with members nominated by the constituent bodies in the rights, privileges and duties inherent in membership of the Council other than qualification for election to the vice-chairmanship.

5. RETIREMENT

On nomination to the Council a person shall be entitled to membership for three consecutive years. At the end of this period the nominee, if he is qualified, shall be eligible for re-election. On first appointment of the group of members specified in Clause 3 (ii) seven shall serve for only one year before retirement and a further seven for an initial period of two years. These members shall be decided by lot. They will be eligible for re-election and thereafter the normal period of their membership of the Council and that of their successors shall be three years. On first appointment of the group of members specified in Clause 3 (iii) one shall retire at the end of the first year of service and a further two at the end of two years' membership in similar manner and conditions.

6. CASUAL VACANCIES

A person filling a casual vacancy shall be appointed to membership in like manner to that by which the person whose vacancy he fills was appointed. On initial appointment he shall retain membership only for the unexpired portion of the period which remained to the person whose place in the Council he takes.

7. PROCEDURE

The Council is empowered by the constituent bodies to regulate and control all its procedure and action for the furtherance and attainment of the objects defined in Clause 2 hereof as the Council may decide. The chairman and members shall each be entitled to cast one vote in any matter decided by them on a show of hands or by ballot, but if a division should result in an equal number of votes being cast for and against a motion the chairman shall be entitled to exercise a casting vote.

8. QUORUM

A quorum at a Council meeting shall be 13 members.

9. VICE-CHAIRMAN

At its first meeting following the thirtieth day of June in each and every year the Council shall appoint from its members nominated under the provisions of Clause 3 (ii) a vice-chairman, who shall hold office until the first meeting of the Council in the following financial year and subject to possession of qualification, shall then be eligible for re-election. Nominations in writing, duly proposed and seconded, with the written consent of the nominee, must be submitted to the secretary not later than fourteen days before the meeting of the Council at which the election is to take place. In the absence of written nomination, oral nomination may be made at the appropriate meeting of the Council. If no nomination is made, the existing holder of the office shall be declared to have been re-elected. In the absence of the chairman the vice-chairman shall preside at Council meetings and he shall fulfil all the functions of the chairman should that office be not occupied.

10. MEETINGS

Meetings shall be held at least five times a year. The Chairman is empowered to call a special meeting, if, in his opinion, the business to be transacted warrants this action. A special meeting shall be convened by the secretary on the requisition of not fewer than eight members. Such requisition shall be addressed to the secretary at the office of the Council for the time being. Not less than seven days' notice shall be given in writing of any meeting of the Council unless members agree to accept shorter notice.

11. COMMITTEES

The Council shall have power to appoint committees of its members for the discharge of such duties as shall be specified. A committee shall not have executive authority unless this is expressly delegated to it by the Council. Members of committees shall hold office until the first Council meeting following the next succeeding thirtieth day of June when they shall be automatically eligible for re-election unless they signify prior intention not to continue to serve in this capacity. At this meeting if the names of eligible sitting members and those of new nominees exceed the number of places on a committee the choice of members shall be decided by a vote of the members present. Each committee shall appoint a chairman from amongst its members. The Council chairman and vice-chairman shall be ex-officio members of all committees.

12. NOTICES

Notice of meetings shall be sent to members of the Council at the addresses indicated by them to the secretary. Accidental omission to notify any of the said persons or non-receipt by any of them of such notice shall not invalidate the proceedings of the meeting to which the notice relates.

13. FINANCE

The monetary expenditure of the Council shall be met by annual subscriptions payable by the constituent bodies as set out in the Schedule hereto. No variation in these amounts shall be made without the prior written consent of the constituent bodies. Subscriptions shall be payable on the first day of July in each year.

All cheques issued in the name of the Council shall be signed by the chairman and secretary and in the absence of either by the remaining signatory and vice-chairman or other specially designated member of the Council.

14. TRAVELLING EXPENSES

A member attending a meeting of the Council or of any of its committees shall be entitled to receive his first-class return railway fare from the funds of the Council.

15. SUBSISTENCE ALLOWANCES

Members of the Council appointed under Clause 3 (iii) shall be entitled to receive from Council funds subsistence expenses incurred in attending council and/or committee meetings in accordance with rates to be fixed by the Council from time to time.

16. DISSOLUTION

The Council may at any time terminate its existence if it appears to the members that the Council's voluntary nature and independence are threatened. A resolution to dissolve the Council, to be binding, must be passed by a two-thirds majority of its members present and voting at a meeting specially called for the purpose, which two-thirds majority shall be not less than a simple majority of the membership of the Council. Not less than twenty-one days' notice shall be given of any such meeting and this shall give particulars of the purpose for which the meeting is called. The Council shall notify secretaries of the constituent bodies of such meeting at the time it summons members.

17. ALTERATION OF CONSTITUTION

Alteration of these Articles of Constitution shall require the approval of a two-thirds majority of members present and voting at a meeting, which two-thirds majority shall be not less than a simple majority of the membership of the Council. No alteration shall be effective unless at least 28 days' notice of a proposed alteration shall have been given to Council members and secretaries of the constituent bodies.

18. STAFF

The secretarial and administrative work of the Council shall be carried out by an appointed secretary and a staff engaged for the purpose on terms and conditions decided by the Council from time to time.

19. REVOCATION OF PREVIOUS ARTICLES OF CONSTITUTION

These Articles of Constitution shall have effect on and from the first day of July, 1963. They supersede the original Articles of Constitution, dated the first day of July, 1953, as amended in January, 1959, and again in the financial year 1961–62 which are hereby revoked by resolution of the General Council of the Press this eighteenth day of June, 1963.

Appendix II

RECOMMENDED ROUTINE PROCEDURE AT HOSPITALS

AS APPROVED BY THE CONFERENCE OF REPRESENTATIVES OF THE MEDICAL PROFESSION AND THE PRESS, 16 MAY 1956

INTRODUCTION

1. The following recommendations are put forward as guiding principles which hospitals could reasonably adopt.

SICKNESS CASES

2. Information should not be divulged to the Press without the consent of the patient beyond the statement that the person named in an enquiry is a patient. Where, however, even this statement would be deleterious to the patient's interests, his presence in the hospital should not be disclosed without his consent. For example, in certain special hospitals, such as mental hospitals and sanatoria, where the mere admission of the patient implies the nature of the diagnosis, no information should be given to the Press without the patient's consent, and that of the doctor in charge, who should satisfy himself that to give the information would not be prejudicial to the patient's interests.

3. In the case of well-known people (and subject always to the patient's consent), a brief indication of progress may be given, in terms authorised by the doctor in charge.

4. In the circumstances referred to under 2 and 3, where the patient is too ill to give his consent, or is a minor, the consent of the nearest competent relative should be obtained.

ACCIDENT CASES

5. (a) *Individual Cases*. The Press should be given, on enquiry only and at the time of the enquiry or as soon as possible afterwards, the name and address of the patient and a general indication of his condition but not necessarily a diagnosis. The patient's relatives should, if possible, be informed before any statement is given to the Press; but if it has not been possible to

do so, this should be made clear to the Press. Further information should be given only with the patient's consent. Where the patient is too ill to give his consent, or is a minor, the consent of the nearest competent relative should be obtained.

(*b*) *Multiple Cases.* In accidents involving a number of people (for example, a railway or air accident) all reasonable steps should be taken to ensure that relatives of the injured have been informed before the publication of names, bearing in mind the necessity of early publication to dispel the anxiety of the next-of-kin of all other persons who were, or might have been, involved in the accident. Further information should be given only with the patient's consent. Where the patient is too ill to give his consent, or is a minor, the consent of the nearest competent relative should be obtained.

6. Hospitals admitting accident cases should maintain a casualty book or other similar records by reference to which enquiries may be answered.

GENERAL

7. All hospitals should ensure that a sufficiently experienced and responsible officer of the hospital is at all times available, whether in person or by telephone, to answer Press enquiries, and should nominate an officer or officers for this purpose.

8. When dealing with representatives of the Press, broadcasting or television authorities who call at hospitals and are unknown to them, such hospital officers are advised to ask to see evidence of accreditation in the form of a document issued by the representative's newspaper, news agency, photographic news agency, or other authority, or a membership card of the Institute of Journalists or the National Union of Journalists. Telephone enquiries not known to the officer receiving the call can, if necessary, be asked to give a number which can be rung back for the purpose of checking.

9. Satisfactory co-operation between hospitals and the Press will depend on the observance of conduct that will promote mutual confidence and good personal relations. Difficulties and misunderstandings should be taken up between the hospitals or board concerned and the national or local Press.

Appendix III

REPORTING PROCEEDINGS IN COURTS OF LAW

PRESS RIGHTS AND OBLIGATIONS

An important declaration on the right of the Press to publish evidence given in open court was issued by the Council in May 1964.

This was the outcome of a request to consider statements made by Defence Counsel and the Chairman of the Magistrates during committal proceedings at Aylesbury in the Great Mail Train Robbery case. The declaration said that these statements were viewed with the utmost concern. It also called attention to the fact that subsequently, though in another matter altogether, an Oldham magistrates' bench had requested the Press at noon on a Monday to withhold publication of evidence given in open court on the previous Friday. Having considered both these matters the Council issued the following statement:

1. The first object of the Press Council is to maintain the freedom of the Press, and in relation to this object, the Council has had to consider certain difficulties that have recently arisen over the reporting of proceedings in courts of law. It is a fundamental principle of British justice, as laid down by the highest court in the land, that justice should as a rule be administered openly and in public and it is plain that without the services of the Press only a tiny fraction of the public could be kept informed of what takes place in court. There are, of course, statutory restrictions on the reporting of certain matters. But in general it is the duty as well as the right of the Press to publish full and fair reports of court proceedings and this duty is recognised by the special privilege that is granted to newspapers for the purpose.

2. From time to time a request is made to the Press by judges and magistrates not to publish evidence of a specified description. Quite often such a request is made as an alternative to the exercise by the court of a power to hear the evidence in private. But whether the request is made for that or for any other reason, it should, in the opinion of the Council, be complied

with. If any editor considers that a particular request is unreasonable the Council would wish to be informed. But the Council believes that judges and magistrates have always in mind the fundamental principle that justice must be done openly and therefore that such requests are not made except in the overriding interest of a fair trial.

3. There is one occasion which occurs often enough to make a specific request unnecessary and that is in a trial by jury when evidence is given by witnesses or mentioned by Counsel in the absence of the jury. Otherwise a reporter can expect to receive a clear and specific request so that he may know where his duty lies and exactly what it is that he is being asked not to report.

4. In the committal proceedings in what has become known as the Great Mail Train Robbery case, counsel for some of the defendants submitted to the magistrates that evidence tendered by the prosecution was inadmissible. The submission was rejected. A submission that the evidence should be heard in camera was also rejected. Counsel then made an application that the Press should be asked to exercise great discretion in reporting the evidence in view of the fact that it might prejudice a fair trial. The Chairman of the magistrates thereupon asked the Press to be considerate, 'only reporting what is absolutely necessary.' The Press Council considers, with respect, that that is the sort of request which it is quite impossible for the Press to comply with. The only definitive characteristic which this evidence possessed to distinguish it from any other evidence in the case was that one counsel was contending that it was admissible and the other that it was not. A reporter cannot in such a situation be expected to judge what should be reported and what should not.

5. After some of the disputed evidence had been received one of the counsel for the defence made use of his right of audience to state in open court that if any part of the evidence were reported in the Press, B.B.C. or Television, his instructing solicitors would report the matter to the Attorney-General to see if he thought fit to bring proceedings for Contempt of Court to ensure that the defendants had a fair trial and remedy the injustice already done to them. The Council acknowledges with gratitude the assistance it has received from observations made by the Bar Council and by members of the Bar concerned and is very ready to believe that Counsel were acting out of a sense of duty to their clients. But in the interests of the freedom of the Press the Press Council must express itself quite clearly. There is no authority whatever for the suggestion that newspapers which publish what has taken place in open court, there being no ruling from the Bench to the contrary, can be punished for Contempt of Court. The further suggestion that the Press will be acting contemptuously unless it takes steps, which the court

itself has not taken, to ensure for the defendants what their counsel thinks necessary for a fair trial and to remedy what he deems to be the injustice done by the ruling of the court, is, in the opinion of the Council, absurd. The Council hopes that editors and reporters will not be deterred by threats of this sort from the performance of their duty to the public.

6. The Council has expressed itself strongly because this is not the only occasion upon which suggestions of Contempt of Court have been made by members of the Bar. In recent committal proceedings at Oldham, Counsel for one of four defendants in a case of considerable public interest asked for the hearing to be held *in camera* on the ground that he might object, at a later stage, to the admissibility of some of the evidence. The magistrates said that having taken into account the interests of the defendants, the general public and the Press they were of the opinion that the proceedings should be held in open court, but, they added 'we ask the Press not to report or make mention of statements made by M—— [one of the defendants] on which there is any doubt about their admissibility and likely to be prejudicial'.

The *Oldham Evening Chronicle*, that day, published in a column adjoining the report of the hearing a protest against what it called the attempt by the Bench to place on the shoulders of newspaper editors the burden of decisions which properly belonged to the Court. The defence Counsel referred to represented to the magistrates that the comment constituted Contempt of Court but the magistrates refused to take note of the objection.

Five days later — on the following Monday — Counsel entered his objection to certain police evidence. The magistrates then decided to hear the remainder of this evidence *in camera*. Announcing their decision, the chairman said: 'We again ask the Press not to print any of the evidence relating to the defendant M—— by this witness'. Some of this had been given on the previous Friday.

7. Nothing that the Council has said is intended to derogate from the right and duty of an editor or reporter to exercise his own discretion in refraining from reporting details of legal proceedings when the pain and distress that publicity may cause to an innocent individual outweighs the public interest. The only principle that can govern the use of this discretion is that it must be exercised always without fear or favour. The danger that suppression may be ascribed to fear or to favouritism is sufficiently great and the need for publicity for legal proceedings so important that exceptions to the rule must be rare.

Appendix IV

CHEQUE-BOOK JOURNALISM

The Press Council has closely examined the subject of cheque-book journalism which has agitated the public mind in recent years and today issues the following observations:

The term 'cheque-book journalism' is of recent introduction into colloquial language. It has escaped definition and like 'democracy', 'progress' and other expressions which, in the mouth of the political orator, can convey different meanings every time they are employed, the import of what the user means by 'cheque-book journalism' can vary from the cost of entertaining a contact to luncheon to payment of thousands of pounds for the discreditable memoirs of a notorious person.

There is a considerable body of people which uses the term by way of opprobrium solely in regard to special articles or interviews on vice or immorality contributed by notorieties of the moment. This is a serious aspect of the subject on which the Press Council has spoken bluntly, but it is by no means the whole of it. Cheque-book journalism fundamentally is the power of the purse — a power which, in misuse, could give the wealthy newspaper an unfair advantage over its less well-to-do rivals in this competitive world. The term, therefore, could strictly be applied to all sources of benefit — news, features and personal ability — that a newspaper obtains by reason of its financial affluence.

Normally, however, the critic of cheque-book journalism has in mind the purchase from non-journalists of news or views. It should be clearly understood that there is nothing inherently wrong in the purchase of knowledge from a willing seller, nor has the notable individual in the community a greater right to benefit himself financially by the sale of autobiographical matter than the rogue.

What then are the objectionable elements of the practice? In the wider aspect of acquisition of exclusive news they centre on exercise of the power of the purse to deny competitors legitimate access to news or facts that the public ought to know. This limitation of circulation of news is a grave matter. It is at the heart of the anti-social side of cheque-book journalism. If the public good requires that news shall be generally known it is completely unethical for any newspaper, by exercise of the power of the purse, to block dissemination for private gain.

The yardstick of measurement of public interest is not always national. A news event that may be trivial considered nationally may be of great importance to the public of a given provincial area. The Press Council, for instance, has knowledge of cases in which national newspapers have bought exclusive rights to news and pictures of local events not only to the exclusion of national competitors but to the deprivation of the local Press. Because local people rely primarily upon their town or county newspapers for their local news such instances of artificial restriction of news must, on the face of things, be against public interest.

The difficulty of enunciating a standard of conduct applicable to all cases of purchase of exclusive rights to news is obvious. Circumstances can be almost infinitely variable and the Press Council cannot do otherwise than judge each case on its merits.

The second objectionable element of cheque-book journalism is its tendency to induce unseemly conduct in the quest of special-purchase stories. In one instance which the Press Council considered there was a street fracas between journalists of rival newspapers when some of them tried to interview a man leaving a Court on a 'Not Guilty' finding in a charge of murder. Others claimed that their newspapers had 'bought his story' and the conflict between the groups was unedifying. Such conduct serves only to bring the Press into discredit. There is no redeeming feature about behaviour of this kind. The best antidote to it is removal of the cause.

The third element is 'body-snatching', a term devised to describe extreme steps sometimes taken to ensure that a bought source of information shall not be in a position to divulge anything of what he knows to persons other than his paymasters. It is one thing to rely on a seller's promise of silence and another to take almost forcible steps to make certain that it is kept. The Council finds this practice most objectionable.

The glamorisation of vice and the rewarding of criminals are the aspects of cheque-book journalism that make the biggest impact on the public. The Press Council has not hesitated to condemn this practice and it is heartened to note that since its outspoken comments on the Christine Keeler memoirs in 1963 there has been marked improvement in the standards of newspaper approach to the publication of unsavoury matters which are not dealt with in the way of public duty.

This point of public duty, although of primary importance, is sometimes overlooked by critics of the newspapers. The Press has a responsibility to the community to record what is going on. It would err ethically if it ignored unpleasant matters of public consequence simply because they were unpleasant. Vice and sex should not be swept under the carpet. They should be adequately reported and commented upon in an adult manner, and this generally can be achieved without going into excessive detail.

When the Press exceeds its duty to inform in these events it panders to the baser element in man's nature and descends to the level of trafficking in scandal. The claim that a large section of the population demands this sort of journalism is no excuse for providing it. One does not give a sick man poison because he fancies it!

The Council unhesitatingly condemns as immoral the practice of financially rewarding criminals for disclosure of their nefarious practices by way of public entertainment. Crime is anti-social and it cannot be other than wrong that an evil-doer should benefit — oftentimes substantially — by his offences against the community. These payments for revelations by the notorious might also be held to constitute encouragement to others. To some people the prospect of wide publicity and a monetary reward being obtainable for details of their illegal exploits could be a vivid and compelling inducement to criminal activity.

Some degree of reservation was expressed within the Council about publication of revelations by convicted spies because the spy, in the minds of many, is a criminal only to the side he injures. When he spies for his country he could even be something of a hero to his compatriots. It was also advanced in discussion that publication of a foreign spy's work in Britain served the positive good of exposing weaknesses in the nation's defensive mechanism. In the final analysis, however, the Council felt that it is contrary to public welfare to reward criminals whether they be vicious or treasonable.

The Press Council regrets that it cannot provide an all-embracing definition of cheque-book journalism. The facets of the subject are so many and varied that each case must be considered in light of its facts and circumstances. The Council will, however, keep the matter under review and will issue, from time to time, its views on individual cases which come to its notice.

Appendix V

DECLARATION OF PRINCIPLE

In the course of the Moors Murder trial earlier this year public concern was expressed at the possible effects of newspapers making payments to witnesses in criminal proceedings for the purpose of obtaining information for news stories and articles.

Misgivings were felt that such action might lead to the colouring of evidence and that a long process of questioning witnesses might prejudice the proper conduct of a trial.

The matter was raised in both Houses of Parliament and it was stated that the Press Council was giving urgent consideration to the problem. This the Council has done in consultation with newspaper editors. The Press Council now makes the following Declaration of Principle:

1. No payment or offer of payment should be made by a newspaper to any person known or reasonably expected to be a witness in criminal proceedings already begun in exchange for any story or information in connection with the proceedings until they have been concluded.

2. No witness in committal proceedings should be questioned on behalf of any newspaper about the subject matter of his evidence until the trial has been concluded.

3. No payment should be made for feature articles to persons engaged in crime or other notorious misbehaviour where the public interest does not warrant it; as the council has previously declared, it deplores publication of personal articles of an unsavoury nature by persons who have been concerned in criminal acts or vicious conduct.

In making this declaration the Press Council acknowledges the wide support given by editors to the broad principles set out.

The Council does not intend that the principles enunciated shall preclude reasonable contemporaneous enquiries in relation to the commission of crime when these are carried out with due regard to the administration of justice. There may be occasions on which the activities of newspapers are affected by overriding questions of public interest such as the exposure of wrongdoing.

No code can cover every case. Satisfactory observance of the principles must depend upon the discretion and sense of responsibility of editors and newspaper proprietors.

Index